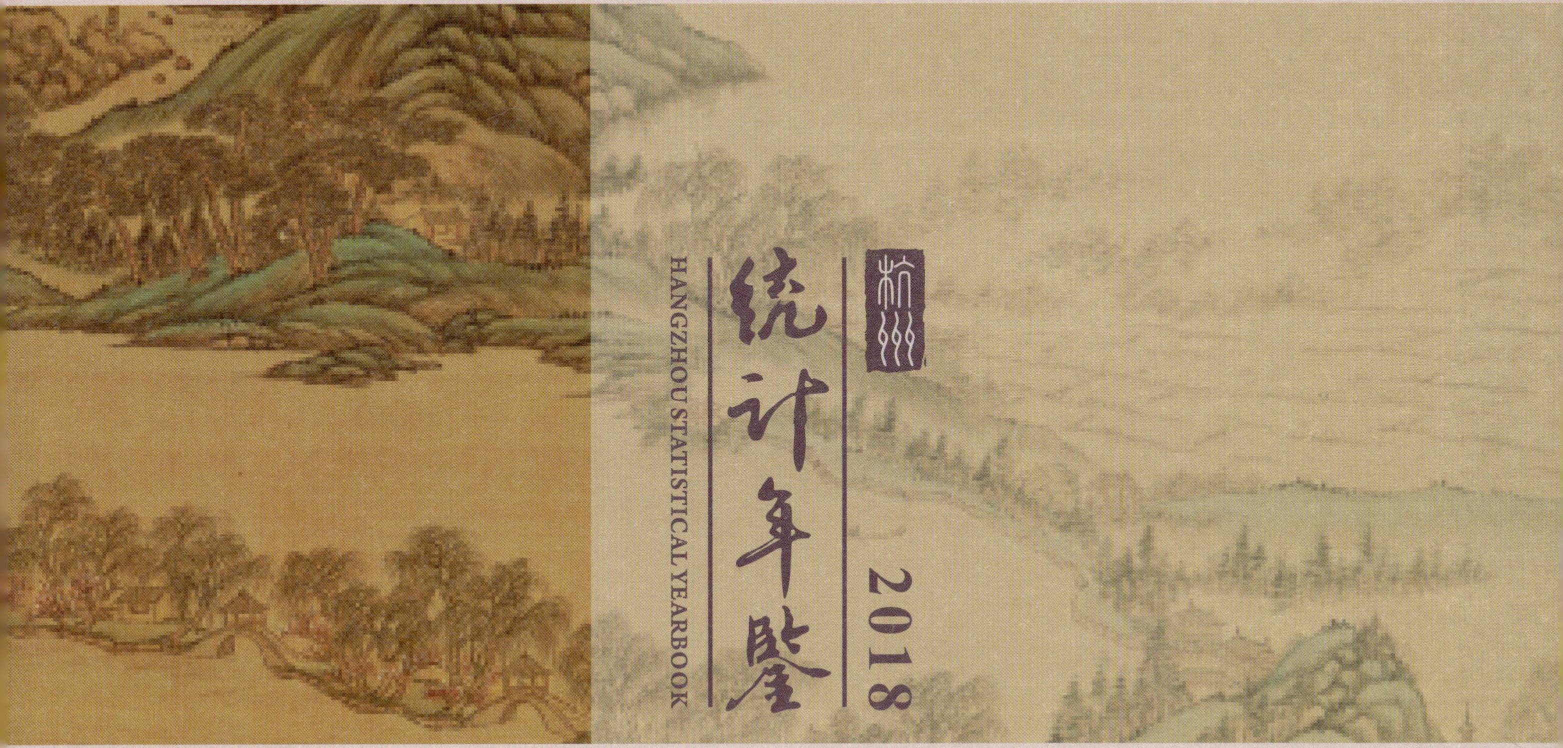

杭州统计年鉴 2018

HANGZHOU STATISTICAL YEARBOOK

杭州统计年鉴 2018

HANGZHOU STATISTICAL YEARBOOK

杭州市统计局
国家统计局杭州调查队
杭州市社会经济调查局

中国统计出版社
China Statistics Press

图书在版编目（CIP）数据

杭州统计年鉴. 2018 / 杭州市统计局, 国家统计局杭州调查队, 杭州市社会经济调查局编. -- 北京 : 中国统计出版社, 2018.9
ISBN 978-7-5037-8569-6

Ⅰ. ①杭… Ⅱ. ①杭… ②国… ③杭… Ⅲ. ①统计资料－杭州－2018－年鉴 Ⅳ. ①C832.551-54

中国版本图书馆CIP数据核字(2018)第171267号

杭州统计年鉴2018

作　　者/ 杭州市统计局
国家统计局杭州调查队
杭州市社会经济调查局
责任编辑/ 陈越月
装帧设计/ 张子杰
出版发行/ 中国统计出版社
地　　址/ 北京市丰台区西三环南路甲6号　邮政编码/100073
电　　话/ 邮购（010）63376909　书店（010）68783171
网　　址/ http://csp.stats.gov.cn
印　　刷/ 浙江新中商务印刷有限公司
经　　销/ 新华书店
开　　本/ 890mm×1240mm　1/16
字　　数/ 974千字
印　　张/ 28.25
版　　别/ 2018年9月第1版
版　　次/ 2018年9月第1次印刷

ISBN 978-7-5037-8569-6

定价：300.00元

如有印装差错，由本社发行部调换

HANGZHOU STATISTICAL YEARBOOK

杭州统计年鉴

2018 编委会和编辑人员

HANGZHOU
STATISTICAL YEARBOOK
杭州统计年鉴

2018 Editorial Board and Staff

编者说明

一、《杭州统计年鉴—2018》是一部信息密集的资料性年刊。本年鉴系统收集了全市和各区、县（市）2017年经济和社会各方面的统计数据，以及多个重要历史年份和近年全市主要统计数据。

二、本年鉴分为13个篇章：综合；人口和就业人员；农业；工业、能源；建筑业；交通运输、邮电；固定资产投资；国内贸易；对外经济、旅游；财政、金融、保险；城市建设、环境保护；科技、教育、文化、卫生、体育；人民生活、物价、民政。为便于读者使用，各篇章附有简要说明和主要统计指标解释。

三、本年鉴中涉及到历史数据，均以最新版本为准；本年鉴中部分数据合计数或相对数由于单位取舍不同而产生的计算误差，均未做机械调整。

四、2001年起，萧山、余杭撤市建区，市区数据含萧山、余杭区；2014年起富阳撤市建区，市区数据包括富阳区；2017年起临安撤市建区，市区数据包括临安区。萧山区数据未做特殊说明的均含大江东产业集聚区数据。

五、本年鉴表中符号使用说明：“-”表示这一栏没有数字；“…”表示该数字不足本表最小计量单位；“#”表示其中的主要项；“空格”表示该项统计数据不详或无该项数据；“*”表示表下有注解。

六、本年鉴所使用的度量衡单位均采用国际统一标准计量单位，金额除特别标明外，均以人民币计量。

七、与2017年版《杭州统计年鉴》相比较，本年鉴在篇章结构和内容上主要做了以下修订：第一篇删除了全市十大产业主要指标（2011-2015年）、分地区生产总值（主要年份）、分地区生产总值指数（主要年份）、分地区第一产业增加值（主要年份）、分地区第二产业增加值（主要年份）、分地区工业增加值（主要年份）、分地区第三产业增加值（主要年份）、分地区建筑业增加值（主要年份）；增加全市分地区和产业生产总值指数（2017年）；第三篇增加乡镇基本情况2017；第九篇删除出口企业前20位排名。

八、《杭州统计年鉴》公开出版以来，受到了社会各界的关心和支持，对此我们深表谢意。限于我们的水平，欢迎各界人士继续对年鉴的不足之处给予批评指正，帮助我们进一步提高统计年鉴的编辑工作，更好地为社会各界服务（网址：http：//tjj. hangzhou. gov. cn）。

Editorial Note

Ⅰ. *Hangzhou Statistical Yearbook 2018* is an informative annuals that covers comprehensive data series of Hangzhou's social and economic development. Which contains very comprehensive statistics of Hangzhou's social and economic development in 2017. It covers Hangzhou's data in recent years and some historically important years.

Ⅱ. The Yearbook contains 13 chapters: 1. General Survey; 2. Population and Employment; 3. Agriculture; 4. Industry and Energy; 5. Construction; 6. Transportation, Post and Telecommunications; 7. Investment in Fixed Assets; 8. Domestic Trade; 9. Foreign Economic Cooperation and Tourism; 10. Finance, Banking and Insurance; 11. Urban Construction and Environmental Protection; 12. Science and Technology, Education, Culture, Public Health and Sports; 13. People's Livelihood, Price Indices and Civil Administration. To facilitate readers, each chaper provides brief introduction and explanatory notes on main statistical indicators.

Ⅲ. Please refer to the newly published version of the Yearbook for updated historical data. Statistical discrepancies on totals and relative figures due to rounding are not adjusted in the Yearbook.

Ⅳ. Because of the change of urban administrative division, the data of Xiaoshan District and Yuhang District have been included into the urban districts since 2001, and it is the same for Fuyang District since 2014, Lin'an District since 2017. Without special notes, the data of Xiaoshan District include the data of Dajiangdong industry cluster district.

Ⅴ. Notations used in this book:"—" indicates that the column has no figure;"…" indicates that the figure is not large enough to be measured with the smallest unit in the table;"blank space" indicates that the date are unknown, or are not available;"#" indicates the major items of the total;" * " indicates"see footnotes below".

Ⅵ. The international standard unit of measurement is applied in this book, all amounts are denominated in RMB, except those with special notes.

Ⅶ. In comparison with Hangzhou Statistical Yearbook 2017, following revisions have been made in this new version in terms of the statistical contents and editing : Chapter 1 deleted Ten Major Industries (2011 ~2015)、Gross Domestic Product by Region (Main Years)、Indices of Gross Domestic Product by Region (Main Years)、Value Added of Primary Industry by Region (Main Years)、Value Added of Secondary Industry by Region (Main Years)、Value Added of Industry by Region (Main Years)、Value Added of Tertiary Industry by Region (Main Years)、Value Added of Construction by Region (Main Years), added Indices of Gross Donestic Product by Region and Industry (2017); Chapter 3 added Statistics on Towns and Townships (2017); Chapter 9 deleted The List of Top Twenty Export Enterprises.

Ⅷ. Since published openly, Previous Editions of Hangzhou Statistics Yearbook have enjoyed wide concern and support; and we express heartfelt thanks. In order to get further improvement in the yearbook editing, we welcome all candid comments and criticism from our readers (website: http: //tjj. hangzhou. gov. cn).

目　　录
Contents

一、综合
Ⅰ. General Survey

二、人口和就业人员

Ⅱ. Population and Employment

三、农业

Ⅲ. Agriculture

四、工业、能源

Ⅳ. Industry and Energy

五、建筑业
Ⅴ. Construction

六、交通运输、邮电

Ⅵ. Transportation, Post and Telecommunications

七、固定资产投资

Ⅶ. Investment in Fixed Assets

八、国内贸易
Ⅷ. Domestic Trade

九、对外经济、旅游
Ⅸ. Foreign Economic Cooperation and Tourism

十、财政、金融、保险

Ⅹ. Finance, Banking and Insurance

十一、城市建设、环境保护

Ⅺ. Urban Construction and Environmental Protection

十二、科技、教育、文化、卫生、体育

Ⅻ. Science and Technology，Education，Culture，Public Health and Sports

十三、人民生活、物价、民政

XIII. People's Livelihood, Price Indices and Civil Administration

2017年杭州市国民经济和社会发展统计公报

杭 州 市 统 计 局

国家统计局杭州调查队

2017年,全市上下认真学习贯彻党的十九大精神,深入领会把握习近平新时代中国特色社会主义思想的精神实质和实践要求,全面落实省第十四次、市第十二次党代会决策部署,以强化供给侧结构性改革为主线,加快建设独特韵味别样精彩世界名城,全面推进拥江发展。全市经济结构持续优化,发展质量不断提高,民生福祉持续增进,社会事业实现新进步。

一、综　　合

(一)经济总量。

2017年,全市实现地区生产总值12603亿元,比上年增长8.1%。其中第一产业增加值311亿元,第二产业增加值4362亿元,第三产业增加值7930亿元,分别增长1.8%、4.8%和10.5%。全市常住人口人均GDP为135113元,比上年提高10827元,增长5.5%。按国家公布的年平均汇率折算,为20011美元。三次产业结构调整为2.5∶34.6∶62.9,服务业占GDP比重比上年提高2个百分点。

图1　2011年－2017年地区生产总值及增长速度

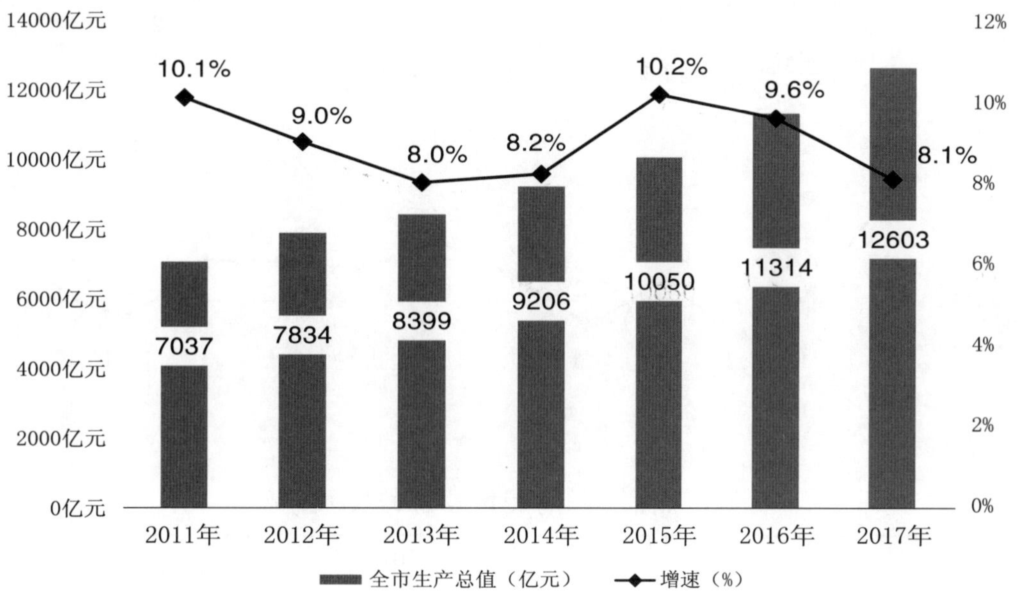

(二)民营经济。

全年民营经济实现增加值7561亿元,占GDP的60.2%。年末,全市私营企业48.10万户,比上年末增长20.1%;个体工商户47.14万户,增长10.6%。全年新设个体工商户9.38万户,增长8.4%。私营企业和个体工商户从业人员分别为312.25万人和92.41万人,增长10.9%和16.3%。

(三)财政收支。

全年财政总收入2921.30亿元,一般公共预算收入1567.42亿元,分别增长14.2%和17.4%。其中企业所得税270.22亿元,个人所得税146.20亿元,分别增长22.0%和26.6%。全市一般公共预算支出1540.92亿元,增长9.7%。其中民生类支出1213.09亿元,增长11.9%,民生支出占比78.7%,比上年提高1.5个百分点。

图 2　2011 年－2017 年一般公共预算收入及增长速度

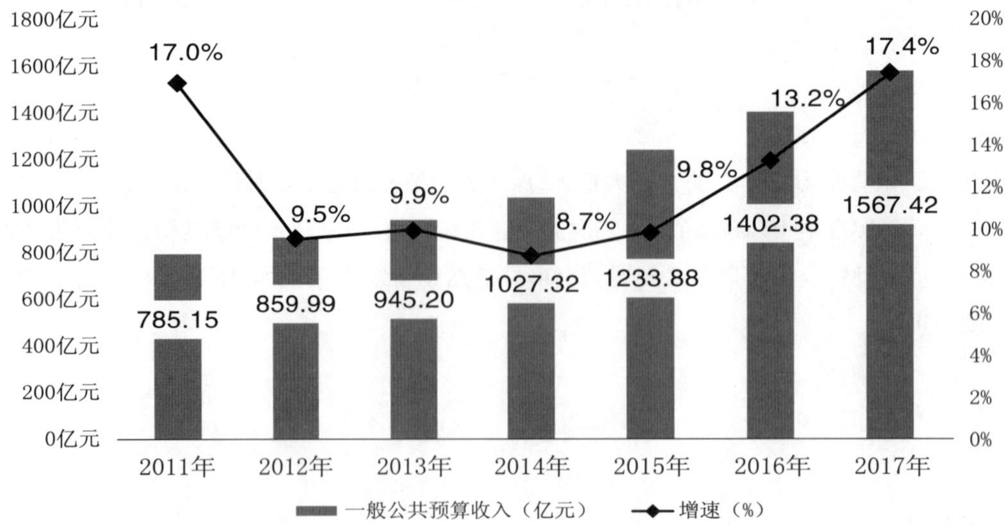

(四)市场价格。

全年市区居民消费价格比上年上涨 2.5%。其中居住类价格上涨 5.7%、教育文化和娱乐类价格上涨 4.1%、食品烟酒类价格上涨 0.9%。

图 3　2017 年市区居民消费价格月度涨跌幅度

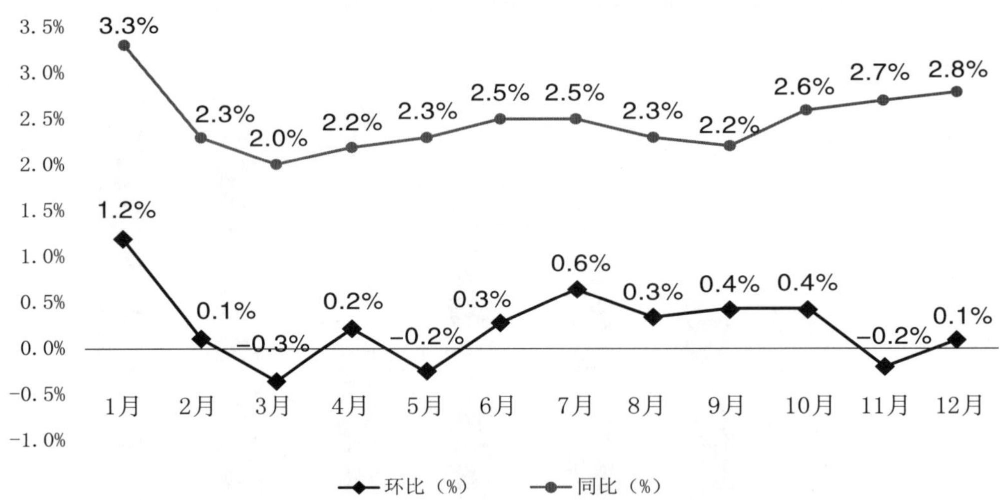

表 1　市区居民消费价格涨跌幅度(%)

项　　目	2016 年	2017 年
市区居民消费价格	2.6	2.5
1. 食品烟酒	6.0	0.9
2. 衣着	0.3	0.0
3. 居住	2.2	5.7
4. 生活用品及服务	-0.4	0.2
5. 交通和通信	-1.0	1.5
6. 教育文化和娱乐	3.7	4.1
7. 医疗保健	0.8	1.7
8. 其他用品和服务	2.7	1.4

全年工业生产者出厂价格上涨4.4%，工业生产者购进价格上涨8.4%。

（五）人口就业。

年末全市常住人口946.80万人，比上年末增加28.00万人，其中城镇人口727.14万人，占常住人口的76.8%，比2016年提高0.6个百分点；人口出生率为12.5‰，自然增长率为7.4‰。全市户籍人口753.88万人，人口出生率为14.70‰，自然增长率为6.19‰。全市新增城镇就业人员29.71万人，安置失业人员再就业11.04万人。年末城镇登记失业率1.70%。

二、质量效益

（一）结构优化。

全年信息经济实现增加值3216亿元，增长21.8%，占GDP的25.5%，同比提高1.2个百分点。其中电子商务产业增加值1316亿元，增长36.6%，连续七年增速保持在30%以上。六大产业群中的文化创意产业增加值3041亿元，增长19.0%，占GDP的24.1%。

（二）企业增效。

全年规模以上工业企业实现利税1775亿元，增长8.5%，其中利润999亿元，增长7.7%，分别比上年提高1.7和1.0个百分点。全员劳动生产率为30.2万元/人，提高2.4万元/人；亩产增加值为150万元、增加13.2万元。规模以上信息传输、软件和信息技术服务业企业实现利税1381亿元，增长34.3%，其中利润1226亿元，增长35.4%。

三、农　　业

全年农林牧渔业增加值306亿元，增长2.4%。其中农业195亿元，林业43亿元，渔业28亿元，农林牧渔专业及辅助性活动6亿元，分别增长4.6%、3.1%、3.1%、14.4%；牧业33亿元，下降11.5%。粮食总产量47.26万吨，增长2.9%；蔬菜产量338.34万吨，增长0.9%；水果产量81.99万吨，增长7.3%；水产品产量20.10万吨，增长3.2%；肉类产量21.27万吨，下降4.2%。市级“菜篮子”基地502个，其中新建42个；创建省级现代农业园区3个，特色农业强镇4个，全年新建粮食功能区9.6万亩。新建美丽乡村精品示范线12条，村庄生态修复850个；农家乐（民宿）共接待游客4964万人次，实现经营收入52亿元，分别增长27.9%和18.2%。

四、工业和建筑业

（一）工业。

全年工业增加值3968亿元，增长6.3%，其中规模以上工业增加值3184亿元，增长7.0%。规模以上工业企业中高新技术产业、战略性新兴产业、装备制造业增加值分别增长13.6%、15.0%和11.0%，占规模以上工业的50.1%、30.6%和43.2%，比上年提高4.1、3.4和1.3个百分点；八大高耗能行业增加值占比24.6%，下降1.5个百分点。新产品产值率为37.7%。工业产品产销率为98.5%。

（二）建筑业。

全年建筑业增加值396亿元，占GDP的3.1%。具有总承包和专业承包资格的建筑企业1410家，完成施工产值4324亿元，增长5.3%。新签合同额5037亿元，增长23.2%。实现利税总额198亿元，增长3.7%。

五、固定资产投资和房地产开发

（一）固定资产投资。

全年完成固定资产投资5857亿元，增长1.4%，其中民间投资3301亿元，增长10.4%，占56.4%。从投资产业结构看，农林牧渔业投资40亿元，增长2.4%；工业投资861亿元，增长0.5%；服务业投资4956亿元，增长1.5%。

（二）房地产开发。

全年房地产开发投资2734亿元，增长4.9%，其中住宅投资1713亿元，增长9.8%。房屋施工面积11523万平方米，下降0.3%；新开工面积2177万平方米，增长1.9%；竣工面积2086万平方米，增长8.5%。商品房销售面积2054万平方米，下降11.7%。

六、国内贸易

全年批发和零售业增加值982亿元，增长8.1%；住宿餐饮业增加值193亿元，增长6.0%。社会消费品零售总额5717亿元，增长10.5%。其中限额以上批发和零售企业实现网上零售656亿元，增长24.9%，占社会消费品零售额11.5%。按经营地分，城镇消费品零售额5421亿元，增长10.4%；乡村消费品零售额297亿元，增长11.4%。全市商品交易市场684个，交易额4289亿元，增长11.5%。

图4　2011年-2017年全市社会消费品零售总额

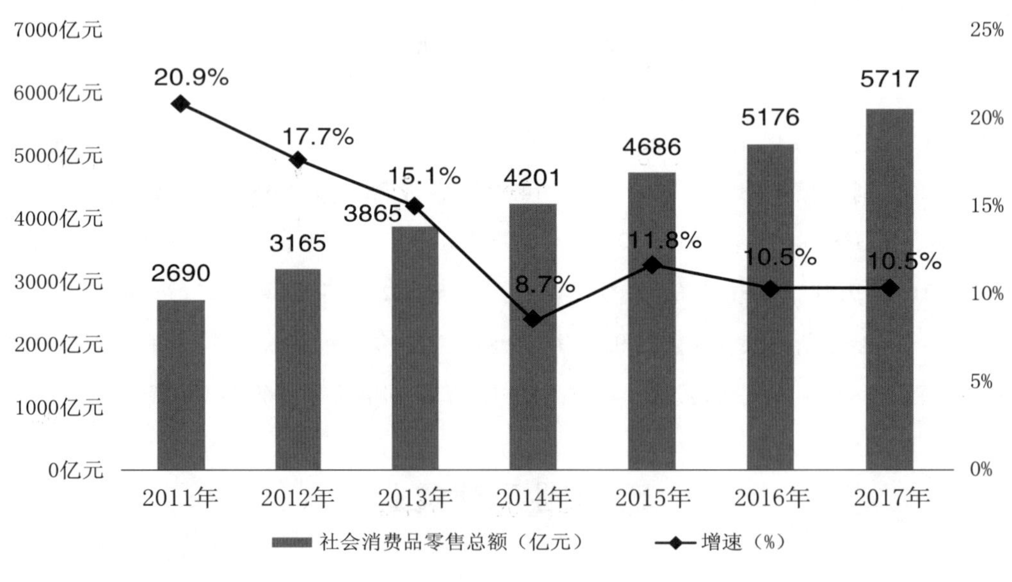

七、对外经济

（一）对外贸易。

全年货物进出口总额5085亿元，增长13.3%，其中出口3456亿元，增长4.3%，进口1629亿元，增长38.8%。高新技术产品出口478亿元，增长12.8%，机电产品出口1456亿元，增长7.3%。民营企业出口2325亿元，增长6.8%。对“一带一路”沿线国家出口1049亿元，占出口总额30.4%。

全年服务进出口总额1619亿元，增长15.7%，占货物和服务贸易进出口比重为24.1%，其中出口1088亿元，增长15%；进口531亿元，增长17%。

跨境电商交易额99.36亿美元，增长22.5%，其中出口70.22亿美元，进口29.14亿美元，分别增长15.9%和42.0%。

（二）对外合作。

年末全市设立各类境外投资企业（机构）1781个，增长12.3%。全年对外承包工程和劳务合作营业额23.50亿美元，增长22.0%。离岸服务外包合同执行额64.65亿美元，增长10.1%。

（三）利用外资。

全年新引进外商投资企业575家，增长24.5%。实际利用外资66.1亿美元，下降8.3%。其中服务业实际利用外资57.1亿美元，增长1.0%，占实际利用外资的86.4%。年末120家世界500强企业来杭投资208个项目，其中当年新进企业8家，项目10个。

（四）浙商回归。

全年引进浙商回归项目985个，到位资金761.8亿元，增长7.3%，其中服务业项目829个，到位资金666.7亿元。

八、交通、邮电和旅游

（一）交通运输。

全年交通运输、仓储和邮政业增加值342亿元，增长3.8%。全社会货物运输总量3.48亿吨，增长15.3%。旅客运输量2.23亿人次，增长8.5%。年末萧山国际机场已开通航线286条，其中国际航线49条，港澳台航线8条。航空客运吞吐量达3557万人次，货物吞吐量58.95万吨，分别增长12.6%和20.8%。其中出入境旅客452.9万人次、货邮6.53万吨，分别增长8.3%和34.4%。

全年地铁客运量3.40亿人次，增长26.5%。主城区公共交通日均客运量430.2万人次。

年末社会机动车辆保有量279.36万辆，增长6.1%。民用汽车保有量245.12万辆，增长4.7%，其中私人汽车199.85万辆，增长9.4%。

（二）邮政电信。

全年邮政企业和规模以上快递服务企业实现业务收入275.09亿元，增长27.9%，其中快递业务收入251.05亿元，增长28.3%。

电信行业实现业务收入230.81亿元，增长8.9%。年末固定电话用户246.70万户，下降2.5%；移动电话用户1724.2万户，下降0.6%；宽带用户505万户，增长14.0%。光网络覆盖率达99.5%。

（三）旅游业。

全年旅游休闲产业增加值928亿元，增长12.6%，占GDP的7.4%。旅游总收入3041.34亿元，增长18.3%，其中旅游外汇收入35.43亿美元，增长12.5%。旅游总人数16286.63万人，增长15.8%。接待国内游客15884.4万人次，增长16.0%；接待入境旅游者402.23万人次，增长10.7%。年末各类旅行社767家，增长7.0%；星级宾馆143家，其中五星级23家，四星级42家；A级景区91个，其中5A级3个，4A级34个。

九、金　　融

全年金融业增加值1056亿元，增长6.9%。年末全市金融机构499家，当年新增37家。全市金融机构本外币存款余额36483.24亿元，增长9.3%；贷款余额29270.94亿元，增长11.9%，其中住户贷款9653.68亿元，增长

23.8%，非金融企业及机关团体贷款19325.94亿元，增长6.6%。

表2　2017年末全市金融机构本外币存贷款余额及增速

指　　标	年末数(亿元)	比上年末增长(%)
各项存款	36483.24	9.3
其中:住户存款	8670.60	2.1
非金融企业存款	16313.18	12.7
各项贷款	29270.94	11.9
其中:住户贷款	9653.68	23.8
非金融企业及机关团体贷款	19325.94	6.6

年末上市公司163家，其中境内上市128家。境内上市公司总市值19955.22亿元。全年新增上市公司28家，融资187.7亿元。新三版挂牌企业381家。

全年保费收入633.7亿元，增长22.2%。其中，财产险保费收入194亿元，增长12.5%；人身险保费收入439.71亿元，增长27.1%。支付各类保险赔款169.61亿元，增长6.8%。其中财产险105.96亿元，增长5.9%；人身险63.64亿元，增长8.2%。

十、教育和科技

(一)教育。

年末共有小学458所，在校学生56.04万人；初中251所，在校学生22.48万人；普通高中80所，在校学生11.31万人；普通高等学校39所，在校学生(含研究生)48.41万人。学前三年幼儿入园率为98.95%；初中毕业生升入各类高中比例为99.69%；高等教育毛入学率63.26%。全市累计解决义务教育阶段外来务工人员子女入学28.20万人。全市各级各类中外合作办学项目72个，其中市属高校项目8个，高中段学校项目7个。

(二)科学技术。

全年发明专利申请25578件、发明专利授权9872件，分别增长2.5%、14.2%。发明专利授权量中企业专利占比达47.4%。新认定国家重点扶持高新技术企业589家，累计达2844家。年末培育认定研发中心2189家，其中省级研发中心835家。省科技型中小企业9238家。省级以上企业研发机构1203家。新增省级企业研究院76家。科技企业孵化器113家，其中国家级32家，省级60家。拥有省级众创空间101家，23家入选2017年省级优秀众创空间。

全年研究与试验发展(R&D)经费支出与生产总值之比为3.15%。财政一般公共预算支出中科技支出92.32亿元，增长23.2%。

十一、文化、卫生和体育

(一)文化。

年末有各类专业艺术表演团体11个，文化馆15个，博物馆、纪念馆88个，全国重点文物保护单位39处，档案馆16个，公共图书馆15个，图书馆藏书1590万册(不含省)。全市有线电视接入户353.02万户，其中数字电视313.09万户，分别增长1.9%和4.8%。全年拍摄电视剧44部，共1331集。生产原创动画片36036分钟。摄制完成17部电影。全市拥有非物质文化遗产保护项目335个,比上年增加4个。

(二)卫生。

年末拥有各类医疗卫生机构4933个,其中医院302个,比上年末分别增长5.2%和9.0%。社区卫生服务中心(站)1275个,疾病预防控制中心15个。拥有床位7.59万张,其中医院床位7.02万张,分别增长9.3%和9.7%。各类专业卫生技术人员11.04万人,其中执业(助理)医师4.18万人,注册护士4.63万人,分别增长9.1%、9.5%和10.2%。全市医疗机构完成诊疗人数12924.98万人次,增长6.2%。全市婴儿死亡率和5岁以下儿童死亡率分别为1.73‰和2.27‰。每十万孕产妇死亡率为6.5人。

(三)体育。

全年运动员共获得国际性比赛奖牌47枚,其中金牌22枚,银牌15枚,获得全国性奖牌318枚,其中金牌148枚,银牌90枚。成功举办第十三届全国学生运动会、杭州马拉松、杭州西湖国际名校赛艇挑战赛、国际冲浪挑战赛、国际(杭州)毅行大会等大型体育赛事。创建4所国家高水平体育后备人才基地、8所省高水平体育后备人才基地(其中重点4所)、5所省体育传统项目学校阳光后备要才基地。

十二、人民生活和社会保障

(一)人民生活。

全年居民人均可支配收入49832元,增长8.1%,扣除价格因素实际增长5.5%。其中城镇居民人均可支配收入56276元、增长7.8%,扣除价格因素实际增长5.2%;农村居民人均可支配收入30397元、增长8.9%,扣除价格因素实际增长6.2%。

全年居民人均生活消费支出34146元,增长7.0%,扣除价格因素实际增长4.4%。其中城镇居民人均生活消费支出38179元,农村居民人均生活消费支出21983元,分别增长7.0%和6.9%,扣除价格因素分别增长4.4%和4.3%。

表3　2017年全市居民人均收支主要指标

指标名称	城镇居民		农村居民	
	绝对数(元)	增幅(%)	绝对数(元)	增幅(%)
人均可支配收入	56276	7.8	30397	8.9
(一)工资性收入	32144	6.8	18232	6.9
(二)经营净收入	4893	6.2	7770	9.3
(三)财产净收入	8329	5.4	1280	12.6
(四)转移净收入	10910	13.9	3115	19.6
人均生活消费支出	38179	7.0	21983	6.9

年末城镇居民人均现住房建筑面积36.4平方米。每百户居民家庭拥有家用汽车55.8辆、空调235.3台、家用电脑115.1台,分别增长6.7%、3.8%和2.8%;农村居民人均现住房建筑面积70.9平方米。每百户农村居民家庭拥有家用汽车46.5辆、空调186.7台、家用电脑76.4台,分别增长9.7%、11%和1.9%。

(二)社会保障。

年末职工基本养老保险参保人数、职工基本医疗保险参保人数分别为628.32万人和580.50万人,比上年末增加52.34万人和51.18万人;年末失业、生育保险参保人数分别为413.20万人和390.73万人,增加39万人和41.4万人。全年推出公共租赁住房配租房源8514套,新增货币补贴保障家庭1691户。主城区居民最低生活保障标准调整至每人每月917元，增长12%，其余区、县(市)最低生活保障标准同步提高。年末全市最低生活保障对象12.27万人，全年发放低保金7.49亿元。

(三)社会福利。

年末全市拥有社区老年食堂(含社区助餐服务点)1176家。城乡社区居家养老服务照料中心2815个，社区级居家养老照料中心实现全覆盖，城区15分钟、农村20分钟的养老服务步行圈基本形成。拥有各类福利院、敬老院303所，床位7.03万张，收养人员2.27万人。全年发行各类福利彩票28.17亿元，增长7.1%。开展第十七次"春风行动"，市本级募集帮扶资金8538万元。

十三、城市建设

(一)城市基础设施建设。

全年基础设施投资1597亿元，占全市固定资产投资的27.3%。快速路网建设完成182公里。全年境内公路总里程达到16424公里，其中高速公路632公里。

年末主城区公共交通运营线路371条，其中新辟线路16条，优化线路40条。全市新开通地铁线路35.8公里，通车总里程达到117.6公里。建成启用运河水陆交通集散服务中心。

年末市区建成区园林绿地21726公顷，市区人均公园绿地面积达13.4平方米，建成区绿化覆盖率为40.0%。

(二)公用事业。

全年电网投资51.1亿元，110千伏及以上输变电工程投产37项，新增容量408万千伏安、线路252.11公里。全市用电量738.03亿千瓦时，增长8.8%，其中城乡居民生活用电114.86亿千瓦时，增长7.0%。

城区自来水日供水设计能力达到390.7万立方米，最高日供水量358.1万立方米。

城区新建成停车泊位56916个，其中公共泊位6222个。

十四、环境保护和安全生产

(一)环境保护。

全年环境空气日优良天数累计271天，比上年增加11天，优良率74.2%。市区PM2.5平均浓度44.6微克/立方米，下降8.6%。全市9个县控以上劣V类水断面、1256个劣V类水体完成"剿劣"任务。52个市控以上断面中，满足功能要求的断面48个，达标率为92.3%。组织减排项目124个，淘汰老旧汽车23119辆，新增清洁能源和新能源公交车879辆。淘汰落后和过剩产能170家(项)，实施"低小散"块状行业整治提升3753家。削减挥发性有机物排放量9974吨。全年规模以上工业单位增加值能耗下降4.1%。

生态环境质量综合指数(EI)继续位于全国、全省前列。获得国家生态园林城市、省级生态文明建设示范市称号。累计建成国家级生态县(市、区)8个，国家级生态乡镇119个，省级生态县(市、区)9个。

(二)安全生产。

全年共发生各类生产安全事故462起、死亡449人、受伤91人，分别下降17.8%，19.4%和15.7%。

公报注释：

1. 全市生产总值和各产业增加值绝对数按现行价格计算，增长速度按不变价格计算；三次产业划分执行国家统计局2012年制定的《三次产业划分规定》。

2. 2016年、2017年地区生产总值数据含研究与开发支出。

3. 根据第三次农业普查结果对农业相关数据和2016年固定资产投资基数进行调整,2017年固定资产投资增速按可比口径计算。

资料来源:

本公报中城镇新增就业、登记失业率、社会保障数据来自市人力社保局;私营企业和个体工商户数据来自市市场监管局;财政数据来自市财政局;农业园区、粮食功能区数据来自市农业局;教育数据来自市教育局;货物进出口数据来自杭州海关;低保、社会服务和救助、福利彩票数据来自市民政局;公路里程、公路货运量、水运货运量、公路客运量、水运客运量数据来自市交通局;货物出港量、客运出港量、通航线路数据来自萧山机场;地铁运营数据来自市地铁集团;停车泊位、人均公园绿地面积数据来自市建委;生态建设、环境监测数据来自市环保局;各类事故发生起数、死亡人数来自市安监局;浙商回归、实际利用外资来自市投资促进局;美丽乡村、农家乐(民宿)数据来自市农办;对外承包工程、服务贸易数据来自市商务委;电网投资、用电量数据来自国网杭州供电公司;户籍人口、机动车拥有数据来自市公安局;邮政业务数据来自市邮政管理局;旅游数据来自市旅委;货币金融数据来自人民银行杭州中心支行;保险业数据来自中国保监会浙江监管局;博物馆、纪念馆数据来自市园文局;档案馆数据来自市档案局;科技创新、高新技术企业、研发中心、众创空间、专利数据来自市科委;艺术表演团体、公共图书馆、文化馆、影视制作数据来自市文广新局;上市公司数据来自市金融办;卫生数据来自市卫生计生委;体育数据来自市体育局;“春风行动”数据来自市总工会;价格、城乡居民收支、人均住房面积、百户居民耐用品数据来自国家统计局杭州调查队;其它数据均来自于市统计局。

Statistical Communiqué of Hangzhou on the 2017 National Economic and Social Development

Hangzhou Municipal Bureau of Statistics

Hangzhou Survey Office of National Bureau of Statistics

In 2017, Hangzhou studied and implemented the spirit of the 19th National Congress of the Communist Party of China conscientiously, understood the spiritual essence and practical requirements of Xi Jinping Thought on Socialism with Chinese Characteristics for a New Era thoroughly, fully implemented the decisions and arrangements of 14th provincial Party Congress and 12th municipal Party Congress, to strengthen the reform of supply side as the principal line, speed up the building of unique and splendid world famous city, promoted the development of Yong Jiang strategy comprehensively. The city's economic structure was continuously optimized, the quality of development was constantly improving, people's livelihood and welfare were promoted continuously, and the social undertakings made new progress.

I. General Outlook

Economic Aggregate

In 2017, the gross domestic product (GDP) was 1260. 3 billion yuan, up by 8. 1% over the previous year. Of this total, the added value of the primary industry was 31. 1 billion yuan with an annual increase of 1. 8%, that of the secondary industry was 436. 2 billion yuan with an annual increase of 4. 8%, and that of the tertiary industry was 793 billion yuan with an annual increase of 10. 5%. The city's per capita GDP was 135,113 yuan, increased by 10,827 yuan over the previous year, up by 5. 5%. According to the average exchange rate in 2017 which published by the Central Bank, the per capita GDP was 20,011 US dollars. The proportions of the three industries adjusted to 2. 5: 34. 6: 62. 9, showing that the proportion of tertiary industry increased by 2 percentage points over the previous year.

Figure 1 Hangzhou GDP and Growth 2011 – 2017

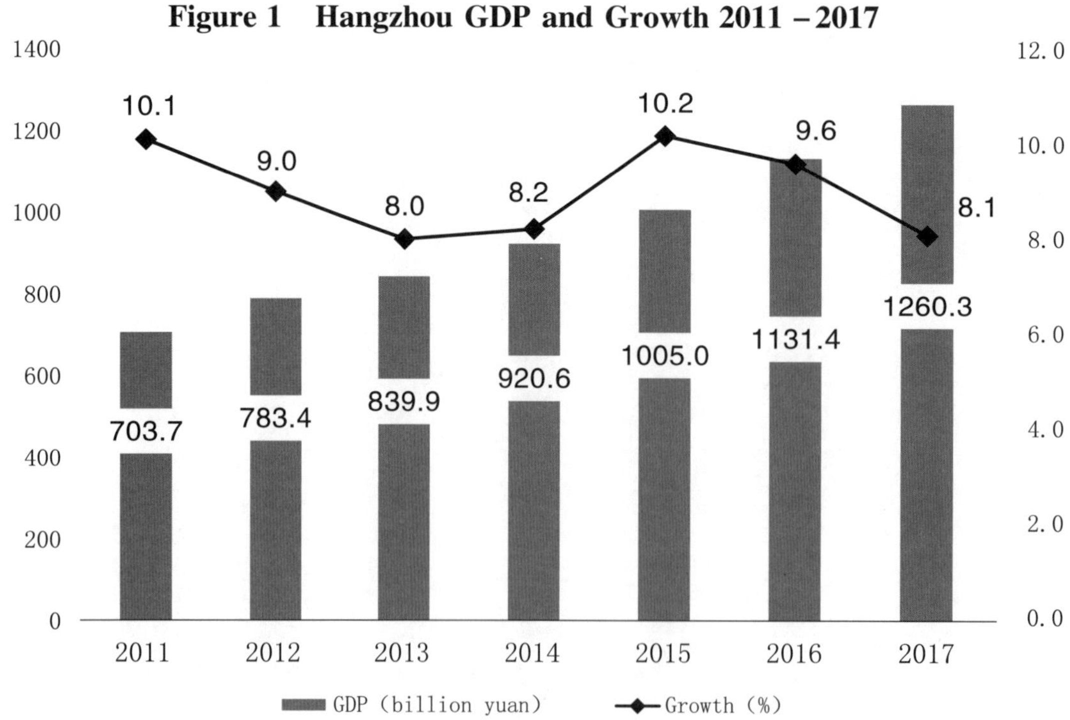

Non – State – Owned Economy

In 2017, the added value of the non – state – owned economy was 756. 1 billion yuan, accounting for 60. 2% of Hangzhou's GDP. At the end of the year, there were 481 thousand private enterprises and 471. 4 thousand individual businesses, up by 20. 1% and 10. 6% respectively. A total of 93. 8 thousand individual businesses were newly set up throughout the year, up by 8. 4%. The employees of private enterprises reached 3. 1225 million with an annual increase of 10. 9% , and that of individual businesses reached 924. 1 thousand with an annual increase of 16. 3%.

Fiscal Revenue and Expenditure

In 2017, the general fiscal revenue of the city reached 292. 13 billion yuan, up by 14. 2% , and the general budgetary revenue of the local government was 156. 742 billion yuan, up by 17. 4%. Of this total, the corporate income tax was 27. 022 billion yuan, and the personal income tax was 14. 62 billion yuan, up by 22. 0% and 26. 6% respectively. The fiscal expenditure of the local government was 154. 092 billion yuan, up by 9. 7%. Of this total, the fiscal expenditure for promoting people's livelihood reached 121. 309 billion yuan, up by 11. 9% , accounting for 78. 7% , increased by 1. 5 percentage points compare to previous year.

Figure 2 The General Budgetary Revenue of The Local Government 2011 – 2017

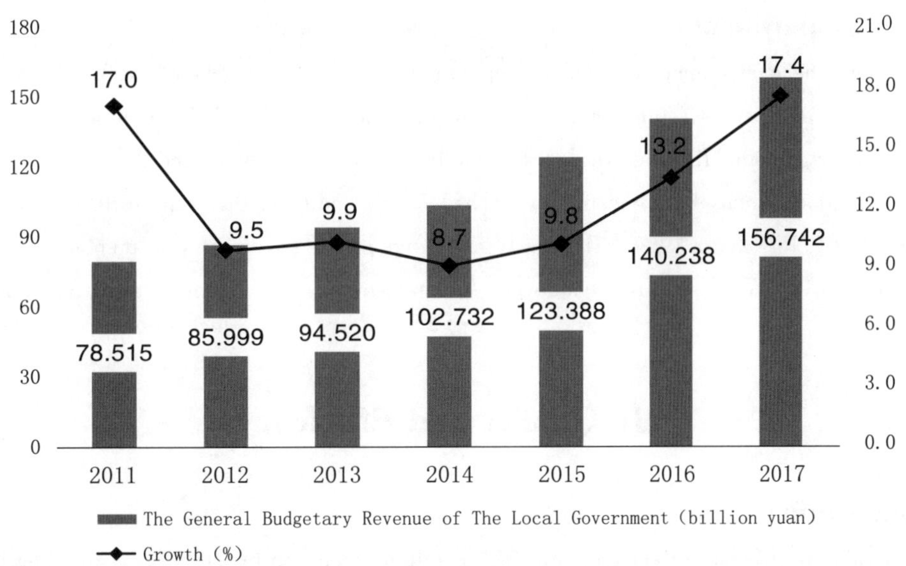

Commodity Price

The consumer price in urban area went up by 2. 5% over the previous year, of which, the price of residence up by 5. 7% , the price of education culture and entertainment up by 4. 1% , and the price of food and tobacco up by 0. 9%.

Figure 3 Monthly Changes in Urban Consumer Price in 2017

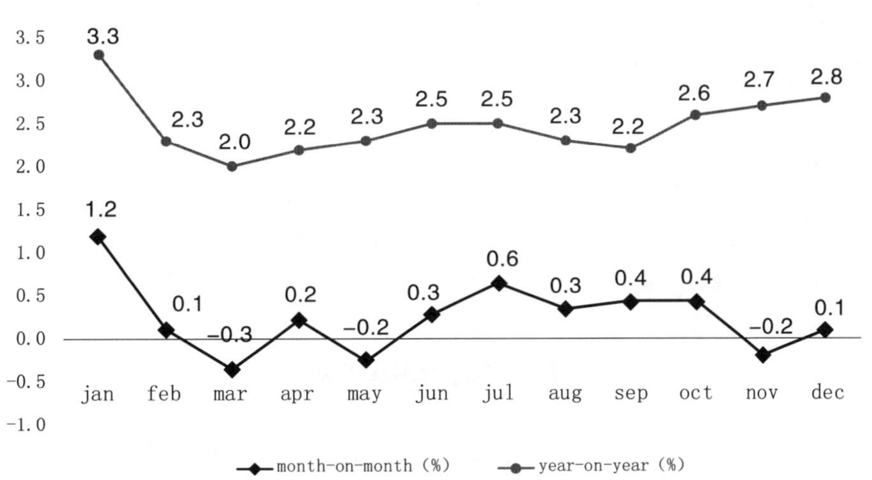

Table 1 The Changes of Consumer Price in Urban District

Item	2016	2017
General level of CPI in urban district	2.6	2.5
1. Food Tobacco and Liguor	6.0	0.9
2. Clothing	0.3	0.0
3. Residence	2.2	5.7
4. Household facilities, articles and Services	-0.4	0.2
5. Transportation and Telecommunication	-1.0	1.5
6. Education, Culture and Recreation	3.7	4.1
7. Health Care and Medical Services	0.8	1.7
8. Miscellaneous Goods and Services	2.7	1.4

The producer prices for manufactured goods and the producer purchasing prices up by 4.4% and 8.4% respectively.

Population and Employment

By the end of the year, the total number of resident population in Hangzhou reached 9.468 million, an increase of 280 thousand over the previous year. Of this total, urban population reached 7.2714 million, accounting for 76.8%, increased by 0.6 percentage points than last year; the crude birth rate was 12.5‰, and the rate of natural increase(RNI) was 7.4‰. The population of household registration reached 7.5388 million, the crude birth rate was 14.70‰, and the rate of natural increase(RNI) was 6.19‰. The newly employed people in urban area numbered 297.1 thousand, and 110.4 thousand unemployed people were re-employed. The registered urban unemployment rate was 1.7% at the year end.

II. Quality and Efficiency

Structure Optimization

In 2017, the added value of information economy was 321.6 billion yuan, up by 21.8%, accounting for 25.5% of GDP, increased by 1.2 percentage points over last year. Of this total, the added value of e-commerce industry was 131.6 billion yuan, up by 36.6%, and the growth rate of e-commerce industry remained above 30% for seven consecutive years. As one of the six industrial clusters, the cultural and creative industry achieved an added value of of 304.1 billion yuan, up by 19.0%, accounting for 24.1% of GDP.

Enterprise Efficiency

In 2017, the profit and tax of industrial enterprises above designated size was 177.5 billion yuan, up by 8.5%. Of this total, the profit was 99.9 billion yuan, up by 7.7%, increased by 1.7 percentage points and 1.0 percentage points over the previous year respectively. The total labour productivity was 302 thousand yuan / person, raising 24 thousand yuan / person; The added value per mu was 1.5 million yuan, increased by 132 thousand yuan. The profit and tax of information transmission & software & information technology service above designated size enterprises was 138.1 billion yuan, up by 34.3%, and the profit was 122.6 billion yuan, up by 35.4%.

III. Agriculture

In 2017, the added value of agriculture, forestry, animal husbandry and fishery achieved 30.6 billion yuan, up by 2.4%.

Of this total, the added value of agriculture was 19. 5 billion yuan, that of forestry was 4. 3 billion yuan, that of fishery was 2. 8 billion yuan, and that of agriculture & forestry & animal husbandry & Fishery Services was 0. 6 billion yuan, up by 4. 6% , 3. 1% , 3. 1% and 14. 4% respectively. The added value of animal husbandry was 3. 3 billion yuan, down by 11. 5%. The total output of grain was 0. 4726 million tons, up by 2. 9% ; the output of vegetable was 3. 3834 million tons, up by 0. 9% ; the output of fruit was 0. 8199 million tons, up by 7. 3% ; the output of meat was 21. 27 million tons, down by 4. 2% ; and that of aquatic products was 0. 201 million tons, up by 3. 2%. In 2017, there were 502 municipal vegetable bases in Hangzhou, of which 42 were newly built. 3 provincial - level modern agricultural parks and 4 distinctive agriculture towns were constructed, and 96 thousand mu of grain functional areas were newly - built throughout the year. 12 beautiful countryside quality demonstration lines were newly built , ecological restoration was implemented to 850 villages. The farmhouse (Home Hostel) received 49. 64 million tourists and the business revenue reached 5. 2 billion yuan, up by 27. 9% and 18. 2% respectively.

IV. Industry and Construction

Industry

In 2017, the added value of the industrial sector was 396. 8 billion yuan, up by 6. 3%. Of this total, the added value of industrial enterprises above designated size was 318. 4 billion yuan, up by 7. 0%. Among the industrial enterprises above designated size, the added value of high - tech industries, strategic emerging industries and equipment manufacturing industries up by 13. 6% , 15. 0% and 11. 0% respectively, accounting for 50. 1% , 30. 6% and 43. 2% of industrial enterprises above designated size, increased by 4. 1, 3. 4 and 1. 3 percentage points respectively; the added value of eight high energy consuming industries accounted for 24. 6% , decreased by 1. 5 percentage points. The output value ratio of new products was 37. 7%. The sales - output ratio of industrial products reached 98. 5%.

Construction

The added value of construction industry was 39. 6 billion yuan, accounting for 3. 1% of GDP. There were 1, 410 construction enterprises with the qualification of general contract and special contract, which construction output value amounted to 432. 4 billion yuan, up by 5. 3%. The new contract was 503. 7 billion yuan, up by 23. 2%. Total profits and taxes reached 19. 8 billion yuan, up by 3. 7%.

V. Investment in Fixed Assets and Real Estate

Investment in Fixed Assets

In 2017, the completed investment in fixed assets was 585. 7 billion yuan, up by 1. 4% over the previous year. Of this total, the private investment was 330. 1 billion yuan, up by 10. 4% , accounting for 56. 4%. Grouped by sectors, the investment in the primary industry was 4 billion yuan, up by 2. 4% ; the industrial investment was 86. 1 billion yuan, up by 0. 5% ; the investment in the tertiary industry was 495. 6 billion yuan, up by 1. 5%.

Investment in Real Estate

In 2017, the completed investment in real estate development was 273. 4 billion yuan, up by 4. 9% over the previous year, of which, the residential investment was 171. 3 billion yuan, up by 9. 8%. The floor space under construction was 115. 23 million square meters, down by 0. 3%. The new housing floor space under construction was 21. 77 million square meters, up by 1. 9%. The completed floor space was 20. 86 million square meters, up by 8. 5% . The sold floor space of commercial buildings was 20. 54 million square meters, down by 11. 7%.

VI. Domestic Trade

In 2017,the added value of wholesale and retail trades was 98. 2 billion yuan, up by 8. 1% , and the added value of lodging and catering services was 19. 3 billion yuan, up by 6. 0%. The total retail sales of consumer goods reached 571. 7 billion yuan, a growth of 10. 5% over the previous year. Of this total, the online retail sales by wholesale and retail enterprises above designated size was 65. 6 billion yuan, up by 24. 9% , accounting for 11. 5%. Group by business area, the retail sales of consumer goods in urban areas was 542. 1 billion yuan, up by 10. 4% ; and that in rural areas was 29. 7 billion yuan, up by 11. 4%. The number of city's commodity trading market was 684 with an annual turnover of 428. 9 billion yuan, up by 11. 5%.

Figure 4 Total Retail Sales of Consumer Goods and Growth Rates 2011 – 2017

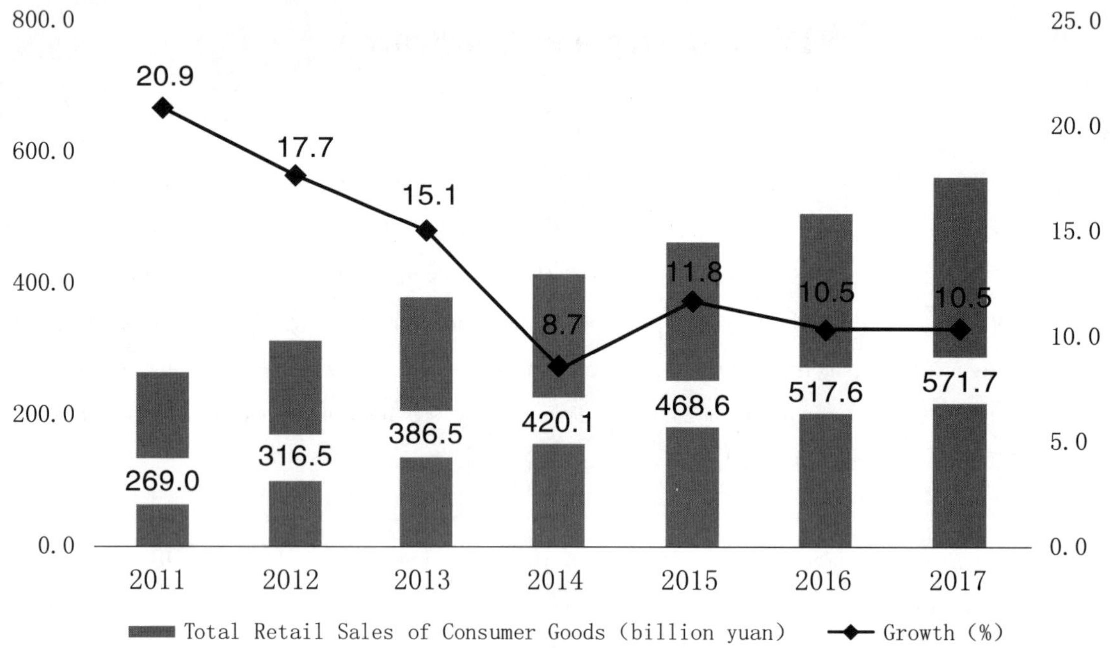

VII. Foreign Economic Relations

International Trade

The total value of import and export of goods in 2017 was 508. 5 billion yuan, up by 13. 3%. Of this total, the export was 345. 6 billion yuan, up by 4. 3% ; the import was 162. 9 billion yuan, up by 38. 8%. The export of high – tech products was 47. 8 billion yuan, up by 12. 8% , and the export of electromechanical products was 145. 6 billion yuan, up by 7. 3%. The export by private enterprises was 232. 5 billion yuan, up by 6. 8%. The export to the countries which along the Belt and Road was 104. 9 billion yuan, accounting for 30. 4% of total export.

The total import and export of service trade was 161. 9 billion yuan, up by 15. 7% , accounting for 24. 1% of total import and export in goods and service trade. Of this total, the export was 108. 8 billion yuan, up by 15% ; the import was 53. 1 billion yuan, up by 17%.

The trading volume of cross border e – commerce was 9. 936 billion U. S. dollars, up by 22. 5%. Of this total, the export was 7. 022 billion U. S. dollars, and the import was 2. 914 billion U. S. dollars, up by 15. 9% and 42. 0% respectively.

International Cooperation

By the end of 2017, the total number of overseas enterprises (institutions) which had been set up by Hangzhou investors was 1,781, up by 12.3%. The accomplished business revenue through contracted overseas engineering projects and labor cooperation was 2.35 billion U.S. dollars, up by 22.0%. The executed value of offshore service outsourcing was 6.465 billion U.S. dollars, up by 10.1%.

Utilization of Foreign Capital

In 2017, 575 foreign - invested enterprises were newly set up, up by 24.5%. The actually utilized foreign capital was 6.61 billion US dollars, down by 8.3%. Of this total, the actually utilized foreign capital in service industry was 5.71 billion US dollars, up by 1.0%, accounting for 86.4%. By the end of 2017, 120 companies of Fortune Global 500 invested 208 projects in Hangzhou, of which 8 enterprises and 10 projects were newly introduced this year.

Return of Zhejiang Merchants

In 2017, 985 projects of Return Zhejiang merchants were introduced, with a total investment of 76.18 billion yuan, up by 7.3%. Of this total, the projects in service industry was 829, with a total investment of 66.67 billion yuan.

VIII. Transportation, Post, Telecommunications and Tourism

Transportation

In 2017, the added value of transportation, storage and post achieved 34.2 billion yuan, up by 3.8%. The annual total freight traffic was 0.348 billion tons, up by 15.3%. The total passenger traffic was 0.223 billion persons, up by 8.5%. By the end of 2017, 286 air routes had been opened, including 49 international routes and 8 routes to Hongkong, Macao and Taiwan. The aviation passenger throughput was 35.57 million persons, and the cargo throughput was 0.5895 million tons, up by 12.6% and 20.8% respectively. Of this total, the entry - exit passengers were 4.529 million persons, and that of cargo were 65.3 thousand tons, up by 8.3% and 34.4% respectively.

The annual subway passengers were 340 million, up by 26.5%. The daily average public traffic passengers in urban area were 4.302 million.

The total possession of motor vehicles reached 2.7936 million, up by 6.1%. The total possession of civil vehicles reached 2.4512 million, up by 4.7%, of which private cars numbered 1.9985 million, up by 9.4%.

Post and Telecommunications

In 2017, the business income of postal enterprises and express delivery enterprises above designated size totaled 27.509 billion yuan, up by 27.9%, of which the business income of express delivery was 25.105 billion yuan, up by 28.3%. The business income of telecommunication services totaled 23.081 billion yuan, up by 8.9%. At the end of 2017, there were 2.467 million fixed - line telephone subscribers and 17.242 million mobile phone users, down by 2.5% and 0.6% respectively. The broadband subscribers amounted to 5.05 million, up by 14.0%. The coverage rate of optical network was 99.5%.

Tourism

In 2017, the added value of tourism industry achieved 92.8 billion yuan, up by 12.6%, accounting for 7.4% of GDP. The total revenue from tourism reached 304.134 billion yuan, up by 18.3%, of which the foreign exchange earnings from international tourism was 3.543 billion US dollars, up by 12.5%. The number of total tourists was 162.8663 million, up by 15.8%. The number of domestic visitors was 158.844 million, up by 16.0%; and that of overseas visitor arrivals was 4.0223 million, up by 10.7%. At the end of 2017, there were 767 travel agencies, up by 7.0%, and 143 star - rated hotels, including 23 5 - star hotels and 42 4 - star hotels, and 91 A - rated scenic spots, including 3 AAAAA scenic spots and 34 AAAA scenic spots.

IX. Finance

In 2017, the added value of Finance achieved 105. 6 billion yuan, up by 6. 9%. There were 499 financial institutions in Hangzhou at year – end, increased by 37 over the previous year. The balance of RMB and foreign currency deposits was 3648. 324 billion yuan, up by 9. 3% ; and the loans balance was 2927. 094 billion yuan, up by 11. 9% , of which, the loans balance of household was 965. 368 billion yuan, up by 23. 8% , and the loans balance of non – financial institutions was 1932. 594 billion yuan, up by 6. 6%.

Table 2 Deposit and Loan Balance in RMB and Foreign Currency in all Financial Institutions at the End of 2017

Item	Year – end Figure (100 million yuan)	Increase/Decrease over the previous year(%)
Total Deposit Balance	36483. 24	9. 3
Of which: Household Deposits	8670. 60	2. 1
Non – financial Institutions Deposits	16313. 18	12. 7
Total Loan Balance	29270. 94	11. 9
Of which: Household Loans	9653. 68	23. 8
Non – financial Enterprise Loans	19325. 94	6. 6

There were 163 listed companies in Hangzhou at the year – end, of which 128 were listed domestically. The total value of companies listed domestically was 1995. 522 billion yuan. There were 28 newly authorized listed companies in Hangzhou, raising 18. 77 billion yuan. 381 companies were listed on the New Third Board.

In 2017, the premiums received by the insurance companies totalled 63. 37 billion yuan, up by 22. 2%. Of this total, the property insurance premium was 19. 4 billion yuan, up by 12. 5% , and the life insurance premium was 43. 971 billion yuan, up by 27. 1%. The payments of insurance indemnity of various kinds totalled 16. 961 billion yuan, up by 6. 8% , of which, the property insurance indemnity was 10. 596 billion yuan, up by 5. 9% , and life insurance indemnity was 6. 364 billion yuan, up by 8. 2%.

X. Education, Science & Technology

Education

By the end of 2017, there were 458 primary schools with 560. 4 thousand students, 251 junior secondary schools with 224. 8 thousand students, 80 regular senior secondary schools with 11. 31 thousand students, and 39 regular institutions of higher education with 484. 1 thousand students in Hangzhou. The ratio of enrollment to kindergartens of those who were 3 years younger than school age reached 98. 95%. The enrollment rate to senior schools from junior secondary schools was 99. 69% , and the gross enrollment rate to general colleges and universities was 63. 26%. 282 thousand children of migrant workers were enrolling in the stage of compulsory education. There were 72 home and abroad cooperative projects at all levels, of which 8 projects were municipal colleges and universities, and 7 projects were senior secondary schools.

Science & Technology

In 2017, 25,578 invention patents were applied and 9,872 were authorized, up by 2. 5% and 14. 2% respectively.

Among all authorized invention patents, the enterprise patents accounted for 47.4%. There were accumulated 2,844 national - level supported high - tech enterprises, an annual increase of 589. At the year - end, there were 2,189 foster identified research and development centers, of which 835 were provincial level. There were 9,238 scientific small and medium sized enterprises, including 1,203 enterprise research centers above provincial level. 76 enterprise research institutes at provincial level were newly increased in the year. There were a total of 113 scientific enterprise incubators, of which 32 at national level, and 60 at provincial level. There were 101 public innovation spaces in Hangzhou, of which 23 were named provincial level outstanding public innovation spaces.

The expenditures on research and development activities (R&D) accounted for 3.15% of Hangzhou's GDP. The expenditure on science and technology in general public budget expenditure was 9.232 billion yuan, up by 23.2%.

XI. Culture, Public Health and sports

Culture

By the end of 2017, there were 11 professional arts performing organizations, 15 cultural centers, 88 museums, 39 national key cultural relics protection units, 16 archives, and 15 public libraries with 15.90 million books (excluding the province - owned). The city's cable TV access households reached 3.5302 million, of which 3.1309 million were digital TV, up by 1.9% and 4.8% over the previous year respectively. During the whole year, a total of 1,331 episodes in 44 TV dramas were produced, 36,036 minutes of original animation was created, and 17 films were completed. There were 335 intangible cultural heritage protection projects in Hangzhou, increased by 4 over the previous year.

Public Health

At the year - end, there were 4,933 medical and health institutions in Hangzhou, including 302 hospitals, up by 5.2% and 9.0% over the previous year respectively. There were 1,275 community health service centers (stations) and 15 disease prevention and control centers. The number of beds was 75,900, of which 70,200 were hospital beds, up by 9.3% and 9.7% respectively. There were 110,400 professional medical personnel, of whom 41,800 were licensed (assistant) doctors and 46,300 were registered nurses, up by 9.1%, 9.5% and 10.2% respectively. A total of 129.2498 million patients received diagnosis and treatment in medical institutions, up by 6.2%. The infant mortality rate and mortality rate of children under five - year old were 1.73‰ and 2.27‰ respectively. The mortality per 100,000 pregnant women was 6.5 persons.

Sports

Hangzhou athletes won 47 medals in international competitions throughout the year, including 22 gold medals, 15 silver medals, and won 318 medals in national competitions, including 148 gold medals, 90 silver medals. Hangzhou successfully held the 13th National Student Games, Hangzhou Marathon, Hangzhou West Lake International Collegiate Rowing Challenge, International surfing challenge and International (Hangzhou) trailwalk etc. Hangzhou established 4 national high - level sports reserve talents bases, 8 provincial high - level sports reserve talents bases (including 4 key bases), 5 provincial sports traditional project school backup bases.

XII. People's Livelihood and Social Security

People's Livelihood

The annual per capita disposable income in Hangzhou was 49,832 yuan, up by 8.1% or a real increase of 5.5% after deducting price factors. In terms of residence area, the annual per capita disposable income of urban households reached 56,276 yuan, up by 7.8% or a real increase of 5.2% after deducting price factors, and the annual per capita disposable income of rural households was 30,397yuan, up by 8.9%, a real increase of 6.2% after deducting price factors. The annual per capita consumption expenditure in Hangzhou was 34,146 yuan, up by 7.0%, a real increase of 4.4% after deducting price factors. In terms of residence area, the annual per capita consumption expenditure of urban households was 38,179 yuan, and that of rural households was 21,983 yuan, up by 7.0% and 6.9% respectively, after deducting price factors, the real increase were 4.4% and 4.3% respectively.

Table 3 Per Capita Disposable Income and Consumption Expenditure in Hangzhou 2017

Item	Urban Residents		Rural Residents	
	Income (yuan)	Increase over the previous year (%)	Income (yuan)	Increase over the previous year (%)
Disposable Income	56,276	7.8	30,397	8.9
1. Income from Wages	32,144	6.8	18,232	6.9
2. Net Business Income	4,893	6.2	7,770	9.3
3. Property Income	8,329	5.4	1,280	12.6
4. Transfer Income	10,910	13.9	3,115	19.6
Consumption Expenditure	38,179	7.0	21,983	6.9

By the end of the year, the per capita floor space of residential building in urban areas reached 36.4 square meters, and every 100 urban households had 55.8 family cars, 235.3 air conditioners, 115.1 home computers, up by 6.7%, 3.8% and 2.8% respectively; the per capita floor space of residential building in rural areas reached 70.9 square meters, and every 100 rural households had 46.5 family cars, 186.7 air conditioners, 76.4 home computers, up by 9.7%, 11% and 1.9% respectively.

Social Security

By the end of the year, a total of 6.2832 million people participated in the basic social pension insurance for employees, an increase of 523.4 thousand; a total of 5.805 million people participated in the basic medical insurance program for employees, an increase of 511.8 thousand; a total of 4.1320 million people participated in the unemployment insurance, 3.9073 million people participated in the maternity insurance, a year - on - year increase of 390 thousand and 414 thousand respectively. 1,691 households were newly added as low - rent housing security families, and 8,541 units of public rental housing were available. The minimum subsistence guarantee for residents in urban areas was raised to 917 yuan per person per month, up by 12%, and that for residents in rural areas was raised by the same percentage. By the end of the year, 122.7 thousand people were benefitted from the city's minimum living guarantee system, and the annual payment of minimum living guarantee system reached 0.749 billion yuan.

Social Welfare

By the end of the year, there were 1,176 canteens for the aged in Hangzhou. The number of community home care service centers reached 2,815, covering all urban and rural areas. The Elderly services were basically available on a 15 - minute walk in urban areas and 20 - minute walk in rural areas. There were 303 welfare institutions and nursing homes for the aged, providing 70,300 beds, accommodating 22,700 persons. The fund raised by all kinds of welfare lotteries issued this year reached 2.817 billion yuan, up by 7.1%. A total of 85.38 million yuan of social funds was raised by the 17th 'Spring Breeze Action'.

XIII. Urban Construction

Urban Infrastructure Construction

In 2017, the investment in infrastructure amounting to 159. 7 billion yuan, accounting for 27. 3% of the city's investment in fixed assets. The construction of high – speed road network of 182 km was completed . The total mileage of roads reached 16,424 km, including 632 km of expressways.

At the end of the year, there were 371 public transport operation lines in the main urban area, of which 16 were newly opened, and 40 were optimized. The city had newly opened 35. 8 kilometers length of subway, with a total mileage of 117. 6 km. The construction of canal transportation service center was completed and opened to the public.

At the end of the year, the green space in urban built – up area were 21,726 hectares. The per capita green space in urban area was 13. 4 square meters, and the green coverage rate of the built – up area was 40. 0%.

Public Utilities

The annual investment in construction of power grids amounted to 5. 11 billion yuan. A total of 37 power transmission projects, each of which was 110 KV or above, were newly under construction. An additional capacity of 4. 08 million KVA and 252. 11 km of electrical wires were added respectively. The electricity consumption of the whole city was 73. 803 billion KWH, up by 8. 8% , of which the consumption of residents in urban and rural areas was 11. 486 billion KWH, up by 7. 0%.

The daily capacity of water supply in urban areas reached 3. 907 million cubic meters, and the highest daily water supply reached 3. 581 million cubic meters.

A total of 56,916 parking spaces were newly completed, of which 6,222 were public parking spaces.

XIV. Environment Protection and Work Safety

Environment Protection

The total days with urban air quality rated excellent or good accumulated to 271 throughout the year, increased by 11 days over the previous year, accounting for 74. 2% of the year. The average concentration of PM2. 5 in the urban area was 44. 6 micrograms per cubic meter, down by 8. 6%. Water quality of 9 county controlled sections and 1256 sites which failed to meet Enade standard was improved. Among the 52 municipal level flow sections, 48 met the functional requirements, accounting for 92. 3%. The city implemented 124 emission reduction projects, eliminated 23,119 old cars, and newly added 879 green energy buses. The number of eliminated backward & surplus production capacity projects reached 170, and 3,753 small blocky industries were promoted. The city reduced emissions of volatile organic compounds by 9,974 tons. The energy consumption per unit added value of industrial enterprises above designated size decreased by 4. 1%.

The comprehensive index of eco – environmental quality (EI) continues to be ranked in the forefront of the whole country and the whole province. The city was awarded titles of national ecological garden city and provincial demonstration city of ecological construction. The constructed national ecological counties accumulated to 8, the constructed national ecological towns accumulated to 119, and the constructed provincial ecological counties accumulated to 9.

Work Safety

There were 462 work accidents throughout the year, resulting in 499 deaths and 91 injured, down by 17. 8% , 19. 4% and 15. 7% respectively.

Notes:

1. GDP and absolute added value of various industries are calculated based on current price, whereas their growth rates are calculated based on constant price. The classification on industries is subject to the Classification on Primary, Secondary and Tertiary Industries regulations formulated by National Statistics Office in 2012.

2. GDP of year 2016 and 2017 included the expenditure of research and development.

3. According to the results of the 3rd agricultural census, the data of agriculture related and investment in fixed assets were adjusted; the growth of investment in fixed assets in 2017 was calculated on a comparable basis.

Source of Statistics:

In this communigue, Statistics on newly increased employed people in urban areas, registered urban unemployment rate and social security are from Hangzhou Municipal Bureau of Human Resources and Social Security; fiscal statistics are from Hangzhou Bureau of Finance; statistics on agricultural park and grain production functional zone are from Hangzhou Agriculture Bureau; statistics on education are from Hangzhou Municipal Commission of Education; statistics on import and export are from Hangzhou Customs; statistics on subsistence allwance, social services and assistance, welfare lottery are from Hangzhou Municipal Bureau of Civil Affairs; statistics on highway mileage, freight traffic and passenger traffic are form Hangzhou Traffic Management Bureau; statistics on aviation, air routes are form Xiaoshan International Airport; statistics on passenger capacity of metro are from Hangzhou Metro Group; statistics on'Spring Breeze Action' are from Federation of trade Unions; statistics on garbage classification area are from Hangzhou Urban Management Committee; statistics on parking space, centralized disposal rate of urban sewage and per capita green land of parks are from Hangzhou Municipal Commission of Housing and Urban – Rural Development; statistics on ecological construction and environmental monitoring are from Hangzhou Municipal Bureau of Environmental Protection; statistics on safety production are from Hangzhou Administration of Work Safety; statistics on online retail are from Zhejiang Provincial Department of Commerce; statistics on actually utilized foreign direct investment are from Hangzhou Municipal Commission of Commerce; statistics on tourism are from Hangzhou Municipal Commission of Tourism Development; statistics on money and finance are from People's Bank of China Hangzhou Center Branch; statistics on insurance are from Zhejiang Bureau of China Insurance Regulatory Commission; statistics on patent are from Hangzhou Municipal Science and Technology Commission; statistics on public library are from Hangzhou Municipal Administration of Press, Publication, Radio, Film and Telecision; statistics on newly authorized listed company are from Hangzhou Finance Office; statistics on healthcare are from Hangzhou Municipal Commission of Health and Family Planning; statistics on sports are from Hangzhou Municipal Bureau of Sports; statistics on price are from Hangzhou Survey Office of National Bureau of Statistics; other statistics are from Hangzhou Municipal Bureau of Statistics.

一、综合

GENERAL SURVEY

1 综　　合
General Survey

主要统计指标
Major Statistical Indicators

全市生产总值	Gross Domestic Product	12603.36	亿元	(100 million yuan)
为上年	As Compared with the Preceding Year	108.1	%	(%)
第一产业	Primary Industry	311.08	亿元	(100 million yuan)
为上年	As Compared with the Preceding Year	101.8	%	(%)
第二产业	Secondary Industry	4362.48	亿元	(100 million yuan)
为上年	As Compared with the Preceding Year	104.8	%	(%)
第三产业	Tertiary Industry	7929.80	亿元	(100 million yuan)
为上年	As Compared with the Preceding Year	110.5	%	(%)
常住居民人均生产总值	Per Capita GDP (Long-term Residents)	135113	元	(yuan)
为上年	As Compared with the Preceding Year	105.5	%	(%)
生产总值构成	Composition of Gross Domestic Product	100	%	(%)
第一产业	Primary Industry	2.5	%	(%)
第二产业	Secondary Industry	34.6	%	(%)
第三产业	Tertiary Industry	62.9	%	(%)

1－01 行政区划(2017年末)
Administrative Division(End of 2017)

单位:个 (unit)

地 区	Region	街 道 Subdistrict Offices	乡(镇) Towns and Townships	镇 Towns	村、社区 Villages and Communities	村 Villages
全 市	**Whole City**	**92**	**98**	**75**	**3126**	**2036**
市 区	Urban District	85	52	46	2232	1202
上城区	Shangcheng	6	–	–	54	–
下城区	Xiacheng	8	–	–	74	–
江干区	Jianggan	10	–	–	182	4
拱墅区	Gongshu	10	–	–	99	–
西湖区	Xihu	10	2	2	206	41
高新(滨江)区	Hi－Tech(Binjiang)	3	–	–	60	–
萧山区	Xiaoshan	14	12	12	595	411
余杭区	Yuhang	14	6	6	355	183
富阳区	Fuyang	5	19	13	304	276
临安区	Lin'an	5	13	13	303	287
桐庐县	Tonglu	4	10	6	200	182
淳安县	Chun'an	–	23	11	438	423
建德市	Jiande	3	13	12	256	229

注:萧山区含大江东产业集聚区、江干区含经济技术开发区、西湖区含风景名胜区。

a) Figures of Xiaoshan include Dajiangdong, figures of Jianggan include Economic and Technological Development Zone, figures of Xihu include the West Lake Scenic Zone.

1－02 土地面积和人口密度(2017年末)

Land Area and Population Density(End of 2017)

地　区	Region	土地面积(平方千米) Land Area (sq. km)	年末总人口(万人) Population (10000 persons)	人口密度(人/平方千米) Population Density (person/sq. km)
全　市	**Whole City**	**16596**	**946.8**	**570**
市　区	Urban District	8000	824.1	1030
上城区	Shangcheng	18	34.8	19333
下城区	Xiacheng	31	53.1	17129
江干区	Jianggan	210	112.8	5371
拱墅区	Gongshu	88	56.2	6386
西湖区	Xihu	263	86.0	3270
高新(滨江)区	Hi－Tech(Binjiang)	73	35.1	4808
萧山区	Xiaoshan	1163	165.5	1423
余杭区	Yuhang	1222	147.6	1208
富阳区	Fuyang	1808	73.9	409
临安区	Lin'an	3124	59.1	189
桐庐县	Tonglu	1780	42.9	241
淳安县	Chun'an	4452	35.3	79
建德市	Jiande	2364	44.5	188

注:萧山区含大江东产业集聚区、江干区含经济技术开发区、西湖区含风景名胜区。

a) Figures of Xiaoshan include Dajiangdong, figures of Jianggan include Economic and Technological Development Zone, figures of Xihu include the West Lake Scenic Zone.

1-03 平均每天主要社会经济活动(2010-2017年)

Selected Indicators on Average Daily Social and Economic Activities(2010-2017)

指标 Item	2010	2011	2012	2013	2014	2015	2016	2017
全市生产总值 (万元) Gross Domestic Product (10,000 yuan)	163444	192802	214620	230098	252224	275349	309118	345298
工业增加值 (万元) Value-Added of Industry (10,000 yuan)	67212	79181	84749	86477	93559	95831	101809	108716
规模以上工业企业利税总额 (万元) Total Pre-tax Profits of Industrial Enterprises above Designated Size (10,000 yuan)	33324	36452	36711	39748	42139	42731	45236	48617
农林牧渔业总产值 (万元) Gross Output Value of Farming, Forestry, Animal Husbandry and Fishery (10,000 yuan)	8667	9783	10530	10942	11468	12066	12768	13041
固定资产投资 (万元) Investment in Fixed Assets (10,000 yuan)	72654	84932	101993	116818	135690	152228	159629	160456
住宅竣工面积 (平方米) Floor Space of Residential Buildings Completed (sq. m)	21981	23038	18466	23154	25425	29323	30419	40297
社会消费品零售总额 (万元) Total Retail Sales of Consumer Goods (10,000 yuan)	60959	73705	86718	105886	115108	128691	141426	156642
住户存款新增额 (万元) The Increased Amount of Household Deposits (10,000 yuan)	19289	15247	14863	8729	9825	8739	23921	4858
财政总收入 (万元) Total Financial Revenue (10,000 yuan)	34121	40792	44600	47534	52606	61335	69902	80036

1－04 国民经济

Major Indicators of

指　标		Item	
年末常住人口	（万人）	Long－term Residents（End of 2017）	（10,000 persons）
年末户籍人口	（万人）	Household Registration Population（End of 2017）	（10,000 persons）
#城镇人口	（万人）	Urban Population	（10,000 persons）
年末从业人员数	（万人）	Total Number of Employed Persons（End of 2017）	（10,000 persons）
全市生产总值	（亿元）	Gross Domestic Product	（100 million yuan）
第一产业	（亿元）	Primary Industry	（100 million yuan）
第二产业	（亿元）	Secondary Industry	（100 million yuan）
第三产业	（亿元）	Tertiary Industry	（100 million yuan）
人均生产总值（户籍）	（元）	Per Capita GDP（Household）	（yuan）
人均生产总值（常住）	（元）	Per Capita GDP（Long－term）	（yuan）
主要农产品产量		Output of Major Farm Products	
粮食	（万吨）	Grain	（10,000 tons）
棉花	（吨）	Cotton	（ton）
油菜籽	（吨）	Rapeseeds	（ton）
茶叶	（吨）	Tea	（ton）
蚕茧	（吨）	Silk－worm Cocoons	（ton）
生猪年末存栏	（万头）	Hogs in Stock at Year End	（10,000 heads）
肉类产量	（万吨）	Output of Meat	（10,000 tons）
淡水产品产量	（吨）	Freshwater Aquatic Products	（ton）
全部工业总产值	（亿元）	The Total Output Value of Industrial Enterprises	（100 million yuan）
规模以上工业总产值	（亿元）	The Output Valne of Industrial Enterprises Above Designated Size	（100 million yuan）
规模以上工业企业利税总额	（亿元）	Total Pre－tax Profits of Industrial Enterprises Above Designated Size	（100 million yuan）
客运量	（万人次）	Total Passenger Traffic	（10,000 person－times）
货运量	（万吨）	Total Freight Traffic	（10,000 tons）
固定资产投资	（亿元）	Investment in Fixed Assets	（100 million yuan）
社会消费品零售总额	（亿元）	Total Retail Sales of Consumer Goods	（100 million yuan）

注：1. 规模以上工业的计算口径，1997 年以前为乡及乡以上，1998 年－2010 年为主营业务收入 500 万元及以上，2011 年起为 2000 万元及以上的工业企业。

2. 从 2014 年起，粮食数据按粮食生产统计监测抽样调查口径。

主要指标（主要年份）
National Economy (Main Years)

1985	1990	1995	2000	2005	2010	2012	2013	2014	2015	2016	2017
	583.21		701.70	771.30	870.54	880.20	884.40	889.20	901.80	918.80	946.80
543.05	574.78	597.96	621.58	660.45	689.12	700.52	706.61	715.76	723.55	736.00	753.88
153.46	169.00	191.43	226.99	297.54	365.24	384.09	393.88	404.27	447.24	463.86	482.55
330.37	363.49	422.55	408.11	481.10	626.33	644.43	650.51	654.92	663.03	676.95	681.06
90.49	189.62	762.01	1382.56	2943.84	5965.71	7833.62	8398.58	9206.16	10050.21	11313.72	12603.36
15.97	30.94	69.25	103.96	148.21	208.41	255.11	261.60	274.35	287.95	304.21	311.08
52.08	96.17	410.00	709.32	1494.36	2819.81	3500.13	3574.25	3845.58	3909.01	4120.93	4362.48
22.44	62.51	282.76	569.28	1301.27	2937.49	4078.37	4562.73	5086.24	5853.25	6888.59	7929.80
1675	3310	12797	22342	44871	86932	112211	119372	129448	139653	155030	169187
				38542	70024	89323	95190	103813	112230	124286	135113
180.00	189.56	174.50	153.08	103.50	58.00	54.98	47.53	47.53	45.91	45.91	47.26
6704	6693	8038	2112	1038	704	577	509	426	378	300	255
51849	60683	61446	80436	70733	67946	64102	64816	50181	51186	43526	47223
22742	26429	19824	24810	25551	30500	32283	28503	26548	28139	28150	30103
7980	11085	13240	9308	16339	11700	9724	8267	6364	4880	3482	3013
166.10	159.00	147.58	172.16	165.28	192.53	210.76	174.89	153.95	137.26	114.08	104.08
11.16	14.93	19.21	25.24	30.74	31.78	33.47	30.27	26.98	24.31	22.19	21.27
30400	47588	63294	91626	147800	208945	210527	197992	186026	178880	175308	172845
				6589.51	12810.52	15595.28	15211.78	15851.40	15018.77	15054.78	15688.35
128.59	292.26	1020.03	1543.57	5441.13	11081.04	12959.68	12418.00	12853.05	12415.68	12420.96	12963.76
24.81	31.54	63.05	161.61	450.68	1224.48	1339.94	1450.55	1538.07	1559.68	1655.64	1774.52
6724	8119	16620	18607	24124	33772	35819	36409	24070	23942	20541	22289
2488	6522	10347	11459	19909	25915	30089	30734	29335	29384	30170	34785
14.19	22.92	156.63	376.65	1277.80	2651.88	3722.75	4263.87	4952.70	5556.32	5842.42	5856.65
47.81	98.17	299.35	514.68	978.43	2225.00	3165.19	3864.84	4201.46	4697.23	5176.20	5717.43

a) The standard for above designated size of industry, before 1997, it was above the sub – district level; 1998 – 2010, it was the annual sales income over 5 million yuan; since 2011, it was the annual sales income over 20 million yuan.

b) The data of grain was obtained from the sampling survey of grain production in 2014.

1-04 续表

指　标		Item	
境外旅游者人数	（万人次）	Number of Foreign Tourists	(10,000 person-times)
财政总收入	（亿元）	Total Financial Revenue	(100 million yuan)
一般公共预算支出	（亿元）	General Public Budget Revenue	(100 million yuan)
金融机构存款余额（本外币）	（亿元）	Deposits of Financial Institutions	(100 million yuan)
住户存款余额	（亿元）	Household Deposits	(100 million yuan)
金融机构贷款余额（本外币）	（亿元）	Loans of Financial Institutions	(100 million yuan)
非私营单位就业人员工资总额	（亿元）	Total Wages of Employed Persons in Non-private Units	(100 million yuan)
非私营单位就业人员平均工资	（元）	Average Wage of Employed Persons in Non-private Units	(yuan)
市区居民消费价格指数	（以1978年为100）	Consumer Price Index in Urban District	(Year of 1978 = 100)
市区商品零售价格指数	（以1978年为100）	Retail Price Index in Urban District	(Year of 1978 = 100)
全体居民人均可支配收入	（元）	Per Capita Annual Disposable Income of Urban and Rural Residents	(yuan)
城镇居民人均可支配收入	（元）	Per Capita Annual Disposable Income of Urban Residents	(yuan)
农村居民人均可支配收入	（元）	Per Capita Annual Disposable Income of Rural Residents	(yuan)
高等学校在校学生数	（人）	Student Enrollment in Institutions of Higher Education	(person)
中等专业学校在校学生数	（人）	Student Enrollment in Secondary Specialized Schools	(person)
普通中学在校学生数	（人）	Student Enrollment in Secondary Schools	(person)
小学在校学生数	（人）	Student Enrollment in Primary Schools	(person)
卫生机构数	（个）	Number of Health Institutions	(unit)
#医院	（个）	Number of Hospitals	(unit)
卫生技术人员	（人）	Number of Medical Technical Personnel	(person)
#执业（助理）医师	（人）	Number of Lisensed (Assistant) Doctors	(person)
床位数	（张）	Number of Beds in Health Institutions	(unit)
#医院	（张）	Beds in Hospital	(unit)

continued

1985	1990	1995	2000	2005	2010	2012	2013	2014	2015	2016	2017
23.84	38.83	44.13	70.71	151.36	275.71	331.12	316.01	326.13	341.56	363.23	402.23
18.65	25.25	55.13	142.85	520.79	1245.43	1627.89	1734.98	1920.11	2238.75	2558.41	2921.30
5.77	11.82	24.91	73.43	238.33	616.58	786.28	855.74	961.18	1205.48	1404.31	1540.92
48.50	133.77	707.97	2088.47	6748.72	17084.35	20148.77	22174.71	24450.51	29863.83	33386.04	36483.24
15.96	69.75	342.34	788.56	2191.66	4990.97	6089.98	6408.59	6767.20	7617.75	8493.27	8670.60
58.01	162.27	567.20	1686.64	5545.30	15078.73	18090.90	19350.46	21316.83	23327.95	26169.00	29270.94
13.01	27.79	89.05	126.75	297.02	933.06	1483.90	1758.23	1982.27	2152.40	2417.60	2646.72
1266	2382	7156	14257	31069	48772	56417	63664	69209	76073	85022	93891
140.21	246.68	503.06	611.07	623.07	701.33	753.36	772.19	787.63	801.81	822.66	843.23
142.61	256.45	476.99	504.42	470.47	526.76	560.39	568.80	573.35	574.50	583.12	588.95
							35763	39237	42642	46116	49832
1026	1985	6301	9668	16601	30035	37511	40925	44632	48316	52185	56276
624	1171	3012	4894	7655	13186	17017	21208	23555	25719	27908	30397
36996	39866	63124	122386	351918	434811	459181	471820	474652	485558	480953	484070
16527	23564	42784	45238	20344	3999	3909	3656	3974	3968	4402	4566
244399	199940	257071	342533	362257	352997	331353	327346	324414	321306	326187	337851
414839	460514	513988	485679	458942	453897	472613	483489	502688	524513	543038	560411
1582	1738	1712	1599	2196	2819	3017	4139	4198	4428	4691	4933
404	440	414	396	127	151	198	208	218	244	277	302
25593	30990	34245	35487	42353	61117	71618	78340	85614	93036	101194	110395
11503	14483	16465	16317	17833	24345	27369	29686	31977	34832	38172	41833
19637	24121	26684	27166	33251	42828	49471	52056	55779	63632	69452	75948
15010	18879	21360	23303	25907	33611	44019	46636	50805	58400	63994	70187

1－05　全市生产总值及发展指数(1978－2017年)

Gross Domestic Product and its Indices(1978－2017)

单位:万元　(10000 yuan)

年份 Year	地区生产总值(当年价格) Gross Domestic Product (Current Price)	第一产业 Primary Industry	第二产业 Secondary Industry	第三产业 Tertiary Industry	人均生产总值(元)(按户籍) Per Capita GDP (Household Registered)	人均生产总值(元)(按常住) Per Capita GDP (Long－term Residents)	地区生产总值指数(%) Indices of Gross Domestic product(%) (1978＝100)	第一产业 Primary Industry	第二产业 Secondary Industry	第三产业 Tertiary Industry
1978	284046	63372	169344	51330	565	－	100	100	100	100
1979	335285	83852	194132	57301	659	－	113.3	114.2	114.0	110.0
1980	406508	81524	253545	71439	791	－	135.7	105.6	151.1	130.7
1981	468206	90955	287632	89619	904	－	154.0	108.7	172.2	162.3
1982	501854	108769	294725	98360	957	－	165.1	129.8	177.7	176.3
1983	558947	101106	334413	123428	1054	－	183.6	115.6	203.1	219.9
1984	694690	126443	405535	162712	1298	－	225.3	140.1	245.4	283.7
1985	904897	159684	520853	224360	1675	－	268.9	139.9	300.8	352.8
1986	1053589	177589	601277	274723	1917	－	299.9	145.0	335.3	409.9
1987	1260162	204366	718892	336904	2276	－	338.4	148.7	382.2	471.6
1988	1525427	256838	855305	413284	2717	－	363.3	145.5	419.8	497.2
1989	1662945	282746	896736	483463	2928	－	352.1	145.1	396.5	509.0
1990	1896216	309404	961673	625139	3310	－	372.4	154.4	422.2	528.0
1991	2279545	334024	1131088	814433	3952	－	439.8	161.1	492.4	669.5
1992	2900690	349033	1487838	1063819	4996	－	540.5	161.6	637.5	814.8
1993	4247094	419364	2264440	1563290	7263	－	703.2	171.2	878.7	1004.7
1994	5855239	575131	3143430	2136678	9924	－	888.1	185.0	1161.6	1225.7
1995	7620055	692510	4100008	2827537	12797	－	1064.8	198.2	1434.6	1445.1
1996	9066133	839985	4776225	3449923	15095	－	1203.3	208.9	1644.0	1621.4
1997	10363299	913611	5415017	4034671	17113	－	1360.9	223.1	1852.8	1861.3
1998	11348899	960558	5879589	4508752	18611	－	1513.3	244.0	2071.4	2060.5
1999	12252795	975821	6307510	4969464	19961	－	1667.7	257.4	2280.6	2287.1
2000	13825616	1039641	7093233	5692742	22342	－	1867.8	272.1	2565.7	2563.9
2001	15680138	1114569	7935809	6629760	25074	－	2095.7	292.3	2891.6	2884.4
2002	17818302	1146388	9018225	7653689	28150	－	2372.3	304.2	3276.2	3308.4
2003	20997744	1265890	10757812	8974042	32819	－	2732.9	322.5	3885.6	3725.3
2004	25431796	1322341	13182254	10927201	39293	－	3142.8	338.9	4534.4	4258.0
2005	29438430	1482145	14943581	13012704	44871	－	3551.4	350.5	5037.8	4956.3
2006	34434972	1548594	17283905	15602473	51908	44128	4059.5	364.7	5672.8	5820.3
2007	41040117	1634719	20458811	18946588	61315	51416	4651.7	372.8	6483.5	6761.1
2008	47889748	1798300	23725807	22365641	70948	58862	5165.2	386.7	7062.8	7705.1
2009	51114007	1905093	23657646	25551268	75111	61821	5680.2	398.7	7486.6	8822.4
2010	59657106	2084144	28198060	29374902	86932	70024	6361.8	408.7	8332.6	9995.8
2011	70372782	2367708	32805209	35199865	101634	80689	7004.3	418.9	9057.5	11195.2
2012	78336168	2551127	35001330	40783711	112211	89323	7634.7	429.4	9709.6	12449.1
2013	83985753	2615974	35742503	45627276	119372	95190	8245.5	435.4	10389.3	13606.9
2014	92061634	2743492	38455759	50862382	129448	103813	8921.6	443.3	11220.4	14777.1
2015	100502079	2879492	39090099	58532488	139653	112230	9831.6	450.8	11837.6	16934.5
2016	113137223	3042063	41209307	68885853	155030	124286	10775.4	458.9	12370.2	19220.7
2017	126033629	3110811	43624809	79298010	169187	135113	11653.6	467.1	12967.1	21242.5

注:2016年起研究与试验发展支出计入地区生产总值。

a) From 2016, research and test development expenditure was included in the GDP.

1-06 市区生产总值及发展指数(1978-2017年)

Gross Domestic Product and its Indices of Urban District (1978-2017)

单位:万元 (10000 yuan)

年份 Year	地区生产总值(当年价格) Gross Domestic Product (Current Price)	第一产业 Primary Industry	第二产业 Secondary Industry	第三产业 Tertiary Industry	人均生产总值(元)(按户籍) Per Capita GDP (Household Registered)	人均生产总值(元)(按常住) Per Capita GDP (Long-term Residents)	地区生产总值指数(%) Indices of Gross Domestic product(%) (1978=100)	第一产业 Primary Industry	第二产业 Secondary Industry	第三产业 Tertiary Industry
1978	141995	5215	106663	30117	1389	-	100	100	100	100
1979	167206	6527	126517	34162	1555	-	116.4	109.4	118.1	111.6
1980	208220	5943	159161	43116	1863	-	145.3	94.0	150.9	133.9
1981	229243	6165	171946	51132	2005	-	159.9	90.3	163.9	157.2
1982	248297	7327	183284	57686	2125	-	173.7	107.3	176.0	175.6
1983	282171	5938	200334	75899	2369	-	197.9	83.1	193.8	229.5
1984	353781	8469	244445	100867	2919	-	245.4	114.9	235.5	298.4
1985	448574	11233	293579	143762	3633	-	289.9	120.7	270.1	382.2
1986	513639	12245	324585	176809	4042	-	317.3	122.6	287.7	445.1
1987	605234	15408	370668	219158	4724	-	353.2	137.1	313.8	517.4
1988	708474	19602	425319	263553	5441	-	370.8	136.0	332.7	534.0
1989	772208	23869	435847	312492	5848	-	347.0	146.7	296.7	545.2
1990	896496	23919	470844	401733	6722	-	366.5	147.6	314.6	573.6
1991	1096628	25767	547949	522912	8158	-	426.0	151.4	356.3	691.1
1992	1413278	27611	712697	672969	10420	-	535.3	153.1	447.4	877.8
1993	2086571	36208	1052187	998176	15196	-	687.6	157.7	583.7	1117.4
1994	2788314	48257	1395127	1344931	19945	-	870.9	172.3	779.6	1335.3
1995	3697794	57784	1866784	1773226	25969	-	1041.6	183.5	945.7	1574.3
1996	4727377	110881	2356408	2260088	28552	-	1194.9	194.7	1103.6	1769.5
1997	5414265	130062	2630349	2653853	32227	-	1354.9	214.2	1230.3	2052.6
1998	5905726	134320	2786159	2985247	34620	-	1482.5	230.7	1337.2	2266.1
1999	6317335	145242	2915614	3256479	36394	-	1599.3	254.5	1431.1	2467.8
2000	7111586	145715	3278310	3687561	40127	-	1785.5	255.5	1596.7	2763.9
2001	12260891	582492	6026353	5652046	32607	-	2017.2	275.7	1805.3	3126.0
2002	14042278	605433	6901224	6535621	36640	-	2300.8	290.0	2038.6	3607.4
2003	16647332	665083	8343138	7639111	42675	-	2664.8	302.2	2448.4	4058.3
2004	20362738	664676	10368453	9329609	51241	-	3077.4	313.1	2873.9	4630.5
2005	23495459	732463	11582930	11180067	57934	-	3461.2	318.2	3141.5	5406.6
2006	27483121	755663	13254773	13472684	66731	51073	3955.9	320.5	3493.9	6399.6
2007	32738842	773208	15546960	16418675	78541	58907	4525.3	322.7	3948.4	7455.8
2008	38139834	830741	17926048	19383045	90400	66808	5018.5	324.8	4266.5	8505.2
2009	41086525	874987	17987776	22223762	96251	70418	5539.5	334.6	4539.5	9704.4
2010	47768030	941591	21358545	25467894	110541	78665	6198.7	339.3	5029.8	10975.7
2011	56297165	1054368	24746674	30496123	128656	89967	6818.5	345.7	5437.2	12281.8
2012	62711287	1128362	26276722	35306203	141597	99616	7432.2	353.0	5796.0	13657.4
2013	67258795	1123778	26756092	39378925	150089	105497	8011.9	350.8	6196.0	14845.6
2014	79773702	1563084	32020016	46190602	153152	112322	8668.9	353.7	6697.8	16107.5
2015	87219983	1628558	32394494	53196931	164886	121681	9570.5	358.2	7052.8	18475.2
2016	98354845	1704347	34069866	62580632	182554	134798	10498.8	360.8	7334.9	20987.9
2017	116214609	2150036	39058651	75005922	191605	143392	11360.5	365.3	7691.7	23172.4

1－07　全市生产总值指数(1978－2017 年)

Indices of Gross Domestic Product (1978－2017)

(上年＝100)　　(Preceding Year＝100)

年　份 Year	地区生产总值 Gross Domestic Product	第一产业 Primary Industry	第二产业 Secondary Industry	第三产业 Tertiary Industry	人均生产总值(元)(按户籍) Per Capita GDP(yuan)(Household Registered)	人均生产总值(元)(按常住) Per Capita GDP(yuan)(Long－term Residents)
1978	120.2	119.1	123.7	111.6	119.0	
1979	113.3	114.2	114.0	110.0	112.1	
1980	119.7	92.5	132.5	118.8	118.4	
1981	113.6	102.9	114.0	124.2	112.6	
1982	107.2	119.4	103.2	108.6	105.9	
1983	111.2	89.1	114.3	124.7	109.9	
1984	122.7	121.2	120.8	129.0	121.6	
1985	119.4	99.9	122.6	124.4	118.2	
1986	111.5	103.7	111.5	116.2	110.3	
1987	112.8	102.5	114.0	115.1	111.3	
1988	107.4	97.8	109.8	105.4	105.8	
1989	96.9	99.8	94.4	102.4	95.8	
1990	105.8	106.4	106.5	103.7	104.9	
1991	118.1	104.4	116.6	126.8	117.3	
1992	122.9	100.3	129.5	121.7	122.1	
1993	130.1	105.9	137.8	123.3	129.1	
1994	126.3	108.1	132.2	122.0	125.2	
1995	119.9	107.1	123.5	117.9	118.8	
1996	113.0	105.4	114.6	112.2	112.0	
1997	113.1	106.8	112.7	114.8	112.1	
1998	111.2	109.4	111.8	110.7	110.5	
1999	110.2	105.5	110.1	111.0	109.4	
2000	112.0	105.7	112.5	112.1	111.1	
2001	112.2	107.4	112.7	112.5	111.1	
2002	113.2	104.1	113.3	114.7	111.8	
2003	115.2	106.0	118.6	112.6	114.0	
2004	115.0	105.1	116.7	114.3	113.7	
2005	113.0	103.4	111.1	116.4	111.5	
2006	114.3	104.1	112.6	117.4	113.0	
2007	114.6	102.2	114.3	116.2	113.6	112.0
2008	111.0	103.7	108.9	114.0	110.1	108.9
2009	110.0	103.1	106.0	114.5	109.1	108.2
2010	112.0	102.5	111.3	113.3	111.0	108.7
2011	110.1	102.5	108.7	112.0	109.1	107.6
2012	109.0	102.5	107.2	111.2	108.2	108.4
2013	108.0	101.4	107.0	109.3	107.1	107.3
2014	108.2	101.8	108.0	108.6	107.0	107.6
2015	110.2	101.7	105.5	114.6	108.9	109.1
2016	109.6	101.8	104.5	113.5	108.1	107.8
2017	108.1	101.8	104.8	110.5	105.9	105.5

注:本表按可比价格计算。

a) The indices in this table are calculated at comparable prices.

1-08 市区生产总值指数(1978-2017年)

Indices of Gross Domestic Product of Urban District (1978-2017)

(上年=100) (Preceding Year=100)

年 份 Year	地区生产总值 Gross Domestic Product	第一产业 Primary Industry	第二产业 Secondary Industry	第三产业 Tertiary Industry	人均生产总值(元)(按户籍) Per Capita GDP(yuan) (Household Registered)	人均生产总值(元)(按常住) Per Capita GDP(yuan) (Long-term Residents)
1978	120.1	118.8	122.3	113.6	118.0	
1979	116.4	109.4	118.1	111.6	111.4	
1980	124.8	85.9	127.8	120.0	119.7	
1981	110.1	96.1	108.6	117.4	107.6	
1982	108.6	118.8	107.4	111.7	106.3	
1983	113.9	77.5	110.1	130.7	111.7	
1984	124.0	138.2	121.5	130.0	121.8	
1985	118.2	105.0	114.7	128.1	116.0	
1986	109.4	101.6	106.5	116.7	107.4	
1987	111.3	111.8	109.1	116.0	109.4	
1988	105.0	99.2	106.0	103.2	103.3	
1989	93.6	107.9	89.2	102.1	92.2	
1990	105.6	100.6	106.0	105.2	104.6	
1991	116.2	102.6	113.3	120.5	115.3	
1992	125.7	101.1	125.6	127.3	124.5	
1993	128.5	103.0	130.5	127.3	126.9	
1994	126.6	109.3	133.6	119.5	124.4	
1995	119.6	106.5	121.3	117.9	117.4	
1996	114.7	106.1	116.7	112.4	105.3	
1997	113.4	110.0	111.5	116.0	104.7	
1998	109.4	107.7	108.7	110.4	107.8	
1999	107.9	110.3	107.0	108.9	106.0	
2000	111.6	100.4	111.6	112.0	109.3	
2001	113.0	107.9	113.1	113.1	111.2	
2002	114.1	105.2	112.9	115.4	111.9	
2003	115.8	104.2	120.1	112.5	113.8	
2004	115.5	103.6	117.4	114.1	113.4	
2005	112.5	101.6	109.3	116.8	110.2	
2006	114.3	100.7	111.2	118.4	112.5	
2007	114.4	100.7	113.0	116.5	113.0	110.8
2008	110.9	100.7	108.1	114.1	109.5	108.0
2009	110.4	103.0	106.4	114.1	109.1	108.0
2010	111.9	101.4	110.8	113.1	110.5	107.5
2011	110.0	101.9	108.1	111.9	108.6	106.7
2012	109.0	102.1	106.6	111.2	107.7	108.4
2013	107.8	99.4	106.9	108.7	106.8	106.7
2014	108.2	100.8	108.1	108.5	106.7	107.6
2015	110.4	101.3	105.3	114.7	108.7	109.3
2016	109.7	100.7	104.0	113.6	107.7	107.8
2017	108.2	101.3	104.9	110.4	105.6	105.3

1－09 全市分行业

Composition of

单位:万元

行　业	Sector	全 Whole	
		2017	为上年(%) As Compared with the Preceding Year(%)
全市生产总值	Gross Domestic Product	126033629	108.1
按行业分	Grouped by Sector		
#农、林、牧、渔业	Farming, Forestry, Animal Husbandry & Fishery	3167716	101.9
工业	Industry	39681260	106.3
建筑业	Construction	3958415	91.4
批发和零售业	Wholesale and Retail Trade	9817762	108.1
交通运输、仓储和邮政业	Transportation, Storage and Post	3416034	103.8
住宿和餐饮业	Hotels and Catering Services	1931494	106.0
信息传输、软件和信息技术服务业	Information Transmission, Software and Information Technology Services	22538650	125.6
金融业	Financial Intermediation	10555278	106.9
房地产业	Real Estate	7896825	100.1
租赁和商务服务业	Leasing and Busyness Service	4497594	108.4
科学研究、技术服务业	Scientific Research, Technical Service	3466762	106.2
水利环境和公共设施管理业	Management of Water Conservancy, Enviroment and Public Facilities	891164	100.9
居民服务、修理和其他服务业	Service for the Residents, Repair and Others	1636350	113.2
教育	Education	4322969	105.1
卫生和社会工作	Health Care and Social Work	2744089	108.6
文化、体育和娱乐业	Culture, Sports and Entertainment	1299007	90.0
公共管理、社会保障和社会组织	Public Administration ,Social Security and Social Organization	4212260	102.5
第一产业	Primary Industry	3110811	101.8
第二产业	Secondary Industry	43624809	104.8
第三产业	Tertiary Industry	79298010	110.5
按构成分	by Structure		
劳动者报酬	Labourer's Remuneration	55102648	
生产税净额	Net Taxes on Production	19137495	
固定资产折旧	Depreciation of Fixed Assets	13903204	
营业盈余	Operating Surplus	37890282	

生产总值构成(2017 年)
Gross Domestic Product(2017)

(10000 yuan)

市 City		#市 区 Urban District			
比 重 (%) Proportion(%)		2017	为上年(%) As Compared with the Preceding Year(%)	比 重 (%) Proportion(%)	
2017	2016			2017	2016
100.0	100.0	116214609	108.2	100.0	100.0
2.5	2.7	2193892	101.4	1.9	1.8
31.5	32.9	35682510	106.4	30.7	31.3
3.1	3.5	3386783	89.6	2.9	3.3
7.8	7.8	9260498	108.1	8.0	7.9
2.7	2.9	2916887	101.7	2.5	2.6
1.5	1.5	1715626	106.1	1.5	1.4
17.9	15.3	22152696	125.7	19.1	16.8
8.4	8.7	10079912	106.9	8.7	9.3
6.3	6.1	7297091	98.3	6.3	6.3
3.6	3.5	4233215	107.9	3.6	3.8
2.8	2.7	3415440	106.1	2.9	3.1
0.7	0.7	836696	100.7	0.7	0.8
1.3	1.2	1476996	112.1	1.3	1.2
3.4	3.5	4010706	105.6	3.5	3.4
2.2	2.1	2565629	108.2	2.2	2.2
1.0	1.2	1245517	89.4	1.1	1.4
3.3	3.4	3744513	101.8	3.2	3.3
2.5	2.7	2150036	101.3	1.9	1.7
34.6	36.4	39058651	104.9	33.6	34.6
62.9	60.9	75005922	110.4	64.5	63.6
43.7	45.0	49936880		43.0	44.2
15.2	16.7	17649469		15.2	16.9
11.0	11.4	12835772		11.0	11.3
30.1	26.9	35792488		30.8	27.6

1－10 全市分地区和产业生产总值构成(2017 年)

Gross Domestic Product by Region and Industry(2017)

单位:万元 (10000 yuan)

地区	Region	地区生产总值 Gross Domestic Product	第一产业 Primary Industry	第二产业 Secondary Industry	第三产业 Tertiary Industry	工业 Industry	建筑业 Construction	户籍人口人均 GDP(元) Per Capita GDP (yuan)(Household Registered)	常住人口人均 GDP(元) Per Capita GDP (Long－term Residents)
全市	**Whole City**	**126033629**	**3110811**	**43624809**	**79298010**	**39681260**	**3958415**	**169187**	**135113**
市区	Urban District	116214609	2150036	39058651	75005922	35682510	3386783	191605	143392
#上城区	Shangcheng	10114403	－	3858672	6255731	3676093	182581	312494	288488
下城区	Xiacheng	8605212	－	336748	8268464	131114	205693	213553	161297
江干区	Jianggan	6240457	5977	1250635	4983845	538784	712049	144108	82491
拱墅区	Gongshu	5375017	－	947337	4427679	823446	123954	152014	93969
西湖区	Xihu	11211093	38199	1105619	10067276	756374	349535	164410	136330
高新(滨江)区	Hi－Tech (Binjiang)	12243357	10123	5950710	6282524	5841090	109720	527823	356637
萧山区	Xiaoshan	20072357	666306	9232353	10173698	8604739	630544	156102	124403
大江东产业集聚区	Dajiangdong Industry Cluster District	2954407	124842	2483126	346440	2354535	128591	193089	158839
余杭区	Yuhang	20344726	503763	5860116	13980847	5467204	395164	200928	143525
富阳区	Fuyang	7248770	462611	3245747	3540412	2987854	261153	107481	98262
临安区	Lin'an	5309162	432722	2639140	2237299	2402888	237623	99545	90024
经济技术开发区	Economic and Technological Development Zone	6523077	3451	4539014	1980612	4451271	87861	581890	192848
西湖风景名胜区	The West Lake Scenic Zone	401660	8438	7897	385325	1654	6243	201323	135012
桐庐县	Tonglu	3831267	251554	1986003	1593709	1802468	185542	92731	89936
淳安县	Chun'an	2402801	362469	790091	1250241	623612	167299	52154	68397
建德市	Jiande	3584953	346752	1790064	1448137	1572669	218790	70267	80380
经济技术开发区(含前进园区)	Economic and Technological Development Zone(Including Qianjin Zone)	7461338	3451	5477275	1980612	5389533	87861	－	－

1－11 全市分地区和产业生产总值指数(2017 年)
Indices of Gross Domestic Product by Region and Industry(2017)

(上年＝100)　　(Preceding Year＝100)

地　区	Region	地区生产总值 Gross Domestic Product	第一产业 Primary Industry	第二产业 Secondary Industry	第三产业 Tertiary Industry	工　业 Industry	建筑业 Construction
全　市	**Whole City**	**108.1**	**101.8**	**104.8**	**110.5**	**106.3**	**91.4**
市　区	Urban District	108.2	101.3	104.9	110.4	106.4	89.6
#上城区	Shangcheng	106.5	–	107.1	106.1	108.1	90.1
下城区	Xiacheng	105.4	–	91.1	106.1	105.4	81.8
江干区	Jianggan	105.1	134.0	95.5	107.9	92.9	97.8
拱墅区	Gongshu	107.2	–	106.0	107.5	112.1	76.5
西湖区	Xihu	107.5	92.6	103.5	108.0	102.2	106.7
高新(滨江)区	Hi－Tech(Binjiang)	113.6	77.9	114.3	113.1	116.2	60.3
萧山区	Xiaoshan	106.8	100.2	100.7	114.7	101.9	84.1
大江东产业集聚区	Dajiangdong Industry Cluster District	100.2	95.3	100.3	102.0	100.6	93.4
余杭区	Yuhang	114.2	101.3	105.9	118.4	107.2	91.0
富阳区	Fuyang	106.5	102.0	104.3	109.7	107.0	77.3
临安区	Lin'an	107.6	102.0	105.8	111.5	105.4	111.1
经济技术开发区	Economic and Technological Development Zone	106.5	87.0	105.3	109.7	105.2	107.4
西湖风景名胜区	The West Lake Scenic Zone	106.2	108.6	54.6	108.4	31.5	68.9
桐庐县	Tonglu	107.5	102.0	104.1	113.6	104.4	102.0
淳安县	Chun'an	107.7	104.1	102.5	112.9	102.9	100.9
建德市	Jiande	107.3	102.6	105.7	111.0	105.5	108.1
经济技术开发区(含前进园区)	Economic and Technological Development Zone (Including Qianjin Zone)	104.1	87.0	102.4	109.7	102.3	107.4

1-12 主要指标占全省比重(2017年)
Proportion of Main Indicators in Whole Province(2017)

指标 Item		全省 Zhejiang Province	杭州市 Hangzhou City	杭州市占全省(%) Proportion of Hangzhou in Zhejiang(%)
年末常住人口 Long-term Residents(End of 2017)	(万人) (10000 persons)	5657.00	946.80	16.7
年末户籍人口 Household Registration Population(End of 2017)	(万人) (10000 persons)	4957.63	753.88	15.2
年末就业人员数 Total Number of Employed Persons	(万人) (10000 persons)	3796.00	681.06	17.9
地区生产总值 Gross Domestic Product	(亿元) (100 million yuan)	51768.26	12603.36	24.3
第一产业 Primary Industry	(亿元) (100 million yuan)	1933.92	311.08	16.1
第二产业 Secondary Industry	(亿元) (100 million yuan)	22232.08	4362.48	19.6
第三产业 Tertiary Industry	(亿元) (100 million yuan)	27602.26	7929.80	28.7
常住人口人均生产总值 Per Capita GDP of Long-term Residents	(元) (yuan)	92057	135113	-
农林牧渔业总产值 Gross Output Value of Farming, Forestry, Animal Husbandry and Fishery	(亿元) (100 million yuan)	3093.36	457.70	14.8
主要农产品产量 Output of Major Farm Products				
#粮食 Grain	(万吨) (10000 tons)	580.14	47.26	8.2
蚕茧 Silk-worm Cocoons	(万吨) (10000 tons)	1.63	0.3013	44.0
生猪年末存栏 Hogs in Stock at Year End	(万头) (10000 heads)	542.55	104.08	21.0
肉类产量 Output of Meat	(万吨) (10000 tons)	86.99	21.27	28.3
淡水产品总产量 Freshwater Aquatic products	(万吨) (10000 tons)	122.08	17.28	14.2

1－12 续表1 continued 1

指 标 Item		全 省 Zhejiang Province	杭州市 Hangzhou City	杭州市占全省(%) Proportion of Hangzhou in Zhejiang(%)
规模以上工业增加值 Value－added of Industrial Enterprises above Designated Size	(亿元) (100 million yuan)	14510.06	3184.05	21.9
规模以上工业企业利税总额 Total Pre－tax Profits of Industrial Enterprises above Designed Size	(亿元) (100 million yuan)	7637.42	1774.52	23.2
主要工业产品产量 Output of Major Industrial Products				
#发电量 Electricity	(亿千瓦时) (100 million kwh)	3259	150.22	4.6
氢氧化钠(烧碱)(折100%) Caustic Soda(100% discount)	(万吨) (10000 tons)	188.83	21.00	11.1
碳酸钠(纯碱) Soda Ash	(万吨) (10000 tons)	32.28	32.28	100
合成氨 Synthetic Ammonia	(万吨) (10000 tons)	62.11	22.02	35.5
水泥 Cement	(万吨) (10000 tons)	11231	1583	14.1
钢材 Steels	(万吨) (10000 tons)	3148	441	14.0
化学纤维 Chemical Fiber	(万吨) (10000 tons)	2055.70	625.63	30.4
纱 Yarn	(万吨) (10000 tons)	190.42	52.88	27.8
自行车 Bicycles	(万辆) (10000 units)	720	192	26.7
彩色电视机 Colour TV Sets	(万台) (10000 units)	610	2	0.3
电冰箱 Household Refrigerator	(万台) (10000 units)	677	76	11.2
洗衣机 Washing Machine	(万台) (10000 units)	1227	289	23.6
客运量 Volume of Passenger Transport	(万人次) (10000 person－times)	107293	22289	20.8

1－12　续表2　continued 2

指　标 Item		全　省 Zhejiang Province	杭州市 Hangzhou City	杭州市占全省(%) Proportion of Hangzhou in Zhejiang(%)
货运量 Volume of Goods Transport	(万吨) (10000 tons)	241993	34785	14.4
固定资产投资 Investment in Fixed Assets	(亿元) (100 million yuan)	31125.99	5856.65	18.8
社会消费品零售总额 Total Retail Sales of Consumer Goods	(亿元) (100 million yuan)	24308.48	5717.43	23.5
出口额 Total Exports	(亿美元) (100 million USD)	2868.91	509.95	17.8
实际利用外资 Foreign Capital Actually Used	(亿美元) (100 million USD)	179.02	66.10	36.9
境外旅游者人数 Number of International Tourists	(万人次) (10000 person－times)	1211.73	402.23	33.2
财政总收入 Total Financial Revenue	(亿元) (100 million yuan)	10300.16	2921.30	28.4
#一般公共预算收入 General Public Budget Revenue	(亿元) (100 million yuan)	5803.38	1567.42	27.0
一般公共预算支出 Financial Expenditure	(亿元) (100 million yuan)	7530.27	1540.92	20.5
金融机构存款余额(本外币) Deposits of Financial Institutions	(亿元) (100 million yuan)	107320.53	36483.24	34.0
住户存款余额 Deposits of Households	(亿元) (100 million yuan)	40804.3	8670.60	21.6
金融机构贷款余额(本外币) Loans of Financial Institutions	(亿元) (100 million yuan)	90233.3	29270.94	32.4
非私营单位就业人员平均工资 Average Wage of Employed Persons of Non－private Units	(元) (yuan)	80750	93891	116.3
全体居民人均可支配收入 Per Capita Annual Disposable Income of Urban and Rural Residents	(元) (yuan)	42046	49832	118.5
城镇居民人均可支配收入 Per Capita Annual Disposable Income of Urban Residents	(元) (yuan)	51261	56276	109.8
农村居民人均可支配收入 Per Capita Annual Disposable Income of Rural Residents	(元) (yuan)	24956	30397	121.8
高等学校在校学生数 Number of Institutions of Higher Education	(万人) (10000 persons)	107.68	48.41	45.0
普通中学在校学生数 Number of Secondary Schools	(万人) (10000 persons)	233.18	33.79	14.5
小学在校学生数 Number of Primary Schools	(万人) (10000 persons)	354.01	56.04	15.8

1-13 国民经济主要指标人均水平(2010-2017年)
Major Per Capita Indicators of National Economy(2010-2017)

指 标 Item	2010	2011	2012	2013	2014	2015	2016	2017
全市生产总值 (元) Gross Domestic Product (yuan)	70024	80689	89323	95190	103813	112230	124286	135113
规模以上工业总产值 (元) Gross Industrial Output Value above Designatted Size (yuan)	130064	141634	147773	106639	144937	138645	136449	138977
农林牧渔业总产值 (元) Gross Output Value of Farming, Forestry, Animal Husbandry and Fishery (yuan)	3713	4094	4382	4526	4720	4918	5133	5027
社会消费品零售总额 (元) Total Retail Sales of Consumer Goods (yuan)	26117	30845	36091	43804	47378	52454	56863	60387
财政总收入 (元) Financial Revenue (yuan)	14618	17071	18562	19664	21652	25000	28105	31318
#一般公共预算收入 (元) General Public Budget Revenue (yuan)	7880	9002	9806	10713	11585	13779	15406	16803
一般公共预算支出 (元) General Public Budgetary Expenditure (yuan)	7237	8571	8966	9699	10839	13462	15427	16519
全体居民可支配收入 (元) Annual Disposable Income of Urban and Rural Residents (yuan)	-	-	-	35763	39237	42642	46116	49832
全体居民消费性支出 (元) Annual Living Expendituer of Urban and Ruarual Residents (yuan)	-	-	-	26827	28492	30181	31905	34146
城镇居民可支配收入 (元) Annual Disposable Income of Urban Residents (yuan)	30035	34065	37511	40925	44632	48316	52185	56276
城镇居民消费性支出 (元) Annual Living Expenditure of Urban Residents (yuan)	20219	22642	22800	30659	32165	33818	35686	38179
农村居民可支配收入 (元) Annual Disposable Income of Rural Residents (yuan)	13186	15245	17017	21208	23555	25719	27908	30397
农村居民消费性支出 (元) Annual Living Expenditure of Rural Residents (yuan)	10267	12125	13612	16021	17816	19334	20563	21983

1－14 信息经济主要指标(2016－2017 年)
Information Economy(2016－2017)

指标 Item	2016 年 主营业务收入(亿元) Revenne from Principal Business (100 million yuan)	2016 年 增速(%) Growth (%)	2016 年 增加值(亿元) Added Value (100 million yuan)	2016 年 增速(%) Growth (%)	2017 年 主营业务收入(亿元) Revenne from Principal Business (100 million yuan)	2017 年 增速(%) Growth (%)	2017 年 增加值(亿元) Added Value (100 million yuan)	2017 年 增速(%) Growth (%)
剔重合计 Total(eliminate repetition)	**6814**	**26.8**	**2688**	**22.8**	**8936**	**28.6**	**3216**	**21.8**
分产业 By Sector								
电子商务产业 E－commerce	1574	44.4	1027	45.2	2399	45.0	1316	36.6
云计算与大数据产业 Cloud Computing and Big Data	1588	26.1	961	28.2	2080	31.6	1207	31.9
物联网产业 Internet of Things	1105	23.6	335	8.8	1416	28.8	430	18.0
互联网金融产业 Internet Finance	－	－	230	7.0	－	－	191	6.6
智慧物流产业 Wisdom Logistics	532	27.6	96	18.5	656	23.0	119	15.8
数字内容产业 Digital Content	3207	42.2	1499	35.0	4710	43.9	1870	28.5
软件与信息服务产业 Soft－ware and Information Service	4116	34.5	1869	28.8	5690	35.7	2318	27.8
电子信息产品制造产业 Electronic Information Products Manufacturing Industry	2284	12.7	621	11.0	2696	16.5	733	10.7
移动互联网产业 Mobile Internet	1450	42.5	1034	45.1	2104	45.0	1333	35.0
集成电路产业 Integrate Circuit Industry	140	20.0	53	21.5	165	18.8	59	18.8
信息安全产业 Information Security Industry	529	23.9	250	14.6	672	27.2	336	24.9
机器人产业 Robot Industry	60	3.6	20	4.2	69	14.2	21	9.8

1－15 "1＋6"产业集群主要指标(2016－2017 年)
"1＋6" Industrial Cluster(2016－2017)

产业分组	Industry Grouping	2016 年 增加值(亿元) Added Value (100 million yuan)	2016 年 速度(%) Growth (%)	2017 年 增加值(亿元) Added Value (100 million yuan)	2017 年 速度(%) Growth (%)
信息经济产业	Information Economy Industry	2688	22.8	3216	21.8
文化创意产业	Cultural and Creative Industry	2542	21.2	3041	19.0
金融产业	Financial Industry	996	6.7	1065	6.7
旅游休闲产业	Tourism Leisure Industry	809	13.3	928	12.6
健康产业	Health Industry	663	16.5	749	10.4
时尚产业(制造业)	Fashion Industry (Manufacturing)	298	11.7	275	－8.0
高端装备产业(制造业)	High－end Equipment Industry(Manufacturing)	380	15.2	399	－0.4

1－16 按机构类型和登记注册类型分组的法人单位数(2017年)

Number of Corporation Units by Types of Organization and Registration(2017)

单位:个 (unit)

指标名称	Item	法人单位数 Number of Corporation Units		
		合计 Total	单产业法人单位 Containing Single Industrial Activity	多产业法人单位 Containing Multiple Industrial Activity
合计	**Total**	**450348**	**438371**	**11976**
按机构类型分组	**By Type of Organization**	**450348**	**438371**	**11976**
企业	Enterprises	426503	415279	11223
事业单位	Publlic Institution	5303	4882	421
机关	Office	1261	1061	200
社会团体	Social Group	4082	4035	47
民办非企业单位	Private Non－enterprise Unit	3785	3761	24
基金会	Foundation	124	123	1
居委会	Neighborhood Committees	1063	1050	13
村委会	Villagers Committees	2012	1992	20
农民专业合作社	Specialty Cooperative of Peasants	4287	4275	12
其他组织机构	Other	1928	1913	15
按登记注册类型分组	**Grouped By Registered Type**	**450348**	**438371**	**11976**
内资	Domestic－funded	444826	433274	11551
国有	State－owned	8318	7546	772
集体	Collective－owned	2475	2398	77
股份合作	Cooperative	451	430	21
联营	Joint Ownership	167	165	2
国有联营	State Joint Ownership	12	11	1
集体联营	Collective Joint	85	85	－
国有与集体联营	Joint State－collective	19	19	－
其他联营	Other Joint Ownership	51	50	1
有限责任公司	Limited Liability Corporations	19128	17343	1784

单位:个　　1-16 续表 continued　　(unit)

指标名称	Item	法人单位数 Number of Corporation Units 合计 Total	单产业法人单位 Containing Single Industrial Activity	多产业法人单位 Containing Multiple Industrial Activity
国有独资公司	State - funded Corporations	617	496	121
其他有限责任公司	Other Limited Liability Corporations	18511	16847	1663
股份有限公司	Share - holding Corporations Ltd.	1619	1283	336
私营	Private	397426	388976	8450
私营独资	Private - funded	30923	30506	417
私营合伙	Private Partnership	8607	8579	28
私营有限责任公司	Private Limited Liability Corporations	356733	348815	7918
私营股份有限公司	Private Share - holding Corporations Ltd.	1163	1076	87
其他内资	Other Domestic - funded	15242	15133	109
港澳台商投资	Enterprises With Investment from Hong Kong, Macao and Taiwan	2591	2382	209
与港澳台商合资经营	Joint - venture Enterprises with funds from Hong Kong, Macao and Taiwan	983	899	84
与港澳台商合作经营	Cooperative Enterprises with funds from Hong Kong, Macao and Taiwan	30	27	3
港澳台商独资	Enterprises With Sole Investment from Hong Kong, Macao and Taiwan	1523	1411	112
港澳台商投资股份有限公司	Share - holding Corporations Ltd. With Investment from Hong Kong, Macao and Taiwan	27	21	6
其他港、澳、台商投资	Other Enterprises With Investment from Hong Kong, Macao and Taiwan	28	24	4
外商投资	With Foreign Investment	2931	2715	216
中外合资经营	Joint - venture	1200	1114	86
中外合作经营	Cooperation Enterprises	40	38	2
外资企业	With Sole Foreign Investment	1602	1480	122
外商投资股份有限公司	Share - holding Corporations Ltd. With Foreign Investment	41	37	4
其他外商投资	Other Enterprises With Foreign Investment	48	46	2

1－17 按行业和地区分组的法人单位数(2017 年)

Number of Corporation Units by Sector and Region(2017)

单位:个 (unit)

指标名称 Item	法人单位数 Number of Corporation Units		
	合计 Total	单产业法人单位 Containing Single Industrial Activity	多产业法人单位 Containing Multiple Industrial Activity
合计 Total	**450348**	**438371**	**11976**
一、按国民经济行业分组 Grouped by Sector	**450348**	**438371**	**11976**
农、林、牧、渔业 Farming, Forestry, Animal Husbandry and Fishery	7836	7780	56
农业 Agriculture	4265	4235	30
林业 Forestry	1129	1122	7
畜牧业 Animal Husbandry	817	809	8
渔业 Fishery	990	981	9
农、林、牧、渔、专业及辅助性活动 Services for Farming, Forestry, Animal Husbandry and Fishery	635	633	2
采矿业 Mining and Quarrying	265	260	5
煤炭采选业和洗选业 Coal Mining and Processing	3	2	1
石油和天然气开采业 Petroleum and Natural gas Mining			
黑色金属矿采选业 Ferrous Metals Mining and Processing	8	8	–
有色金属矿采选业 Nonferrous Metals Mining and Processing	16	15	1
非金属矿采选业 Nonmetal Minerals Mining and Processing	230	227	3
开采专业及辅助性活动 Supplementary Activities for Mining	4	4	–
其他采矿业 Other Minerals Mining	4	4	–
制造业 Manufacturing Industry	58185	57014	1170
农副食品加工业 Agricultural Products Processing	1025	976	49
食品制造业 Food Manufacturing	809	755	54
酒、饮料和精制茶制造业 Wine, Beverage and Tea Manufacturing	595	566	29
烟草制品业 Tobacco Processing	4	4	–
纺织业 Textile Industry	4849	4756	93

单位:个　　1－17　续表1　continued 1　　(unit)

指标名称 Item	法人单位数 Number of Corporation Units		
	合计 Total	单产业法人单位 Containing Single Industrial Activity	多产业法人单位 Containing Multiple Industrial Activity
纺织服装、服饰业 Textile Products and Costune Indnstry	5481	5404	77
皮革、毛皮、羽毛及其制品和制鞋业 Leather. Furs. Downand Related and Shoes Products	1254	1237	17
木材加工和木、竹、藤、棕、草制品业 Timber Processing, Bamboo, Cane, Palm Fiber and Straw Products	1156	1141	15
家具制造业 Furniture Manufacturing	1135	1109	26
造纸和纸制品业 Paper Making and Paper Products	2594	2569	25
印刷和记录媒介复制业 Printing and Record Media	1472	1448	24
文教、工美、体育和娱乐用品制造业 Cultural, Educational. Industrial Arts. Sports and Entertainment Goods	2540	2515	25
石油、煤炭及其他燃料加工业 Petroleum, Coal and other Fuel Processing	100	97	3
化学原料和化学制品制造业 Raw Chemical Materials and Chemical Products	2199	2141	58
医药制造业 Medical and Pharmaceutical Products	330	313	17
化学纤维制造业 Chemical Fiber	258	253	5
橡胶和塑料制品业 Rubber and Plastic Products	3802	3754	48
非金属矿物制品业 Nonmetal Minerals Products	2912	2857	55
黑色金属冶炼和压延加工业 Smelting and Processing of Ferrous Metal	559	548	11
有色金属冶炼和压延加工业 Smelting and Processing of Nonferrous Metals	402	394	8
金属制品业 Metals Products	6103	6025	78
通用设备制造业 Ordinary Machinery	6107	5986	121
专用设备制造业 For Special Purpose Equipment Manufacturing	2875	2811	64
汽车制造业 Automobile Manufacturing	1741	1709	31
铁路、船舶、航空航天和其他运输设备制造业 Railway. watercraft. Avigation spaceflight and other Equipment Manufacturing	561	547	14
电气机械和器材制造业 Electric Equipment and Machinery	3715	3615	100

单位:个　　　1-17　续表2　continued 2　　　(unit)

指标名称　Item	法人单位数 Number of Corporation Units		
	合计 Total	单产业法人单位 Containing Single Industrial Activity	多产业法人单位 Containing Multiple Industrial Activity
计算机、通信和其他电子设备制造业 Computers. Telecommunications and Other Electronic Equipment Manufacturing	1894	1828	66
仪器仪表制造业 Instruments and Meters Manufacturing	964	924	40
其他制造业 Other Manufacturing	343	337	6
废弃资源综合利用业 Multiple Utilization of Waste Resouces	206	197	9
金属制品、机械和设备修理业 Metal Products, Machinery and Equipment Repair	200	198	2
电力、热力、燃气及水生产和供应业 Produotion and supply of electricity, gas & water	704	662	42
电力、热力生产和供应业 Production and Supply of Electric Power and Hot Water	456	436	20
燃气生产和供应业 Production and Supply of Gas	67	53	14
水的生产和供应业 Production and Supply of Tap Water	181	173	8
建筑业 Construction	18502	17571	931
房屋建筑业 Housing	2233	1964	269
土木工程建筑业 Civil Engineering	3741	3442	299
建筑安装业 Installation	2275	2147	128
建筑装饰、装修和其他建筑业 Building Decoration and Others	10253	10018	235
批发和零售业 Wholesale and Retail Trade	144693	141706	2987
批发业 Wholesale	91186	89643	1543
零售业 Retail Trade	53507	52063	1444
交通运输、仓储和邮政业 Transportation, Storage and Post	7091	6751	340
铁路运输业 Railway Transport	12	12	-
道路运输业 Highway Transport	4920	4735	185
水上运输业 Water Transport	99	93	6

单位:个　　1-17　续表3　continued 3　　(unit)

指标名称 Item	法人单位数 Number of Corporation Units		
	合计 Total	单产业法人单位 Containing Single Industrial Activity	多产业法人单位 Containing Multiple Industrial Activity
航空运输业 Air Transport	44	38	6
管道运输业 Pipeline Transport	1	1	-
多式联运和运输代理业 Multimodal Transport and Transport Agency	1254	1180	74
装卸搬运和仓储业 Carrying and Storage	355	339	16
邮政业 Postal Services	406	353	53
住宿和餐饮业 Lodging and Catering Services	8351	7707	644
住宿业 Lodging	2474	2278	196
餐饮业 Catering Services	5877	5429	448
信息传输、软件和信息技术服务业 Information Transmission , Software and Information Technology Services	45984	45315	669
电信、广播电视和卫星传输服务 Telecommunication, Radio and Television, Satellite Transmission Services	350	313	37
互联网和相关服务 Internet and Related Services	2173	2119	54
软件和信息技术服务业 Software and Information Technology Services	43461	42883	578
金融业 Banking and Insurance	3373	3121	252
货币金融服务 Monetary and Financial Services	370	289	81
资本市场服务 Capital Market Services	1676	1628	48
保险业 Insurance	216	111	105
其他金融业 Others	1111	1093	18
房地产业 Real Estate	13118	12289	829
房地产业 Real Estate	13118	12289	829
租赁和商务服务业 Renting and Business Service	77173	75255	1918
租赁业 Renting	3047	2943	104

指标名称　Item	法人单位数 Number of Corporation Units		
	合计 Total	单产业法人单位 Containing Single Industrial Activity	多产业法人单位 Containing Multiple Industrial Activity
商务服务业 Commercial Service	74126	72312	1814
科学研究和技术服务业 Scientific Research and Technical Service	29801	29011	790
研究和试验发展 Research and Experiment	3457	3411	46
专业技术服务业 Technical Services	13674	13085	589
科技推广和应用服务业 Promotion and Application of Service and Technology Services	12670	12515	155
水利、环境和公共设施管理业 Water Conservancy,Environment and Public Utility	1885	1786	99
水利管理业 Water Conservancy	120	110	10
生态保护和环境治理业 Ecological Protection and Environmental Management	236	212	24
公共设施管理业 Public Facilities	1529	1464	65
土地管理业 Land Management			
居民服务、修理和其他服务业 Service for the Residents ,Repair and Others	7213	6961	252
居民服务业 Resident Services	3461	3309	152
机动车、电子产品和日用产品修理业 Motor Vehicles , Electronics and Household Goods Repair Industry	2585	2518	67
其他服务业 Other Services	1167	1134	33
教育 Education	5301	5032	269
教育 Education	5301	5032	269
卫生和社会工作 Health Care,Sports & Social Welfare	2752	2475	277
卫生 Health Care	1711	1445	266
社会工作 Sports & Social Welfare	1041	1030	11
文化、体育和娱乐业 Culture,Sports and Entertainment	7442	7306	136
新闻和出版业 News and Publishing	179	177	2
广播、电视、电影和录音制作业 Television, Radio, Film and Television Sound Recording Production	1456	1435	21
文化艺术业 Culture and Arts	2178	2158	20
体育 Sports	1125	1068	57

指标名称 Item	法人单位数 Number of Corporation Units		
	合计 Total	单产业法人单位 Containing Single Industrial Activity	多产业法人单位 Containing Multiple Industrial Activity
娱乐业 Recreation	2504	2468	36
公共管理、社会保障和社会组织 Public Administration ,Social Security and Social Organization	10679	10369	310
中国共产党机关 Communist Party Agencies	163	155	8
国家机构 Government Agencies	2535	2316	219
人民政协、民主党派 The CPPCC, Democratic Parties	42	41	1
社会保障 Social Security	76	74	2
群众团体、社会团体和其他成员组织 Mass Organizations,Social Groups and Other Members of Organization	4788	4741	47
基层群众自治组织及其他组织 Basic Level Mass Autonomous Organization and Other Organizations	3075	3042	33
二、按地区分组	**450348**	**438371**	**11976**
杭州市 HangZhou	450348	438371	11976
上城区 Shangcheng	22402	21495	907
下城区 Xiacheng	29341	28206	1135
江干区 Jianggan	50907	49545	1361
拱墅区 Gongshu	38010	36910	1101
西湖区 Xihu	64625	62537	2088
高新(滨江区) Hi-Tech(Binjiang)	25609	24968	641
萧山区 Xiaoshan	74867	73406	1460
余杭区 Yuhang	64836	63326	1510
富阳区 Fuyang	26981	26439	542
临安区 Lin'an	17492	17094	398
桐庐县 Tonglu	15515	15220	295
淳安县 Chun'an	8248	7969	279
建德市 Jiande	11515	11256	259

1－18　市区分月气象概况(2017 年)
Monthly Meteorological Conditions in Urban District(2017)

月　份	Month	平均气温(度) Average Temperature(℃)	日照时数(小时) Sunshine Hours(hours)	降雨天数(天) Rainfall Days (day)	降水量(毫米) Precipitation(mm)
全　年	**Whole Year**	**18.3**	**1818.4**	**145**	**1442**
1　月	January	7.3	119.3	11	71.7
2　月	February	7.8	132.7	7	27.2
3　月	March	11.3	121.3	14	189
4　月	April	18.7	181.4	14	142.9
5　月	May	22.8	197	9	87.8
6　月	June	24.1	101.1	19	307.2
7　月	July	31.6	272.9	10	77.5
8　月	August	30.3	222.7	16	95.3
9　月	September	24.9	101.6	15	168.3
10　月	October	19.1	125.8	9	89.2
11　月	November	13.7	115.2	14	139.1
12　月	December	7.4	127.4	7	46.8

1－19 气　　象
Meteorological

指　标	Item	市　区 Urban District	萧山区 Xiaoshan
一、气　温	**The Atmospheric Temperature**		
全年平均气温（度）	Annual Average Temperature（℃）	18.3	18.0
极端最高气温（度）	The Highest Temperature of the Year（℃）	41.3	40.8
出现日期（日/月）	Date（d/m）	24/7	25/7
极端最低气温（度）	The Lowest Temperature of the Year（℃）	－2.5	－2.4
出现日期（日/月）	Date（d/m）	21/1	21/1
二、降　雨	**Rainfall**		
本年降雨日数（日）	Total Rainy Days（day）	145	148
全年降雨总量（毫米）	Annual Rainfall（millimeters）	1442.0	1519.5
最长连续降雨日数（日）	Longest Consecutive Days of Rain（day）	11	11
最长连续降雨总量（毫米）	Rainfall（millimeters）	171.9	153.2
最长连续降雨起止日期（日/月）	Start/End（d/m）	19－29/6	19－29/6
日最大降雨量（毫米）	Maximum Daily Rainfall（millimeters）	75.1	68.7
出现日期（日/月）	Date（d/m）	24/6	24/6
三、全年日照总时数（小时）	**Total Sunshine Hours（hours）**	**1818.4**	**1943.6**
四、降　霜	**Frost**		
全年降霜日数（日）	Annual Frost Days（day）	28	25
初霜日期（日/月）	Start Date（d/m）	17/12	6/12
终霜日期（日/月）	End Date（d/m）	9/3	3/3
五、降　雪	**Snow**		
全年降雪日数（日）	Annual Frost Days（day）	3	1
初雪日期（日/月）	Start Date（d/m）	23/11	9/2
终雪日期（日/月）	End Date（d/m）	8/2	9/2

概　　况(2017 年)
Conditions by Region(2017)

余杭区 Yuhang	富阳区 Fuyang	临安区 Lin'an	桐庐县 Tonglu	淳安县 Chun'an	建德市 Jiande
18.0	18.1	17.0	18.1	18.2	18.0
41.8	40.6	40.2	42.2	40.2	40.9
22/7	25/7	4/8	24/7	24/7	23/7
-3.8	-3.5	-5.5	-3.3	-1.3	-2.4
21/1	21/1	21/1	21/1	21/1	21/1
143	136	144	144	145	148
1471.4	1415.6	1381.1	1471.2	1510.7	1493.1
18	8	18	9	11	12
273.1	134.5	188.3	85.0	226.3	257.5
19/6-6/7	19-26/6	19/6-6/7	12/3-20/3	19/6-29/6	19/6-30/6
115.9	77.3	83	134.2	83.3	82.0
24/6	13/6	24/6	13/6	13/6	13/6
暂缺	**1816.0**	**1787.6**	**1631.3**	**1870.1**	**1764.8**
暂缺	14	26	26	13	27
17/12	6/12	7/12	15/12	17/12	16/12
13/2	13/2	3/3	14/2	13/2	3/3
					2
	-	2	1	1	1
		11/1	9/2	23/2	23/2
		9/2	9/2	23/2	23/2

主要统计指标解释

地区生产总值(GDP) 指一个国家(或地区)所有常住单位在一定时期内生产活动的最终成果。地区生产总值有三种表现形态,即价值形态、收入形态和产品形态。从价值形态看,它是所有常住单位在一定时期内生产的全部货物和服务价值超过同期投入的全部非固定资产货物和服务价值的差额,即所有常住单位的增加值之和;从收入形态看,它是所有常住单位在一定时期内创造并分配给常住单位和非常住单位的初次收入分配之和;从产品形态看,它是所有常住单位在一定时期内最终使用的货物和服务价值与货物减去进出口货物和服务。在实际核算中,生产总值有三种计算方法,即生产法、收入法和支出法。三种方法分别从不同的方面反映生产总值及其构成。

三次产业 是根据社会生产活动历史发展的顺序对产业结构的划分,产品直接取自自然界的部门称为第一产业,对初级产品进行再加工的部门称为第二产业,为生产和消费提供各种服务的部门称为第三产业。它是世界上较为通用的产业结构分类,但各国的划分不尽一致。2012 年前的三次产业划分标准按照当年《统计年鉴》,从 2013 年起,三次产业划分调整为:

第一产业是指农、林、牧、渔业(不含农、林、牧、渔服务业)。

第二产业是指工业[采矿业(不含开采辅助活动),制造业(不含金属制品、机械和设备修理业),电力、热力、燃气及水生产和供应业]和建筑业。

第三产业即服务业,是指除第一产业、第二产业以外的其他行业。

劳动者报酬 指劳动者因从事生产活动所获得的全部报酬。包括劳动者获得的各种形式的工资、奖金和津贴,既包括货币形式,也包括实物形式的;还包括劳动者所享受的公费医疗和医药卫生费上下班交通补贴和单位支付的社会保险费等。对于个体经济来说其所有者所获得的劳动报酬和经营利润不易区分,这两部分统一作为劳动报酬处理。

生产税净额 指生产税减生产补贴后的余额。生产税指政府对生产单位生产销售和从事经营活动以及因从事生产活动使用某些生产要素(如固定资产土地劳动力)所征收的各种税、附加费和规费。生产补贴和生产税相反,指政府对生产单位的单方面收入转移,因此视为负生产税,包括政策亏损补贴、粮食系统价格补贴、外贸企业出口退税收入等。

固定资产折旧 在一定时期内为弥补固定资产损耗按照核定的固定资产损耗率提取的固定资产折旧,或按国民经济核算统一规定的折旧率虚拟计算的固定资产折旧。它反映了固定资产在当期生产中的转移价值。各类企业和企业化管理的事业单位的固定资产折旧是指实际计提并计入成本费中的折旧费;不计提折旧的政府机关非企业化管理的事业单位和居民住房的固定资产折旧是按照统一固定的折旧率和固定资产原值计算的虚拟折旧。原则上,固定资产折旧应按照固定资产的重置价值计算,但是目前我国尚不具备对全社会固定资产进行重估价的基础,所以暂时只能采用上述方法。

营业盈余 指常住单位创造的增加值扣除劳动者报酬生产税净额和固定资产折旧后的余额。它相当于企业的营业利润加上生产补贴,但要扣除从利润中开支的工资和福利等。

可比价格 指在不同时期的价值指标对比时,扣除了价格变动的因素,以确切反映物量的变化。按可比价格计算有两种方法:一种是直接用产品产量乘每一年的不变价格计算;另一种使用价格指数换算。

不变价格 指用同类产品的年平均价格作为固定价格,来计算各年产品价值。按不变价格计算的产品价值消除了价格变动因素,不同时期对比可反映出生产的发展速度。新中国成立后,随着工农业产品价格的变化,国家统计局先后五次制定了全国统一的工业产品不变价格和农业产品不变价格,从 1949 年到 1957 年使用 1952 工(农)业产品不变价格,从 1957 年到 1971 年使用 1957 年不变价格,从 1981 年到 1990 年使用 1980 年不变价格,从 1990 年开始使用 1990 年不变价格。

信息经济 2014 年,杭州发布了关于加快发展信息经济的若干意见,发展目标是到 2020 年,率先成为特色鲜明、全国领先的信息经济强市和智慧经济创新城市。确立发展电子商务、云计算与大数据、物联网、互联网金融、智慧物流、数字内容等六大核心产业以及软件与信息服务、电子信息产品制造、移动互联网、集成电路、信息安全、机器人等六大重点领域。

"1+6 产业集群" 2016 年,杭州在国民经济和社会发展第"十三个"五年规划纲要中,提出:构建以信息经济为引领、现代服务业为主导、先进制造业为支撑、都市现代农业为基础的现代产业新体系,推进产业迈向中高端。确立发展万亿信息产业集群以及文化创意、旅游休闲、金融服务、健康、时尚、高端装备制造等六大千亿产业集群的目标。

降水量 从天空降落到地面的液态或固态(经融化后)降水,未经蒸发、渗透、流失而在水平面上积聚的深度。降水量以毫米为单位。

空气的温度(简称气温) 表示空气冷热程度的物理量。

日照时数 太阳在一地实际照射地面的时数。

Explanatory Notes on Main Statistical Indicators

Gross Domestic Product (GDP) refers to the final products of all resident units in a country (or a region) during a certain period of time. Gross domestic product is expressed in three different forms, i. e. value, income, and products respectively. The form of value refers to the total value of all products and services produced by all resident units during a certain period of time minus total value of intermediate input of materials and services of the nature of non – fixed assets or the summation of the value – added of all resident units; the form of income includes all the income created by all resident units and distributed primarily to all resident and non – resident units; the form of products refers to the value of all final goods and services for final use by all resident units minus imports of goods and services during a given period of time. In the practice of national accounting, gross domestic product is calculated with three approaches, i. e. production approach, income approach, and expenditure approach, which reflect gross domestic product and its composition from different aspects.

Three Industries Industry structure has been classified according to the historical sequence of development. Primary industry refers to extraction of natural resources; secondary industry involves processing of primary products; and tertiary industry provides services of various kinds for production and consumption. The above classification is universal although it varies to someextent from country to country. The explanatory notes on Three Industries were available on Hangzhou Statistical Yearbook of the year before 2012, and the indicators of Three Industry have been revised according to the national standards since 2013.

Primary Industry refers to argriculture, forestry, animal husbandry and fishery industries (excluding their service activities).

Second Industry refers to industry [mining and quarrying (excluding its support activities), manufacturing (excluding the repair services of metal product, machine and equipment), production and supply of electricity, heat, water and gas] and construction.

Tertiary Industry is the service industry, refers to all other economic acitivities not included in the primary or secondary industries.

Labourer's Remuneration refers to the whole payment of various forms earned by the labourers from the productive activities they are engaged in. It includes wages, bonuses and allowances the labourers earned in monetary form and in kind. It also includes the free medical services provided to the labourers and the medicine expenses, traffic subsidies and social insurance free paid by the labourers' working units for them. As the individual economy is concerned, since the labourers' remuneration is not easily distingushed from the operating profit, both are treated as labourers remuneration.

Net Taxes on Production refers to the residual of the taxes on production minus the subsidies on production. The taxes on production refer to the various taxes, extra charges and fees levied on the production units on their production, sail and business activities as well as on some factors of production, such as fixed assets, land and labour force, used in the production activities they are engaged in. In contrast to the taxes on production, the subsidies on production refer to the unilateral transfer of part of the government's revenue to the production units and is therefore regarded as negative taxes on production. They include sunsidies on the loss due to implementation of government policies, price subsidies to the grain institutions, foreign trade corporations' receipts from drawback, ect.

Depreciation of Fixed Assets refers to the depreciation of fixed assets of a given period, drawn in accordance with the stipulated depreciation rate for purpose of compensating the wear loss of the fixed assets of the depreciation of fixed assets calculated in a fictitious way in accordance with the stipulated unified depreciation rate in the national economic accounting system. It reflects the value of transfer of the fixed assets in the production of the current period. The depreciation of fixed assets in various enterprises and institutions managed as enterprises refers to the depreciation expenses actually drawnand calculated as part of the cost. In government agencies and institutions not managed as enterprises which do not draw the depreciation expenses, as well as for the house of residents, the depreciation of fixed assets is the imputed depreciation, which is calculated in accordance with the stipulated unified depreciation rate. In principle, the depreciation of fixed assets should bs calculated on the basis of the repurchased value of the fixed assets. However, there is no actual condition to reevaluated all the fixed assets in China. Therefore, the abovementioned methods are temporarily adopted at present.

Operating Surplus refers to the balance of the value added created by the resident units deducting the laboures' remuneration, net taxes on production and the depreciation of fixed assets. It is equivalent to the business profit of the enterprises plus subsidies on production, but the wages and welfare expenses paid from the profits should be deducted.

Comparable Price is applied when comparing value indicators of different periods to reflect accurately the changes in physical value. The price is not considered here. Two methods are used for calculating comparable prices: 1. Multipling the output of products by their constant price of a certain year; 2. Conversion of the data in current prices by relevant price index.

Constant Prices refer to the average price of a given produce in a certain year, which is used to calculate the output value over time. As the output value at constant prices removes the factor of price changes, it reflects the trend of production development over time. Since 1949, with the changes in general price level, the State Statistical Bureau has issued nationally unified constant prices for five times, the 1952 constant prices for 1949 – 1957; the 1957 constant prices for 1958 – 1970; the 1970 constant prices for 1971 – 1981; the 1980 constant prices for 1981 – 1990; the 1990 constant prices have been used since 1991.

Information Economy In 2014, Hangzhou issued a document on speeding up the development of the information economy. By 2020, Hangzhou will be a national – leading information economy city with distinctive features and an innovative smart economy city. Hangzhou will promote the development of six key industries of E – commerce, Cloud Computing and Big Data, Internet of Things, Internet Finance, Wisdom Logistics, Digital Content, as well as six key areas of Soft – ware and Information Service, Electronic Information Products Manufacturing, Mobile Internet, Integrate Circuits, Information Security, Robot.

"1 +6" Industrial Cluster In 2016, in the outline of the 13th five – year plan for national economic and social development, hangzhou will quicken the establishment of a new system of modern industry based on the information economy as the lead, the modern service industry as the predominance, the advanced manufacturing industry as the support, the urban modern agriculture as the foundation, and promote the development of industries toward the medium – high end. We will build a series of large – scale industrial clusters, including a trillion scale information industry clusters, and six hundred billion scale industry clusters of Cultural and Creative Industry, Tourism Leisure Industry, Financial Industry, Health Industry, Fashion Industry (Manufacturing) and High – end Equipment Industry (Manufacturing).

Precipitation refers to the depth of rainfall onto the ground (as well as liquefied from solid forms) from above the air prior to its vaporization, seepage, running off.

It is calculated in the unit of millimeter (mm).

Air Temperature refers to the physical quantity reflecting the extent of coldness and hotness of the air.

Duration of sunshine refers to the real time for the ground to receive sunshine at a certain place.

二、人口和就业人员

POPULATION AND EMPLOYMENT

2 人口和就业人员 Population and Employment

主要统计指标 Major Statistical Indicators

年末常住人口	Long-term Residents(year-end)	946.8	万人	(10, 000 persons)
为上年	As Compared with the Preceding Year	103.0	%	(%)
#城镇人口	Urban Population	727.14	万人	(10, 000 persons)
年末户籍登记户数	Total Registration Households(year-end)	235.26	万户	(10, 000 Subscribers)
为上年	As Compared with the Preceding Year	102.5	%	(%)
年末户籍登记人口	Total Registration Population(year-end)	753.88	万人	(10, 000 persons)
为上年	As Compared with the Preceding Year	102.4	%	(%)
#男性	Male	374.75	万人	(10, 000 persons)
为上年	As Compared with the Preceding Year	102.3	%	(%)
户籍人口自然增长率	Natural Growth Rate of Household Registered Population	6.19	‰	(‰)
年末就业人员	Number of Employed Persons(year-end)	681.06	万人	(10, 000 persons)
为上年	As Compared with the Preceding Year	100.6	%	(%)

2-01 历次普查常住人口情况

Long-term Residents in the Past Population Census

单位:万人 (10000 person)

地区 Region		第一次人口普查 1953.7.1 the First Population Census (1953.7.1)	第二次人口普查 1964.7.1 the Second Population Census (1964.7.1)	第三次人口普查 1982.7.1 the Third Population Census (1982.7.1)	第四次人口普查 1990.7.1 the Fourth Population Census (1990.7.1)	第五次人口普查 2000.11.1 the Fifth Population Census (2000.11.1)	第六次人口普查 2010.11.1 the Sixth Population Census (2010.11.1)
杭州市	**Hangzhou**	**301.13**	**421.90**	**526.05**	**583.21**	**687.87**	**870.04**
市　区	Urban District	227.49	318.88	405.55	454.38	564.52	752.64
#上城区	Shangcheng				21.10	33.51	34.46
下城区	Xiacheng				25.66	41.24	52.61
江干区	Jianggan				36.12	56.54	99.88
拱墅区	Gongshu				29.34	42.93	55.19
西湖区	Xihu				35.40	59.33	82.00
高新(滨江)区	Hi-Tech(Binjiang)					11.59	31.90
萧山区	Xiaoshan	56.32	82.34	106.11	113.06	123.33	151.13
余杭区	Yuhang	52.28	64.96	80.50	86.08	81.77	117.03
富阳区	Fuyang	29.22	39.66	54.13	58.07	62.86	71.77
临安区	Lin'an	26.01	35.57	45.65	49.55	51.42	56.67
桐庐县	Tonglu	19.73	26.20	34.83	37.66	37.81	40.64
淳安县	Chun'an	27.49	38.66	42.03	43.55	38.23	33.68
建德市	Jiande	26.42	38.15	43.64	47.63	47.31	43.08

注:历年普查市区口径均已按现行行政辖区调整。

a) The data of the past population censuses in urban district were adjusted according to the current administrative division.

2－02 全市户籍人口和总户数(1978－2017年)

Household Registered Population and Households(1978－2017)

年份 Year	总户数 (万户) Total Households (10000 households)	总人口数 (万人) Total Population (10000 persons)	城镇人口(万人) Urban Population (10000 persons)	按性别分 By Sex 男(万人) Male (10000 persons)	按性别分 By Sex 女(万人) Female (10000 persons)
1978	117.89	505.55	116.06	260.74	244.81
1979	116.61	511.83	124.60	263.97	247.86
1980	119.11	515.53	128.88	266.02	249.51
1981	125.96	520.73	134.56	268.69	252.04
1982	131.53	528.06	139.94	272.72	255.34
1983	135.55	533.06	143.34	275.64	257.41
1984	139.24	537.49	147.46	278.04	259.45
1985	145.23	543.05	153.46	281.11	261.94
1986	151.59	549.53	157.19	284.57	264.96
1987	157.66	557.63	161.12	288.70	268.93
1988	164.41	565.04	164.87	292.21	272.83
1989	169.09	570.98	167.28	295.15	275.83
1990	171.94	574.78	169.00	297.02	277.76
1991	174.78	578.73	171.25	298.85	279.88
1992	177.68	582.40	174.03	300.63	281.77
1993	179.17	587.10	179.11	303.03	284.07
1994	180.65	592.93	186.50	306.00	286.93
1995	182.55	597.96	191.43	308.25	289.71
1996	184.33	603.22	196.68	310.76	292.46
1997	186.28	607.96	204.39	313.02	294.94
1998	187.80	611.64	210.52	314.69	296.95
1999	191.60	616.05	219.05	316.63	299.42
2000	193.48	621.58	227.00	319.09	302.49
2001	195.56	629.14	237.77	322.78	306.36
2002	198.27	636.81	252.02	326.62	310.19
2003	201.12	642.78	263.67	329.04	313.74
2004	204.52	651.68	282.58	332.62	319.06
2005	207.42	660.45	297.54	336.12	324.33
2006	209.91	666.31	309.78	338.23	328.08
2007	211.99	672.35	323.75	340.50	331.85
2008	213.74	677.64	340.76	342.45	335.19
2009	215.28	683.38	354.48	344.51	338.87
2010	216.51	689.12	365.24	346.56	342.56
2011	218.26	695.71	376.03	349.09	346.62
2012	218.95	700.52	384.09	350.90	349.62
2013	220.66	706.61	393.88	353.32	353.29
2014	222.35	715.76	404.27	357.26	358.50
2015	225.79	723.55	447.24	360.68	362.87
2016	229.57	736.00	463.86	366.47	369.53
2017	235.26	753.88	482.55	374.75	379.12

注:1. 按公安户籍人口统计。

2. 城镇人口2015年前为非农业人口。

a) Figures in this table are based on the household registered statistics which published by Public Security Bureau.

b) Since 2015, the donotation of Non－agriculture Population has been adjusted to Urban Population.

2－03 市区户籍人口和总户数(1978－2017年)

Household Registered Population and Households of Urban District(1978－2017)

年 份 Year	总户数 (万户) Total Households (10000 households)	总人口数 (万人) Total Population (10000 persons)	城镇人口(万人) Urban Population (10000 persons)	按性别分 By Sex 男(万人) Male (10000 persons)	女(万人) Female (10000 persons)
1978	25.52	104.53	78.73	53.95	50.58
1979	26.23	110.50	85.05	57.09	53.41
1980	27.23	113.08	87.93	58.56	54.52
1981	29.88	115.59	90.53	59.96	55.63
1982	31.24	118.05	92.72	61.28	56.77
1983	32.69	120.13	94.94	62.43	57.70
1984	34.07	122.29	97.34	63.63	58.66
1985	35.36	124.67	100.01	64.96	59.71
1986	37.02	127.07	102.59	66.29	60.78
1987	38.70	129.16	104.09	67.38	61.78
1988	40.05	131.26	107.30	68.46	62.80
1989	41.19	132.84	108.88	69.28	63.56
1990	42.26	133.89	109.97	69.75	64.14
1991	42.98	134.97	111.20	70.33	64.64
1992	43.63	136.30	112.70	71.08	65.22
1993	44.55	138.33	115.13	72.22	66.11
1994	45.04	141.27	118.48	73.82	67.45
1995	46.06	143.52	121.38	74.91	68.61
1996	52.39	166.73	128.76	87.15	79.58
1997	53.14	169.29	131.76	88.53	80.76
1998	53.92	171.89	134.62	89.86	82.03
1999	54.64	175.27	139.29	91.65	83.62
2000	55.34	179.18	143.69	93.64	85.54
2001	115.81	379.49	193.26	194.59	184.90
2002	117.11	387.01	205.98	198.47	188.54
2003	119.01	393.19	216.13	201.14	192.05
2004	120.56	401.59	233.08	204.43	197.16
2005	122.02	409.52	245.56	207.70	201.82
2006	123.31	414.18	256.42	209.45	204.73
2007	124.40	419.50	269.30	211.59	207.91
2008	125.56	424.30	285.11	213.54	210.76
2009	126.92	429.44	297.83	215.56	213.88
2010	128.43	434.82	307.52	217.65	217.16
2011	130.14	440.34	317.63	219.86	220.48
2012	131.48	445.43	325.50	221.99	223.43
2013	133.27	450.82	334.38	224.24	226.58
2014	157.11	525.07	358.56	261.17	263.90
2015	160.47	532.86	389.14	264.71	268.15
2016	164.22	544.68	403.20	270.31	274.38
2017	188.48	615.23	440.61	304.86	310.37

注:城镇人口2015年前为非农业人口。

a) Since 2015, the donotation of Non－agriculture Population has been adjusted to Urban Population.

2-04 分地区户籍人口和总户数(2017年末)
Household Registered Population and Households by Region(End of 2017)

地　区 Region	总户数 (户) Total Households (household)	总人口数 (人) Total Population (person)	按性别分 By Sex 男(人) Male (person)	 女(人) Female (person)
全　市 Whole City	**2352575**	**7538771**	**3747545**	**3791226**
市　区 Urban District	1884833	6152286	3048565	3103721
#上城区 Shangcheng	112106	320431	159422	161009
下城区 Xiacheng	130088	403170	200259	202911
江干区 Jianggan	172285	562880	279945	282935
经济技术开发区 Economic and Technological Development Zone	33536	117876	60422	57454
拱墅区 Gongshu	126358	361609	179510	182099
西湖区 Xihu	199865	712763	357342	355421
西湖风景名胜区 The West Lake Scenic Zone	6333	19820	9280	10540
高新(滨江)区 Hi-Tech(Binjiang)	68196	242803	123228	119575
萧山区 Xiaoshan	377496	1295770	635157	660613
大江东产业集聚区 Dajiangdong Industry Cluster District	42078	154110	75087	79023
余杭区 Yuhang	294189	1040496	508563	531933
富阳区 Fuyang	216058	677210	339360	337850
临安区 Lin'an	188192	535154	265779	269375
桐庐县 Tonglu	148647	414883	206516	208367
淳安县 Chun'an	146647	460769	233277	227492
建德市 Jiande	172448	510833	259187	251646

2-05 分地区户籍人口年龄构成(2017 年末)

Age Structure of Household Registered Population by Region(End of 2017)

地 区 Region	0-17 岁 0~17 years old		18-34 岁 18~34 years old		35-59 岁 35~59 years old		60 岁以上 over 60 years old	
	人数(人) Number of people (person)	占总人口% of the total population	人数(人) Number of people (person)	占总人口% of the total population	人数(人) Number of people (person)	占总人口% of the total population	人数(人) Number of people (person)	占总人口% of the total population
全 市 Whole City	**1258969**	**16.7**	**1684384**	**22.3**	**2925033**	**38.8**	**1670385**	**22.2**
市 区 Urban District	1056631	17.2	1382191	22.5	2358225	38.3	1355239	22.0
#上城区 Shangcheng	38023	11.9	67723	21.1	116677	36.4	98008	30.6
下城区 Xiacheng	53518	13.3	96260	23.8	146195	36.3	107197	26.6
江干区 Jianggan	115432	20.5	136404	24.2	205006	36.5	106038	18.8
经济技术开发区 Economic and Technological Development Zone	28850	24.5	45310	38.4	35224	29.9	8492	7.2
拱墅区 Gongshu	59611	16.5	76607	21.2	135960	37.6	89431	24.7
西湖区 Xihu	134814	18.9	180799	25.4	269604	37.8	127546	17.9
西湖风景名胜区 The West Lake Scenic Zone	2527	12.7	3872	19.5	7771	39.3	5650	28.5
高新(滨江)区 Hi-Tech(Binjiang)	54800	22.6	70839	29.2	84464	34.7	32700	13.5
萧山区 Xiaoshan	213993	16.5	271568	21.0	498646	38.5	311563	24.0
大江东产业集聚区 Dajiangdong Industry Cluster District	24978	16.2	33126	21.5	58281	37.8	37725	24.5
余杭区 Yuhang	202451	19.5	224573	21.6	400662	38.5	212810	20.4
富阳区 Fuyang	107639	15.9	144921	21.4	279192	41.2	145458	21.5
临安区 Lin'an	76350	14.3	112497	21.0	221819	41.4	124488	23.3
桐庐县 Tonglu	62509	15.1	90729	21.9	164966	39.7	96679	23.3
淳安县 Chun'an	68631	14.9	96751	21.0	195830	42.5	99557	21.6
建德市 Jiande	71198	13.9	114713	22.5	206012	40.3	118910	23.3

2-06 全市户籍人口自然变动情况(1978-2017年)

Natural Changes of Household Registered Population(1978-2017)

年 份 Year	出 生 Birth		死 亡 Death		自然增长 Natural Growth	
	人数(人) Birth Population (person)	出生率(‰) Birth Rate(‰)	人数(人) Death Population (person)	死亡率(‰) Death Rate(‰)	人数(人) Natural Growth Population (person)	自然增长率(‰) Natural Growth Rate(‰)
1978	73550	14.63	29928	2.95	43622	8.68
1979	71442	14.04	29500	5.80	41942	8.24
1980	52145	10.15	30727	5.98	21418	4.17
1981	73015	14.09	31352	6.05	41663	8.04
1982	82910	15.81	30805	5.87	52105	9.94
1983	69940	13.18	33598	6.33	36342	6.85
1984	60091	11.23	33070	6.18	27021	5.05
1985	66757	12.36	33715	6.24	33042	6.12
1986	84702	15.50	33576	6.15	51126	9.35
1987	94127	17.00	33238	6.00	60889	11.00
1988	85472	15.23	35356	6.30	50116	8.93
1989	81048	14.27	34031	5.99	47017	8.28
1990	76579	13.37	34977	6.11	41602	7.26
1991	66144	11.47	33534	5.81	32610	5.66
1992	61708	10.63	34681	5.97	27027	4.66
1993	62465	10.68	34127	5.84	28338	4.84
1994	63580	10.78	35099	5.95	28481	4.83
1995	62586	10.51	36186	6.08	26400	4.43
1996	63680	10.60	25417	5.90	28263	4.70
1997	58471	9.65	34663	5.72	23808	3.93
1998	53951	8.85	38302	6.28	15649	2.57
1999	59085	9.63	36866	6.01	22219	3.62
2000	62300	10.07	40218	6.50	22082	3.57
2001	52088	8.33	33827	5.41	18261	2.92
2002	53064	8.38	35867	5.67	17197	2.72
2003	51420	8.04	36662	5.73	14758	2.31
2004	59940	9.26	34078	5.27	25862	3.99
2005	57233	8.72	35417	5.39	21816	3.33
2006	57790	8.71	38892	5.86	18898	2.85
2007	60296	9.01	37833	5.65	22463	3.36
2008	61332	9.09	42648	6.32	18684	2.77
2009	62441	9.18	39159	5.76	23282	3.42
2010	69606	10.14	46193	6.73	23413	3.41
2011	70337	10.16	38225	5.52	32112	4.64
2012	77349	11.08	49789	7.13	27560	3.95
2013	70850	10.07	37544	5.34	33306	4.73
2014	89743	12.62	40415	5.68	49328	6.94
2015	70617	9.81	40326	5.60	30291	4.21
2016	90896	12.46	35614	4.88	55282	7.58
2017	109496	14.70	63366	8.51	46130	6.19

注:本表按公安部门统计。

a) Figures in this table are based on the Public Security Bureau.

2－07　市区户籍人口自然变动情况(1978－2017年)

Natural Changes of Household Registered Population of Urban District(1978－2017)

年　份 Year	出　生 Birth		死　亡 Death		自然增长 Natural Growth	
	人数(人) Birth Population (person)	出生率(‰) Birth Rate(‰)	人数(人) Death Population (person)	死亡率(‰) Death Rate(‰)	人数(人) Natural Growth Population (person)	自然增长率(‰) Natural Growth Rate(‰)
1978	11923	11.56	6449	6.25	5474	5.31
1979	13184	12.26	5808	5.40	7376	6.86
1980	9708	8.68	6511	5.82	3197	2.86
1981	14938	13.06	6599	5.77	8339	7.29
1982	18092	15.49	6494	5.56	11598	9.93
1983	17107	14.36	6949	5.84	10158	8.52
1984	16257	13.41	6892	5.69	9365	7.72
1985	15824	12.81	7403	6.84	8421	6.82
1986	17120	13.60	6865	5.45	10255	8.15
1987	18701	14.60	7070	5.52	11631	9.08
1988	18503	14.21	7503	5.76	11000	8.45
1989	15868	12.02	6985	5.29	8883	6.73
1990	14085	10.56	7490	5.62	6595	4.94
1991	10195	7.58	7025	5.22	3170	2.36
1992	9994	7.37	7259	5.35	2735	2.02
1993	10099	7.35	7196	5.24	2903	2.11
1994	9918	7.09	7082	5.06	2836	2.03
1995	9806	6.89	7367	5.17	2439	1.72
1996	12098	7.80	8221	5.30	3877	2.50
1997	12304	7.32	8630	5.13	3674	2.19
1998	11714	6.87	9060	5.31	2654	1.56
1999	13694	7.89	8148	4.69	5546	3.20
2000	15058	8.50	10996	6.20	4062	2.30
2001	30902	8.22	19439	5.17	11463	3.05
2002	33156	8.65	19922	5.20	13234	3.45
2003	29019	7.44	21176	5.43	7843	2.01
2004	34858	8.77	19445	4.89	15413	3.88
2005	34056	8.39	21310	5.25	12746	3.14
2006	33260	8.08	21156	5.14	12104	2.94
2007	37029	8.88	20051	4.81	16978	4.07
2008	38703	9.17	21428	5.08	17275	4.09
2009	40293	9.44	22178	5.20	18115	4.24
2010	47052	10.89	25404	5.88	21648	5.01
2011	47256	10.80	22140	5.06	25116	5.74
2012	51892	11.72	27271	6.16	24621	5.56
2013	48107	10.74	21332	4.76	26775	5.97
2014	69577	13.36	27249	5.23	42328	8.13
2015	55275	10.45	26492	5.01	28783	5.44
2016	71427	13.26	23544	4.37	47883	8.89
2017	92571	15.96	52817	9.11	39754	6.85

2-08 分地区户籍人口自然变动情况(2017年)
Natural Changes of Household Registered Population by Region(2017)

地　区 Region	出　生 Birth		死　亡 Death		自然增长 Natural Growth	
	人数(人) Birth Population (person)	出生率(‰) Birth Rate(‰)	人数(人) Death Population (person)	死亡率(‰) Death Rate(‰)	人数(人) Natural Growth Population (person)	自然增长率(‰) Natural Growth Rate(‰)
全　市 Whole City	**109496**	**14.70**	**63366**	**8.51**	**46130**	**6.19**
市　区 Urban District	92571	15.96	52817	9.11	39754	6.85
#上城区 Shangcheng	3178	9.82	7383	22.81	-4205	-12.99
下城区 Xiacheng	4898	12.16	5599	13.89	-701	-1.73
江干区 Jianggan	10586	19.42	4558	8.36	6028	11.06
经济技术开发区 Economic and Technological Development Zone	3071	27.39	218	1.94	2853	25.45
拱墅区 Gongshu	5567	15.74	4786	13.53	781	2.21
西湖区 Xihu	11371	16.20	5172	7.37	6199	8.83
西湖风景名胜区 The West Lake Scenic Zone	210	10.53	353	17.69	-143	-7.16
高新(滨江)区 Hi-Tech(Binjiang)	5811	25.05	901	3.88	4910	21.17
萧山区 Xiaoshan	18140	14.11	8752	6.81	9388	7.30
大江东产业集聚区 Dajiangdong Industry Cluster District	2370	15.49	909	5.94	1461	9.55
余杭区 Yuhang	18608	18.38	6247	6.17	12361	12.21
富阳区 Fuyang	8504	12.61	4718	7.00	3786	5.61
临安区 Lin'an	5908	11.08	4701	8.81	1207	2.27
桐庐县 Tonglu	5302	12.83	2860	6.92	2442	5.91
淳安县 Chun'an	5361	11.64	3924	8.52	1437	3.12
建德市 Jiande	6262	12.27	3765	7.38	2497	4.89

2－09 分地区户籍人口机械变动情况(2017年)
Mechanical Changes of Household Registered Population by Region(2017)

单位:人 (person)

地区 Region	本年迁入人数 Number of the Persons Moved in(person)		本年迁出人数 Number of the Persons Moved Out(person)		本年净迁入人数 Net Persons Moved in
	省内 From Zhejiang Province	省外 From Other Provinces	省内 To Zhejiang Province	省外 To Other Provinces	
全市 Whole City	**63616**	**100789**	**15251**	**16191**	**132963**
市区 Urban District	61744	95968	8775	14480	134457
#上城区 Shangcheng	2991	3654	256	793	5596
下城区 Xiacheng	5285	8103	656	1407	11325
江干区 Jianggan	12145	14700	1559	2764	22522
经济技术开发区 Economic and Technological Development Zone	5502	8031	1296	2293	9944
拱墅区 Gongshu	5776	5512	506	591	10191
西湖区 Xihu	11531	15907	1884	4774	20780
西湖风景名胜区 The West Lake Scenic Zone	131	209	29	55	256
高新(滨江)区 Hi－Tech(Binjiang)	6406	7220	452	862	12312
萧山区 Xiaoshan	3407	7245	463	977	9212
大江东产业集聚区 Dajiangdong Industry Cluster District	5502	8031	1296	2293	9944
余杭区 Yuhang	11584	27911	898	1179	37418
富阳区 Fuyang	1046	2461	346	615	2546
临安区 Lin'an	1573	3255	1755	518	2555
桐庐县 Tonglu	806	2113	1394	505	1020
淳安县 Chun'an	458	1190	2462	531	－1345
建德市 Jiande	608	1518	2620	675	－1169

2－10　婚姻登记情况（2016－2017年）

Marriage Registration Situations（2016－2017）

地　　区 Region	2016			2017		
	准予登记结婚对数（对） Marriages Legally Registered（couples）	再婚人数（人） Re－married（person）	离婚对数（对） Divorces（couples）	准予登记结婚对数（对） Marriages Legally Registered（couples）	再婚人数（人） Re－married（person）	离婚对数（对） Divorces（couples）
全　市 Whole City	**63260**	**29963**	**21033**	**65633**	**22736**	**24740**
市　区 Urban District	47806	22174	15369	54768	19039	20358
#萧山区 Xiaoshan	9488	3395	2180	9012	2609	2756
余杭区 Yuhang	7262	3542	2755	8278	3187	3281
富阳区 Fuyang	4939	2184	1773	5266	1974	1926
临安区 Lin'an	4201	2361	1663	4280	1753	2076
桐庐县 Tonglu	3318	1847	1303	3122	1178	1444
淳安县 Chun'an	3780	1711	1250	3809	1178	1316
建德市 Jiande	4155	1870	1448	3934	1341	1622

2-11 三次产业就业人员及构成(2010-2017年)

Number of Employed Persons by Three Industries(2010-2017)

单位:万人 (10000 persons)

指标名称	Item	2010	2011	2012	2013	2014	2015	2016	2017
全市总计	**Total**	**626.33**	**637.77**	**644.43**	**650.51**	**654.92**	**663.03**	**676.95**	**681.06**
第一产业	Primary Industry	75.70	72.21	70.39	70.07	66.39	67.01	66.11	66.29
第二产业	Secondary Industry	286.26	289.12	290.01	291.51	286.99	271.90	261.78	257.60
第三产业	Tertiary Industry	264.37	276.44	284.03	288.93	301.54	324.12	349.06	357.17
全市构成(以合计为100)	**Composition (Total=100)**	**100**	**100**	**100**	**100**	**100**	**100**	**100**	**100**
第一产业	Primary Industry	12.1	11.3	10.9	10.8	10.1	10.1	9.8	9.7
第二产业	Secondary Industry	45.7	45.4	45.0	44.8	43.9	41.0	38.7	37.8
第三产业	Tertiary Industry	42.2	43.3	44.1	44.4	46.0	48.9	51.5	52.5

2－12　全市非私营及规上

Number of Employed Persons of Non－private Units

单位:人

地区、行业	Region,Sector	就业人员合计 Number of Employed Persons	非私营单位 Non－private
全市	**Total**	**4522705**	**2870218**
市区	Urban District	4254961	2741717
#上城区	Shangcheng District	242166	180096
下城区	Xiacheng District	295246	238966
江干区	Jianggan District	474059	204470
拱墅区	Gongshu District	322032	154055
西湖区	Xihu District	651987	533941
高新(滨江)区	Hi－Tech(Binjiang) District	358926	277580
萧山区	Xiaoshan District	829686	491561
大江东产业集聚区	Dajiangdong Industry Cluster District	110145	57478
余杭区	Yuhang District	473357	266018
富阳区	Fuyang District	227774	120019
临安区	Lin'an District	146165	80474
经济技术开发区	Economic and Technological Development Zone	204846	168020
西湖风景名胜区	The West Lake Scenic Zone	28717	26517
桐庐县	Tonglu County	116284	45179
淳安县	Chun'an County	71119	40361
建德市	Jiande City	80341	42961
按国民经济行业分组	**Grouped by Sector**		
农、林、牧、渔业	Farming,Forestry,Animal Husbandry & Fishery	1202	1077
采矿业	Mining	1739	613
制造业	Manufacturing	1069614	656656
电力、热力、燃气及水生产和供应业	Production & Supply of Electricity,Heat,Gas & Water	19987	18581
建筑业	Construction	1526074	710028
批发和零售业	Wholesale & Retail Trades	281787	172071
交通运输、仓储和邮政业	Transportation,Storage and Posts	154937	113731
住宿和餐饮业	Hotels and Catering Services	101155	68136
信息传输、软件和信息技术服务业	Information Transmission, Software and Information Technology	218332	161076
金融业	Financial Intermediation	116339	114924
房地产业	Real Estate	149596	113017
租赁和商务服务业	Leasing and Business Services	195420	125346
科学研究、技术服务业	Scientific Research,Technical Services	140392	114182
水利、环境和公共设施管理业	Management of Water Conservancy,Environment and Public Facilities	38775	24981
居民服务、修理和其他服务业	Service to Households,Repair and Other Services	27074	10956
教育	Education	191174	186867
卫生和社会工业	Health Care and Social Work	125458	117606
文化、体育和娱乐业	Culture,Sports and Entertainment	25739	22459
公共管理、社会保障和社会组织	Public Management,Social Security and Social Organizations	137911	137911

私营单位就业人员数(2017年末)

and Private Units Above Designated Size(End of 2017)

(person)

女性 Female	非私营单位 Non - private	在岗职工 Staff and Workers	非私营单位 Non - private	其他就业人员 Other Employed Persons	非私营单位 Non - private
1436021	**990263**	**4198058**	**2699418**	**324647**	**170800**
1337321	937050	3946362	2578157	308599	163560
97250	78965	219321	168566	22845	11530
122604	102840	250590	210276	44656	28690
108619	64527	390059	191867	84000	12603
82874	53726	298894	137906	23138	16149
188524	156928	601060	496157	50927	37784
116481	93998	350337	270833	8589	6747
237665	140465	805577	477287	24109	14274
30732	17070	107296	56255	2849	1223
171495	101845	453712	252972	19645	13046
73570	40830	214646	111818	13128	8201
52795	29122	141199	76627	4966	3847
76782	66277	199859	164851	4987	3169
8662	7527	21108	18997	7609	7520
39525	20373	111144	42528	5140	2651
29189	15962	65817	38295	5302	2066
29986	16878	74735	40438	5606	2523
311	284	1104	979	98	98
322	135	1707	581	32	32
427119	242803	1053563	647041	16051	9615
5213	4885	19679	18280	308	301
143941	59539	1339909	657372	186165	52656
147492	87929	272646	165190	9141	6881
37453	28410	150936	111102	4001	2629
56090	38372	86380	54428	14775	13708
80702	59817	216380	160217	1952	859
66834	66144	91398	90231	24941	24693
62601	47599	139177	103693	10419	9324
67081	42959	181547	114148	13873	11198
48871	41196	134323	109524	6069	4658
13548	9786	36075	22905	2700	2076
15122	5729	25379	10441	1695	515
120381	118486	178481	174217	12693	12650
86697	81416	116740	109507	8718	8099
12834	11365	21754	18682	3985	3777
43409	43409	130880	130880	7031	7031

2－13 全市非私营及规上

Average Number of Employed Persons of Non－private Units

单位:人

地区、行业	Region, Sector	就业人员年平均人数 Annual Average Number of Staff and Workers	非私营单位 Non－private
全市	**Total**	**4471209**	**2818936**
市区	Urban District	4207536	2692241
#上城区	Shangcheng District	238518	177666
下城区	Xiacheng District	288570	234693
江干区	Jianggan District	491432	199739
拱墅区	Gongshu District	319710	154177
西湖区	Xihu District	653688	539387
高新(滨江)区	Hi－Tech(Binjiang) District	347566	269075
萧山区	Xiaoshan District	800889	464462
大江东产业集聚区	Dajiangdong Industry Cluster District	109351	56316
余杭区	Yuhang District	462552	259683
富阳区	Fuyang District	221701	117060
临安区	Lin'an Districty	144679	79188
经济技术开发区	Economic and Technological Development Zone	210029	171113
西湖风景名胜区	The West Lake Scenic Zone	28202	25998
桐庐县	Tonglu County	111519	44297
淳安县	Chun'an County	73454	40032
建德市	Jiande City	78700	42366
按国民经济行业分组	**Grouped by Sector**		
农、林、牧、渔业	Farming, Forestry, Animal Husbandry & Fishery	1205	1083
采矿业	Mining	1813	678
制造业	Manufacturing	1064238	653579
电力、热力、燃气及水生产和供应业	Production & Supply of Electricity, Heat, Gas & Water	19986	18581
建筑业	Construction	1514335	682552
批发和零售业	Wholesale & Retail Trades	281369	173110
交通运输、仓储和邮政业	Transportation, Storage and Posts	143327	109641
住宿和餐饮业	Hotels and Catering Services	100832	68643
信息传输、软件和信息技术服务业	Information Transmission, Software and Information Technology	211171	153815
金融业	Financial Intermediation	114002	112616
房地产业	Real Estate	148654	112900
租赁和商务服务业	Leasing and Business Services	190917	122566
科学研究、技术服务业	Scientific Research, Technical Services	136906	111452
水利、环境和公共设施管理业	Management of Water Conservancy, Environment and Public Facilities	38687	25416
居民服务、修理和其他服务业	Service to Households, Repair and Other Services	26852	10487
教育	Education	190683	186174
卫生和社会工作	Health Care and Social Work	122551	115235
文化、体育和娱乐业	Culture, Sports and Entertainment	25693	22420
公共管理、社会保障和社会组织	Public Management, Social Security and Social Organizations	137988	137988

私营单位平均人员数(2017 年)

and Private Units Above Designated Size(2017)

(person)

在岗职工年平均人数 Staff and Workers	非私营单位 Non - private	其他就业人员年平均人数 Average Number of Other Employed Persons	非私营单位 Non - private
4125624	**2642272**	**345585**	**176664**
3877321	2522656	330215	169585
216351	166577	22167	11089
245964	207147	42606	27546
385191	182101	106241	17638
295739	137105	23971	17072
602105	500098	51583	39289
340242	263903	7324	5172
776130	449996	24759	14466
106684	55241	2667	1075
442712	246262	19840	13421
208999	109287	12702	7773
139757	75440	4922	3748
203394	166118	6635	4995
20737	18622	7465	7376
106442	41539	5077	2758
68543	37979	4911	2053
73318	40098	5382	2268
1109	987	96	96
1781	646	32	32
1048373	644128	15865	9451
19659	18262	327	319
1305677	622770	208658	59782
271805	165913	9564	7197
139808	107171	3519	2470
86458	55274	14374	13369
209231	152946	1940	869
90580	89414	23422	23202
138625	103924	10029	8976
177925	112230	12992	10336
130957	106942	5949	4510
35827	23204	2860	2212
25097	10007	1755	480
176259	171799	14424	14375
114017	107284	8534	7951
21662	18597	4031	3823
130774	130774	7214	7214

2－14 分行业非私营单位

The Education Level of the Staff and Workers in

单位:人

行　业	Sector	单位就业人员 The Education Level
		大学本科及以上 Bachelor's Degree of above
总　计	**Total**	**863831**
农、林、牧、渔业	Farming, Forestry, Animal Husbandry & Fishery	164
采矿业	Mining	40
制造业	Manufacturing	129376
电力、热力、燃气及水生产和供应业	Production & Supply of Electricity, Heat, Gas & Water	7477
建筑业	Construction	42794
批发和零售业	Wholesale & Retail Trades	46354
交通运输、仓储及邮政业	Transportation, Storage and Posts	20134
住宿和餐饮业	Hotels and Catering Services	5681
信息传输、软件和信息技术服务业	Information Transmission, Software and Information Technology	114852
金融业	Financial Intermediation	78354
房地产业	Real Estate	22656
租赁和商务服务业	Leasing and Business Services	30547
科学研究和技术服务业	Scientific Research, Technical Services	59066
水利、环境和公共设施管理业	Management of Water Conservancy, Environment and Public Facilities	4810
居民服务、修理和其他服务业	Service to Households, Repair and Other Services	1497
教育	Education	133125
卫生和社会工作	Health Care and Social Work	71182
文化、体育和娱乐业	Culture, Sports and Entertainment	13576
公共管理、社会保障和社会组织	Public Management, Social Security and Social Organizations	82146

职工素质情况(2017 年末)

Non - private Units by Sector(End of 2017)

(persons)

文化程度 of the Employed Persons in Onits			单位就业人员中专业技术人员 Professional and Technical Personnel	单位就业人员中技术工人 Skilled Workers
大专 College Degree	中专及高中 Technical Secondary School and High School	初中及以下 Junior High School and Below		
472278	**645888**	**888221**	**703962**	**736586**
180	240	493	138	380
50	99	424	78	324
101554	191467	234259	120139	258441
4824	4241	2039	3297	9272
62953	179588	424693	91253	341724
42265	48882	34570	20829	20655
31631	40835	21131	8783	50359
12644	21906	27905	3244	5914
32672	10756	2796	82343	5704
22996	11729	1845	42413	2451
26233	34453	29675	15267	4191
25521	33607	35671	13715	12557
20202	10352	24562	59016	4663
4384	5355	10432	3867	3984
1336	2698	5425	824	1151
22153	16205	15384	124154	6128
24774	13118	8532	90836	4916
4756	2810	1317	13258	655
31150	17547	7068	10508	3117

主要统计指标解释

人口数 指一定时点、一定地区范围内的有生命的个人的总和。

年度统计的年末人口数是指每年 12 月 31 日 24 时的人口数。

出生率(又称粗出生率) 指一定时期内(通常为一年)平均每千人所出生的人数的比率,一般用千分率表示。计算公式:

$$出生率 = \frac{年出生人数}{年平均人数} \times 1000‰$$

出生人数是指活产婴儿,即胎儿脱离母体时(不管怀孕月数),有过呼吸或其他生命现象。

年平均人数是年初、年底人口数的平均数,也可用年中人口数代替。

死亡率(又称粗死亡率) 指一定时期内(通常为一年)一定地区的死亡人数与同期平均人数(或期中人数)之比,一般用千分率表示。计算公式:

$$死亡率 = \frac{年死亡人数}{年平均人数} \times 1000‰$$

人口自然增长率 指一定时期内(通常为一年)人口自然增加数(出生人数减死亡人数)与该时期内平均人数(或期中人数)之比,一般用千分率表示。计算公式:

$$人口自然增长率 = \frac{本年出生人数 - 本年死亡人数}{年平均人数} \times 1000‰$$

人口自然增长率 = 人口出生率 - 人口死亡率

就业人员 指从事一定社会劳动并取得劳动报酬或经营收入人员,包括各级机关企事业单位就业人员、个体户主、个体就业人员、农村就业人员及其他未包括的就业人员(包括宗教职业者、现役军人等)。

单位就业人员 是指在各级国家机关、政党机关、社会团体及企业、事业单位中工作,并取得劳动报酬的全部人员。包括在岗职工、再就业的离退休人员、民办教师、在各单位中工作的外方人员和港、澳、台方人员以及聘用的外单位下岗职工、兼职人员、从事第二职业人员、使用的劳务派遣人员。各单位的就业人员反映了实际参加生产或工作的全部劳动力。

在岗职工 指在本单位工作并由单位支付劳动报酬的人员,以及在本单位有工作岗位,但由于学习、病伤产假等原因暂未工作,仍由单位支付劳动报酬的人,包括本单位临时性用工并支付劳动报酬的人员。2012 年开始在岗职工包含劳务派遣人员。

非私营单位 包括独立核算的机关、事业单位和国有、集体、股份制、港澳台投资及外商投资企业等。

非私营单位及规上私营单位 包括独立核算的非私营单位、规模以上私营工业企业、限额以上私营批发零售住宿餐饮企业、私营房地产开发经营企业、具有资质的私营建筑企业、规模以上私营服务企业、100 人及以上的规模以下私营企业。

Explanatory Notes on Main Statistical Indicators

Total Population refers to the total number of people alive at a certain point of time within a given area. The annual statistics on total population is taken at midnight, the 31st of December.

Birth Rate (or Crude Birth Rate) refers to the ratio of the number of births to the average population during a certain period of time (usually a year), which is often expressed in ‰. The following formula is used:

$$\text{Birth Rate} = \frac{\text{Number of Births}}{\text{Average Number of Population}} \times 1000‰$$

Number of births refers to live births, i. e. the births when babies had showed any vital phenomena regardless of the length of pregnancy.

Annual Average Number of Population is the average of the number of population at the beginning of the year and that at the end of the year. Sometimes it is substituted for with the mid - year population.

Death Rate (or Crude Death Rate) refers to the ratio of the number of deaths to the average population (or mid - year population) during a certain period of time (usually a year), which is often expressed in ‰. The following formula is used:

$$\text{Death Rate} = \frac{\text{Number of Deaths}}{\text{Annual Average Number of Population}} \times 1000‰$$

Natural Growth Rate of Population refers to the ratio of natural increase in population (number of births minus number of deaths) in a certain period of time (usually a year) to the average population (or mid - year population) of the same period, which is often expressed in ‰. The following formulas are applied:

$$\text{Natural Growth Rate of Population} = \frac{\text{Number of Births} - \text{Number of Deaths}}{\text{Average Number of Population}} \times 1000‰$$

Natural Growth Rate of Population = Birth Rate - Death Rate

Employed Persons refer to persons who are engaged in social labour and receive remuneration payment or earn business income, including all employees of government, enterprises and institutions, self - employed workers, employed persons in the rural areas and other employed workers (including religious professionals, servicemen, etc.).

Persons Employed in Various Units refer to all the persons who are working in government agencies of various levels, political and party organizations, social organizations, enterprises, institutions, and receiving wages or other forms of payment. Including fully employed staff and works, re - employed retirees, teachers in schools run by the local people, foreigners and Chinese compatriots from Hong Kong, Macao, and Taiwan working in various units, part - time employees, employees of other units working temporarily, employees holding the second job, dispatch personnels. Persons Employed in various units reflect the actual total labor force which are engaged in the production or work.

Fully Employed Staff and Workers refer to persons who work in, and receive wages from their working units, as well as persons who have their work posts, but are temporarily absent from work for reasons of study or on sick, injury or maternal leave and still receive wages from their working units. including persons who are engaged in temporary employment and receive remuneration payment. Since 2012, the number of fully employed staff included the labor dispatch personnel.

Non - private Units include independent accounting units of government organizations and institutions, state - owned enterprises, collective - owned enterprises, and enterprises with funds from Hongkong, Macao and Taiwan.

Including Units above Designated Size include independent accounting units of non - private, private industrial enterprises above designated size, private enterprises above designated size of wholesale & retail trades, hotels, catering serrices, private enterprises for real estate development, private construction enterprises with qualification grade, private enterprises of service industry above designated size, private enterprises below designated size with at least 100 employed persons.

三、农业

AGRICULTURE

3-01 全市分地区农林牧渔业增加值(2017年)

The added Value of Agriculture, Forestry, Animal Husbandry and Fishery(2017)

单位:万元 (10000 yuan)

地 区 Region	农林牧渔业合计 Total	为上年%	农业 Agriculture	为上年%	林业 Forestry	为上年%	畜牧业 Animal Husbandry	为上年%	渔业 Fishery	为上年%	农、林、牧、渔专业及辅助性活动 Services for Farming, Forestry, Animal Husbandry and Fishery	为上年%
全 市 Whole City	**3056039**	**102.4**	**1951535**	**104.6**	**428898**	**103.1**	**334289**	**88.5**	**284845**	**103.1**	**56472**	**114.4**
市区 Urban District	2133712	127.3	1320356	122.8	305423	195.9	224761	118.2	239749	108.6	43423	125.5
#江干区 Jianggan	5178	115.7	3619	104.7	15	100	1418	184.6	91	46.2	35	94.6
西湖区 Xihu	39377	89.3	20183	86.0	497	161.4	15	16.0	17638	90.8	1044	126.5
高新(滨江)区 Hi-Tech(Binjiang)	10483	77.8	9241	73.8	-	-	-	-	1242	130.2	-	-
萧山区 Xiaoshan	670026	101.3	475532	103.4	7865	109.4	93131	90.8	75636	99.0	17862	116.1
大江东产业集聚区 Dajiangdong Industry Cluster District	122821	94.1	83858	101.9	150	102.7	18691	71.1	17568	89.9	2554	110.8
余杭区 Yuhang	511891	101.8	325312	103.9	54626	89.1	15107	73.4	99041	107.8	17805	111.0
富阳区 Fuyang	438584	103.3	266286	104.9	90192	103.6	58274	91.8	21235	118.1	2597	112.7
临安区 Lin'an	427795	102.1	210507	102.7	152188	105.9	55392	89.6	5628	101.1	4080	142.7
经济技术开发区 Economic and Technological Development Zone	3653	80.8	1359	81.8	-	-	1424	53.3	870	455.5	-	-
西湖风景名胜区 The West Lake Scenic Zone	8357	110.8	8317	110.9	40	100	-	-	-	-	-	-
桐庐县 Tonglu	238425	102.5	152110	108.3	44046	100.1	25067	86.0	13915	87.5	3287	105.6
淳安县 Chun'an	347874	104.7	246744	107.0	52409	107.7	26966	85.3	17333	98.4	4422	112.2
建德市 Jiande	336028	103.4	232325	108	27020	114.4	57495	88.5	13848	84.1	5340	110.2

注:按第三次农业普查数据修订。

a) Data in this table are adjusted according to the 3rd agricultural census.

3 农　　业
Agriculture

主要统计指标
Major Statistical Indicators

农村机械总动力	Total Power of Agricultural Machinery	255.77	万千瓦	(10, 000 kw)
为上年	As Compared with the Preceding Year	90.1	%	(%)
农村从业人员数	Total Employed Persons in Rural Areas	282.19	万人	(10, 000 persons)
为上年	As Compared with the Preceding Year	100.2	%	(%)
农林牧渔业增加值	Value-added of Farming,Forestry,Animal Husbandry and Fishery	305.60	亿元	(100 million yuan)
为上年	As Compared with the Preceding Year	102.4	%	(%)
粮食总产量	Total Output of Grain Crops	47.26	万吨	(10, 000 tons)
为上年	As Compared with the Preceding Year	102.9	%	(%)
肉类产量	Total Output of Meat	21.27	万吨	(10, 000 tons)
为上年	As Compared with the Preceding Year	93.6	%	(%)

3－02 农林牧渔业总产值（1978－2017年）

Gross Output Value of Agriculture, Forestry, Animal Husbandry and Fishery (1978－2017)

单位：万元 (10000 yuan)

年份 Year	农林牧渔业 Gross Output Value	#农业 Farming	种植业 Planting	林业 Forestry	畜牧业 Animal Husbandry	渔业 Fishery	农、林、牧、渔专业及辅助性活动 Services for Farming, Forestry, Animal Husbandary and Fishery
1978	85922	67365	64378	3430	14474	653	－
1979	115649	84727	81989	4629	25216	1077	－
1980	112377	79006	76059	7262	25015	1094	－
1981	120792	87354	81659	8309	23799	1330	－
1982	150606	107566	103346	8912	31801	2327	－
1983	148878	103685	96272	9800	32693	2700	－
1984	177029	122567	115286	14769	35922	3771	－
1985	212961	136893	126026	19095	50110	6863	－
1986	238285	150803	138254	19990	58197	9295	－
1987	281326	173080	155960	26427	70129	11690	－
1988	358500	208838	187648	31434	101013	17215	－
1989	386805	225969	201389	27857	113952	19027	－
1990	421045	260031	233055	26962	113424	20628	－
1991	463578	284275	254834	37763	117458	24082	－
1992	497915	300828	256833	35589	133867	27631	－
1993	600760	365124	300736	47476	154766	33394	－
1994	812473	496392	415366	58627	217217	40237	－
1995	996440	620057	526328	81321	244054	51008	－
1996	1173294	740202	617573	95740	271652	65700	－
1997	1287650	797812	665172	114510	294153	81175	－
1998	1367578	845106	701850	121197	289085	112190	－
1999	1414737	876685	737406	126000	293495	118557	－
2000	1526530	903322	754311	136848	331563	154797	－
2001	1649978	965005	816884	149264	362303	173406	－
2002	1685036	932995	886285	162227	391844	197970	－
2003	1890129	991556	949138	182595	417798	232599	65581
2004	1982683	1010947	972594	206787	457619	234080	73250
2005	2194799	1136559	1103981	233039	495900	270810	58491
2006	2253822	1224822	1191816	267748	490448	206082	64722
2007	2471427	1308047	1279758	294707	585536	222601	60536
2008	2737605	1408124	1374083	320212	636633	309270	63366
2009	2897371	1497362	1462791	362317	642892	325626	69174
2010	3163392	1698775	1673470	329278	705596	349011	80732
2011	3570744	1907895	1882876	348535	836532	389985	87797
2012	3843403	2077191	2041481	381802	868504	420006	95900
2013	3993712	2161055	2120540	408170	911324	407292	105871
2014	4185804	2333804	2291071	470164	828184	442023	111629
2015	4404121	2524163	2468981	498051	807001	452309	122597
2016	4490065	2621544	2558927	530464	768795	436050	133212
2017	4577017	2738813	2677779	549138	685811	453211	150044

注：按第三次农业普查数据修订。

a) Data in this table are adjusted according to the 3rd agricultural census.

3－03　农林牧渔业总产值构成(1978－2017 年)

Composition of Gross Output Value of Agriculture, Forestry, Animal Husbandry and Fishery(1978－2017)

单位:%　　　　(%)

年份 Year	农林牧渔业 Gross Output Value	#农业 Farming	种植业 Planting	林业 Forestry	畜牧业 Animal Husbandry	渔业 Fishery	农、林、牧、渔专业及辅助性活动 Services for Farming, Forestry, Animal Husbandary and Fishery
1978	100	78.4	74.9	4.0	16.8	0.8	–
1979	100	73.3	70.9	4.0	21.8	0.9	–
1980	100	70.3	67.7	6.5	22.2	1.0	–
1981	100	72.3	67.6	6.9	19.7	1.1	–
1982	100	71.4	68.6	5.9	21.1	1.6	–
1983	100	69.6	64.7	6.6	22.0	1.8	–
1984	100	69.2	65.1	8.3	20.3	2.2	–
1985	100	64.3	59.2	9.0	23.5	3.2	–
1986	100	63.3	58.0	8.4	24.4	3.9	–
1987	100	61.5	55.4	9.4	24.9	4.2	–
1988	100	58.2	52.3	8.8	28.2	4.8	–
1989	100	58.4	52.1	7.2	29.5	4.9	–
1990	100	61.8	55.4	6.4	26.9	4.9	–
1991	100	61.3	55.0	8.2	25.3	5.2	–
1992	100	60.4	51.6	7.2	26.9	5.5	–
1993	100	60.8	50.1	7.9	25.8	5.5	–
1994	100	61.1	51.1	7.2	26.7	5.0	–
1995	100	62.2	52.8	8.2	24.5	5.1	–
1996	100	63.1	52.6	8.2	23.1	5.6	–
1997	100	62.0	51.7	8.9	22.8	6.3	–
1998	100	61.8	51.3	8.9	21.1	8.2	–
1999	100	62.0	52.1	8.9	20.7	8.4	–
2000	100	59.2	49.4	9.0	21.7	10.1	–
2001	100	58.5	52.2	9.0	22.0	10.5	–
2002	100	55.4	52.6	9.6	23.3	11.7	–
2003	100	52.5	50.2	9.7	22.1	12.3	3.4
2004	100	51.0	49.1	10.4	23.1	11.8	3.7
2005	100	51.8	50.3	10.6	22.6	12.3	2.7
2006	100	54.3	52.9	11.9	21.8	9.1	2.9
2007	100	52.9	51.8	11.9	23.7	9.0	2.5
2008	100	51.4	50.2	11.7	23.3	11.3	2.3
2009	100	51.7	50.5	12.5	22.2	11.2	2.4
2010	100	53.7	52.9	10.4	22.3	11.0	2.6
2011	100	53.4	52.7	9.8	23.4	10.9	2.5
2012	100	54.0	53.1	9.9	22.6	10.9	2.6
2013	100	54.1	53.1	10.2	22.8	10.2	2.7
2014	100	55.8	54.7	11.2	19.8	10.6	2.6
2015	100	57.3	56.1	11.3	18.3	10.3	2.8
2016	100	58.4	57.0	11.8	17.1	9.7	3.0
2017	100	59.8	58.5	12.0	15.0	9.9	3.3

3-04 农林牧渔业分项产值(2010-2017年)

Gross Output Value of Agriculture, Forestry, Animal Husbandry and Fishery by Branch(2010-2017)

单位:万元 (10000 yuan)

指标	Item	2010	2011	2012	2013	2014	2015	2016	2017
农林牧渔业总产值(现价)	**Gross Output Value (Current Price)**	**3163392**	**3570744**	**3843403**	**3993712**	**4185804**	**4404121**	**4490065**	**4577017**
一、农业产值	**Farming**	**1698775**	**1907895**	**2077191**	**2161055**	**2333804**	**2524163**	**2621544**	**2738813**
1.种植业产值	Planting	1673470	1882876	2041481	2120540	2291071	2468981	2558927	2677779
粮食	Grain	215990	230246	241471	248550	224164	228341	171736	177764
油料	Oil-bearing Crops	31137	35245	35482	37649	37530	48373	34737	37332
棉花	Cotton	1255	1155	1424	1571	1152	1094	467	397
麻类	Fiber Crops	42	21	16	25	8	6	5	3
甘蔗	Sugarcane	18756	20067	18417	18496	17347	16322	5770	5214
烟叶	Tobacco	1	2	2	1	1	1	1	1
药材类	Crude Drugs	42927	50530	60454	67623	75180	86538	98954	112902
蔬菜	Vegetables	535623	607469	664937	665429	686995	748644	834633	829020
茶、桑、果、坚果	Tea, Mulberry & Fruits	484261	565641	605200	630899	749516	802647	828571	908024
其他	Others	343478	372500	414078	450297	499178	537015	584053	607122
2.其他农业产值	Other Farming	25305	25019	35710	40515	42733	55182	62617	61034
二、林业产值	**Forestry**	**329278**	**348535**	**381802**	**408170**	**470164**	**498051**	**530464**	**549138**
人造林木生长	Artificial Forestry	27964	23828	32802	33734	31640	32574	31490	31415
林产品	Forest Products	184740	197815	214198	227962	267839	294806	327864	349421
竹木采伐	Lumbering	82063	90806	93552	103425	130794	127670	125112	122773
采集野生植物	Wild Plant collected	34511	36086	41250	43049	39891	43001	45998	45529
三、畜牧业产值	**Animal Husbandry**	**705596**	**836532**	**868504**	**911324**	**828184**	**807001**	**768795**	**685811**
牲畜	Livestock Raising	430193	534840	556742	589952	522674	522001	572122	498108
家禽饲养	Poultry Raising	70201	69653	82132	77869	72333	72394	36208	30122
活的畜禽产品	Livestock Products	109625	124024	125886	132151	127075	112964	92066	88831
捕猎野兽野禽	Hunting Wild Beast and Wild Fowl	4455	4698	5454	5126	6260	5256	6032	6043
其他动物饲养	Other Animals Raising	91122	103317	98290	106226	99842	94386	62367	62707
四、渔业产值	**Fishery**	**349011**	**389985**	**420006**	**407292**	**442023**	**452309**	**436050**	**453211**
五、农、林、牧、渔专业及辅助性活动	**Services for Farming, Forestry, Animal Husbandary and Fishery**	**80732**	**87797**	**95900**	**105871**	**111629**	**122597**	**133212**	**150044**

注:按第三次农业普查数据修订。

a) Data in this table are adjusted according to the 3rd agricultural census.

3－05 农林牧渔业分项产值构成(2010－2017年)

Composition of Gross Output Value of Agriculture, Forestry, Animal Husbandry and Fishery by Branch(2010－2017)

单位:%　　　　　　　　　　　　　　　　　　　　(%)

指　　标	Item	2010	2011	2012	2013	2014	2015	2016	2017
农林牧渔业总产值(现价)	**Gross Output Value (Current Price)**	**100**	**100**	**100**	**100**	**100**	**100**	**100**	**100**
一、农业产值	**Farming**	**53.7**	**53.4**	**54.0**	**54.1**	**55.8**	**57.3**	**58.4**	**59.8**
1. 种植业产值	Planting	52.9	52.7	53.1	53.1	54.7	56.1	57.0	58.5
粮食	Grain	6.8	6.4	6.3	6.2	5.4	5.2	3.8	3.9
油料	Oil Plants	1.0	1.0	0.9	0.9	0.9	1.1	0.8	0.8
棉花	Cotton	–	–	–	–	–	–	–	–
麻类	Fiber Crops	–	–	–	–	–	–	–	–
甘蔗	Sugarcane	0.6	0.6	0.6	0.5	0.4	0.4	0.1	0.1
烟叶	Tobacco	–	–	–	–	–	–	–	–
药材类	Crude Drugs	1.4	1.4	1.6	1.7	1.8	2.0	2.2	2.5
蔬菜	Vegetables	16.9	17.0	17.3	16.7	16.4	16.9	18.6	18.1
茶、桑、果、坚果	Tea, Mulberry & Fruits	15.3	15.8	15.7	15.8	17.9	18.2	18.5	19.8
其他	Others	10.9	10.5	10.7	11.3	11.9	12.2	13.0	13.3
2. 其他农业产值	Other Farming	0.8	0.7	0.9	1.0	1.0	1.3	1.4	1.3
二、林业产值	**Forestry**	**10.4**	**9.8**	**9.9**	**10.2**	**11.2**	**11.3**	**11.8**	**12.0**
人造林木生长	Artificial Forestry	0.9	0.7	0.8	0.8	0.8	0.7	0.7	0.7
林产品	Forest Products	5.8	5.5	5.6	5.7	6.4	6.7	7.3	7.6
竹木采伐	Lumbering	2.6	2.5	2.4	2.6	3.1	2.9	2.8	2.7
采集野生植物	Wild Plant collected	1.1	1.1	1.1	1.1	0.9	1.0	1.0	1.0
三、畜牧业产值	**Animal Husbandry**	**22.3**	**23.4**	**22.6**	**22.8**	**19.8**	**18.3**	**17.1**	**15.0**
牲畜	Livestock Raising	13.6	15.0	14.5	14.8	12.5	11.9	12.7	10.9
家禽饲养	Poultry Raising	2.2	2.0	2.1	1.9	1.7	1.6	0.8	0.7
活的畜禽产品	Livestock Products	3.5	3.5	3.3	3.3	3.0	2.6	2.1	1.9
捕猎野兽野禽	Hunting Wild Beast and Wild Fowl	0.1	0.1	0.1	0.1	0.1	0.1	0.1	0.1
其他动物饲养	Other Animals Raising	2.9	2.8	2.6	2.7	2.4	2.1	1.4	1.4
四、渔业产值	**Fishery**	**11.0**	**10.9**	**10.9**	**10.2**	**10.6**	**10.3**	**9.7**	**9.9**
五、农、林、牧、渔专业及辅助性活动	**Services for Farming, Forestry, Animal Husbandary and Fishery**	**2.6**	**2.5**	**2.6**	**2.7**	**2.6**	**2.8**	**3.0**	**3.3**

3-06 分地区农林牧

Gross Output Value of Agriculture, Forestry,

单位:万元

指　　标	Item	全市 Whole City	市区 Urban District	江干区 Jianggan	西湖区 Xihu	高新(滨江)区 Hi-Tech(Binjiang)
合　　计	**Gross Output Value**	**4577017**	**3220292**	**7833**	**61576**	**15110**
一、农业产值	**Farming**	**2738813**	**1853396**	**5757**	**28379**	**13291**
(一)种植业产值	Planting	2677779	1827205	5757	28269	13291
#副产品产值	By-products	8926	5601	-	11	4
1.粮食作物	Grain	177764	121002	-	47	112
谷　　物	Cereal	136271	95849	-	35	112
豆　　类	Beans	14175	9283	-	8	-
薯　　类	Tubers	27318	15870	-	4	-
2.油　　料	Oil Plants	37332	16551	-	53	-
3.棉　　花	Cotton	397	181	-	-	-
4.麻　　类	Fiber Crops	3	-	-	-	-
5.甘　　蔗	Sugarcane	5214	4550	-	115	-
6.烟　　叶	Tobacco	1	-	-	-	-
7.药 材 类	Crude Drugs	112902	34086	-	60	-
8.蔬　　菜	Vegetables	829020	642709	2605	7546	2727
9.茶、桑、果、坚果	Tea, Mulberry & Fruits	908024	478597	81	6724	1487
10.其　　他	Others	607122	529529	3071	13724	8965
(二)其他农业产值	Other Farming	61034	26191	-	110	-
二、林业产值	**Forestry**	**549138**	**390558**	**17**	**577**	**-**
1.人造林木生长	Artificial Forestry	31415	19019	17	576	-
2.林产品	Forest Products	349421	250277	-	-	-
3.村及村以下竹木采伐	Lumbering	122773	94315	-	1	-
4.采集野生植物	Wild Plant collected	45529	26947	-	-	-
三、畜牧业产值	**Animal Husbandry**	**685811**	**469887**	**1878**	**29**	**-**
1.牲畜	Livestock	498108	379772	1878	-	-
2.家禽饲养	Poultry Raising	30122	21362	-	5	-
3.活的畜禽产品	Livestock Products	88831	30712	-	24	-
4.捕猎野兽野禽	Hunting Wild Beast and Wild Fowl	6043	4261	-	-	-
5.其他动物饲养	Other Animals Raising	62707	33780	-	-	-
四、渔业产值	**Fishery**	**453211**	**387813**	**105**	**30821**	**1819**
五、农、林、牧、渔专业及辅助性活动	**Services for Farming, Forestry, Animal Husbandary and Fishery**	**150044**	**118638**	**76**	**1770**	**-**

注:按第三次农业普查数据修订。

渔业总产值(2017 年)

Animal Husbandry and Fishery by Region(2017)

(10000 yuan)

萧山区 Xiaoshan	大江东产业集聚区 Dajiangdong Industry Cluster District	余杭区 Yuhang	富阳区 Fuyang	临安区 Lin'an	经济技术开发区 Economic and Technological Development Zone	西湖风景名胜区 The West Lake Scenic Zone	桐庐县 Tonglu	淳安县 Chun'an	建德市 Jiande
1065012	**189334**	**775376**	**617583**	**615915**	**6893**	**13395**	**350572**	**484449**	**521704**
668386	**120370**	**455678**	**367663**	**297482**	**3433**	**13327**	**218318**	**327188**	**339911**
668333	120356	450765	353704	290326	3433	13327	213292	326019	311263
1881	598	1431	1552	692	30	–	857	1141	1327
32300	8331	34519	33951	19484	589	–	16316	17222	23224
24270	5546	32348	28666	9834	584	–	13593	8974	17855
6553	2785	1005	1354	360	3	–	941	2162	1789
1477	–	1166	3931	9290	2	–	1782	6086	3580
6533	2358	2206	5013	2746	–	–	5945	6298	8538
125	14	56	–	–	–	–	–	145	71
–	–	–	–	–	–	–	–	3	–
3481	673	637	296	21	–	–	172	41	451
–	–	–	–	–	–	–	–	1	–
5719	–	7633	10249	10425	–	–	10843	36674	31299
311903	82009	163316	89587	62592	2433	–	63357	62282	60672
49548	7641	135654	122794	148571	411	13327	89916	178279	161232
258724	19330	106744	91814	46487	–	–	26743	25074	25776
53	14	4913	13959	7156	–	–	5026	1169	28648
15694	**194**	**75450**	**104394**	**194358**	**–**	**68**	**53858**	**71254**	**33468**
5145	108	12669	283	261	–	68	2351	8658	1387
8150	85	45710	61862	134555	–	–	37668	41183	20293
2161	1	15272	27522	49359	–	–	6479	13765	8214
238	–	1799	14727	10183	–	–	7360	7648	3574
216649	**37687**	**34357**	**110561**	**104226**	**2187**	**–**	**48282**	**51764**	**115878**
195497	35183	22842	79884	78488	1183	–	29265	38068	51003
6319	861	6684	7070	1282	2	–	1210	925	6625
6500	362	2807	11827	8252	1002	–	3219	5075	49825
320	320	536	2381	1024	–	–	1047	142	593
7713	961	1488	9399	15180	–	–	13541	7554	7832
115469	**25717**	**160541**	**27902**	**8284**	**1273**	**–**	**21027**	**25801**	**18570**
48814	**5366**	**49350**	**7063**	**11565**	**–**	**–**	**9087**	**8442**	**13877**

a) Data in this table are adjusted according to the 3rd agricultural census.

3－07 主要农作物播种面积及产量(2016－2017年)
Sown Areas and Yield of Major Farm Crops(2016－2017)

指 标	Item	2016			2017		
		播种面积(千公顷) Sown Area (1000 hectares)	总产量(吨) Total Output (ton)	公顷产量(公斤) Yield per Hectare (kg/hectare)	播种面积(千公顷) Sown Area (1000 hectares)	总产量(吨) Total Output (ton)	公顷产量(公斤) Yield per Hectare (kg/hectare)
农作物总计	**Total Farm Crops**	**269.88**			**273.23**		
一、粮 食	**Grain Crops**	**84.97**	**459143**	**5403**	**86.48**	**472646**	**5465**
#春粮	#Spring Grain	14.04	44065	3139	15.64	58488	3739
秋粮	Autumn Grain	49.80	331836	6664	49.83	331923	6662
(一)谷 物	Cereals	60.00	375938	6265	63.19	393491	6228
1.稻谷	Rice	37.23	286247	7689	38.5	291611	7574
①早稻及早中稻	Early Rice & Semi－late Rice	1.47	8925	6076	1.47	8769	5965
②晚稻及迟中稻	Late Rice & Semi－late Rice	35.76	277322	7756	37.03	282842	7638
#单季稻	#Single－crop Rice	34.32	267035	7782	36.36	278592	7663
2.小麦	Wheat	10.06	30556	3037	11.79	43546	3693
3.大麦	Barley	0.30	1161	3896	0.5	1884	3753
4.玉米	Corn	12.29	57458	4675	12.3	56110	4561
5.其他谷物	Other Cereals	0.13	516	3969	0.09	340	3736
(二)豆 类	Beans	16.78	42299	2521	14.26	37904	2657
1.大豆	Soybeans	15.17	38477	2536	13.46	34917	2593
2.蚕(豌)豆	Broad Beans	1.25	3023	2415	0.64	2370	3703
3.杂豆	Other Beans	0.36	799	2232	0.16	617	3856
(三)薯 类	Tubers	8.19	40906	4996	9.03	41251	4568

3－07 续表 continued

指 标	Item	2016 播种面积（千公顷）Sown Area (1000 hectares)	2016 总产量（吨）Total Output (ton)	2016 公顷产量（公斤）Yield per Hectare (kg/hectare)	2017 播种面积（千公顷）Sown Area (1000 hectares)	2017 总产量（吨）Total Output (ton)	2017 公顷产量（公斤）Yield per Hectare (kg/hectare)
二、油料	**Oil Plants**	**23.62**	**53525**	**2266**	**23.29**	**57310**	**2461**
1.油菜籽	Rapeseeds	20.15	43526	2160	19.68	47223	2400
2.花生	Peanuts	1.92	7254	3772	1.88	7137	3798
3.芝麻	Sesame						
4.其他	Others	1.55	2745	1774	1.73	2950	1705
三、棉花（皮棉）	**Cotton**	**0.19**	**300**	**1571**	**0.18**	**255**	**1433**
四、麻类	**Fiber Cropers**	**0.006**	**15**	**2500**	**0.005**	**10**	**2000**
五、糖类	**Sugar Crops**	**0.58**	**33694**	**57794**	**0.52**	**30817**	**58699**
六、烟叶	**Tobacco**	**－**	**1**	**－**	**－**	**1**	**－**
七、药材	**Crude Drugs**	**5.24**	**31755**	**6064**	**6.55**	**38371**	**5861**
八、蔬菜	**Vegetables**	**96.90**	**3353377**	**34607**	**96.44**	**3383444**	**35083**
九、果用瓜	**Melon as Fruit**	**11.54**	**369905**	**32049**	**11.53**	**379064**	**32876**
#西瓜	Watermelon	8.20	279223	34023	8.06	285348	35416
草莓	Strawberry	1.29	38326	29595	1.47	42132	28700
十、花卉苗木	**Flower Gardening**	**35.36**	**－**	**－**	**36.84**	**－**	**－**
十一、其他作物	**Others**	**11.47**	**－**	**－**	**11.4**	**－**	**－**
#绿肥	Green Manure	1.51	－	－	1.4	－	－

注：按第三次农业普查数据修订。
a) Data in this table are adjusted according to the 3rd agricultural census.

3－08 分地区粮食

Sown Areas and Yield of

指 标		Item		全市 Whole City	市区 Urban District	江干区 Jianggan	西湖区 Xihu	高新(滨江)区 Hi－Tech (Binjiang)
一、播种面积总计	**(公顷)**	**Sown Area of Grain Crops**	**(hectare)**	**86479**	**55385**	**–**	**45**	**50**
春粮	(公顷)	Spring Grain	(hectare)	15643	11533	–	12	7
早稻	(公顷)	Early Rice	(hectare)	1470	1002	–	–	–
晚稻	(公顷)	Late Rice	(hectare)	37030	27463	–	16	43
薯类	(公顷)	Tubers	(hectare)	9030	4199	–	3	–
玉米	(公顷)	Corn	(hectare)	12302	4838	–	7	–
大豆	(公顷)	Soybeans	(hectare)	13464	7794	–	5	–
杂豆	(公顷)	Other Beans	(hectare)	160	51	–	1	–
其他谷物	(公顷)	Other Cereals	(hectare)	91	33	–	3	–
二、总产量	**(吨)**	**Yield of Grain Crops**	**(ton)**	**472646**	**321569**	**–**	**237**	**320**
春粮	(吨)	Spring Grain	(ton)	58488	44055	–	47	21
早稻	(吨)	Early Rice	(ton)	8769	5961	–	–	–
晚稻	(吨)	Late Rice	(ton)	282842	211348	–	121	299
薯类	(吨)	Tubers	(ton)	41251	20309	–	17	–
玉米	(吨)	Corn	(ton)	56110	22309	–	29	–
大豆	(吨)	Soybeans	(ton)	34917	23336	–	13	–
杂豆	(吨)	Other Beans	(ton)	617	247	–	5	–
其他谷物	(吨)	Other Cereals	(ton)	340	165	–	15	–
三、公顷产量	**(公斤)**	**Yield per Hectare**	**(kg)**	**5465**	**5806**	**–**	**5235**	**6400**
春粮	(公斤)	Spring Grain	(kg)	3739	3820	–	3917	3000
早稻	(公斤)	Early Rice	(kg)	5965	5949	–	–	–
晚稻	(公斤)	Late Rice	(kg)	7638	7696	–	8444	6953
薯类	(公斤)	Tubers	(kg)	4568	4837	–	6250	–
玉米	(公斤)	Corn	(kg)	4561	4611	–	4417	–
大豆	(公斤)	Soybeans	(kg)	2593	2994	–	3167	–

注:按第三次农业普查数据修订。

播种面积及产量(2017 年)
Grain Crops by Region(2017)

萧山区 Xiaoshan	大江东产业集聚区 Dajiangdong Industry Cluster District	余杭区 Yuhang	富阳区 Fuyang	临安区 Lin'an	经济技术开发区 Economic and Technological Development Zone	西湖风景名胜区 The West Lake Scenic Zone	桐庐县 Tonglu	淳安县 Chun'an	建德市 Jiande
18482	**5739**	**14149**	**15114**	**7256**	**289**	**–**	**7629**	**11725**	**11740**
3033	500	3531	3112	1838	1	–	1194	958	1958
822	554	117	5	–	58	–	127	108	233
6195	1225	9009	9243	2828	129	–	3722	900	4945
453	–	389	1418	1935	1	–	699	2860	1272
2117	631	532	1138	947	97	–	1141	4460	1863
5976	2824	732	773	306	2	–	822	3040	1808
12	3	8	26	4	–	–	7	20	82
6	2	2	12	9	1	–	6	44	8
93741	**26634**	**92631**	**93499**	**39457**	**1684**	**–**	**43329**	**44376**	**63372**
13473	2438	12342	11748	6421	3	–	4496	3193	6744
4946	3130	730	30	–	255	–	719	704	1385
46377	9563	73605	68949	21093	904	–	27582	6224	37688
2424	–	2003	6604	9255	6	–	3542	11634	5766
9594	2998	2391	5637	4151	507	–	5097	19622	9082
17483	8485	2281	2779	772	8	–	2125	5359	4097
49	11	34	143	16	–	–	31	59	280
28	9	10	66	45	1	–	32	112	31
5072	**4641**	**6547**	**6186**	**5438**	**5827**	**–**	**5679**	**3785**	**5398**
4442	2938	3495	3775	3493	3000	–	3765	3333	3444
6017	5650	6750	6000	–	4396	–	5659	6774	5956
7486	7807	8170	7460	7459	7008	–	7410	6916	7621
5351	–	6307	4657	4783	6000	–	5066	4068	4531
4532	4751	5077	4953	4383	5226	–	4467	4400	4876
2926	3005	3116	3595	2523	4000	–	2586	1763	2266

a) Data in this table are adjusted according to the 3rd agricultural census.

3－09 分地区油、菜、茶、
Statistics on Rapeseeds, Vegetables, Tea,

指标		Item		全市 Whole City	市区 Urban District	江干区 Jianggan	西湖区 Xihu	高新(滨江)区 Hi－Tech (Binjiang)
一、油料		**Oil Plants**						
播种面积	(公顷)	Sown Area	(hectare)	23289	10456	－	122	－
每公顷产量	(公斤)	Yield per Hectare	(kg)	2461	2679	－	2210	－
总产量	(吨)	Total Output	(ton)	57310	28015	－	249	－
二、蔬菜		**Vegetables**						
播种面积	(公顷)	Sown Area	(hectare)	96442	71775	899	1506	439
总产量	(吨)	Total Output	(ton)	3383444	2658545	22224	28681	14355
三、茶叶		**Tea**						
(一)茶园面积	(公顷)	Tea Garden Area	(hectare)	34636	14030	22	1124	49
(二)总产量	(吨)	Output of Tea	(ton)	30103	19273	5	450	8
春　茶	(吨)	Spring Tea	(ton)	20409	13287	5	293	8
夏　茶	(吨)	Summer Tea	(ton)	6393	4362	－	39	－
秋　茶	(吨)	Autumn Tea	(ton)	3301	1624	－	118	－
四、桑蚕		**Silkworm Cocoons & Mulberry**						
(一)桑园总面积	(公顷)	Mulberry Garden Area	(hectare)	10680	2583	－	－	－
(二)蚕茧总产量	(吨)	Output of Silkworm Cocoons	(ton)	3013	971	－	－	－
春　茧	(吨)	Spring Silkworm Cocoons	(ton)	1333	381	－	－	－
夏　茧	(吨)	Summer Silkworm Cocoons	(ton)	268	121	－	－	－
秋　茧	(吨)	Autumn Silkworm Cocoons	(ton)	1412	469	－	－	－

蚕、果生产情况(2017 年)
Silkworm Cocoons and Fruits Production by Region(2017)

萧山区 Xiaoshan	大江东产业集聚区 Dajiangdong Industry Cluster District	余杭区 Yuhang	富阳区 Fuyang	临安区 Lin'an	经济技术开发区 Economic and Technological Development Zone	西湖风景名胜区 The West Lake Scenic Zone	桐庐县 Tonglu	淳安县 Chun'an	建德市 Jiande
4003	1461	1536	3054	1741	–	–	2866	4688	5279
2852	2990	2382	2621	2543	–	–	2428	1959	2492
11418	4368	3916	8004	4428	–	–	6959	9182	13154
27449	7782	22306	10383	8203	590	–	6880	9211	8576
1292462	374470	692017	387821	209925	11060	–	223323	256432	245144
1270	–	3679	4025	3499	–	362	4083	12387	4136
600	–	8512	7018	2546	–	134	3387	4591	2852
490	–	5762	4740	1879	–	110	1545	3599	1978
47	–	1550	2241	477	–	8	957	480	594
63	–	1200	37	190	–	16	885	512	280
19	–	783	784	997	–	–	802	5924	1371
–	–	28	494	449	–	–	714	960	368
–	–	22	113	246	–	–	417	408	127
–	–	3	113	5	–	–	–	141	6
–	–	3	268	198	–	–	297	411	235

3-09 续表

指标	Item	全市 Whole City	市区 Urban District	江干区 Jianggan	西湖区 Xihu	高新(滨江)区 Hi-Tech (Binjiang)
五、水果生产	**Fruits**					
(一)果园面积合计 (公顷)	Area of Orchards (hectare)	29666	11211	-	62	47
柑桔园 (公顷)	Citrus (hectare)	7669	456	-	5	-
梨 园 (公顷)	Pears (hectare)	4154	1869	-	9	-
桃 园 (公顷)	Peaches (hectare)	4393	1801	-	8	-
杨梅园 (公顷)	Red Bayberry (hectare)	3246	1565	-	5	47
枇杷园 (公顷)	Loquat (hectare)	2523	887	-	-	-
柿子园 (公顷)	Persimmons (hectare)	821	250	-	1	-
葡萄园 (公顷)	Grapes (hectare)	1367	1099	-	21	-
其他果园 (公顷)	Others (hectare)	4251	2743	-	10	-
(二)水果总产量 (吨)	Yield of Fruits (ton)	819929	385434	-	1287	4560
柑 桔 (吨)	Citrus (ton)	177819	4614	-	70	-
梨 头 (吨)	Pears (ton)	69533	33242	-	110	-
桃 子 (吨)	Peaches (ton)	77499	47180	-	100	-
杨 梅 (吨)	Red Bayberry (ton)	13771	7463	-	58	28
枇 杷 (吨)	Loquat (ton)	14858	6184	-	-	-
柿 子 (吨)	Persimmons (ton)	8948	3544	-	4	-
葡 萄 (吨)	Grapes (ton)	24586	19345	-	488	-
果用瓜 (吨)	Melon as Fruit (ton)	379064	234069	-	333	4532
其他水果 (吨)	Others (ton)	39682	23493	-	108	-

注:按第三次农业普查数据修订。

continued

萧山区 Xiaoshan	大江东产业集聚区 Dajiangdong Industry Cluster District	余杭区 Yuhang	富阳区 Fuyang	临安区 Lin'an	经济技术开发区 Economic and Technological Development Zone	西湖风景名胜区 The West Lake Scenic Zone	桐庐县 Tonglu	淳安县 Chun'an	建德市 Jiande
2661	100	3386	2927	2128	–	–	3860	8525	6070
24	2	41	259	127	–	–	124	4619	2470
122	2	881	587	270	–	–	1377	556	352
155	3	475	797	366	–	–	873	1003	716
643	–	243	400	227	–	–	560	423	698
2	1	804	65	16	–	–	124	860	652
73	–	29	106	41	–	–	37	449	85
203	75	404	320	151	–	–	124	91	53
1385	14	413	283	652	–	–	406	333	769
124880	32986	75018	120865	57827	997	–	93859	117600	223036
386	98	621	2746	791	–	–	2457	59748	111000
1242	84	14354	14079	3457	–	–	24975	5471	5845
1510	85	7767	31656	6147	–	–	10131	10370	9818
2866	–	1252	1583	1676	–	–	1845	1688	2775
62	42	5803	145	174	–	–	357	5465	2852
1039	7	598	979	924	–	–	387	3688	1329
4016	1471	6720	5068	3053	–	–	1793	949	2499
108422	30880	33513	61082	25190	997	–	46736	24030	74229
4271	276	3057	2839	13218	–	–	3273	3878	9038

a) Data in this table are adjusted according to the 3rd agricultural census.

3－10 分地区畜牧业

Statistics on Animal Husbanday

指 标		Item		全市 Whole City	市区 Urban District	江干区 Jianggan	西湖区 Xihu
一、生猪		**Hogs**					
生猪年末存栏	（万头）	Being Raised at Year－end	（10000 heads）	104.08	79.45	－	－
#能繁殖的母猪	（万头）	#Reproducible	（10000 heads）	8.67	7.25	－	－
年内肥猪出栏	（万头）	Slaughtered Hogs of the Year	（10000 heads）	237.13	183.85	－	－
全年饲养量	（万头）	Number of Hogs Raised in the year	（10000 heads）	341.21	263.3	－	－
二、牛		**Cattle & Buffaloes**					
牛年末存栏	（头）	Being Raised at Year－end	（head）	27280	17877	－	－
#良种及改良种乳牛	（头）	#Improved Milk Cows	（head）	5988	5361	－	－
牛年内出栏	（头）	Slaughtered Cattle & Buffaloes of the Year	（head）	30862	23679	－	－
三、羊		**Sheep & Goats**					
羊年末存栏	（万只）	Being Raised at Year－end	（10000 heads）	21.64	17.93	－	－
羊年内出栏	（万只）	Slaughtered Sheep & Goats of the Year	（10000 heads）	27.41	25.1	3.97	－
四、兔		**Rabbits**					
兔年末存栏	（万只）	Being Raised at Year－end	（10000 heads）	14.77	13.05	－	－
兔年内出栏	（万只）	Slaughtered Rabbits of the Year	（10000 heads）	55.98	44.31	－	－
五、家禽		**Poultry**					
家禽年末存栏	（万只）	Being Raised at Year－end	（10000 heads）	932.88	448.84	－	－
家禽年内出栏	（万只）	Slaughtered Poultry of the Year	（10000 heads）	1203.9	872.64	－	0.42
六、年末养蜂箱数	**（箱）**	**Beehives**	**（case）**	**100982**	**35009**	**－**	**－**
七、畜禽产品产量		**Output of Livestock Products**					
1.肉类产量	（吨）	Output of Meat	（ton）	212658	163211	1022	5
#猪 肉	（吨）	Pork	（ton）	181771	139811	－	－

渔业生产(2017 年)
and Fishery by Region(2017)

高新(滨江)区 Hi－Tech(Binjiang)	萧山区 Xiaoshan	大江东产业集聚区 Dajiangdong Industry Cluster District	余杭区 Yuhang	富阳区 Fuyang	临安区 Lin'an	经济技术开发区 Economic and Technological Development Zone	西湖风景名胜区 The West Lake Scenic Zone	桐庐县 Tonglu	淳安县 Chun'an	建德市 Jiande
－	54.81	9.82	3.29	9.88	11.47	－	－	5.03	12.43	7.17
－	5.54	0.95	0.41	0.64	0.66	－	－	0.33	0.42	0.67
－	99.65	20.66	8.58	40.05	35.56	0.01	－	13.31	20.49	19.48
－	154.46	30.48	11.87	49.93	47.03	0.01	－	18.34	32.92	26.65
－	4824	－	777	3188	6512	2576	－	2834	2801	3768
－	2270	－	－	9	1835	1247	－	－	－	627
－	1837	－	805	12373	7508	1156	－	3193	1928	2062
－	7.15	1.09	4.59	2.71	3.44	0.04	－	1	0.63	2.08
－	7.69	1.48	3.81	5.57	4.04	0.02	－	0.75	0.43	1.13
－	1.64	0.66	2.53	8.5	0.38	－	－	0.03	0.38	1.31
－	2.94	2.15	8.19	28.64	4.54	－	－	0.01	0.01	11.65
－	120.64	19.46	112.71	163.23	52.18	0.08	－	44.73	53.39	385.92
－	244.56	34.2	241.19	331.82	54.56	0.09	－	48.47	31.25	251.54
－	**9398**	**4499**	**1796**	**16736**	**7079**	**－**	**－**	**35865**	**20238**	**9870**
－	81858	14442	11703	37791	30606	226	－	11537	16343	21567
－	76511	13636	6212	29617	27463	8	－	9941	15493	16526

3－10 续表

指 标		Item		全市 Whole City	市区 Urban District	江干区 Jianggan	西湖区 Xihu
牛 肉	(吨)	Beef	(ton)	4878	3670	–	–
羊 肉	(吨)	Mutton	(ton)	4821	4437	1022	–
兔 肉	(吨)	Rabbit Meat	(ton)	970	796	–	–
禽 肉	(吨)	Poultry Meat	(ton)	19844	14184	–	5
2. 禽蛋产量	(吨)	Poultry Eggs	(ton)	91379	22230	–	47
3. 蜂蜜产量	(吨)	Honey	(ton)	19344	12850	–	–
4. 蜂皇浆产量	(公斤)	Honey Tonic	(kg)	532050	209754	–	–
5. 牛奶产量	(吨)	Milk	(ton)	25661	21552	–	–
6. 兔毛产量	(吨)	Rabbit Wool	(ton)	65	65	–	–
八、渔业生产		**Fishery**					
(一)淡水产品产量总计	(吨)	Total Output of Freshwater Aquatic Products	(ton)	172845	140452	100	18207
其中:养殖产量	(吨)	Artificially Cultured	(ton)	161172	135148	–	17132
1. 鱼 类	(吨)	Fish	(ton)	102462	80238	–	12467
#鲫 鱼	(吨)	#Crucians	(ton)	14741	10896	–	2417
编 鱼	(吨)	Breams	(ton)	7090	4289	–	749
黑 鱼	(吨)	Snake Heads	(ton)	2466	2455	–	1180
2. 虾蟹类	(吨)	Shrimps, Prawns & Crabs	(ton)	25376	25172	–	791
3. 贝 类	(吨)	Shellfish	(ton)	928	252	–	47
4. 其 他	(吨)	Others	(ton)	32406	29486	–	3827
#甲 鱼	(吨)	Turtles	(ton)	30632	28067	–	3821
(二)淡水养殖面积合计	(公顷)	Freshwater Aquiculture Area	(hectare)	66415	13836	–	1709

注:按第三次农业普查数据修订。

continued

高新(滨江)区 Hi-Tech(Binjiang)	萧山区 Xiaoshan	大江东产业集聚区 Dajiangdong Industry Cluster District	余杭区 Yuhang	富阳区 Fuyang	临安区 Lin'an	经济技术开发区 Economic and Technological Development Zone	西湖风景名胜区 The West Lake Scenic Zone	桐庐县 Tonglu	淳安县 Chun'an	建德市 Jiande
–	333	–	177	1767	1180	213	–	611	280	317
–	1162	240	815	697	739	2	–	134	61	189
–	55	43	200	459	82	–	–	–	–	174
–	3797	523	4299	5200	880	3	–	796	509	4355
–	1621	176	2797	12714	5051	–	–	2738	5157	61254
–	1483	379	158	3563	7646	–	–	1964	854	3676
–	83723	32216	6994	64248	54789	–	–	261791	46326	14179
–	9387	–	–	–	7808	4357	–	21	–	4088
–	–	–	22	–	43	–	–	–	–	–
996	42347	8000	58845	14179	5218	560	–	8923	13339	10131
626	41551	7935	57230	13443	4616	550	–	8583	10414	7027
308	15395	2546	35484	12368	4076	140	–	5826	10246	6152
41	24	–	3254	4303	836	21	–	1335	1498	1012
–	8	–	1879	1356	297	–	–	319	1161	1321
–	1178	–	45	52	–	–	–	11	–	–
210	22177	5163	1221	334	29	410	–	166	–	38
–	–	–	–	205	–	–	–	–	–	676
108	3979	226	20525	536	511	–	–	2591	168	161
108	3517	–	19902	335	384	–	–	2335	168	62
60	3481	570	4243	1503	2716	124	–	1420	49258	1901

a) Data in this table are adjusted according to the 3rd agricultural census.

3-11 分地区林业
Statistics on Forestry

指 标	Item	全市 Whole City	市区 Urban District
一、营林情况	**Afforestation**		
1. 当年造林面积 （公顷）	Afforested Areas (hectare)	1020	289
2. 迹地更新面积 （公顷）	Area of Forest Updating (hectare)	1655	379
3. 封山育林面积 （公顷）	Area of Afforestation in Enclosed Mountain (hectare)	94844	42147
4. 零星(四旁)植树 （万株）	Planting Trees (10000 plant)	163	64
5. 中、幼龄林抚育面积(公顷)	Area of Grown Forest Cultivated (hectare)	14897	6034
二、林产品产量	**Output of Forest Products**		
1. 油茶籽 （吨）	Camellia Seeds (ton)	10058	248
2. 竹笋干 （吨）	Dried Bamboo Shoots (ton)	61869	44666
3. 核 桃 （吨）	Walnuts (ton)	20705	12293
4. 板 栗 （吨）	Chestnuts (ton)	12559	2451
三、竹木采伐量	**Lumbering**		
1. 木 材 （万立方米）	Timber Cut (10000 cu. m)	19.39	5.91
2. 竹 材 （万支）	Bamboo Cut (10000 pieces)	3612	2746

生产(2017 年)
by Region(2017)

				桐庐县 Tonglu	淳安县 Chun'an	建德市 Jiande
萧山区 Xiaoshan	余杭区 Yuhang	富阳区 Fuyang	临安区 Lin'an			
135	8	107	39	103	222	405.73
	39	127	213	236	426	614
13339		23400	3958	40981	8077	3639
30		18	16	30	19	50
835	1000	1333	2733	2433	2430	4000
		15	233	320	7810	1680
1993	9830	10563	22280	7639	7358	2206
	18	150	12125	1300	7014	98
400	181	1050	820	3003	4305	2800
	0.50	2.13	3.28	1.36	6.98	5.14
135	806	1202	603	120	516	230

3－12 分地区主要农
Possession of Major Agricultural

指　标		Item		全市 Whole City	市区 Urban District
一、农业机械总动力	**（千瓦）**	**Total Power of Agricultural Machinery**	**(kw)**	**2557650**	**1828590**
耕作机械动力	（千瓦）	Cultivation Machinery	(kw)	219496	166634
收获机械动力	（千瓦）	Harvest Machinery	(kw)	47009	34119
植保机械动力	（千瓦）	Plant Protection Machinery	(kw)	52530	43044
排灌机械动力	（千瓦）	Drainage & Irrigation Machinery	(kw)	384651	285135
农副产品加工机械动力	（千瓦）	Processing Machinery of Agricultural Products	(kw)	170704	86069
运输机械动力	（千瓦）	Transport Machinery	(kw)	285775	195881
渔业机械动力	（千瓦）	Fishery Machinery	(kw)	117011	99452
其他机械动力	（千瓦）	Other Machinery	(kw)	1280474	918256
二、主要农机具		**Agricultural Machinery and Machinery For Processing Farm Products**			
大中型拖拉机	（台）	Large & Medium Tractors	(unit)	1347	1177
机引农具	（台）	Mechanized Farm Implement	(unit)	2842	2645
农用小型拖拉机	（台）	Mini－tractors	(unit)	11528	7028
联合收获机	（台）	Combine Harvesters	(unit)	901	713
机动割晒机	（台）	Motorized Harvesters	(unit)	7	6
机动脱粒机	（台）	Motorized Thresher	(unit)	44747	36899
谷物烘干机	（台）	Cereal Dryer	(unit)	625	418
机动喷雾（粉）器	（架）	Motorized Sprayer	(unit)	32522	27421
农用水泵	（台）	Water Pump for Agricultural Use	(unit)	133466	91803
节水喷灌机械	（套）	Saving Water and Sprinkling Machinery	(set)	4315	729
粮食加工机械	（台）	Grain Processing Machinery	(unit)	19413	9156
棉花加工机械	（台）	Cotton Processing Machinery	(unit)	235	138
油料加工机械	（台）	Oil Processing Machinery	(unit)	1685	513
农用运输机械	（台）	Vehicles for Agricultural Use	(unit)	15050	10892

机具年末拥有量(2017 年)
Machinery at the Year - end by Region(2017)

萧山区 Xiaoshan	大江东产业集聚区 Dajiangdong Industry Cluster District	余杭区 Yuhang	富阳区 Fuyang	临安区 Lin'an	桐庐县 Tonglu	淳安县 Chun'an	建德市 Jiande
547712	**109749**	**410865**	**325464**	**358406**	**155623**	**309487**	**263950**
60460	15848	44528	34865	25672	12514	14576	25772
11956	3202	8584	11569	1347	6306	1478	5106
4657	569	3341	4039	30444	1584	3042	4860
88895	10885	76265	48631	57318	30023	22410	47083
30412	4019	14495	11005	27036	11627	50230	22778
72125	10780	56381	35431	25232	27161	38122	24611
79763	15161	8979	1397	147	1529	13799	2231
199444	49285	198292	178527	191210	64879	165830	131509
643	268	287	165	79	76	26	68
1792	634	593	168	89	73	27	97
1662	66	2541	2444	284	953	1291	2256
348	73	127	202	26	82	31	75
–		4	2			1	
4009	217	25348	6994	496	121	2547	5180
144	54	122	91	61	78	24	105
3241	278	1738	1670	19258	730	2237	2134
16992	1117	17595	14318	40400	11411	4842	25410
239	54	417	8	58	53	550	2983
1425	250	1033	1103	5510	1232	7122	1903
73	21	8	51	6	21	60	16
179	95	45	84	198	241	615	316
4260	555	2570	2214	1457	1524	1492	1142

3-13 农业物资
Agricultural Material

指 标		Item		全市 Whole City	市区 Urban District
一、农村用电量	**(万千瓦时)**	**Electricity Consumed in Rural Area**	**(10000 kwh)**	**1139632**	**1035189**
二、农业化肥施用量		**Consumption of Chemical Fertilizer**			
(一)按实物量计算	(吨)	Physical Quantity Consumption	(ton)	452741	311869
1. 氮 肥	(吨)	Nitrogenous Fertilizer	(ton)	190512	122397
2. 磷 肥	(吨)	Phosphate Fertilizer	(ton)	71700	50933
3. 钾 肥	(吨)	Potash Fertilizer	(ton)	36975	22228
4. 复合肥	(吨)	Compound Fertilizer	(ton)	153554	116311
(二)按折纯法计算	(吨)	Pure Consumption	(ton)	92236	57349
1. 氮 肥	(吨)	Nitrogenous Fertilizer	(ton)	40991	25992
2. 磷 肥	(吨)	Phosphate Fertilizer	(ton)	11047	6445
3. 钾 肥	(吨)	Potash Fertilizer	(ton)	7063	3911
4. 复合肥	(吨)	Compound Fertilizer	(ton)	33135	21001
三、农用塑料薄膜使用量	**(吨)**	**Use of Plastic Film**	**(ton)**	**10610**	**4053**
四、农用柴油使用量	**(吨)**	**Consumption of Diesel Oil**	**(ton)**	**25810**	**15697**
五、农药使用量	**(吨)**	**Consumption of Pesticide**	**(ton)**	**6632**	**4361**

消耗情况(2017 年)
Consumption(2017)

萧山区 Xiaoshan	大江东产业集聚区 Dajiangdong Industry Cluster District	余杭区 Yuhang	富阳区 Fuyang	临安区 Lin'an	桐庐县 Tonglu	淳安县 Chun'an	建德市 Jiande
179073	**23969**	**207845**	**454253**	**124996**	**65304**	**14563**	**24576**
168846	31483	49835	24406	62988	35423	56691	48758
64924	13054	25447	12439	17305	16485	30376	21254
33546	6354	7512	2627	6513	7392	6484	6891
11365	865	4909	608	4977	3852	6079	4816
59011	11210	11967	8732	34193	7694	13752	15797
19908	3682	11977	10316	13163	10059	7133	17695
9115	1853	5343	5224	5540	3962	2938	8099
3026	580	1128	946	1107	1451	753	2398
1366	106	1079	304	1045	1132	386	1634
6401	1143	4427	3842	5471	3514	3056	5564
2061	**323**	**406**	**274**	**1174**	**748**	**4088**	**1721**
6088	**1194**	**2324**	**443**	**6672**	**4829**	**1818**	**3466**
1481	**261**	**930**	**809**	**1035**	**680**	**608**	**983**

3-14 乡(镇)
Statistics on Towns

乡镇名称	Town	社区(居民委员会) Number of communities (residents committees)	村民委员会(个) Number of Villagers' Committees (unit)	乡镇常住户数(户) Resident Households in Towns (household)
全　市	**Whole City**	**717**	**2047**	**2732299**
江干区	**Jianggan District**	**83**	**4**	**185576**
彭埠街道	Pengbu Subdistrict	18	–	30888
笕桥街道	Jianqiao Subdistrict	20	–	51498
丁兰街道	Dinglan Subdistrict	24	2	50932
九堡街道	Jiubao Subdistrict	21	2	52258
经济技术开发区	**Economic and Technological Development Zone**	**18**	**–**	**104185**
下沙街道	Xiasha Subdistrict	18	–	104185
西湖区	**Xihu District**	**90**	**32**	**169774**
留下街道	Liuxia Subdistrict	12	1	28819
转塘街道	Zhuantang Subdistrict	34	8	18254
三墩镇	Sandun	35	2	105430
双浦镇	Shuangpu	9	21	17271
高新(滨江)区	**Hi-Tech(Bingjiang) District**	**59**	**–**	**153064**
西兴街道	Xixing Subdistrict	16	–	53239
长河街道	Changhe Subdistrict	22	–	55260
浦沿街道	Puyan Subdistrict	21	–	44565
西湖风景名胜区	**The West Lake Scenic Zone**	**6**	**9**	**9806**
西湖街道	West Lake Subdistrict	6	9	9806
萧山区	**Xiaoshan District**	**158**	**421**	**518875**
城厢街道	Chengxiang Subdistrict	34	–	48199
北干街道	Beigan Subdistrict	16	13	39051
蜀山街道	Shushan Subdistrict	19	8	15219
新塘街道	Xintang Subdistrict	23	17	25762
靖江街道	Jingjiang Subdistrict	3	13	14195

基本情况(2017 年)

and Townships(2017)

乡镇常住人口数(人) Resident Population in Towns (person)	乡镇就业人员数(人) Employed Persons in Towns (person)	乡镇常用耕地面积(公顷) Commonly used cultivated area of township (hectare)	公共财政总收入(万元) Public Finance Income (10000 yuan)	公共财政支出(万元) Public Finance Expenditure (10000 yuan)
8829997	**4487149**	**155279.18**	**4809450.11**	**3111291.39**
576259	**224493**	**362.93**	**417743**	**72627**
88507	41051	–	254600	20021
163853	120173	178	21397	18993
140995	35869	19	129335	17000
182904	27400	165.93	12411	16613
224174	**74554**	**1012**	**20106**	**17759**
224174	74554	1012	20106	17759
522934	**103693**	**6313**	**223723.18**	**58264.17**
72027	28112	21.7	14077.9	17340.11
69288	39823	1156	177340.46	17780.58
310475	870	3477.3	14488.69	14409.11
71144	34888	1658	17816.13	8734.37
626093	**173632**	**550.8**	**164171**	**70034**
197136	87192	151.8	25549	18713
193875	63070	291	83328	25276
235082	23370	108	55294	26045
29000	**15552**	**–**	**7995**	**15212**
29000	15552	–	7995	15212
1792921	**920466**	**38096.98**	**1758813.43**	**1394876.5**
144337	82168	–	315030.37	315186.59
116197	29394	–	256372	256372
63081	47098	722.6	60961	60961
97193	40373	614	75407	18782
56930	23260	1414	38830	38830

3－14 续表1

乡镇名称	Town	社区(居民委员会) Number of Communities (residents committees)	村民委员会(个) Number of Villagers´ Committees (unit)	乡镇常住户数(户) Resident Households in Towns (household)
南阳街道	Nanyang Subdistrict	2	13	15061
义蓬街道	Yipeng Subdistrict	4	22	25007
河庄街道	Hezhuang Subdistrict	1	20	14812
新湾街道	Xinwan Subdistrict	1	12	10222
临江街道	Linjiang Subdistrict	1	2	3680
前进街道	Qianjin Subdistrict	1	3	3500
闻堰街道	Wenyan Subdistrict	6	6	18600
宁围街道	Ningwei Subdistrict	7	15	43540
新街街道	Xinjie Subdistrict	4	15	25650
楼塔镇	Louta	1	12	9180
河上镇	Heshang	1	15	8723
戴村镇	Daicun	1	22	11814
浦阳镇	Puyang	–	18	16719
进化镇	Jinhua	1	25	14205
临浦镇	Linpu	14	20	18169
义桥镇	Yiqiao	2	21	12700
所前镇	Suoqian	1	19	13503
衙前镇	Yaqian	2	11	11903
瓜沥镇	Guali	11	63	72821
益农镇	Yinong	1	19	14420
党湾镇	Dangwan	1	17	12220
余杭区	**Yuhang District**	**165**	**183**	**615465**
临平街道	Linping Subdistrict	15	–	30831
南苑街道	Nanyuan Subdistrict	24	–	58700
东湖街道	Donghu Subdistrict	33	5	57843

continued 1

乡镇常住人口数（人）Resident Population in Towns (person)	乡镇就业人员数（人）Employed Persons in Towns (person)	乡镇常用耕地面积（公顷）Commonly used cultivated area of township (hectare)	公共财政总收入（万元）Public Finance Income (10000 yuan)	公共财政支出（万元）Public Finance Expenditure (10000 yuan)
53982	28105	3000	44868	15679
87642	54723	3096	69654	69289
58323	29667	2511.2	25902	26319.8
32188	11058	1287	8684	14677
16410	11487	889.73	7271	7271
16867	4537	532	3150	8133
56755	45196	266	22820	22175
115444	69342	1524	144632.08	37062.19
77183	37681	1919	113716	81147
28175	24004	780	16143	16089
27959	14516	828.95	25000	24900
41831	3250	1181	10047	18681
52981	27683	1296	18320	17998
48516	30534	1145	29174	29068
88103	44202	1028	105309	104990
47398	28040	1387	44161.01	26808.26
66124	31903	848.5	22486.7	15607.5
42238	35916	522.27	49350.13	48468.71
254872	119287	6213	210842	82143
47275	22708	2793	15914	15000
54917	24334	2298.73	24769.14	23238.45
2152903	**1158928**	**25651.47**	**1576166.37**	**871788.88**
77727	47331	67.7	22622.26	12851.27
170394	79527	525.6	54241.7	9451.6
201696	106029	816.8	471600	65700

3－14 续表2

乡镇名称	Town	社区(居民委员会) Number of Communities (residents committees)	村民委员会(个) Number of Villagers' Committees (unit)	乡镇常住户数(户) Resident Households in Towns (household)
星桥街道	Xingqiao Subdistrict	15	–	19872
五常街道	Wuchang Subdistrict	13	–	32042
乔司街道	Qiaosi Subdistrict	4	11	83956
运河街道	Yunhe Subdistrict	5	14	13407
崇贤街道	Chongxian Subdistrict	2	11	26185
仁和街道	Renhe Subdistrict	1	18	23150
良渚街道	Liangzhu Subdistrict	14	23	48265
闲林街道	Xianlin Subdistrict	5	8	37024
仓前街道	Cangqian Subdistrict	3	8	34451
余杭街道	Yuhang Subdistrict	7	14	58031
中泰街道	Zhongtai Subdistrict	4	10	17953
塘栖镇	Tangqi	9	18	26938
径山镇	Jingshan	2	13	11138
瓶窑镇	Pingyao	6	13	23192
鸬鸟镇	Luniao	1	6	3632
百丈镇	Baizhang	1	6	3770
黄湖镇	Huanghu	1	5	5085
富阳区	**Fuyang District**	**30**	**276**	**276966**
富春街道	Fuchun Subdistrict	22	12	99216
春江街道	Chunjiang Subdistrict	–	9	12431
鹿山街道	Lushan Subdistrict	1	9	7065
东洲街道	Dongzhou Subdistrict	–	15	13520
银湖街道	Yinghu Subdistrict	1	22	17074
万市镇	Wanshi	1	15	6555

continued 2

乡镇常住人口数（人）Resident Population in Towns (person)	乡镇就业人员数（人）Employed Persons in Towns (person)	乡镇常用耕地面积（公顷）Commonly used cultivated area of township (hectare)	公共财政总收入（万元）Public Finance Income (10000 yuan)	公共财政支出（万元）Public Finance Expenditure (10000 yuan)
64714	26965	245.8	4125	5000
118363	74085	–	188098.99	336997.92
231126	129146	886.27	130944	56190
63069	34523	679	19889	19607
135180	86574	911	45852	17481
135706	43837	2600	30118	22500
236845	152553	2800	119060	44759
104106	28359	426	107203	42921
124883	74655	1670	113199	26990
150156	81430	2795.73	54990.98	23307.66
58267	32045	1168	22653.88	13597.87
122686	71122	1813	67600	71200
36438	21125	3175	31324.85	30384.62
77887	46585	2580	76779.7	57483.18
12170	3363	1400	4568	3880
12431	7620	133.57	6633	4279
19059	12054	958	4663.01	7207.76
860718	**481550**	**18801.02**	**221460.74**	**213942.38**
284010	83979	1235	36768.3	36556.8
41710	31570	224.01	13456	13100
24550	14502	839.4	5835.7	5835.7
48951	26261	980	15073	14001
57065	53513	1632	21414	18769
21777	14134	1184	6289	6286

3－14　续表3

乡镇名称	Town	社区(居民委员会) Number of Communities (residents committees)	村民委员会(个) Number of Villagers´ Committees (unit)	乡镇常住户数(户) Resident Households in Towns (household)
洞桥镇	Dongqiao	－	11	5784
渌渚镇	Luzhu	－	13	5232
永昌镇	Yongchang	－	5	3647
里山镇	Lishan	－	5	2895
常绿镇	Changlu	－	8	4105
场口镇	Changkou	1	24	13260
常安镇	Chang´an	－	16	4085
龙门镇	Longmen	－	4	2104
新登镇	Xindeng	4	28	36176
胥口镇	Xukou	－	13	6363
大源镇	Dayuan	－	15	10924
灵桥镇	Lingqiao	－	13	7953
新桐乡	Xintong	－	7	3295
上官乡	Shangguan	－	5	2674
环山乡	Huanshan	－	7	3846
湖源乡	Huyuan	－	10	1841
春建乡	Chunjian	－	6	2984
渔山乡	Yushan	－	4	3937
临安区	**Lin´an City**	**30**	**287**	**213804**
玲珑街道	Linlong Subdistrict	1	16	10211
锦南街道	Jinnan Subdistrict	1	9	7017
锦城街道	Jincheng Subdistrict	18	5	45882
锦北街道	Jinbei Subdistrict	7	12	20747
青山湖街道	Qingshanghu Subdistrict	1	19	15461

continued 3

乡镇常住人口数（人）Resident Population in Towns (person)	乡镇就业人员数（人）Employed Persons in Towns (person)	乡镇常用耕地面积（公顷）Commonly used cultivated area of township (hectare)	公共财政总收入（万元）Public Finance Income (10000 yuan)	公共财政支出（万元）Public Finance Expenditure (10000 yuan)
18247	18063	1110	5137	5129
16408	11842	757.46	11723	11462
11930	2600	493	4700	3932
9763	9729	278.6	3120	3120
9394	8897	323	3281.06	3286.8
38674	25671	1457	10899	11095
15396	14957	907	5040	5040
6325	6146	283	3350	3350
111598	73359	2384.4	33762	33581
18521	11152	816.8	2513.98	2513.98
38086	12964	574	10557	10453
27523	15965	504.25	7048	7047.2
10626	10618	598	3007	3000
8318	5024	159.2	3174	3174
12563	12463	387	3768.2	3761.1
6610	2482	576	3515.5	3501.8
9279	6922	503	3547	3219
13394	8737	594.9	4482	2728
629101	**396082**	**20556.62**	**224345.16**	**123253.8**
43022	21977	1216	18000	17900
17543	13000	165	12094	4575
117886	80694	322.73	27826.19	6819.69
53942	14215	320	18550.8	4829.4
55300	28107	724	84653	18072

3－14　续表4

乡镇名称 Town		社区(居民委员会) Number of Communities (residents committees)	村民委员会(个) Number of Villagers' Committees (unit)	乡镇常住户数(户) Resident Households in Towns (household)
高虹镇	Gaohong	–	9	6083
太湖源镇	Taihuyuan	–	20	10488
於潜镇	Yuqian	1	30	19897
太阳镇	Taiyang	–	18	8736
潜川镇	Qianchuan	–	16	7513
昌化镇	Changhua	1	14	7664
河桥镇	Heqiao	–	11	5155
湍口镇	Tuankou	–	13	3756
清凉峰镇	Qingliangfeng	–	17	9567
岛石镇	Daoshi	–	16	8810
板桥镇	Banqiao	–	15	8526
天目山镇	Tianmushan	–	23	11607
龙岗镇	Longgang	–	24	6684
桐庐县	**Tonglu County**	**21**	**183**	**163014**
旧县街道	Jiuxian Subdistrict	–	5	3135
桐君街道	Tongjun Subdistrict	8	6	21349
城南街道	Chengnan Subdistrict	4	19	35427
凤川街道	Fengchuan Subdistrict	–	8	8314
富春江镇	Fuchunjiang	4	15	9681
横村镇	Hengcun	2	24	16318
分水镇	Fenshui	2	26	26191
瑶琳镇	Yaolin	–	16	10631
百江镇	Baijiang	–	15	4729
江南镇	Jiangnan	1	20	14246

continued 4

乡镇常住人口数（人）Resident Population in Towns (person)	乡镇就业人员数（人）Employed Persons in Towns (person)	乡镇常用耕地面积(公顷) Commonly used cultivated area of township (hectare)	公共财政总收入（万元）Public Finance Income (10000 yuan)	公共财政支出（万元）Public Finance Expenditure (10000 yuan)
21416	16927	580	7759.3	3699
31590	23690	2168	10248.2	8298.6
57298	49596	4203	5285.54	7451.56
23841	17828	1299.6	4000	3800
20552	15785	651	2837	5255.8
23138	10167	957.13	3864.09	7190.02
13237	10179	871	3743	3127
11877	6745	652	8800.5	5707.7
27521	13291	1066.9	2664	5260
25996	15571	597.8	305	3761.13
27036	13569	906	6547	5956
36137	29235	2750	2370.04	5510.8
21769	15506	1106.46	4797.5	6040.1
470106	**307369**	**14697.8**	**72840.13**	**23658.56**
9322	5768	428	1556	633
53099	38792	345.5	10452.46	956.66
102304	73613	734	12433	1962
25079	17290	663	5415.17	1847.48
26307	14014	864	8012	1101
50581	23927	2738	8200.5	2412
74032	44375	1857.7	9321.66	4033.74
31218	24019	1898.4	1984.67	1984.67
14399	10022	915	1728	1333
45471	30562	1689.8	4453	3124.01

3－14　续表 5

乡镇名称	Town	社区(居民委员会) Number of Communities (residents committees)	村民委员会(个) Number of Villagers' Committees (unit)	乡镇常住户数(户) Resident Households in Towns (household)
莪山畲族乡	Eshan	–	7	2819
钟山乡	Zhongshan	–	11	5624
新合乡	Xinghe	–	5	1662
合村乡	Hecun	–	6	2888
淳安县	**Chun'an County**	**16**	**423**	**148673**
千岛湖镇	Qiandaohu	12	20	38426
文昌镇	Wenchang	–	16	4012
石林镇	Shilin	–	8	1438
临岐镇	Linqi	1	17	5859
威坪镇	Weiping	1	44	14666
姜家镇	Jiangjia	1	28	7003
梓桐镇	Zitong	–	19	5897
汾口镇	Fenkou	1	51	15598
中洲镇	Zhongzhou	–	19	5696
大墅镇	Dashu	–	17	4303
枫树岭镇	Fengshuling	–	28	5730
里商乡	Lishang	–	16	3269
金峰乡	Jinfeng	–	11	1701
富文乡	Fuwen	–	10	2043
左口乡	Zuokou	–	11	3319
屏门乡	Pingmen	–	15	3768
瑶山乡	Yaoshan	–	11	2826

continued 5

乡镇常住人口数（人）Resident Population in Towns (person)	乡镇就业人员数（人）Employed Persons in Towns (person)	乡镇常用耕地面积（公顷）Commonly used cultivated area of township (hectare)	公共财政总收入（万元）Public Finance Income (10000 yuan)	公共财政支出（万元）Public Finance Expenditure (10000 yuan)
8570	5570	480.4	1151.67	1060
15750	8467	1187	6983	1335
4982	4889	345	276	1064
8992	6061	552	873	812
449883	**319350**	**12043.29**	**23392.4**	**182805.2**
108631	64551	527.81	10853.6	13829.8
13114	8976	428.37	919.5	7320.6
4802	3691	174.27	135.3	3934.5
19720	12849	856.33	1125.3	10880.4
44246	38417	1040.4	1118	17037.4
21359	18048	829.9	1786.5	14142.5
18099	13210	728	265	8595
48373	37767	1542	3900	22310.7
17938	14129	602.56	155.6	7839.2
13631	9797	628	551.1	8878.6
17543	12759	901.7	233.8	10428.1
10770	7165	250.49	260	5852.6
5016	2144	259	457.8	3199.1
6384	4331	290	104.6	3590.3
10708	10070	378.55	147.5	5248.1
11322	10128	306	104.9	5159.3
9445	6117	264.31	154.5	4109.8

3－14 续表6

乡镇名称 Town		社区(居民委员会) Number of Communities (residents committees)	村民委员会(个) Number of Villagers' Committees (unit)	乡镇常住户数(户) Resident Households in Towns (household)
王阜乡	Wangfu	–	18	5917
宋村乡	Songcun	–	8	2038
鸠坑乡	Jiukeng	–	9	2560
浪川乡	Langchuan	–	19	6200
界首乡	Jieshou	–	13	2810
安阳乡	Anyang	–	15	3594
建德市	**Jiande City**	**41**	**229**	**173097**
新安江街道	Xin'anjiang Subdistrict	11	4	38652
洋溪街道	Yangxi Subdistrict	4	2	5798
更楼街道	Genglou Subdistrict	2	14	7404
莲花镇	Lianhua	1	6	3163
乾潭镇	Qiantan	1	24	15130
梅城镇	Meicheng	5	13	17308
杨村桥镇	Yangcunqiao	1	13	5930
下涯镇	Xiaya	1	11	7110
大洋镇	Dayang	3	19	9698
三都镇	Sandu	1	19	7659
寿昌镇	Shouchang	4	23	16141
航头镇	Hangtou	1	18	8517
大慈岩镇	Daciyan	1	12	6105
大同镇	Datong	3	34	16549
李家镇	Lijia	1	10	5523
钦堂乡	Qintang	1	7	2410

continued 6

乡镇常住人口数（人）Resident Population in Towns (person)	乡镇就业人员数（人）Employed Persons in Towns (person)	乡镇常用耕地面积（公顷）Commonly used cultivated area of township (hectare)	公共财政总收入（万元）Public Finance Income (10000 yuan)	公共财政支出（万元）Public Finance Expenditure (10000 yuan)
17610	11607	250	178.1	5905.7
5759	4261	218	89.1	2920.6
7304	3629	112.47	189.2	3717
18429	11922	621.33	232.2	8247.6
8467	5716	319.53	119.1	4135.3
11213	8066	514.27	311.7	5523
495905	**311480**	**17193.27**	**98693.7**	**67069.9**
103481	48057	274	28946	5765
16350	13499	168.5	10341	4500
23045	23044	658	4112	2335
10386	5551	367.67	880.9	1164
45176	30708	1540	7466	7466
42475	31491	1700	6723.2	6723.2
19620	10824	910	2226	2225
26458	18020	1210	8062.6	6937.7
31003	21581	1400.2	3760	3760
20501	14727	1189	3335	2781
46772	19290	1240.1	7547	5669
29263	19438	1577.9	4099	3657
16157	692	1560	1563	3048
45217	38112	2221	2775	4505
13756	11241	719.9	3821	2722
6245	5205	457	3036	3812

3－15 分地区农村
Basic Statistics on

指　　标	Item	全　市 Whole City	市　区 Urban District	江干区 Jianggan	西湖区 Xihu
一、农村人口与从业人员	**Rural Population and Employed Persons**				
农村户数　（万户）	Rural Household　(10000 households)	131.53	96.67	1.43	4
农村人口　（万人）	Rural Population　(10000 persons)	488.22	378.45	6.46	16.65
男	Male	247.31	191.55	3.14	8.23
女	Female	240.91	186.9	3.32	8.42
农村劳动力资源数　（万人）	Rural Laboar Resources　(10000 persons)	317.03	245.05	3.85	10.25
男	Male	165.88	128.17	2.02	5.43
女	Female	151.15	116.88	1.83	4.82
农村从业人员　（万人）	Jobholders in Rural Areas　(10000 persons)	282.19	217.08	2.95	9.3
男	Male	149.66	114.87	1.54	4.97
#从事农业人员	Persons Involved in Agriculture	37.12	22.88	0.17	0.85
女	Female	132.53	102.21	1.41	4.33
#从事农业人员	Persons Involved in Agriculture	29.17	17.44	0.09	0.73
二、农村基础设施	**Public Facilities in Rural Areas**				
自来水受益村数	Number of Villages with Access to Tap Water	2046	1211	4	34
通有线电视村数	Number of Villages Connecting to Cable TV	2046	1211	4	34
通宽带村数	Number of Villages Connecting to Broadband	2046	1211	4	34

基本情况(2017 年末)
Rural Areas by Region(End of 2017)

高新(滨江)区 Hi - Tech(Binjiang)	萧山区 Xiaoshan	大江东产业集聚区 Dajiangdong Industry Cluster District	余杭区 Yuhang	富阳区 Fuyang	临安区 Lin'an	经济技术开发区 Economic and Technological Development Zone	西湖风景名胜区 The West Lake Scenic Zone	桐庐县 Tonglu	淳安县 Chun'an	建德市 Jiande
2.58	35.28	4.97	20.58	16.96	15.56	–	0.28	10.94	11.37	12.55
10.63	127.98	18.21	112.21	56.88	47.07	–	0.57	33.95	35.5	40.32
5.16	63.11	9.11	59.4	28.9	23.36	–	0.25	17.2	17.9	20.66
5.47	64.87	9.1	52.81	27.98	23.71	–	0.32	16.75	17.6	19.66
6.94	79.39	12.24	75.21	36.67	32.42	–	0.32	22.24	24.12	25.62
3.49	40.64	6.35	40.55	19.24	16.65	–	0.15	11.5	12.5	13.71
3.45	38.75	5.89	34.66	17.43	15.77	–	0.17	10.74	11.62	11.91
6.43	71.04	11.21	66.74	32.65	27.68	–	0.29	20.21	23.12	21.78
3.27	36.66	5.84	36.31	17.58	14.4	–	0.14	10.53	12.3	11.96
0.03	6.13	1.02	4.37	6.83	4.44	–	0.06	2.85	5.9	5.49
3.16	34.38	5.37	30.43	15.07	13.28	–	0.15	9.68	10.82	9.82
0.02	4.6	0.72	3.02	5.09	3.82	–	0.07	2.37	5.1	4.26
–	411	59	187	279	287	–	9	183	423	229
–	411	59	187	279	287	–	9	183	423	229
–	411	59	187	279	287	–	9	183	423	229

3-16 农村基本情况(2011-2017年)
Basic Statistics on Rural Areas(2011-2017)

指标 Item	2011	2012	2013	2014	2015	2016	2017
一、农村人口与从业人员 Rural Population and Employed Persons							
农村户数（万户） Rural Household (10000 households)	132.94	129.29	132.18	131.96	132.15	132.00	131.53
农村人口（万人） Rural Population (10000 persons)	434.23	425.49	469.90	480.04	482.63	482.94	488.22
男 Male	218.03	213.81	236.03	241.82	243.47	244.08	247.31
女 Female	216.20	211.68	233.87	238.22	239.16	238.86	240.91
农村劳动力资源数（万人） Rural Laboar Resources (10000 persons)	281.16	276.62	304.14	314.45	313.79	314.83	317.03
男 Male	146.23	143.66	157.27	163.98	163.94	164.54	165.88
女 Female	134.93	132.96	146.87	150.47	149.85	150.29	151.15
农村从业人员（万人） Jobholders in Rural Areas (10000 persons)	262.10	257.30	279.91	286.01	284.73	281.76	282.19
男 Male	137.33	134.85	145.70	151.05	151.21	149.68	149.66
#从事农业人员 Persons Involved in Agriculture				36.50	37.58	37.49	37.12
女 Female	124.77	122.45	134.21	134.96	133.52	132.08	132.53
#从事农业人员 Persons Involved in Agriculture				29.75	30.22	29.74	29.17
二、农村基础设施 Public Facilities in Rural Areas							
自来水受益村数 Number of Villages with Access to Tap Water	2081	2078	2058	2054	2054	2053	2046
通有线电视村数 Number of Villages Connecting to Cable TV	2081	2078	2058	2054	2054	2053	2046
通宽带村数 Number of Villages Connecting to Prroadband		2078	2058	2054	2054	2053	2046
三、农林牧渔业增加值 Value-added of Agriculture, Forestry, Animal Husbandry and Fishery	**2367708**	**2551127**	**2654059**	**2783252**	**2924013**	**2985617**	**3056039**
农业 Farming	1386520	1510382	1571300	1685668	1806178	1866383	1951535
林业 Forestry	277061	302796	324240	371932	393332	415918	428898
畜牧业 Animal Husbandry	421453	435191	458201	405348	395476	377688	334289
渔业 Fishery	253456	270629	262233	280544	284506	276270	284845
农、林、牧、渔专业及辅助性活动 Services for Farming, Forestry, Animal Husbandary and Fishery	29218	32129	38085	39760	44521	49358	56472

注:按第三次农业普查数据修订。

a) Data in this table are adjusted according to the 3rd agricultural census.

主要统计指标解释

农林牧渔业总产值　是以货币表现的农、林、牧、渔业全部产品的总量和对农林牧渔生产活动进行的各种支持性服务活动的价值。它反映一定时期内农林牧渔业生产的总规模和总成果。

农林牧渔业的统计范围是：

(1)农业　包括农作物种植业和其他农业。

农作物种植业　包括谷类、豆类、薯类、棉花、麻类、烟叶、蔬菜、药材、瓜类和其他农作物的种植以及茶园、桑园、果园的生产经营。

其他农业　包括采集野生植物的果实、纤维、树脂、油料以及柴草、野生药材、菌类等。

(2)林业　包括林木的栽培(不包括茶园、桑园和果园的栽培、管理和收获等活动)、林产品的采集、村及村以下合作经济组织和农户的竹木砍伐。

(3)牧业　包括除渔业养殖以外的一切动物饲养和放牧以及野生动物的捕猎和饲养。

(4)渔业　包括水生动物和海藻类植物的养殖和捕捞。

(5)农林牧渔服务业　包括对农林牧渔生产活动进行的各种支持性服务活动。

粮食产量　指全社会的产量,包括国营农场等全民所有制经营、集体统一经营和农民家庭经营的产量,还包括工矿企业家属办的农场和其他生产单位的产量。粮食除包括稻谷、小麦、大麦、玉米、高粱、谷子及其他杂粮外,还包括薯类和豆类。其产量计算方法,豆类按去豆荚后的干豆计算,薯类按5公斤鲜薯折1公斤粮食计算,其他粮食一律按脱粒后的原粮计算。

猪、牛、羊肉产量　指当年出栏并已屠宰的猪、牛、羊的肉产量,即屠宰后除去头蹄下水后带骨的(即胴体重)重量。

水产品产量　指人工养殖的水产品和天然生长的水产品的捕捞量。包括海水的鱼类、虾蟹类、贝类和藻类以及内陆水域的鱼类、虾蟹类和贝类,不包括淡水生植物。

有效灌溉面积　指具有一定水源,地块比较平整、灌溉工程或设备已经配套,在一般年景下当年能够进行正常灌溉的耕地面积。

农业机械总动力　指主要用于农、林、牧、渔业的各种动力机械的动力总和。包括耕作机械、排灌机械、收获机械、农用运输机械、植物保护机械、牧业机械、林业机械和其他农业机械[内燃机按引擎马力折成瓦(特)计算,电动机按功率折成瓦(特)计算]。不包括专门用于乡、镇、村、组办工业、基本建设、非农业运输、科学试验和教学等非农业方面的动力机械与作业机械。

农村用电量　指本年度内扣除在农村中的全民所有制工业、交通、基建单位的用电量以后的农村生产上和生活上的全年用电总度数(全年累计数),包括国家电网的供电量,也包括农村自办电站的供电量。

农用化肥施用量　指本年内实际用于农业生产的化肥数量。包括氮肥、磷肥、钾肥及复合肥。化肥施用量要求按折纯量计算数量。折纯量是指氮肥、磷肥、钾肥分别按含氮、含五氧化二磷、含氧化钾的百分之一百成分进行折算后的数量。复合肥按其所含主要成分折算。

Explanatory Notes on Main Statistical Indicators

Gross Output Value of Farming, Forestry, Animal Husbandry and Fishery refers to the total volume of products of farming, forestry, animal husbandry and fishery in value terms and output value of all kinds of service activities that support farming, forestry, animal husbandry and fishery production. It reflects the total scale and total result of agricultural production during a given period of time.

The statistical scopes for Farming, Forestry, Animal Husbandry and Fishery are:

(1) **Farming** include crop cultivation and other farming crop cultivation, include planting of grain, beans, tubers, cotton, oil – bearing crops, sugar crops, fiber crops, tobacco, vegetables, medicinal materials, melons and others, as well as tea, mulberry and fruit plantation.

Other farming include gathering of wild plant fruits, fiber, gum, oil, firewood, wild medicinal materials, fungi and commodity industry run by rural household.

(2) **Forestry** include planting of trees (not including planting, management & harvest of tea, mulberry and fruit plantation), collection of forest products, cutting and felling of bamboo and trees by villages and other cooperative organizations under villages.

(3) **Animal Husbandry** include raising and grazing of any kind of animal and hunting and raising of wild animal, excluding fish breeding.

(4) **Fishery** include cultivation and catches of aquatic animals and seaweed.

(5) **Service Industry for Farming, Forestry, Animal Husbandry and Fishery** refers to all kinds of service activities that support farming, forestry, animal husbandry and fishery production.

Grain Yield refers to the total yield including grains produced by state farms, collective units, industrial enterprises and mines. Grain includes rice, wheat, corn, sorghum, millet and other miscellaneous grains as well as tubers and beans. Output of beans refers to dry beans without pods. The output of tubers was converted into that of grain at the ratio 5:1. Output of all other grains refers to husked grain.

Output of Pork, Beef, and Mutton refers to the meat of slaughtered hogs, cattle, sheep and goats with head, feet and offal taken away.

Output of Aquatic Products refers to catches of both artificially cultured and naturally grown aquatic products, including fish, shrimps, crabs and shellfish in sea and inland water as well as seaweed. Freshwater plants are not included.

Irrigated Area refers to areas that are effectively irrigated, i. e. level land which has water source and complete sets of irrigation facilities to lift and move adequate water for irrigation purpose under normal conditions.

Total Power of Farm Machinery refers to total mechanical power of machinery used in farming, forestry, animal husbandry, and fishery, including ploughing, irrigation and drainage, harvesting, transport, plant protection, stock breeding, forestry and fishery. The power of internal combustion engines is required to convert horsepower into watts and the power of electric motors is required to be converted into watts. Machinery employed for non – agricultural purposes, such as the machines used in township – run and village – run industry, construction, non – agricultural transport, scientific experiments and teaching, is excluded.

Electricity Consumption in Rural Areas refers to the total degree of electricity consumption in rural production and living (annual aggregate) after discounting the ownership by the whole people in the rural areas of industrial, transport and infrastructure unit of electricity consumption, including the national grid power supply, and also including the power supply in rural areas on their own power station.

Consumption of Chemical Fertilizers in Agriculture refers to the quantity of chemical fertilizers applied in agriculture in the year, including nitrogenous fertilizer, phosphate fertilizer, potash fertilizer, and compound fertilizer. The consumption of chemical fertilizers is required in calculation to convert the gross weight into weight into weight containing 100% effective component (e. g. 100% nitrogen content in nitrogenous fertilizer, 100% phosphorous pentoxide contents in phosphate fertilizer, 100% potassium oxide contents in potash fertilizer). Compound fertilizer is converted with its major component.

四、工业、能源

INDUSTRY AND ENERGY

4 工业、能源
Industry and Energy

主要统计指标
Major Statistical Indicators

规模以上工业企业单位数	Number of Industrial Enterprises above Designated Size	5533	个	(unit)
为上年	As Compared with the Preceding Year	97.3	%	(%)
规模以上工业增加值	Value-added of Industrial Enterprises above Designated Size	3184.05	亿元	(100 million yuan)
为上年	As Compared with the Preceding Year	107.0	%	(%)
规模以上工业总产值	Gross Output Value of Industrial Enterprises above Designated Size	12963.76	亿元	(100 million yuan)
为上年	As Compared with the Preceding Year	104.4	%	(%)
轻工业	Light Industry	4711.50	亿元	(100 million yuan)
为上年	As Compared with the Preceding Year	100.4	%	(%)
重工业	Heavy Industry	8252.27	亿元	(100 million yuan)
为上年	As Compared with the Preceding Year	106.8	%	(%)

4-01 全市工业企业单位数(主要年份)

Number of Industrial Enterprises of the Whole City(Main Years)

单位:个 (unit)

年份 Year	规模以上工业合计 Industry above Designated Size Total	国有经济 State - owned Enterprises	集体经济 Collective - owned Enterprises	其他各种经济类型 Enterprises of Other Types of Ownership
1978	2868	680	2188	-
1980	3519	691	-	-
1985	5800	823	-	-
1990	6183	921	4966	11
1991	6234	933	5219	82
1992	6235	941	5162	132
1995	6744	1086	4722	936
1996	6148	1011	4268	869
1997	4980	760	3250	970
1998	2559	464	815	1280
1999	2474	396	689	1389
2000	2715	282	598	1835
2001	3580	237	252	3091
2002	4015	172	232	3611
2003	4689	144	219	4326
2004	7738	185	192	7361
2005	7359	124	169	7066
2006	7826	110	162	7554
2007	8674	71	131	8472
2008	9907	73	101	9733
2009	10032	71	84	9877
2010	10370	74	68	10228
2011	5868	52	25	5791
2012	5927	56	20	5851
2013	6284	25	11	6248
2014	6169	22	9	6138
2015	6073	17	5	6051
2016	5684	15	4	5665
2017	5533	10	2	5521

注:规模以上工业口径:1997 年及以前为乡及以上工业;1998 -2010 年为主营业务收入 500 万及以上;2011 年为主营业务收入 2000 万及以上(后同)。

a) Industry above Designated Size: Data after 2011 refer to all the industrial enterprises with annual Sales income of over 20 million yuan, data in 1998 - 2010 refer to all the industrial enterprises with annual sales income of over 5 million yuan, data in 1997 and before refer to enterprises at township and above level.

4-02 市区工业企业单位数(主要年份)
Number of Industrial Enterprises in Urban District(Main Years)

单位:个 (unit)

年份 Year	规模以上工业合计 Industry above Designated Size Total	国有经济 State-owned Enterprises	集体经济 Collective-owned Enterprises	其他各种经济类型 Enterprises of Other Types of Ownership
1978	787	313	414	-
1980	894	315	579	-
1985	1250	345	859	7
1990	1360	361	971	28
1991	1411	382	990	39
1992	1490	395	1024	71
1995	1998	440	1102	456
1996	2043	458	1109	476
1997	1733	372	951	410
1998	1019	315	315	389
1999	959	255	284	420
2000	1005	182	253	570
2001	2645	195	200	2250
2002	2838	140	178	2520
2003	3230	115	158	2957
2004	5527	156	122	5249
2005	4995	98	104	4793
2006	5195	85	91	5019
2007	5726	54	77	5595
2008	6530	55	64	6411
2009	6477	52	49	6376
2010	6478	51	37	6390
2011	3867	36	10	3821
2012	3862	37	7	3818
2013	4145	18	5	4122
2014	4716	17	5	4694
2015	4584	12	3	4569
2016	4235	11	2	4222
2017	4726	8	1	4717

4-03 全市工业总产值(主要年份)

Gross Industrial Output Value of the Whole City (Main Years)

单位:万元　　　　(10000 yuan)

年份 Year	规模以上工业 Industry above Designated Size	#轻工业 Light Industry	重工业 Heavy Industry	国有经济 State-owned	集体经济 Collective-owned	其他经济 Other Types of Ownership
1978	429624	-	-	334799	94825	-
1980	617910	-	-	451349	166561	-
1985	1285888	793766	492122	726172	546642	13074
1990	2922600	1848911	1073689	1532900	1300900	88800
1991	3524900	2201757	1323143	1779400	1601400	144200
1992	4527400	2735168	1792232	2141000	2084000	302400
1995	10200259	5600664	4599595	3585284	3999638	2615337
1996	8831167	4606720	4224447	2905614	3320757	2604796
1997	9114651	4871887	4242764	3185886	2971634	2957131
1998	11099357	5726407	5372950	3422316	2824793	4852248
1999	12000796	6129963	5870833	3164602	2543981	6292213
2000	15435682	7623300	7812382	1860336	2698406	10876940
2001	19195133	9957027	9238106	1788783	1911315	15495035
2002	24002972	12435498	11567474	2147066	2151485	19704421
2003	32025226	15652463	16372763	2484171	2444002	27097053
2004	44865779	19761946	25103833	3419970	558890	40886919
2005	54411271	24059690	30351581	6054280	603438	47753553
2006	69754590	29093450	40661140	6776754	667615	62310221
2007	83514029	35878400	47635629	7688908	517878	75307243
2008	93795792	38735329	55060463	7440679	386111	85969002
2009	93907334	40115956	53791378	7576482	354714	85976138
2010	110810397	45764739	65045658	9050510	300262	101459625
2011	123529249	48660810	74868439	10220511	171901	113136837
2012	129596777	51377588	78219189	11507163	167343	117922271
2013	124180035	48663751	75516284	7140899	39776	116999360
2014	128530518	49979222	78551296	6922198	32246	121576073
2015	124156803	48207987	75948816	2309361	14146	121833295
2016	124209589	46939900	77269689	5534102	12292	118663195
2017	129637623	47114960	82522663	1870409	5868	127761346

4-04 市区工业总产值(主要年份)

Gross Industrial Output Value in Urban District(Main Years)

单位:万元 (10000 yuan)

年 份 Year	规模以上工业 Industry above Designated Size	轻 工 业 Light Industry	重 工 业 Heavy Industry	国有经济 State-owned	集体经济 Collective-owned	其他经济 Other Types of Ownership
1978	304242	-	-	248534	55708	-
1980	433623	-	-	335789	97834	-
1985	812246	512767	301998	536498	267613	8135
1990	1533000	1026764	599899	1067400	416500	49100
1991	1814600	1140394	674072	1237600	496800	80200
1992	2291300	1379154	917085	1497400	601200	192700
1995	4760900	2507752	2753196	2252300	908900	1599700
1996	4599778	2460319	2139459	2018768	951432	1629578
1997	4997257	2889406	2609217	2537740	819984	1639533
1998	6110192	3068600	3041592	2989467	1123013	1997712
1999	6280838	3178286	3102552	2668519	979070	2633249
2000	7804302	3635578	4168724	1498595	968509	5337198
2001	16156245	8377563	7778681	1695132	1792228	12668885
2002	20252484	10431428	9821056	2036097	2045450	16170937
2003	26945006	13080771	13864235	2390424	2305431	22249151
2004	37564968	16361706	21203262	3097656	419720	34047592
2005	44775260	19601053	25174207	5592419	390555	38792286
2006	57255453	23722868	33532585	6305071	347788	50602594
2007	67565456	29452269	38113187	7123810	323842	60117804
2008	74564803	31236743	43328060	6812616	219140	67533047
2009	74059755	32178951	41880805	6880470	148937	67030348
2010	86653885	36440816	50213069	8155395	156026	78342464
2011	97800625	39467105	58333520	9253445	70299	88476881
2012	101396009	41428864	59967145	10452692	72743	90870574
2013	94197123	38407906	55789218	6332681	22398	87842044
2014	110230328	42840596	67389732	6463681	22354	103744292
2015	105641721	40775608	64866113	1841145	8633	103791944
2016	105688299	39331082	66357217	5061048	6629	100620622
2017	119823690	42792636	77031054	1689177	2846	118131668

4-05 规模以上工业企业主要经济效益指标(2000-2017年)

Main Economic Indicators of Industrial Enterprises Above Designated Size(2000-2017)

单位:亿元 (100 million yuan)

年份 Year	规模以上工业总产值 Output Value of Industrial Enterprises Above Designated Size	规模以上工业增加值 Added Value of Industrial Enterprises Above Designated Size	资产总计 Total Assets	流动资产合计 Total Current Assets	主营业务收入 Revenne from Principal Business	利润总额 Total Profits	利税总额 Total Profits and Tax
2000	1543.57	360.97	1828.35	946.32	1465.49	76.20	161.61
2001	1919.51	444.91	2148.96	1122.07	1828.28	107.56	208.54
2002	2400.30	597.01	2514.19	1313.92	2288.21	145.48	274.98
2003	3202.52	783.51	3258.93	1783.50	3117.46	194.16	359.54
2004	4486.58	1019.47	4118.31	2300.84	4363.27	226.74	427.23
2005	5441.13	1126.54	4781.34	2692.73	5282.80	234.99	450.68
2006	6975.46	1363.17	5564.68	3215.19	6807.64	314.49	576.51
2007	8351.40	1717.65	6573.12	3880.23	8057.03	414.55	730.50
2008	9379.58	1743.20	7506.26	4437.50	8976.46	453.92	802.13
2009	9390.73	1792.00	8405.62	4968.21	9026.32	510.97	882.62
2010	11081.04	2153.83	9937.41	6011.68	10843.24	764.47	1224.48
2011	12352.92	2369.00	10968.69	6709.76	12022.57	795.53	1330.48
2012	12959.68	2492.00	11983.52	7215.40	12525.39	771.68	1339.94
2013	12418.00	2664.13	12680.28	7609.51	12424.15	853.60	1450.55
2014	12853.05	2813.51	13376.72	7938.51	12833.70	904.60	1538.07
2015	12415.68	2875.05	14015.54	8306.78	12237.39	891.12	1559.68
2016	12420.96	2990.34	14467.36	8502.92	12367.54	946.06	1655.64
2017	12963.76	3184.05	15403.30	9009.58	13209.59	998.56	1774.52

4-05 续表 continued

年份 Year	资产负债率(%) Ratio of Debts to Assets(%)	流动资产周转次数(次) Turnover of Current Assets(times)	成本费用利润率(%) Ratio of Profits to Costs(%)	全员劳动生产率(元/人) Overall Labor Productivity (Yuan/Person)	产品销售率(%) Rate of Production Sold (%)
2000	58.59	1.62	5.49	52713	97.19
2001	57.20	1.70	6.26	59518	97.40
2002	56.82	1.82	6.84	76402	97.76
2003	58.70	1.87	6.69	91284	97.68
2004	59.80	2.00	5.50	98809	98.10
2005	60.12	2.06	4.69	105786	98.25
2006	59.83	2.23	4.87	120289	98.36
2007	60.43	2.21	5.44	138016	98.17
2008	60.42	2.10	5.34	152070	98.14
2009	59.07	1.86	5.86	151002	98.63
2010	58.34	1.96	7.60	166516	98.83
2011	59.12	1.91	6.96	190110	98.61
2012	49.57	1.74	6.60	232587	98.63
2013	58.09	1.63	7.39	222570	99.18
2014	56.83	1.62	7.61	245726	98.48
2015	55.69	1.54	7.91	257020	98.50
2016	54.29	1.53	7.97	278384	99.43
2017	54.66	1.55	7.77	301608	98.45

4－06 分地区工业

Number of Industrial Enterprises

单位:个

项　目	Item	全　市 Whole City	市区 Urban District	上城区 Shangcheng	下城区 Xiacheng	江干区 Jianggan	拱墅区 Gongshu	西湖区 Xihu
规模以上工业合计	**Industrial above Designated Size**	**5533**	**4726**	**33**	**23**	**54**	**75**	**124**
一、按轻重工业分	**Grouped by Light & Heavy Industry**							
轻工业	Light Industry	2778	2331	7	5	22	27	35
重工业	Heavy Industry	2755	2395	26	18	32	48	89
二、按所有制分	**Grouped by Ownership**							
国有企业	State－owned Enterprises	10	8	1				
集体企业	Collective－owned Enterprises	2	1			1		
股份合作企业	Cooperative Enterprises	6	6		1		1	
联营企业	Joint Ownership Enterprises	1	1		1			
有限责任公司	Limited Liability Corporations	920	813	8	12	13	15	46
股份有限公司	Share－holding Corporations Ltd.	227	201	5	2	4	6	6
私营企业	Private Enterprises	3511	2906	16	4	26	46	55
外商及港澳台投资企业	Enterprises with Investment from Foreign、Hong Kong、Macao and Taiwan	850	784	3	3	10	7	17
其他企业	Other Enterprises	6	6					
合计中:国有控股企业	Of the Total:Controlling Share Hold Enterprises	212	185	4	6	2	6	8
三、按企业规模分	**Grouped by Size of Enterprises**							
大型企业	Large	125	120	4	1	2	1	5
中型企业	Medium－sized	641	584	6	2	8	8	18
小微企业	Small	4767	4022	23	20	44	66	101

企业单位数(2017 年末)

by Region(End of 2017)

(unit)

高新(滨江)区 Hi-Tech(Binjiang)	萧山区 Xiaoshan	大江东产业集聚区 Dajiangdong Industry Cluster District	余杭区 Yuhang	富阳区 Fuyang	临安区 Lin'an	经济技术开发区 Economic and Technological Development Zone	西湖风景名胜区 The West Lake Scenic Zone	桐庐县 Tonglu	淳安县 Chun'an	建德市 Jiande
189	**1544**	**266**	**1141**	**644**	**597**	**301**	**1**	**338**	**117**	**352**
50	893	98	582	285	284	141		200	63	184
139	651	168	559	359	313	160	1	138	54	168
1	1		1		1	3		1	1	
										1
	1		3							
44	214	54	180	103	111	67		35	18	54
28	44	10	57	19	23	6	1	8	5	13
69	1006	140	750	456	430	48		244	85	276
47	277	62	150	64	30	176		50	8	8
20	31	12	32	23	22	30	1	10	4	13
15	41	11	15	5	7	24		3		2
39	200	50	134	52	41	76		26	12	19
135	1303	205	992	587	549	201	1	309	105	331

4－07 分地区工业

Gross Industrial

单位:万元

项 目	Item	全 市 Total	市 区 Urban District	上城区 Shangcheng
规模以上工业合计	**Industrial above Designated Size**	**129637623**	**119823690**	**7584529**
一、按轻重工业分	**Grouped by Light & Heavy Industry**			
轻工业	Light Industry	47114960	42792636	3414264
重工业	Heavy Industry	82522663	77031054	4170265
二、按所有制分	**Grouped by Ownership**			
国有企业	State－owned Enterprises	1870409	1689177	940
集体企业	Collective－owned Enterprises	5868	2846	－
股份合作企业	Cooperative Enterprises	35534	35534	－
联营企业	Joint Ownership Enterprises	4787	4787	－
有限责任公司	Limited Liability Corporations	43856526	41564308	7132926
股份有限公司	Share－holding Corporations Ltd.	14068352	13052631	308951
私营企业	Private Enterprises	36399394	31269152	123607
外商及港澳台投资企业	Enterprises with Investment from Foreign、Hong Kong、Macao and Taiwan	33183636	31992140	18105
其他企业	Other Enterprises	213117	213117	－
合计中:国有控股企业	Of the Total:Controlling Share Hold Enterprises	25083114	23869903	3494256
三、按企业规模分	**Grouped by Size of Enterprises**			
大型企业	Large	45603071	44340158	7288730
中型企业	Medium－sized	36246596	33527067	155955
小微企业	Small	47787956	41956465	139843

总产值(2017 年)
Output Value by Region(2017)

(10000 yuan)

下城区 Xiacheng	江干区 Jianggan	拱墅区 Gongshu	西湖区 Xihu	高新 (滨江)区 Hi－Tech (Binjiang)	萧山区 Xiaoshan
406362	**1397773**	**1881421**	**2246361**	**17738976**	**37270896**
50812	218216	855742	769262	1752984	16268807
355551	1179557	1025679	1477100	15985991	21002089
–	–	–	–	6990	909589
–	2846	–	–	–	–
7860	–	2967	–	–	10830
4787	–	–	–	–	–
125665	135255	1099876	720313	7543396	12185844
213764	47840	160827	82553	3478881	2536069
18282	238668	447337	616346	911810	12914471
36005	973164	170413	827150	5797898	8691289
–	–	–	–	–	–
276621	60002	340785	357597	7458428	5223373
210938	861029	680716	752253	10769901	11296829
45203	208603	599710	717802	4020764	12282286
150222	328141	600994	776306	2948310	13691781

单位:万元 4-07 续表

项 目	Item	大江东产业集聚区 Dajiangdong Industry Cluster District	余杭区 Yuhang	富阳区 Fuyang
规模以上工业合计	**Industrial above Designated Size**	**11628048**	**16150215**	**12737908**
一、按轻重工业分	**Grouped by Light & Heavy Industry**			
轻工业	Light Industry	3402920	6413557	3703233
重工业	Heavy Industry	8225128	9736657	9034675
二、按所有制分	**Grouped by Ownership**			
国有企业	State – owned Enterprises	–	552621	–
集体企业	Collective – owned Enterprises	–	–	–
股份合作企业	Cooperative Enterprises	–	13877	–
联营企业	Joint Ownership Enterprises	–	–	–
有限责任公司	Limited Liability Corporations	5628684	4119925	4698670
股份有限公司	Share – holding Corporations Ltd.	610731	3004456	908589
私营企业	Private Enterprises	3215010	6060666	5890741
外商及港澳台投资企业	Enterprises with Investment from Foreign、Hong Kong、Macao and Taiwan	2173623	2398669	1210799
其他企业	Other Enterprises	–	–	–
合计中:国有控股企业	Of the Total:Controlling Share Hold Enterprises	3291079	1637236	1678259
三、按企业规模分	**Grouped by Size of Enterprises**			
大型企业	Large	5236277	2946996	1461269
中型企业	Medium – sized	3478419	5400792	3272904
小微企业	Small	2913352	7802427	8003734

continued (10000 yuan)

临安区 Lin'an	经济技术开发区 Economic and Technological Development Zone	西湖风景名胜区 The West Lake Scenic Zone	桐庐县 Tonglu	淳安县 Chun'an	建德市 Jiande
7410902	**14994524**	**–**	**3912387**	**1881302**	**4020244**
2521133	6824628	–	1694907	1205754	1421663
4889769	8169897	–	2217479	675549	2598580
188887	30150	–	107295	73937	–
–	–	–	–	–	3022
–	–	–	–	–	–
–	–	–	–	–	–
1723081	2079356	–	871415	205275	1215529
2191957	114920	–	67787	196007	751928
2885712	1161513	–	2116676	1156966	1856601
412468	11456179	–	749214	249117	193164
–	–	–	–	–	–
604820	2734703	–	697009	95247	420954
1873412	6198085	–	594806	–	668106
1996815	4826232	–	890685	732303	1096540
3540675	3970208	–	2426895	1148999	2255597

4－08 分地区工业

Value of Industrial

单位:万元

项 目	Item	全 市 Total	市 区 Urban District	上城区 Shangcheng
规模以上工业合计	**Industrial above Designated Size**	**127627244**	**117960521**	**7489845**
一、按轻重工业分	**Grouped by Light & Heavy Industry**			
轻工业	Light Industry	45901122	41614458	3302561
重工业	Heavy Industry	81726122	76346063	4187284
二、按所有制分	**Grouped by Ownership**			
国有企业	State－owned Enterprises	1869153	1687921	843
集体企业	Collective－owned Enterprises	5869	2847	－
股份合作企业	Cooperative Enterprises	35126	35126	－
联营企业	Joint Ownership Enterprises	4787	4787	－
有限责任公司	Limited Liability Corporations	43155861	40913280	7011519
股份有限公司	Share－holding Corporations Ltd.	13987608	12989760	334536
私营企业	Private Enterprises	35869592	30812383	124515
外商及港澳台投资企业	Enterprises with Investment from Foreign、Hong Kong、Macao and Taiwan	32488634	31303802	18433
其他企业	Other Enterprises	210615	210615	－
合计中:国有控股企业	Of the Total:Controlling Share Hold Enterprises	25035820	23853373	3372752
三、按企业规模分	**Grouped by Size of Enterprises**			
大型企业	Large	44892019	43634772	7194917
中型企业	Medium－sized	35507241	32822835	153357
小微企业	Small	47227983	41502914	141571

销售产值(2017 年)

Products Sales by Region(2017)

(10000 yuan)

下城区 Xiacheng	江干区 Jianggan	拱墅区 Gongshu	西湖区 Xihu	高新(滨江)区 Hi-Tech (Binjiang)	萧山区 Xiaoshan
416338	**1388097**	**1872734**	**2241278**	**17115158**	**36482388**
50952	216763	830547	758237	1472024	15816750
365386	1171334	1042187	1483040	15643134	20665639
–	–	–	–	6990	909589
–	2847	–	–	–	–
7860	–	2964	–	–	10216
4787	–	–	–	–	–
127619	137639	1099149	726259	7341777	11932843
215419	49919	158228	77404	3446235	2488787
18779	232351	438974	619530	922460	12639763
41873	965340	173420	818084	5397697	8480886
–	–	–	–	–	–
278399	46964	360675	361796	7370241	5206458
212403	868098	660831	767689	10197815	11097090
45204	203683	617109	709436	3953885	11920954
158731	316317	594795	764153	2963458	13464344

单位:万元　　　　　　　　　　　　　4－08　续表

项　目	Item	大江东产业集聚区 Dajiangdong Industry Cluster District	余杭区 Yuhang	富阳区 Fuyang
规模以上工业合计	**Industrial above Designated Size**	**11431400**	**16011875**	**12647245**
一、按轻重工业分	**Grouped by Light & Heavy Industry**			
轻工业	Light Industry	3320488	6384366	3675083
重工业	Heavy Industry	8110912	9627509	8972162
二、按所有制分	**Grouped by Ownership**			
国有企业	State－owned Enterprises	－	552621	－
集体企业	Collective－owned Enterprises	－	－	－
股份合作企业	Cooperative Enterprises	－	14086	－
联营企业	Joint Ownership Enterprises	－	－	－
有限责任公司	Limited Liability Corporations	5558259	4097602	4687505
股份有限公司	Share－holding Corporations Ltd.	587437	3038775	900395
私营企业	Private Enterprises	3179887	5970916	5837745
外商及港澳台投资企业	Enterprises with Investment from Foreign、Hong Kong、Macao and Taiwan	2105817	2337875	1191652
其他企业	Other Enterprises	－	－	－
合计中:国有控股企业	Of the Total:Controlling Share Hold Enterprises	3287993	1635878	1662088
三、按企业规模分	**Grouped by Size of Enterprises**			
大型企业	Large	5236123	2941998	1460036
中型企业	Medium－sized	3330918	5332636	3235695
小微企业	Small	2864359	7737242	7951514

continued (10000 yuan)

临安区 Lin'an	经济技术开发区 Economic and Technological Development Zone	西湖风景名胜区 The West Lake Scenic Zone	桐庐县 Tonglu	淳安县 Chun'an	建德市 Jiande
7331314	**14960423**	**–**	**3825725**	**1857543**	**3983456**
2510466	6596710	–	1681749	1192122	1412794
4820849	8363714	–	2143976	665420	2570662
188887	28992	–	107295	73937	–
–	–	–	–	–	3021
–	–	–	–	–	–
–	–	–	–	–	–
1703118	2048250	–	830319	199644	1212618
2178497	97740	–	65914	182716	749218
2847770	1159582	–	2084141	1151918	1821149
404709	11473832	–	738055	249327	197449
–	–	–	–	–	–
572287	2982011	–	667349	95247	419851
1853375	6380522	–	589672	–	667575
2003361	4647516	–	874117	718782	1091507
3474579	3932385	–	2361935	1138761	2224374

4－09 全市规模以上工业

Main Economic Indicators of Industrial

单位:万元

项 目	Item	企业单位数（个） Number of Enterprises (unit)	亏损企业(个) Loss Making Enterprises (unit)	工业总产值(当年价格) Gross Industrial Output Value (current price)	新产品产值 Output of New Products
总 计	**Total**	**5533**	**753**	**129637623**	**45282350**
按隶属关系分	**Grouped by Subordination**				
中 央 属	Central	37	7	6333067	328264
省 属	Provincial	44	8	4442398	710773
市 属	Municipal	128	16	7603353	2739969
县(市)属	County and below	56	10	3308420	736927
按所有制分	**Grouped by Ownership**				
国有企业	State－owned Enterprises	10		1870409	5253
集体企业	Collective－owned Enterprises	2		5868	
股份合作企业	Cooperative Enterprises	6		35534	3587
联营企业	Joint Ownership Enterprises	1		4787	
有限责任公司	Limited Liability Corporations	920	133	43856526	18375955
股份有限公司	Share－holding Corporations Ltd.	227	26	14068352	7389350
私营企业	Private Enterprises	3511	426	36399394	9222915
外商及港澳台投资企业	Enterprises with Investment from Foreign、Hong Kong、Macao and Taiwan	850	168	33183636	10148125
其他企业	Other Enterprises	6	－	213117	137165
按企业规模分	**Grouped by Size of Enterprises**				
大型企业	Large	125	8	45603071	21764289
中型企业	Medium－sized	641	82	36246596	13147655
小微企业	Small	4767	663	47787956	10370405
按轻重工业分	**Grouped by Light & Heavy Industry**				
轻工业	Light Industry	2778	386	47114960	10994845
重工业	Heavy Industry	2755	367	82522663	34287505

企业主要经济指标(2017 年)(一)
Enterprises Above Designated Size(2017)(Ⅰ)

(10000 yuan)

工业销售产值 Value of Industrial Products Sales	出口交货值 Export delivery value	实收资本 Total Capital Hold	国家资本 State Capital	个人资本 Personal Capital	港澳台资本 Hongkong, Macau and TaiWan Capital	外商资本 Foreign Capital	就业人员年平均人数(人) Annual Average Number of Staff and Workers (person)
127627244	**17457440**	**33246246**	**3752600**	**7336633**	**1958176**	**3738517**	**1055690**
6249673	10900	1005408	397864	7831	1582	179035	11083
4339322	153811	1551938	441005	152772	9799	193088	16988
7798041	1210483	2071879	852131	203377	45125	195268	59585
3256692	175187	472737	50147	103935	30856	19001	18093
1869153		499811	258469				2923
5869		611					53
35126		4131		4131			612
4787		100					55
43155861	4193069	9109304	2118648	1165842	2909	58891	241060
13987608	1736296	5443023	641357	1952328	24884	31244	110589
35869592	4787261	6893400	8844	4027933		2525	409924
32488634	6740414	11264798	725283	184931	1930383	3645857	289561
210615	401	31068	–	1468	–	–	913
44892019	5924188	9167502	1222349	1348429	455993	1086190	269889
35507241	5731414	9035023	957720	1872987	572634	1089198	322407
47227983	5801839	15043720	1572531	4115216	929548	1563129	463394
45901122	7141814	10391428	312295	2787935	944770	1559329	487719
81726122	10315627	22854818	3440305	4548698	1013406	2179188	567971

单位:万元 4－09 续表1

项 目	Item	企业单位数（个）Number of Enterprises (unit)	亏损企业(个) Loss Making Enterprises (unit)	工业总产值（当年价格）Gross Industrial Output Value (current price)	新产品产值 Output of New Products
按市、县分	**Grouped by County**				
市 区	Urban District	4726	683	119823690	42120141
#萧山区	Xiaoshan	1544	193	37270896	11944861
余杭区	Yuhang	1141	190	16150215	7197204
富阳区	Fuyang	644	87	12737908	3395572
临安区	Lin'an	597	99	7410902	2670762
桐庐县	Tonglu	338	33	3912387	1321573
淳安县	Chun'an	117	8	1881302	230391
建德市	Jiande	352	29	4020244	1610245
按国民经济行业分	**Grouped by Economic Sector**				
采矿业	Mining and Quarrying	23	2	236448	7177
煤炭开采和洗选业	Coal Mining and Dressing	1		2360	
黑色金属矿采选业	Ferrous Metals Mining and Dressing				
有色金属矿采选业	Nonferrous Metals Mining and Dressing	4		55776	
非金属矿采选业	Nonmetal Minerals Mining and Dressing	18	2	178312	7177
制造业	Manufacturing Industry	5425	736	119503190	45127570
农副食品加工业	Agricultural Products Processing	126	14	1247513	160240
食品制造业	Food Manufacturing	110	22	1768133	243494
酒、饮料和精制茶制造业	Wine, Beverage and Tea Manufacturing	53	4	1940828	322790
烟草制品业	Tobacco Processing	2		3385103	55539
纺织业	Textile Industry	658	64	7426443	1608520
纺织服装、服饰业	Textile Products and Costune Indnstry	283	66	2343858	639382
皮革、毛皮、羽毛及其制品和制鞋业	Leather. Furs. Downand Related and Shoes Products	120	21	1324555	221808
木材加工和木、竹、藤、棕、草制品业	Timber Processing, Bamboo, Cane, Palm Fiber and Straw Products	35	3	246133	83298
家具制造业	Furniture Manufacturing	81	7	1282574	427349

continued 1 (10000 yuan)

工业销售产值 Value of Industrial Products Sales	出口交货值 Export delivery value	实收资本 Total Capital Hold	国家资本 State Capital	个人资本 Personal Capital	港澳台资本 Hongkong, Macau and TaiWan Capital	外商资本 Foreign Capital	就业人员年平均人数(人) Annual Average Number of Staff and Workers (person)
117960521	15774316	31103755	3479756	6575506	1896374	3615134	956570
36482388	4062022	10853480	1481711	2038319	821100	1434335	307354
16011875	2562278	3761256	105387	1301433	311291	284131	190761
12647245	981193	2908402	308617	1007615	41980	190121	92307
7331314	1198629	3590572	584825	538261	31847	113567	72758
3825725	903679	922756	61748	272141	38610	77730	45230
1857543	141238	425206	66892	184584	5647	3405	17209
3983456	638207	794529	144205	304402	17544	42248	36681
233122	–	84957	31799	14638	–	–	1724
2289		98		98			15
54717		31900	24719	7181			571
176116		52959	7080	7359			1138
117515980	17457440	30867625	2378163	7293350	1892668	3676116	1034218
1238075	46257	215588	20	86919	31995	20960	9176
1763015	91271	575841	26320	85679	57884	185651	23277
1905660	23162	523604	20550	71937	61404	174814	15031
3271885	9629	70992		3630	1400		3024
7318986	1427619	1479176		644532	134706	177732	104329
2312127	1048642	588254	4230	110484	267689	91039	52033
1312212	698964	224437	449	71857	23034	20243	20590
243966	42832	64291		38762		98	3838
1187725	640884	291516		67363	17534	81783	30228

项　目	Item	企业单位数(个) Number of Enterprises (unit)	亏损企业(个) Loss Making Enterprises (unit)	工业总产值(当年价格) Gross Industrial Output Value (current price)	新产品产值 Output of New Products
造纸和纸制品业	Paper Making and Paper Products	2273	38	3908456	670927
印刷和记录媒介复制业	Printing and Record Media	83	19	656561	123901
文教、工美、体育和娱乐用品制造业	Cultural, Educational. Industrial Arts. Sports and Entertainment Goods	109	11	1682273	449605
石油、煤炭及其他燃料加工业	Petroleum, Coal and Other Fuel Processing	12		105696	22824
化学原料和化学制品制造业	Raw Chemical Materials and Chemical Products	308	28	9685240	2932956
医药制造业	Medical and Pharmaceutical Products	95	4	5043841	1367656
化学纤维制造业	Chemical Fiber	109	7	5279986	1385153
橡胶和塑料制品业	Rubber and Plastic Products	285	39	5629009	1759216
非金属矿物制品业	Nonmetal Minerals Products	296	39	4083620	721893
黑色金属冶炼和压延加工业	Ferrous Metals Smelting and Processing	52	8	1562854	285667
有色金属冶炼和压延加工业	Nonferrous Metals Smelting and Processing	57	10	3716847	500187
金属制品业	Metals Products	348	52	5173740	1571563
通用设备制造业	Ordinary Machinery	484	53	9123228	4116496
专用设备制造业	For Special Purpose Equipment Manufacturing	224	44	2035210	751883
汽车制造业	Automobile Manufacturing	204	26	7594016	4496584
铁路、船舶、航空航天和其他运输设备制造业	Railway. watercraft. Avigation spaceflight and other Equipment Manufacturing	50	7	538290	154103
电气机械和器材制造业	Electric Equipment and Machinery	471	91	11768396	5750351
计算机、通信和其他电子设备制造业	Computers. Telecommunications and Other Electronic Equipment Manufacturing	312	42	17499133	12841757
仪器仪表制造业	Instruments and Meters Manufacturing	135	11	2724383	1258908
其他制造业	Other Manufacturing	23	1	247557	103485
废弃资源综合利用业	Multiple Utilization of Waste Resouces	27	5	479712	100039
金属制品、机械和设备修理业	Metal Products, Machinery and Equipment Repair				
电力、燃气及水的生产和供应业	Produotion and supply of electricity, gas & water	85	15	9897985	147603
电力、热力生产和供应业	Production and Supply of Electric Power and Hot Water	50	6	7171033	137299
燃气生产和供应业	Production and Supply of Gas	15	5	2283623	
水的生产和供应业	Production and Supply of Tap Water	20	4	443330	10304

continued 2 (10000 yuan)

工业销售产值 Value of Industrial Products Sales	出口交货值 Export delivery value	实收资本 Total Capital Hold	国家资本 State Capital	个人资本 Personal Capital	港澳台资本 Hongkong, Macau and TaiWan Capital	外商资本 Foreign Capital	就业人员年平均人数(人) Annual Average Number of Staff and Workers (person)
3895959	210399	662714	2235	315943	28235	17546	34597
636184	12228	204401	22851	51650	35362	3760	9377
1643794	282915	250643	396	57002	22986	93846	17241
102090	1097	24737		21248	334		594
9534727	937549	2224110	48825	330303	45847	239572	49123
4508528	483870	1161084	188124	53820	18151	256751	35984
5110013	367878	1450666		402160	114683	58414	24853
5894620	885263	958007	60046	275296	52348	218363	54021
4044028	141307	912824	62501	329448	55098	123996	34334
1512234	23260	203622	5571	67289	7839	7172	5570
3719598	282593	356967	6875	62416	3026	18812	7467
5090562	900383	953926	11925	464164	135087	27371	46721
9003437	1472614	4342002	572663	794645	95915	334036	97002
2011429	417855	732074	39576	215650	92890	160852	31378
7578597	541777	3257766	1116641	338899	104020	547234	51960
523060	144853	147125	30085	32373		9651	6965
11561250	1911981	3634774	71217	647124	243065	340524	96129
17204218	3893497	4022516	85065	1230167	226449	386196	127563
2672210	491214	1215617	2000	343951	15689	66479	35424
251901	25647	19854		11276		5037	3911
463892		98497		67363		8185	2478
9878142	–	2293664	1342638	28645	65508	62401	19748
7171517		1249540	481587	19420	31700	9819	12349
2287782		477105	358976	1225	31308	52582	2463
418843		567019	502075	8000	2500		4936

4－10 全市规模以上工业

Main Economic Indicators of Industrial

单位:万元

项 目	Item	资产合计 Total Assets	流动资产合计 Total Circulating Funds	应收账款 Receivables	存货 Stock
总 计	**Total**	**154032990**	**90095810**	**30466099**	**18573874**
按隶属关系分	**Grouped by Subordination**				
中 央 属	Central	6627092	3702843	691358	1985684
省 属	Provincial	5384411	2235093	616819	370340
市 属	Municipal	11571854	6015972	1509783	1390758
县(市)属	County and below	3090164	1768989	304973	436089
按所有制分	**Grouped by Ownership**				
国有企业	State－owned Enterprises	1011289	164430	12360	15584
集体企业	Collective－owned Enterprises	10881	10476	806	295
股份合作企业	Cooperative Enterprises	42345	35402	9249	2727
联营企业	Joint Ownership Enterprises	1341	1291	983	270
有限责任公司	Limited Liability Corporations	52254415	27988206	11119565	6175010
股份有限公司	Share－holding Corporations Ltd.	28679706	14514603	3876484	2559258
私营企业	Private Enterprises	34454421	22438139	7430393	5018673
外商及港澳台投资企业	Enterprises with Investment from Foreign、Hong Kong、Macao and Taiwan	37391165	24803752	7931066	4783398
其他企业	Other Enterprises	187428	139511	85194	18661
按企业规模分	**Grouped by Size of Enterprises**				
大型企业	Large	56466438	32589435	12398199	6826354
中型企业	Medium－sized	45976015	25183161	7346302	5096768
小微企业	Small	51590537	32323213	10721598	6650752
按轻重工业分	**Grouped by Light & Heavy Industry**				
轻工业	Light Industry	51541668	29596260	7066049	8022074
重工业	Heavy Industry	102491322	60499550	23400050	10551801

企业主要经济指标(2017 年)(二)

Enterprises Above Designated Size(2017)(Ⅱ)

(10000 yuan)

产成品 Finished Products	固定资产合计 Fixed Assets	累计折旧 Accumulated Depreciation	本年折旧 Depreciation of the year	负债合计 Total Liabilities	流动负债合计 Total Current Liabilities	非流动负债合计 Total Non－current Liabilities	所有者权益合计 Creditors´Equity
7133950	**29806329**	**25241189**	**3430931**	**84200020**	**72797103**	**10862548**	**69800333**
184302	2029392	1688099	213262	3231952	2498062	733890	3395139
182431	1870720	1441730	194885	2352716	1683031	466091	3031694
674921	2617707	2100301	271948	6185912	4626442	1552841	5385940
99459	770377	675054	72315	1715218	1490540	218939	1374945
6330	823587	839344	127155	285697	220068	65628	725592
39	310	1760	110	5163	5163		5718
1760	4841	6453	776	17579	17579		24766
129	50	195	14	985	985		356
1869517	11511277	9760743	1296331	33401570	26872579	6403329	18850407
994384	3523877	2548976	320816	11392602	9462446	1722281	17287101
2119885	7067456	5461852	864704	20557612	19633381	754549	13867728
2126496	6839154	6586832	817386	18397046	16449239	1916761	18993003
15411	35778	35035	3639	141765	135662	–	45662
2145356	8753250	8125193	1072386	29655755	24916606	4733931	26810682
2163446	9517714	8141326	1122999	24967283	21514990	3388892	21008726
2825148	11535365	8974670	1235546	29576983	26365507	2739726	21980924
2952316	10443967	9061202	1232592	26776078	24885897	1680642	24735414
4181634	19362362	16179988	2198339	57423942	47911206	9181907	45064919

项　目	Item	资产合计 Total Assets	流动资产合　计 Total Circulating Funds	应收账款 Receivables	存　货 Stock
按区域分	**Grouped by County**				
市　区	Urban District	144718720	85530009	28876444	17640828
#萧山区	Xiaoshan	49775338	25263746	8598610	5104753
余杭区	Yuhang	18641302	11822920	3878246	2559677
富阳区	Fuyang	15611450	8944440	2442880	1794534
临安区	Lin'an	8916547	5512788	1935225	926497
桐庐县	Tonglu	3854429	2047001	745110	418841
淳安县	Chun'an	1493562	710917	274467	155288
建德市	Jiande	3966279	1807883	570079	358917
按国民经济行业分	**Grouped by Economic Sector**				
采矿业	Mining and Quarrying	366475	176775	27671	11000
煤炭开采和洗选业	Coal Mining and Dressing	2026	559	114	112
黑色金属矿采选业	Ferrous Metals Mining and Dressing				
有色金属矿采选业	Nonferrous Metals Mining and Dressing	96093	32706	2109	3766
非金属矿采选业	Nonmetal Minerals Mining and Dressing	268355	143510	25449	7122
制造业	Manufacturing Industry	143562500	88057633	30226822	18486779
农副食品加工业	Agricultural Products Processing	964402	562677	184217	167339
食品制造业	Food Manufacturing	1929818	1061745	236393	216825
酒、饮料和精制茶制造业	Wine, Beverage and Tea Manufacturing	1975530	1035017	306559	203003
烟草制品业	Tobacco Processing	3366681	2422247	224525	1857838
纺织业	Textile Industry	7597890	4507437	1045103	1111733
纺织服装、服饰业	Textile Products and Costune Indnstry	2346137	1537620	333588	393397
皮革、毛皮、羽毛及其制品和制鞋业	Leather. Furs. Downand Related and Shoes Products	1151038	822775	304607	273138
木材加工和木、竹、藤、棕、草制品业	Timber Processing, Bamboo, Cane, Palm Fiber and Straw Products	217053	116387	31778	25871
家具制造业	Furniture Manufacturing	1434461	932457	221703	168847

continued 1 (10000 yuan)

产成品 Finished Products	固定资产合计 Fixed Assets	累计折旧 Accumulated Depreciation	本年折旧 Depreciation of the year	负债合计 Total Liabilities	流动负债合计 Total Current Liabilities	非流动负债合计 Total Non－current Liabilities	所有者权益合计 Creditors′Equity
6754733	27007561	23085098	3118549	79211587	68295202	10429046	65480058
2169258	9923609	7978365	1143138	29509724	25928991	3485269	20265597
1040245	3864713	2747017	432484	10096787	9050711	1035010	8544502
740943	3205536	2180269	333607	9761942	8219092	1515917	5839076
398539	1542504	1063963	156067	4377887	3831443	405147	4523168
173718	1088396	762539	119212	2236368	2085423	116690	1618057
65085	453499	365643	57147	702370	617026	76218	785637
140414	1256874	1027910	136023	2049696	1799451	240595	1916581
5327	61948	38880	6687	187167	161206	25653	179307
79	729	426	114	1331	1331		695
2747	30559	5665	1082	26625	19664	6709	69468
2501	30661	32790	5490	159212	140211	18944	109144
7112238	23356985	19022237	2730755	77756198	69870820	7546046	65773666
61196	215337	117091	20493	574464	533132	34804	389937
72912	495097	419330	68912	958735	942221	9893	971081
64669	720762	797632	91326	1107782	1060256	47526	867747
147214	497382	425057	56044	857382	857223	159	2509300
543283	1878081	1993505	250687	4421992	4250900	116718	3173461
187746	500542	348326	41523	1172367	1081943	81077	1172659
38064	187170	99664	15146	807600	778184	27287	343436
10947	41407	21997	4034	146742	137546	7447	67187
59002	207855	130070	15326	680624	675624	4541	753836

单位:万元 4-10 续表2

项 目	Item	资产合计 Total Assets	流动资产合计 Total Circulating Funds	应收账款 Receivables	存货 Stock
造纸和纸制品业	Paper Making and Paper Products	4308026	2778556	792804	473241
印刷和记录媒介复制业	Printing and Record Media	817279	490086	180695	109083
文教、工美、体育和娱乐用品制造业	Cultural, Educational. Industrial Arts. Sports and Entertainment Goods	834755	543073	98174	210140
石油、煤炭及其他燃料加工业	Petroleum, Coal and Other Fuel Processing	107821	82638	22203	18909
化学原料和化学制品制造业	Raw Chemical Materials and Chemical Products	11159476	5363958	1509048	903301
医药制造业	Medical and Pharmaceutical Products	5608526	3111926	830547	966521
化学纤维制造业	Chemical Fiber	8240875	3057386	334905	647172
橡胶和塑料制品业	Rubber and Plastic Products	5225970	3057401	1112019	740682
非金属矿物制品业	Nonmetal Minerals Products	4937232	3251942	1646225	458372
黑色金属冶炼和压延加工业	Ferrous Metals Smelting and Processing	1063159	765398	73803	284229
有色金属冶炼和压延加工业	Nonferrous Metals Smelting and Processing	2594277	1819573	252206	469054
金属制品业	Metals Products	4631446	3108918	1038893	927336
通用设备制造业	Ordinary Machinery	13077836	8347697	2620462	1653097
专用设备制造业	For Special Purpose Equipment Manufacturing	2938584	2034328	704948	482916
汽车制造业	Automobile Manufacturing	15111568	7526463	4414877	830922
铁路、船舶、航空航天和其他运输设备制造业	Railway. watercraft. Avigation spaceflight and other Equipment Manufacturing	604171	408220	123115	83312
电气机械和器材制造业	Electric Equipment and Machinery	15491412	9997397	3691400	1840149
计算机、通信和其他电子设备制造业	Computers. Telecommunications and Other Electronic Equipment Manufacturing	20517170	15439901	6715229	2236315
仪器仪表制造业	Instruments and Meters Manufacturing	4574231	3356066	1081462	597799
其他制造业	Other Manufacturing	209826	171194	14059	35965
废弃资源综合利用业	Multiple Utilization of Waste Resouces	525851	347151	81280	100274
金属制品、机械和设备修理业	Metal Products, Machinery and Equipment Repair				
电力、燃气及水的生产和供应业	Produotion and supply of electricity, gas & water	10104015	1861402	211606	76095
电力、热力生产和供应业	Production and Supply of Electric Power and Hot Water	5635213	838164	147848	31798
燃气生产和供应业	Production and Supply of Gas	1613737	260606	35792	20266
水的生产和供应业	Production and Supply of Tap Water	2855066	762631	27965	24032

continued 2 (10000 yuan)

产成品 Finished Products	固定资产合计 Fixed Assets	累计折旧 Accumulated Depreciation	本年折旧 Depreciation of the year	负债合计 Total Liabilities	流动负债合计 Total Current Liabilities	非流动负债合计 Total Non－current Liabilities	所有者权益合计 Creditors´Equity
209678	887051	815387	111348	3139297	2944788	134842	1145245
49257	247788	292707	33016	466692	433067	30360	350585
51357	195595	191184	26400	418262	397104	16850	416493
12009	17223	14843	2022	57186	56207	979	50635
432769	2386489	1751334	249095	5382821	4718656	652797	5776651
438679	1154390	594213	117546	2368004	1926263	438563	3240521
392930	1119267	1185815	144378	4787277	4442462	325486	3453597
414163	1216289	1526949	216937	3035220	2761733	254669	2190746
261007	1035850	986207	126146	3225627	3072839	127174	1711602
152029	153449	250632	25255	623158	565577	53780	440001
96957	435624	226030	39997	1881690	1763103	118587	712587
310361	846384	618741	93163	2647586	2516069	89360	1981430
621910	1888893	1435820	197816	6533863	5865079	628726	6543967
140128	553995	455210	58519	1529610	1385646	141161	1408972
380940	2193258	1189406	238221	10461962	8469369	1991640	4649604
24814	145447	84629	13979	339913	325669	13833	264257
906719	2269055	1492628	232242	7703085	6448694	1245139	7788319
837426	1403050	1172194	187873	10171992	9336963	823518	10345174
147263	341714	324991	42077	1776774	1662457	114113	2797456
10202	25302	26964	2704	74040	74040		135786
36608	97241	33681	8531	404454	388007	15020	121397
16384	6387396	6180073	693489	6256655	2765077	3290849	3847359
3136	4083854	4733532	536679	3579320	1508457	2069136	2055891
6751	1196658	399842	64989	1128574	628312	301260	485163
6498	1106884	1046698	91822	1548760	628307	920454	1306305

4－11 全市规模以上工业

Main Economic Indicators of Industrial

单位：万元

项 目	Item	主营业务收入 Revenues in Main Business	主营业务成本 Costs in Main Business	主营业务税金及附加 Sales Taxes and Extra Charges in Main Business
总　计	**Total**	**132095872**	**105843704**	**2947058**
按隶属关系分	**Grouped by Subordination**			
中央属	Central	6363182	3665860	2087206
省　属	Provincial	4405899	3916426	20582
市　属	Municipal	7895862	6015068	55051
县(市)属	County and Below	3306968	2990246	13203
按所有制分	**Grouped by Ownership**			
国有企业	State－owned Enterprises	1849041	1762213	6826
集体企业	Collective－owned Enterprises	5869	5402	10
股份合作企业	Cooperative Enterprises	36021	28526	232
联营企业	Joint Ownership Enterprises	4787	4586	17
有限责任公司	Limited Liability Corporations	44395963	35523434	2414658
股份有限公司	Share－holding Corporations Ltd.	14345986	11021400	97144
私营企业	Private Enterprises	36504909	31206555	184545
外商及港澳台投资企业	Enterprises with Investment from Foreign、Hong Kong、Macao and Taiwan	34668706	26027728	240830
其他企业	Other Enterprises	284590	263861	2798
按企业规模分	**Grouped by Size of Enterprises**			
大型企业	Large	46588585	34483737	2477881
中型企业	Medium－sized	36001854	29536183	201875
小微企业	Small	49505433	41823784	267302
按轻重工业分	**Grouped by Light & Heavy Industry**			
轻工业	Light Industry	46729114	34988986	2365060
重工业	Heavy Industry	85366758	70854719	581998

企业主要经济指标(2017 年)(三)

Enterprises Above Designated Size(2017)(Ⅲ)

(10000 yuan)

销售费用 Sales Expenses	管理费用 Management Expenses	财务费用 Financial Expenses	利息支出 Interest Expenditure	营业利润 Business Profits	利润总额 Total Profits	利税总额 Total Pre – tax Profits	本年应交增值税 Value Added Tax Payable
6454486	**8146611**	**1335894**	**1398997**	**9135707**	**9985605**	**17745177**	**4795465**
139328	183290	43738	61772	218668	230368	2889952	571023
78235	262202	31415	38498	194222	197483	329347	110923
778686	689799	52488	84537	329134	431036	768485	280586
31359	99013	44607	46409	149232	164658	364539	185732
557	57194	2429	2677	20822	24117	91402	60301
25	270	115	120	47	75	161	77
605	3291	409	443	3015	2072	4046	1741
36	134	–		14	14	159	129
1630862	2099413	431144	443987	2749937	2963986	7146707	1762152
886765	1297734	172561	202375	1385084	1525174	2122351	497529
1082361	2091917	512013	490051	1627668	1839860	3184057	1155844
2851486	2595220	216315	258240	3334731	3618400	5178259	1314361
1790	1439	909	1106	14389	11906	18036	3331
2971672	2793155	250088	292745	4564079	4847678	9364468	2032535
1775163	2286231	383854	404437	2262405	2486266	3828972	1138662
1707652	3067225	701952	701816	2309222	2651662	4551738	1624268
3348369	2832769	554238	584899	3182451	3457535	8078083	2247414
3106117	5313842	781656	814098	5953256	6528071	9667094	2548051

单位:万元 4-11 续表1

项 目	Item	主营业务收入 Revenues in Main Business	主营业务成本 Costs in Main Business	主营业务税金及附加 Sales Taxes and Extra Charges in Main Business
按市、县分	**Grouped by County**			
市 区	Urban District	122766469	98037853	2882460
#萧山区	Xiaoshan	38645476	33382145	340462
余杭区	Yuhang	16155305	13058753	96578
富阳区	Fuyang	13123397	11524733	71056
临安区	Lin'an	7387192	6119597	47866
桐庐县	Tonglu	3606251	3076479	21197
淳安县	Chun'an	1756685	1461637	14814
建德市	Jiande	3966467	3267736	28587
按国民经济行业分	**Grouped by Economic Sector**			
采矿业	Mining and Quarrying	215215	151355	5848
煤炭开采和洗选业	Coal Mining and Dressing	2289	1603	140
黑色金属矿采选业	Ferrous Metals Mining and Dressing			
有色金属矿采选业	Nonferrous Metals Mining and Dressing	38582	24331	937
非金属矿采选业	Nonmetal Minerals Mining and Dressing	174344	125420	4771
制造业	Manufacturing Industry	121962876	96385154	2908446
农副食品加工业	Agricultural Products Processing	1253128	1090291	4506
食品制造业	Food Manufacturing	1799673	1381623	8965
酒、饮料和精制茶制造业	Wine, Beverage and Tea Manufacturing	2163856	1503583	43648
烟草制品业	Tobacco Processing	3225425	721656	2066490
纺织业	Textile Industry	7261535	6335884	35810
纺织服装、服饰业	Textile Products and Costune Indnstry	2354488	1951028	15646
皮革、毛皮、羽毛及其制品和制鞋业	Leather. Furs. Downand Related and Shoes Products	1308084	1160170	6134
木材加工和木、竹、藤、棕、草制品业	Timber Processing, Bamboo, Cane, Palm Fiber and Straw Products	262427	221468	1369
家具制造业	Furniture Manufacturing	1219829	980196	8650

continued 1 (10000 yuan)

销售费用 Sales Expenses	管理费用 Management Expenses	财务费用 Financial Expenses	利息支出 Interest Expenditure	营业利润 Business Profits	利润总额 Total Profits	利税总额 Total Pre - tax Profits	本年应交增值税 Value Added Tax Payable
6064492	7650200	1230329	1297310	8555125	9344556	16711916	4484900
681830	1895677	461815	510821	2169720	2337409	3675567	993576
861534	1258666	160753	162399	938969	1075753	1754902	582570
239144	586961	296848	314728	600877	729712	1413703	612935
287537	504009	73673	72766	443772	493229	776103	235009
97641	219994	48320	43264	179796	202693	339368	115479
87526	64770	16368	16374	134647	145163	223012	63035
204826	211647	40877	42050	266139	293194	453833	132052
4620	15001	6250	6547	36075	35868	52388	10672
94	235			217	219	468	110
531	6622	466	424	5621	5611	9811	3264
3994	8144	5784	6123	30237	30039	42109	7299
6412011	7957597	1235336	1280502	8746201	9566232	17040864	4550494
53470	45753	15868	17368	45589	48581	78737	25437
182859	123822	7962	12577	104960	147660	241620	84713
412067	72462	8933	12798	133066	150469	295711	100616
89132	127789	-1221	3075	255051	250790	2772485	455154
125812	379675	101982	115607	328398	348160	606662	221992
71823	211768	30870	25489	104962	120925	243058	106219
38869	53526	23589	17342	28625	30191	72702	36298
6466	17478	3255	3228	16646	17056	24617	6192
111815	80108	12728	8432	115328	122906	243877	112236

项 目	Item	主营业务收入 Revenues in Main Business	主营业务成本 Costs in Main Business	主营业务税金及附加 Sales Taxes and Extra Charges in Main Business
造纸和纸制品业	Paper Making and Paper Products	3889544	3380523	33423
印刷和记录媒介复制业	Printing and Record Media	662603	562049	3463
文教、工美、体育和娱乐用品制造业	Cultural, Educational. Industrial Arts. Sports and Entertainment Goods	1637650	1491957	5530
石油、煤炭及其他燃料加工业	Petroleum, Coal and Other Fuel Processing	122342	105159	674
化学原料和化学制品制造业	Raw Chemical Materials and Chemical Products	11360827	9276381	53870
医药制造业	Medical and Pharmaceutical Products	4473625	2038325	47074
化学纤维制造业	Chemical Fiber	5552338	5082187	11563
橡胶和塑料制品业	Rubber and Plastic Products	5838610	5065621	27952
非金属矿物制品业	Nonmetal Minerals Products	4074070	3387946	22093
黑色金属冶炼和压延加工业	Ferrous Metals Smelting and Processing	1644781	1537233	3540
有色金属冶炼和压延加工业	Nonferrous Metals Smelting and Processing	4172036	3938749	5354
金属制品业	Metals Products	5154313	4570154	20892
通用设备制造业	Ordinary Machinery	9277101	7443963	58621
专用设备制造业	For Special Purpose Equipment Manufacturing	2031162	1507550	14862
汽车制造业	Automobile Manufacturing	7624211	5998121	210493
铁路、船舶、航空航天和其他运输设备制造业	Railway. watercraft. Avigation spaceflight and other Equipment Manufacturing	537407	440215	7312
电气机械和器材制造业	Electric Equipment and Machinery	11927158	9749159	64636
计算机、通信和其他电子设备制造业	Computers. Telecommunications and Other Electronic Equipment Manufacturing	17679836	12999549	102665
仪器仪表制造业	Instruments and Meters Manufacturing	2665892	1795003	18767
其他制造业	Other Manufacturing	335276	289119	1932
废弃资源综合利用业	Multiple Utilization of Waste Resouces	453652	380297	2513
金属制品、机械和设备修理业	Metal Products, Machinery and Equipment Repair			
电力、燃气及水的生产和供应业	Produotion and supply of electricity, gas & water	9917780	9307195	32764
电力、热力生产和供应业	Production and Supply of Electric Power and Hot Water	7158006	6677370	22783
燃气生产和供应业	Production and Supply of Gas	2313024	2270848	5015
水的生产和供应业	Production and Supply of Tap Water	446750	358978	4967

continued 2 (10000 yuan)

销售费用 Sales Expenses	管理费用 Management Expenses	财务费用 Financial Expenses	利息支出 Interest Expenditure	营业利润 Business Profits	利润总额 Total Profits	利税总额 Total Pre - tax Profits	本年应交增值税 Value Added Tax Payable
83296	191511	113173	111076	85033	164224	426801	228597
17081	51881	6586	6622	34571	35846	61684	21998
30358	57855	14037	12367	40946	43233	82811	33723
4562	5018	2119	2161	5118	6641	9911	2595
610229	678616	107027	102064	782191	873363	1245791	318186
1207907	445227	30146	27405	817262	846605	1228218	334509
30692	125432	112948	124725	287476	293474	379972	73946
229764	303404	32977	53560	205526	222732	382762	131980
222411	192961	65149	66525	204647	214882	374033	136893
13554	23615	14736	16962	59524	60982	80737	16051
19420	58963	47037	59153	105917	110683	276935	160071
97994	272151	57046	57988	161163	186500	340095	132402
329290	769300	86547	87534	781163	852038	1261336	350311
120129	254677	20333	20094	133466	151789	251726	84783
160674	578950	24052	62202	695622	763552	1260792	285076
23379	52791	7983	4963	14862	17601	44279	19357
650873	814293	139989	146930	704623	766428	1142643	308370
1255731	1593016	127258	74639	2087585	2247435	2960573	609374
202404	349956	14785	17440	336725	392036	532662	120145
6036	11948	-1610	988	27247	27047	40170	10724
3914	13652	9053	9190	42913	52405	77465	22547
37856	174013	94308	111949	353431	383505	651925	234300
592	103266	57830	61473	317160	307282	527566	196888
19361	33183	15916	23777	944	6241	27796	16440
17903	37564	20561	26699	35327	69982	96563	20972

4-12 分行业规模以上工业

Main Economic Beneficial Indicators of Industrial

行 业	Sector
总 计	**Total**
煤炭开采和洗选业	Coal Mining and Dressing
黑色金属矿采选业	Ferrous Metals Mining and Dressing
有色金属矿采选业	Nonferrous Metals Mining and Dressing
非金属矿采选业	Nonmetal Minerals Mining and Dressing
农副食品加工业	Agricultural Products Processing
食品制造业	Food Manufacturing
酒、饮料和精制茶制造业	Wine, Beverage and Tea Manufacturing
烟草制品业	Tobacco Processing
纺织业	Textile Industry
纺织服装、服饰业	Textile Products and Costune Indnstry
皮革、毛皮、羽毛及其制品和制鞋业	Leather. Furs. Downand Related and Shoes Products
木材加工和木、竹、藤、棕、草制品业	Timber Processing, Bamboo, Cane, Palm Fiber and Straw Products
家具制造业	Furniture Manufacturing
造纸和纸制品业	Paper Making and Paper Products
印刷和记录媒介复制业	Printing and Record Media
文教、工美、体育和娱乐用品制造业	Cultural, Educational. Industrial Arts. Sports and Entertainment Goods
石油、煤炭及其他燃料加工业	Petroleum, Coal and Other Fuel Processing
化学原料和化学制品制造业	Raw Chemical Materials and Chemical Products
医药制造业	Medical and Pharmaceutical Products

企业主要经济效益指标(2017 年)
Enterprises Above Designated Size by Sector(2017)

每百元固定资产原值实现利税(元) Pre tax Profits per 100 Yuan Original Value of Fixed Assets (yuan)	每百元主营业务收入实现利税(元) Pre tax Profits per 100 yuan Revenues in Main Business (yuan)	产品销售率(%) Rate of Production Sold (%)	出口交货值占工业销售(%) Export delivery Value of the proportion of total sales value (%)	新产品产值率(%) New Product ratio (%)
32.63	**13.43**	**98.45**	**13.68**	**34.93**
40.55	20.45	97.01		
27.3	25.43	98.1		
58.3	24.15	98.77		4.03
23.53	6.28	99.24	3.74	12.84
23.43	13.43	99.71	5.18	13.77
19.66	13.67	98.19	1.22	16.63
300.62	85.96	96.66	0.29	1.64
15.79	8.35	98.55	19.51	21.66
28.3	10.32	98.65	45.35	27.28
25.87	5.56	99.07	53.27	16.75
43.65	9.38	99.12	17.56	33.84
71.39	19.99	92.6	53.96	33.32
25.25	10.97	99.68	5.4	17.17
11.3	9.31	96.9	1.92	18.87
22.28	5.06	97.71	17.21	26.73
31.42	8.1	96.59	1.07	21.59
29.84	10.97	98.45	9.83	30.28
71.66	27.45	89.39	10.73	27.12

4－12 续表

行 业	Sector
化学纤维制造业	Chemical Fiber
橡胶和塑料制品业	Rubber and Plastic Products
非金属矿物制品业	Nonmetal Minerals Products
黑色金属冶炼和压延加工业	Ferrous Metals Smelting and Processing
有色金属冶炼和压延加工业	Nonferrous Metals Smelting and Processing
金属制品业	Metals Products
通用设备制造业	Ordinary Machinery
专用设备制造业	For Special Purpose Equipment Manufacturing
汽车制造业	Automobile Manufacturing
铁路、船舶、航空航天和其他运输设备制造业	Railway. watercraft. Avigation spaceflight and other Equipment Manufacturing
电气机械和器材制造业	Electric Equipment and Machinery
计算机、通信和其他电子设备制造业	Computers. Telecommunications and Other Electronic Equipment Manufacturing
仪器仪表制造业	Instruments and Meters Manufacturing
其他制造业	Other Manufacturing
废弃资源综合利用业	Multiple Utilization of Waste Resouces
金属制品、机械和设备修理业	Metal Products, Machinery and Equipment Repair
电力、热力生产和供应业	Production and Supply of Electric Power and Hot Water
燃气生产和供应业	Production and Supply of Gas
水的生产和供应业	Production and Supply of Tap Water

continued

每百元固定资产原值实现利税（元）Pre tax Profits per 100 Yuan Original Value of Fixed Assets (yuan)	每百元主营业务收入实现利税（元）Pre tax Profits per 100 yuan Revenues in Main Business (yuan)	产品销售率（%）Rate of Production Sold (%)	出口交货值占工业销售（%）Export delivery Value of the proportion of total sales value (%)	新产品产值率（%）New Product ratio (%)
16.83	6.84	96.78	7.2	26.23
13.46	6.56	104.72	15.02	31.25
18.64	9.18	99.03	3.49	17.68
20.5	4.91	96.76	1.54	18.28
47.37	6.64	100.07	7.6	13.46
22.79	6.6	98.39	17.69	30.38
38.3	13.6	98.69	16.36	45.12
25.08	12.39	98.83	20.77	36.94
36.27	16.54	99.8	7.15	59.21
19.69	8.24	97.17	27.69	28.63
33.03	9.58	98.24	16.54	48.86
116.23	16.75	98.31	22.63	73.39
80.08	19.98	98.08	18.38	46.21
76.08	11.98	101.75	10.18	41.8
63.98	17.08	96.7		20.85
5.99	7.37	100.01		1.91
2.06	1.2	100.18		
4.81	21.61	94.48		2.32

4－13 市区规模以上工业

Main Economic Indicators of Industrial Enterprises

单位:万元

项 目	Item	企业单位数（个）Number of Enterprises (unit)	亏损企业(个) Loss Making Enterprises (unit)	工业总产值（当年价格）Gross Industrial Output Value (current price)	新产品产值 Output of New Products
总 计	**Total**	**4726**	**683**	**119823690**	**42120141**
按隶属关系分	**Grouped by Subordination**				
中 央 属	Central	30	7	6108968	320142
省 属	Provincial	41	7	4234805	710773
市 属	Municipal	126	15	7576384	2714985
按所有制分	**Grouped by Ownership**				
国有企业	State－owned Enterprises	8	－	1689177	5253
集体企业	Collective－owned Enterprises	1	－	2846	－
股份合作企业	Cooperative Enterprises	6	－	35534	3587
联营企业	Joint Ownership Enterprises	1	－	4787	－
有限责任公司	Limited Liability Corporations	813	121	41564308	17299022
股份有限公司	Share－holding Corporations Ltd.	201	23	13052631	7054064
私营企业	Private Enterprises	2906	380	31269152	7812937
外商及港澳台投资企业	Enterprises with Investment from Foreign、Hong Kong、Macao and Taiwan	784	159	31992140	9808114
其他企业	Other Enterprises	6	－	213117	137165
按企业规模分	**Grouped by Size of Enterprises**				
大型企业	Large	120	8	44340158	20930932
中型企业	Medium－sized	584	74	33527067	12022846
小微企业	Small	4022	601	41956465	9166364
按轻重工业分	**Grouped by Light & Heavy Industry**				
轻工业	Light Industry	2331	354	42792636	9832585
重工业	Heavy Industry	2395	329	77031054	32287556

企业主要经济指标(2017 年)(一)
Above Designated Size in Urban District(2017)(Ⅰ)

(10000 yuan)

工业销售产值 Value of Industrial Products Sales	出口交货值 Export delivery value	实收资本 Total Capital Hold	国家资本 State Capital	个人资本 Personal Capital	港澳台资本 Hongkong, Macau and TaiWan Capital	外商资本 Foreign Capital	就业人员年平均人数(人) Annual Average Number of Staff and Workers (person)
117960521	**15774316**	**31103755**	**3479756**	**6575506**	**1896374**	**3615134**	**956570**
6025699	10900	955387	357933	7831	1582	179035	9631
4131729	153811	1466909	355975	152772	9799	193088	16286
7774452	1198905	2069259	852131	203377	44605	195268	59298
1687921	–	421090	179748	–	–	–	2253
2847	–	500	–	–	–	–	25
35126	–	4131	–	4131	–	–	612
4787	–	100	–	–	–	–	55
40913280	4013772	8575543	1940680	1028213	2909	58704	221962
12989760	1515017	5101902	633101	1802269	24697	31244	98626
30812383	3972621	6030974	4624	3577012	–	2525	356337
31303802	6272506	10938447	721604	162413	1868768	3522661	275787
210615	401	31068	–	1468	–	–	913
43634772	5754544	8991327	1183341	1342019	455993	1063715	257173
32822835	5343624	8370506	905940	1571391	553109	1070268	293604
41502914	4676148	13741922	1390475	3662096	887271	1481151	405793
41614458	6017416	9594511	289691	2395057	908318	1486460	440356
76346063	9756900	21509244	3190065	4180449	988056	2128674	516214

单位:万元　　4－13　续表1

项　目	Item	企业单位数（个）Number of Enterprises（unit）	亏损企业（个）Loss Making Enterprises（unit）	工业总产值（当年价格）Gross Industrial Output Value（current price）	新产品产值 Output of New Products
按国民经济行业分	**Grouped by Economic Sector**				
采矿业	Mining and Quarrying	9	2	98155	–
煤炭开采和洗选业	Coal Mining and Dressing			–	–
黑色金属矿采选业	Ferrous Metals Mining and Dressing			–	–
有色金属矿采选业	Nonferrous Minerals Mining and Dressing	2	–	12492	–
非金属矿采选业	Nonmetal Minerals Mining and Dressing	7	2	85663	–
制造业	Manufacturing Industry	4653	671	110313730	41972538
农副食品加工业	Agricultural Products Processing	103	9	1013947	132679
食品制造业	Food Manufacturing	93	20	1679644	229682
酒、饮料和精制茶制造业	Wine, Beverage and Tea Manufacturing	34	2	1088479	91296
烟草制品业	Tobacco Processing	2		3385103	55539
纺织业	Textile Industry	538	58	6595401	1474633
纺织服装、服饰业	Textile Products and Costume Industry	203	61	1792409	529859
皮革、毛皮、羽毛及其制品和制鞋业	Leather. Furs. Downand Related and Shoes Products	110	20	1257454	208617
木材加工和木、竹、藤、棕、草制品业	Timber Processing, Bamboo, Cane, Palm Fiber and Straw Products	24	3	165397	52771
家具制造业	Furniture Manufacturing	64	7	1122129	413985
造纸和纸制品业	Paper Making and Paper Products	267	37	3798282	625608
印刷和记录媒介复制业	Printing and Record Media	75	18	605703	123287
文教、工美、体育和娱乐用品制造业	Cultural, Educational. Industrial Arts. Sports and Entertainment Goods	77	11	1500740	383091
石油、煤炭及其他燃料加工业	Petroleum, Coal and Other Fuel Processing	11		99144	20975
化学原料和化学制品制造业	Raw Chemical Materials and Chemical Products	265	25	8537543	2554212

continued 1 (10000 yuan)

工业销售产值 Value of Industrial Products Sales	出口交货值 Export delivery value	实收资本 Total Capital Hold	国家资本 State Capital	个人资本 Personal Capital	港澳台资本 Hongkong, Macau and TaiWan Capital	外商资本 Foreign Capital	就业人员年平均人数(人) Annual Average Number of Staff and Workers (person)
96849	–	62200	28799	7881	–	–	717
–	–	–	–	–	–	–	
–	–	–	–	–	–	–	
11893	–	29300	24719	4581	–	–	263
84955	–	32900	4080	3300	–	–	454
108469017	15774316	28963246	2277436	6542340	1833494	3552733	938802
1018379	42628	170701	20	59835	31126	20928	7629
1679112	73300	534647	26320	66304	56838	185651	21858
1059357	22814	404922	2150	22426	60574	170457	10944
3271885	9629	70992		3630	1400		3024
6495597	1205218	1411791		599807	125236	177732	94423
1768481	687637	521296	3705	80927	264692	84002	46052
1248608	652214	218042	449	68685	22664	19432	18781
164167	26459	56725		37141			2999
1029273	504725	251685		53373	16228	59308	27091
3787523	187240	614473	2235	293523	25136	5555	33307
586043	12222	189547	22851	48096	35362	3760	8581
1458291	243353	234101	396	45754	22633	93597	14644
95639	1020	23326		21248			525
8390444	625974	1941795	37081	277597	28444	195910	42389

单位:万元　　4－13　续表2

项　目	Item	企业单位数(个) Number of Enterprises (unit)	亏损企业(个) Loss Making Enterprises (unit)	工业总产值(当年价格) Gross Industrial Output Value (current price)	新产品产值 Output of New Products
医药制造业	Medical and Pharmaceutical Products	84	4	4850208	1241412
化学纤维制造业	Chemical Fiber	107	7	5254579	1385153
橡胶和塑料制品业	Rubber and Plastic Products	245	34	4850289	1361925
非金属矿物制品业	Nonmetal Mineral Products	221	31	3190396	450803
黑色金属冶炼和压延加工业	Ferrous Metals Smelting and Processing	45	6	1497324	280359
有色金属冶炼和压延加工业	Nonferrous Metals Smelting and Processing	47	7	3641950	488231
金属制品业	Metal Products	299	47	4847146	1437535
通用设备制造业	Ordinary Machinery	437	50	8656519	3922599
专用设备制造业	For Special Purpose Equipment Manufacturing	203	43	1922084	694844
汽车制造业	Automobile Manufacturing	188	26	7408799	4464350
铁路、船舶、航空航天和其他运输设备制造业	Railway. watercraft. Avigation spaceflight and other Equipment Manufacturing	35	5	458720	114787
电气机械和器材制造业	Electric Equipment and Machinery	428	87	11222909	5565298
计算机、通信和其他电子设备制造业	Computers. Telecommunications and Other Electronic Equipment Manufacturing	285	41	16723687	12243735
仪器仪表制造业	Instruments and Meters Manufacturing	131	11	2687577	1258908
其他制造业	Other Manufacturing	20		234280	95268
废弃资源综合利用业	Multiple Utilization of Waste Resouces	12	1	225891	71098
金属制品、机械和设备修理业	Metal Products, Machinery and Equipment Repair			–	–
电力、燃气及水的生产和供应业	Produotion and supply of electricity, gas & water	64	10	9411805	147603
电力、热力生产和供应业	Production and Supply of Electric Power and Hot Water	37	4	6722253	137299
燃气生产和供应业	Production and Supply of Gas	11	3	2261978	
水的生产和供应业	Production and Supply of Tap Water	16	3	427573	10304

continued 2 (10000 yuan)

工业销售产值 Value of Industrial Products Sales	出口交货值 Export delivery value	实收资本 Total Capital Hold	国家资本 State Capital	个人资本 Personal Capital	港澳台资本 Hongkong, Macau and TaiWan Capital	外商资本 Foreign Capital	就业人员年平均人数(人) Annual Average Number of Staff and Workers (person)
4290537	464304	1137354	188124	44163	17631	256751	33346
5084736	367878	1450466		401960	114683	58414	24736
5112680	856854	882733	24823	262688	43662	216318	41057
3155432	129990	703776	27686	230736	52133	123603	28105
1445995	18449	193842	5571	59398	7839	7172	5092
3645510	278842	343517	6875	52466	3026	18812	7025
4768493	787535	881888	11925	420225	131287	27371	41894
8550333	1377035	4135302	572663	734573	93155	329616	91188
1904327	408254	701060	39576	191666	91765	160665	29430
7403158	537741	3183992	1116641	328800	104020	547234	49556
445657	142601	138305	30065	25678		9401	5700
11041592	1798722	3379351	71217	525815	243065	323655	89185
16476528	3796699	3928229	85065	1207780	225207	385875	119859
2634756	490196	1205817	2000	342951	15689	66479	35282
238619	24785	19354		10926		5037	3792
217868		34220		24170			1308
–	–	–	–	–	–	–	
9394655	–	2078309	1173521	25285	62880	62401	17051
6724145		1087603	355260	16060	31700	9819	10160
2266166		454977	341476	1225	28680	52582	2285
404344		535730	476785	8000	2500		4606

4－14 市区规模以上工业

Main Economic Indicators of Industrial

单位:万元

项 目	Item	资产合计 Total Assets	流动资产合计 Total Circulating Funds	应收账款 Receivables	存货 Stock
总 计	**Total**	**144718720**	**85530009**	**28876444**	**17640828**
按隶属关系分	**Grouped by Subordination**				
中 央 属	Central	6450421	3665416	667629	1983670
省 属	Provincial	5177085	2221835	616151	370083
市 属	Municipal	11549461	6002247	1506678	1383357
按所有制分	**Grouped by Ownership**				
国有企业	State－owned Enterprises	853942	153508	12033	15493
集体企业	Collective－owned Enterprises	7669	7484	401	8
股份合作企业	Cooperative Enterprises	42345	35402	9249	2727
联营企业	Joint Ownership Enterprises	1341	1291	983	270
有限责任公司	Limited Liability Corporations	50051007	27078951	10798868	6044675
股份有限公司	Share－holding Corporations Ltd.	27046479	13797296	3712075	2423891
私营企业	Private Enterprises	30476661	20152675	6510501	4504039
外商及港澳台投资企业	Enterprises with Investment from Foreign、Hong Kong、Macao and Taiwan	36051849	24163891	7747140	4631066
其他企业	Other Enterprises	187428	139511	85194	18661
按企业规模分	**Grouped by Size of Enterprises**				
大型企业	Large	55318016	32219046	12354886	6775144
中型企业	Medium－sized	42861533	23704756	6769376	4788964
小微企业	Small	46539171	29606208	9752182	6076721
按轻重工业分	**Grouped by Light & Heavy Industry**				
轻工业	Light Industry	48125799	27853681	6432649	7597299
重工业	Heavy Industry	96592921	57676328	22443795	10043529

企业主要经济指标(2017 年)(二)
Enterprises Above Designated Size in Urban District(2017)(Ⅱ)

(10000 yuan)

产成品 Finished Products	固定资产合计 Fixed Assets	累计折旧 Accumulated Depreciation	本年折旧 Depreciation of the year	负债合计 Total Liabilities	流动负债合计 Total Current Liabilities	非流动负债合计 Total Non - current Liabilities	所有者权益合计 Creditors' Equity
6754733	**27007561**	**23085098**	**3118549**	**79211587**	**68295202**	**10429046**	**65480058**
183344	1896901	1406908	194701	3120763	2402675	718087	3329658
182352	1690226	1324713	172683	2263341	1633857	425889	2913743
671038	2613203	2095224	271168	6173332	4613887	1552841	5376128
6330	683049	712263	107828	242076	190706	51370	611866
6	185	1085	79	4141	4141	–	3529
1760	4841	6453	776	17579	17579	–	24766
129	50	195	14	985	985	–	356
1822933	10628659	8976580	1198815	32105987	25794622	6202521	17942584
919422	3138399	2331515	289380	10724640	8851973	1665897	16321837
1931672	5997083	4711861	730420	18291666	17477169	675031	12161474
2057070	6519518	6310112	787597	17682749	15822366	1834227	18367984
15411	35778	35035	3639	141765	135662	–	45662
2123776	8339738	7876167	1027631	29130658	24402850	4722591	26187357
2026007	8648680	7363330	1025710	23290677	19975585	3253577	19570850
2604950	10019143	7845601	1065207	26790252	23916768	2452879	19721850
2779990	9439531	8365710	1120187	24901624	23181633	1532727	23199559
3974743	17568030	14719388	1998362	54309963	45113570	8896320	42280499

项　目	Item	资产合计 Total Assets	流动资产合计 Total Circulating Funds	应收账款 Receivables	存　货 Stock
按国民经济行业分	**Grouped by Economic Sector**				
采矿业	Mining and Quarrying	212127	113462	17569	5805
煤炭开采和洗选业	Coal Mining and Dressing	–	–	–	–
黑色金属矿采选业	Ferrous Metals Mining and Dressing	–	–	–	–
有色金属矿采选业	Nonferrous Minerals Mining and Dressing	35581	3112	216	1206
非金属矿采选业	Nonmetal Minerals Mining and Dressing	176546	110350	17353	4599
制造业	Manufacturing Industry	135066918	83700164	28667350	17562322
农副食品加工业	Agricultural Products Processing	766252	455080	141572	137176
食品制造业	Food Manufacturing	1810752	989344	211646	201423
酒、饮料和精制茶制造业	Wine, Beverage and Tea Manufacturing	1409464	848210	227952	132529
烟草制品业	Tobacco Processing	3366681	2422247	224525	1857838
纺织业	Textile Industry	7148348	4226565	948900	1053999
纺织服装、服饰业	Textile Products and Costume Industry	2036045	1350776	271098	353948
皮革、毛皮、羽毛及其制品和制鞋业	Leather. Furs. Downand Related and Shoes Products	1070895	801797	294819	267214
木材加工和木、竹、藤、棕、草制品业	Timber Processing, Bamboo, Cane, Palm Fiber and Straw Products	183780	97231	24804	21862
家具制造业	Furniture Manufacturing	1317467	851742	196678	148896
造纸和纸制品业	Paper Making and Paper Products	4164490	2721342	786101	458630
印刷和记录媒介复制业	Printing and Record Media	756423	446698	163452	102775
文教、工美、体育和娱乐用品制造业	Cultural, Educational. Industrial Arts. Sports and Entertainment Goods	745660	484424	77537	197963
石油、煤炭及其他燃料加工业	Petroleum, Coal and Other Fuel Processing	103537	78894	21270	17383
化学原料和化学制品制造业	Raw Chemical Materials and Chemical Products	9485965	4669220	1366568	771282

continued 1 (10000 yuan)

产成品 Finished Products	固定资产合 计 Fixed Assets	累计折旧 Accumulated Depreciation	本年折旧 Depreciation of the year	负债合计 Total Liabilities	流动负债合 计 Total Current Liabilities	非流动负债合 计 Total Non－current Liabilities	所 有 者 权益合计 Creditors´Equity
1400	45498	25542	4926	101679	93838	7840	110447
–	–	–	–	–	–	–	–
–	–	–	–	–	–	–	–
963	22554	2514	392	7692	7692	–	27889
437	22944	23028	4534	93987	86146	7840	82559
6738333	20985823	17348168	2472306	73224789	65682989	7249453	61815055
44949	160262	95999	15990	469563	432735	30300	296688
67721	461184	400241	66186	915527	904452	9569	895224
48222	443829	558363	53639	784996	773096	11901	624467
147214	497382	425057	56044	857382	857223	159	2509300
518810	1766352	1892634	235857	4134179	3982715	103805	3014164
175619	445137	301997	34379	999014	913348	80407	1035920
36094	171631	90495	13887	752709	726476	24568	318185
8819	30129	17206	2810	128453	120850	7402	55328
53528	184439	116356	13189	630375	625375	4541	687091
204418	812146	780497	101726	3025792	2854542	111584	1115213
46692	233563	277056	30931	430373	398722	30360	326049
47608	176031	171849	23152	372759	353337	15637	372901
11092	16778	14032	1892	54997	54018	979	48540
366603	2003332	1482229	216563	4650662	4073884	568219	4835300

单位:万元

4-14 续表2

项 目	Item	资产合计 Total Assets	流动资产合计 Total Circulating Funds	应收账款 Receivables	存 货 Stock
医药制造业	Medical and Pharmaceutical Products	5462028	3032179	800906	943028
化学纤维制造业	Chemical Fiber	8239477	3056460	334824	646963
橡胶和塑料制品业	Rubber and Plastic Products	4766242	2886209	1045586	711500
非金属矿物制品业	Nonmetal Mineral Products	3921610	2733334	1448016	398811
黑色金属冶炼和压延加工业	Ferrous Metals Smelting and Processing	1029140	744681	69313	278544
有色金属冶炼和压延加工业	Nonferrous Metals Smelting and Processing	2545863	1783240	242298	458847
金属制品业	Metal Products	4354163	2958254	973675	887954
通用设备制造业	Ordinary Machinery	12484280	7933574	2356552	1604553
专用设备制造业	For Special Purpose Equipment Manufacturing	2809340	1945915	683106	462293
汽车制造业	Automobile Manufacturing	14778516	7321842	4318807	792520
铁路、船舶、航空航天和其他运输设备制造业	Railway. watercraft. Avigation spaceflight and other Equipment Manufacturing	545814	369982	106598	69902
电气机械和器材制造业	Electric Equipment and Machinery	14691873	9596725	3528493	1734002
计算机、通信和其他电子设备制造业	Computers. Telecommunications and Other Electronic Equipment Manufacturing	20061080	15213803	6644537	2188192
仪器仪表制造业	Instruments and Meters Manufacturing	4555432	3342517	1077895	591158
其他制造业	Other Manufacturing	198390	165144	12064	34626
废弃资源综合利用业	Multiple Utilization of Waste Resouces	257913	172737	67762	36514
金属制品、机械和设备修理业	Metal Products, Machinery and Equipment Repair	-	-	-	-
电力、燃气及水的生产和供应业	Produotion and supply of electricity, gas & water	9439676	1716383	191524	72701
电力、热力生产和供应业	Production and Supply of Electric Power and Hot Water	5113947	748086	131327	28985
燃气生产和供应业	Production and Supply of Gas	1572029	252447	34559	19686
水的生产和供应业	Production and Supply of Tap Water	2753700	715850	25639	24030

continued 2 (10000 yuan)

产成品 Finished Products	固定资产合计 Fixed Assets	累计折旧 Accumulated Depreciation	本年折旧 Depreciation of the year	负债合计 Total Liabilities	流动负债合计 Total Current Liabilities	非流动负债合计 Total Non－current Liabilities	所有者权益合计 Creditors´Equity
423439	1129577	578489	114553	2291944	1850346	438548	3170083
392771	1118796	1185264	144315	4786427	4441612	325486	3453049
405729	980480	1337898	185049	2783178	2514994	249600	1983061
237206	718589	703510	93969	2629413	2560993	59298	1292194
149894	143512	242140	23710	601160	543579	53780	427979
94196	428229	219484	39239	1857638	1739534	118105	688224
291689	765275	565514	83551	2473299	2351175	85439	1878435
609683	1757115	1345631	185290	6305011	5636835	628183	6179263
132989	525097	435929	55269	1488375	1345471	140101	1320963
370903	2110257	1148802	232788	10305935	8317023	1987960	4472578
21398	129433	73391	12136	302224	289143	12879	243590
846266	2114916	1391105	216507	7285045	6066264	1210308	7406821
817828	1257380	1135747	172387	9905930	9077003	817416	10155146
142762	339863	322721	41777	1771159	1657108	113847	2784272
9541	20482	25755	2447	68076	68076	–	130314
14654	44629	12778	3076	163198	153061	9075	94715
–	–	–	–	–	–	–	–
15000	5976240	5711388	641317	5885119	2518375	3171753	3554555
1993	3722064	4295454	489849	3288231	1295826	1992405	1825716
6511	1174896	392341	63324	1104362	611652	297719	467667
6496	1079280	1023593	88145	1492526	610897	881630	1261173

4－15 市区规模以上工业

Main Economic Indicators of Industrial

单位:万元

项　目	Item	主营业务收　入 Revenues in Main Business	主营业务成　本 Costs in Main Business	主营业务税金及附加 Sales Taxes and Extra Charges in Main Business
总　计	**Total**	**122766469**	**98037853**	**2882460**
按隶属关系分	**Grouped by Subordination**			
中　央　属	Central	6139435	3475351	2085096
省　　属	Provincial	4198307	3714759	19664
市　　属	Municipal	7872699	6004332	54831
按所有制分	**Grouped by Ownership**			
国有企业	State – owned Enterprises	1667977	1585794	5888
集体企业	Collective – owned Enterprises	2847	2610	7
股份合作企业	Cooperative Enterprises	36021	28526	232
联营企业	Joint Ownership Enterprises	4787	4586	17
有限责任公司	Limited Liability Corporations	42241207	33647153	2397946
股份有限公司	Share – holding Corporations Ltd.	13304649	10149948	91310
私营企业	Private Enterprises	31682340	27242976	154813
外商及港澳台投资企业	Enterprises with Investment from Foreign、Hong Kong、Macao and Taiwan	33542051	25112400	229450
其他企业	Other Enterprises	284590	263861	2798
按企业规模分	**Grouped by Size of Enterprises**			
大型企业	Large	45388146	33375930	2472366
中型企业	Medium – sized	33439706	27535844	176727
小微企业	Small	43938617	37126080	233366
按轻重工业分	**Grouped by Light & Heavy Industry**			
轻工业	Light Industry	42604631	31659381	2332226
重工业	Heavy Industry	80161838	66378473	550234

企业主要经济指标(2017 年)(三)

Enterprises Above Designated Size in Urban District(2017)(Ⅲ)

(10000 yuan)

销售费用 Sales Expenses	管理费用 Management Expenses	财务费用 Financial Expenses	利息支出 Interest Expenditure	营业利润 Business Profits	利润总额 Total Profits	利税总额 Total Pre－tax Profits	本年应交增值税 Value Added Tax Payable
6064492	**7650200**	**1230329**	**1297310**	**8555125**	**9344556**	**16711916**	**4484900**
136937	179440	42943	60959	193549	204655	2842041	552290
77482	262006	29481	36540	192040	195108	316924	102152
777818	687249	52537	84426	320095	421943	755617	278843
453	56449	1666	1894	18628	21266	78260	51107
–	164	64	68	2	28	82	48
605	3291	409	443	3015	2072	4046	1741
36	134	–	–	14	14	159	129
1579801	2017357	411291	421354	2618230	2819107	6896845	1679792
850142	1213177	155207	186506	1314060	1442321	2008691	475060
837391	1835480	462715	443688	1320916	1502923	2655591	997856
2794274	2522709	198069	242250	3265870	3544919	5050206	1275837
1790	1439	909	1106	14389	11906	18035	3331
2951738	2722978	244298	287724	4525662	4794312	9273886	2007209
1593764	2135553	354255	373193	2054030	2259561	3468779	1032491
1518990	2791669	631776	636393	1975433	2290683	3969251	1445201
3097380	2626833	503350	540233	2902117	3150564	7578373	2095583
2967112	5023367	726979	757077	5653008	6193992	9133543	2389317

单位:万元　　　　4-15　续表1

项　目	Item	主营业务收　入 Revenues in Main Business	主营业务成　本 Costs in Main Business	主营业务税金及附加 Sales Taxes and Extra Charges in Main Business
按国民经济行业分	**Grouped by Economic Sector**			
采矿业	Mining and Quarrying	95073	58601	2818
煤炭开采和洗选业	Coal Mining and Dressing	-	-	-
黑色金属矿采选业	Ferrous Metals Mining and Dressing	-	-	-
有色金属矿采选业	Nonferrous Minerals Mining and Dressing	11566	8192	290
非金属矿采选业	Nonmetal Minerals Mining and Dressing	83507	50409	2527
制造业	Manufacturing Industry	113226479	89091492	2850029
农副食品加工业	Agricultural Products Processing	1034424	900812	3492
食品制造业	Food Manufacturing	1715147	1313292	8602
酒、饮料和精制茶制造业	Wine, Beverage and Tea Manufacturing	1403685	997658	29379
烟草制品业	Tobacco Processing	3225425	721656	2066490
纺织业	Textile Industry	6459760	5619826	31939
纺织服装、服饰业	Textile Products and Costume Industry	1824427	1485203	12972
皮革、毛皮、羽毛及其制品和制鞋业	Leather. Furs. Downand Related and Shoes Products	1245856	1106634	5784
木材加工和木、竹、藤、棕、草制品业	Timber Processing, Bamboo, Cane, Palm Fiber and Straw Products	187389	155949	1143
家具制造业	Furniture Manufacturing	1063402	850560	7869
造纸和纸制品业	Paper Making and Paper Products	3782536	3294786	32256
印刷和记录媒介复制业	Printing and Record Media	610917	515869	3159
文教、工美、体育和娱乐用品制造业	Cultural, Educational. Industrial Arts. Sports and Entertainment Goods	1464152	1349438	4649
石油、煤炭及其他燃料加工业	Petroleum, Coal and Other Fuel Processing	116088	100700	566
化学原料和化学制品制造业	Raw Chemical Materials and Chemical Products	10180570	8278876	48738

continued 1 (10000 yuan)

销售费用 Sales Expenses	管理费用 Management Expenses	财务费用 Financial Expenses	利息支出 Interest Expenditure	营业利润 Business Profits	利润总额 Total Profits	利税总额 Total Pre-tax Profits	本年应交增值税 Value Added Tax Payable
3684	6469	3991	4338	23452	23226	29795	3751
–	–	–	–	–	–	–	–
–	–	–	–	–	–	–	–
346	1818	24	10	896	877	2467	1299
3338	4651	3967	4328	22556	22349	27329	2452
6025329	7478018	1137518	1186774	8213838	8977758	16102441	4274655
41553	36896	12351	13830	40553	41918	66447	21037
179168	116614	6627	11198	100208	142680	234139	82857
267591	56226	5750	9523	52816	57514	141936	55043
89132	127789	-1221	3075	255051	250790	2772435	455154
110183	353960	92305	106189	291730	310867	544720	201914
64634	192653	24951	20738	73853	87998	190512	89541
37203	49173	22089	16260	27801	28466	67429	33179
4881	15101	2996	3009	11519	11634	16945	4168
104092	69835	10689	7586	109200	116510	230076	105698
77445	182511	110188	108533	81929	159354	415817	224207
15441	48608	6049	6086	33690	34918	58715	20639
22622	50855	12665	11058	26662	28068	61222	28504
3906	4381	1996	2033	4844	6371	9378	2442
570260	591154	90170	86853	691224	770993	1118650	298919

单位:万元 4-15 续表2

项　目	Item	主营业务收　入 Revenues in Main Business	主营业务成　本 Costs in Main Business	主营业务税金及附加 Sales Taxes and Extra Charges in Main Business
医药制造业	Medical and Pharmaceutical Products	4285636	1915547	45457
化学纤维制造业	Chemical Fiber	5527061	5058322	11534
橡胶和塑料制品业	Rubber and Plastic Products	5067708	4362477	24092
非金属矿物制品业	Nonmetal Mineral Products	3220454	2716666	15906
黑色金属冶炼和压延加工业	Ferrous Metals Smelting and Processing	1582807	1480389	3145
有色金属冶炼和压延加工业	Nonferrous Metals Smelting and Processing	4098877	3869969	5085
金属制品业	Metal Products	4841717	4306255	18993
通用设备制造业	Ordinary Machinery	8835773	7084454	55593
专用设备制造业	For Special Purpose Equipment Manufacturing	1922937	1445348	13677
汽车制造业	Automobile Manufacturing	7487469	5890997	209014
铁路、船舶、航空航天和其他运输设备制造业	Railway. watercraft. Avigation spaceflight and other Equipment Manufacturing	463405	379454	6892
电气机械和器材制造业	Electric Equipment and Machinery	11401279	9299917	61967
计算机、通信和其他电子设备制造业	Computers. Telecommunications and Other Electronic Equipment Manufacturing	17010478	12384027	99855
仪器仪表制造业	Instruments and Meters Manufacturing	2627821	1761158	18393
其他制造业	Other Manufacturing	321995	278068	1849
废弃资源综合利用业	Multiple Utilization of Waste Resouces	217288	167186	1538
金属制品、机械和设备修理业	Metal Products, Machinery and Equipment Repair	-	-	-
电力、燃气及水的生产和供应业	Produotion and supply of electricity, gas & water	9444917	8887761	29613
电力、热力生产和供应业	Production and Supply of Electric Power and Hot Water	6721535	6287731	19848
燃气生产和供应业	Production and Supply of Gas	2290614	2251434	4949
水的生产和供应业	Production and Supply of Tap Water	432768	348596	4816

continued 2 (10000 yuan)

销售费用 Sales Expenses	管理费用 Management Expenses	财务费用 Financial Expenses	利息支出 Interest Expenditure	营业利润 Business Profits	利润总额 Total Profits	利税总额 Total Pre - tax Profits	本年应交增值税 Value Added Tax Payable
1195136	417525	29508	26648	794480	822424	1191131	323250
30169	124952	112918	124695	287126	293121	377995	73340
215791	273650	28433	49563	188017	202833	331886	104962
184102	147500	54906	53164	116474	127498	242814	99410
12163	21266	14421	16650	58703	60407	78236	14685
18760	57069	46413	58521	104925	109454	273329	158790
88846	250552	51550	53252	150320	174835	317616	123789
307656	731834	82383	83465	763949	833144	1224471	335733
113864	241371	19132	19343	107755	124044	215210	77489
154380	566367	23187	61156	682878	750156	1239327	280157
21364	46662	7332	4349	10136	12602	36195	16700
635604	778498	129536	136895	688072	747491	1107092	297634
1250589	1559953	124749	72790	2062811	2212204	2910378	598318
201936	348826	14715	17333	334442	389654	527847	119800
5697	11392	-2073	525	26458	26373	38678	10456
1165	4843	2803	2455	36216	43438	61817	16840
-	-	-	-	-	-	-	-
35479	165713	88820	106197	317834	343572	579679	206494
483	98167	52258	55726	282907	271133	460967	169985
18099	31759	15931	23777	652	5927	27082	16206
16897	35787	20631	26695	34276	66512	91631	20303

4-16 全市规模以上工业企业

Main Economic Indicators of Industrial Enterprises

单位:万元

项 目	Item	企业单位数(个) Number of Enterprises (unit)	亏损企业(个) Loss Making Enterprises (unit)	工业总产值(当年价格) Gross Industrial Output Value (current price)	新产品产值 Output of New Products
按登记注册类型分组	**Grouped by Status of Registration**				
内资企业	Domestic-funded Enterprises	4683	585	96453987	35134225
国有企业	State-owned Enterprises	10		1870409	5253
中央企业	Central Enterprises	3		1017823	
地方企业	Local Enterprises	7		852585	5253
集体企业	Collective-owned Enterprises	2		5868	
股份合作企业	Cooperative Enterprises	6		35534	3587
联营企业	Joint Ownership Enterprises	1		4787	
集体联营企业	Collective Joint Ownership Enterprises	1		4787	
有限责任公司	Limited Liability Corporations	920	133	43856526	18375955
国有独资公司	State-funded Corporations	30	6	7716388	191914
其他有限责任公司	Other Limited Liability Corporations	890	127	36140139	18184041
股份有限公司	Share-holding Corporations Ltd.	227	26	14068352	7389350
私营企业	Private Enterprises	3511	426	36399394	9222915
私营独资企业	Private-funded Enterprises	109	8	558853	33827
私营合伙企业	Private Partnership Enterprises	15	3	67689	6091
私营有限责任公司	Private Limited Liability Corporations	3289	402	33811291	8105962
私营股份有限公司	Private Share-holding Corporations Ltd.	98	13	1961561	1077036
港、澳、台商投资公司	Enterprises with Investment from Hong Kong, Macao and Taiwan	385	87	14885315	6713016
内地与港澳台合资经营企业	Joint-venture Enterprises with funds from Hong Kong, Macao and Taiwan	224	43	8823825	3148823
内地与港澳台合作经营企业	Cooperative Enterprises with funds from Hong Kong, Macao and Taiwan	1		38698	26334
港澳台商独资经营企业	Enterprises with Sole Investment from Hong Kong, Macao and Taiwan	151	42	4419049	2052098
港澳台商投资股份有限公司	Share-holding Corporations Ltd. with Investment from Hong Kong, Macao and Taiwan	4		1493186	1442327
其他港澳台商投资	Other Enterprises with Investment from Hong Kong, Macao and Taiwan	5	2	110557	43434
外商投资企业公司	Enterprises with Foreign Investment	465	81	18298321	3435109
中外合资经营企业	Joint-venture Enterprises	219	35	8331183	2028412
中外合作经营企业	Cooperation Enterprises	6		89202	14970
外商独资经营企业	Enterprises with Sole Foreign Investment	230	46	9337064	1081706
外商投资股份有限公司	Share-holding Corporations Ltd. with Foreign Investment	5		358884	282007

主要经济指标按登记注册类型分(2017 年)

Above Designated Size by Status of Registration(2017)

(10000 yuan)

工业销售产值 Value of Industrial Products Sales	出口交货值 Export delivery value	实收资本 Total Capital Hold	国家资本 State Capital	个人资本 Personal Capital	港澳台资本 Hongkong, Macau and TaiWan Capital	外商资本 Foreign Capital	就业人员年平均人数(人) Annual Average Number of Staff and Workers (person)
95138610	10717027	21981448	3027318	7151702	27793	92660	766129
1869153		499811	258469				2923
1017726		209194	209194				963
851427		290618	49275				1960
5869		611					53
35126		4131		4131			612
4787		100					55
4787		100					55
43155861	4193069	9109304	2118648	1165842	2909	58891	241060
7577839	30959	447006	317896	26000			12313
35578022	4162111	8662297	1800752	1139842	2909	58891	228747
13987608	1736296	5443023	641357	1952328	24884	31244	110589
35869592	4787261	6893400	8844	4027933		2525	409924
552524	54332	37583		28004			6782
65906	2599	8169		7809			1089
33305069	4481660	6195299	8844	3713541		2525	383400
1946093	248670	652349		278579			18653
14876995	2391981	6557141	535756	121852	1868107	407360	130744
8925277	1410497	4025068	527190	101970	503018	405916	68505
38698	5238	4000				1000	311
4314175	901079	1406053	8566		1299100	144	47520
1502770	55749	1005530		19882	2000		12757
96075	19418	116490			63989	300	1651
17611639	4348433	4707657	189526	63079	62276	3238497	158817
8032196	1494476	1956906	189526	62566	59063	859404	67898
87050	29820	31179		499		27442	1631
8989553	2539576	2622868		15	3212	2303083	78023
321070	265913	85560				42424	10283

4-17 分地区规上

Added Value of Industrial Enterprises Above

单位:亿元

年 份 Year	全 市 Whole City	市 区					
		上城区 Shangcheng	下城区 Xiacheng	江干区 Jianggan	拱墅区 Gongshu	西湖区 Xihu	高新(滨江)区 Hi-Tech (Binjiang)
2000	360.97						
2001	444.91						
2002	597.01						
2003	783.51						
2004	1019.47						
2005	1126.54						
2006	1363.17						
2007	1717.65						
2008	1743.20						
2009	1792.00						
2010	2153.83						
2011	2369.00	215.48	20.83	47.25	119.11	49.03	162.30
2012	2492.00	296.64	22.05	48.00	117.08	49.07	210.02
2013	2664.13	318.89	23.33	53.33	104.34	49.62	278.48
2014	2813.51	328.06	15.16	57.60	78.34	50.45	324.69
2015	2875.05	329.70	7.13	53.79	60.64	52.30	365.67
2016	2990.34	349.57	9.64	47.37	65.80	57.06	374.24
2017	3184.05	362.41	8.16	42.98	74.76	61.04	502.19

注:2000-2010年为主营业务收入500万及以上;2011-2017年为主营业务收入2000万及以上。

工业增加值(2000－2017 年)
Designated Size by Region (2000－2017)

(100 million yuan)

Urban District									
萧山区 Xiaoshan	大江东产业集聚区 Dajiangdong Industry Cluster District	余杭区 Yuhang	富阳区 Fuyang	临安区 Lin'an	经济技术开发区 Economic and Technological Development Zone	西湖风景名胜区 The West Lake Scenic Zone	桐庐县 Tonglu	淳安县 Chun'an	建德市 Jiande
77.95		31.54	22.05	11.83			9.29	2.24	10.13
106.28		38.50	31.69	14.71			11.98	2.99	8.86
145.26		40.29	38.87	18.55			14.08	3.40	13.05
199.34		69.17	52.52	25.09			18.98	5.46	16.82
245.57		86.96	63.65	32.25			29.73	6.59	27.62
311.61		129.16	80.22	37.84			31.60	9.29	28.54
385.34		150.85	103.73	47.54			42.10	12.70	37.88
401.88		195.17	136.42	62.53			57.06	17.35	50.54
482.29		212.97	160.31	74.51			68.41	20.56	61.38
538.91		225.60	167.30	80.02			62.17	23.48	60.03
606.90		297.10	182.30	98.91			76.63	29.18	76.13
721.27		243.41	162.41	98.20			71.74	32.66	68.09
727.65		250.64	165.25	106.67			80.02	38.69	76.19
704.46		275.99	198.03	115.18	380.51	0.06	81.63	43.44	81.74
712.21		301.62	200.53	123.24	405.16	0.12	94.92	47.53	85.18
706.49	189.07	334.30	200.89	127.85	457.66	0.76	102.26	52.06	83.67
742.23	215.14	349.74	201.89	136.80	541.62	－1.77	99.78	49.96	85.75
745.62	225.95	386.71	234.29	138.50	417.58	－	83.38	40.35	86.33

a) Data in 2011－2017 refer to all the industrial enterprises with annual Sales income of over 20 million yuan, data in 2000－2010 refer to all the industrial enterprises with annual sales income of over 5 million yuan.

4 - 18 分地区规上
Index of Added Value of Industrial

（上年 = 100）

年 份 Year	全 市 Whole City	市 区					
		上城区 Shangcheng	下城区 Xiacheng	江干区 Jianggan	拱墅区 Gongshu	西湖区 Xihu	高新(滨江)区 Hi - Tech (Binjiang)
2010	114.9	110.0	121.1	112.2	110.5	109.1	119.6
2011	112.7	112.1	104.0	109.4	112.3	111.8	118.2
2012	110.9	106.6	103.5	105.5	112.2	108.8	113.7
2013	108.0	106.3	107.7	109.4	104.5	109.6	115.1
2014	108.9	108.9	91.6	115.1	105.5	104.9	118.3
2015	105.4	106.0	90.1	100.5	95.2	101.0	117.8
2016	105.6	98.5	102.0	87.5	105.0	105.0	114.9
2017	107.0	108.7	105.5	95.2	111.3	105.1	118.1

工业增加值发展指数(2010－2017 年)

Enterprises Above Designated Size by Region(2010－2017)

(Preceding Year＝100)

Urban District									
萧山区 Xiaoshan	大江东产业集聚区 Dajiangdong Industry Cluster District	余杭区 Yuhang	富阳区 Fuyang	临安区 Lin'an	经济技术开发区 Economic and Technological Development Zone	西湖风景名胜区 The West Lake Scenic Zone	桐庐县 Tonglu	淳安县 Chun'an	建德市 Jiande
114.3		115.0	113.1	122.7	118.5		114.0	114.9	115.5
112.9		109.2	113.3	113.1	111.2		109.1	115.1	113.0
113.5		107.2	112.1	112.4	102.4		109.0	119.6	110.8
108.1		108.0	109.3	105.5	107.3		105.6	112.7	106.1
108.1		107.0	106.2	107.2	109.3		109.0	103.2	108.1
106.2	118.6	102.6	104.1	105.1	106.9	90.9	106.9	103.4	108.2
106.3	117.6	105.0	103.0	109.0	110.2	100.3	108.6	110.6	107.0
101.3	99.7	107.6	106.0	106.7	106.5	－	106.3	104.1	106.7

4-19 全市规上工业三大新兴产业发展情况(2013-2017年)

Statistics on the Three Emerging Industries Above Designated Size(2013-2017)

指标 Item	高新技术产业 High-tech Industries		战略性新兴产业 Strategic Emerging Industries		装备制造业 Equipment Manufacturing Industries	
	增加值(亿元) Value-added (100 million yuan)	为上年(%) As Compared with the Preceding Year (%)	增加值(亿元) Value-added (100 million yuan)	为上年(%) As Compared with the Preceding Year (%)	增加值(亿元) Value-added (100 million yuan)	为上年(%) As Compared with the Preceding Year (%)
2013	785.4	108.9	636.6	107.1	900.5	108.6
2014	1096.6	110.5	813.1	113.0	921.4	109.3
2015	1212.6	109.8	877.3	109.4	1086.1	113.5
2016	1372.9	112.5	812.1	111.6	1249.6	114.6
2017	1605.5	113.6	979.5	115.0	1384.2	111.0

4-20 主要工业产品生产量(2017 年)
Output of Major Industrial Products(2017)

产品名称		Item		全市 Whole City 2017 年	全市 Whole City 为上年(%) As Compared with the Preceding Year(%)	市区 Urban District
发电量	(亿千瓦时)	Electricity	(100 million kwh)	150.22	83.2	111.17
#水力发电	(亿千瓦时)	of which:Hydropower	(100 million kwh)	35.67	70.3	2.8
垃圾发电	(亿千瓦时)	Garbage Power	(100 million kwh)	8.84	96.7	8.84
罐头	(万吨)	Canned Food	(10000 tons)	50492	84.3	18977
乳制品	(吨)	Dairy Products	(ton)	149527	95.6	126719
啤酒	(千升)	Beer	(1000 litres)	1038348	111.3	710170
软饮料	(万吨)	Soft Drinks	(10000 tons)	687	104.4	292
精制茶	(吨)	Tea	(ton)	21206	105.4	7928
卷烟	(亿支)	Cigarettes	(100 million)	537	92.1	537
方便面	(吨)	Instant Noodle	(ton)	248615	87.6	248615
化学纤维	(吨)	Chemical Fiber	(ton)	6256289	107.9	6229109
#合成纤维	(吨)	Synthetic Fibre	(ton)	6098925	107.5	6071745
纱	(万吨)	Yarn	(10000 tons)	528784	96.6	528060
布	(万米)	Cloth	(10000 m)	325592	98.8	276671
印染布	(万米)	Printed Fabric	(10000 m)	619833	100.2	617916
蚕丝及交织机织物(含蚕丝≥50%)	(万米)	Silk and Woven Fabrics (Containing Greater than or Equal 50% silk)	(10000 m)	1575	84.0	1537
服装	(万件)	Garment	(10000 units)	32437	93.5	24074
皮革鞋靴	(万双)	Leather Footwear	(10000 units)	966	79.3	966
家具	(万件)	Furniture	(10000 units)	3880	116.1	3667
塑料制品	(吨)	Plastic Membrane	(ton)	1208837	94.9	997397
机制纸及纸板	(万吨)	Machine Made Paper and Paperboard	(10000 tons)	6739947	102.5	6594089

4－20 续表1 continued 1

产品名称	Item	全市 Whole City 2017年	为上年(%) As Compared with the Preceding Year(%)	市区 Urban District
盐酸(含量31%以上)(吨)	Mariatic Acid(above 31% percent) (ton)	179670	133.1	179670
氢氧化钠(烧碱)(折100%) (吨)	Caustic Soda (ton)	210014	108.2	210014
碳酸钠(纯碱) (吨)	Soda ash (ton)	322835	105.1	322835
初级形态的塑料(塑料树脂及共聚物)(吨)	Plastics in Primary Form(Plastic Resins and Copolymers) (ton)	355814	100.3	208920
合成氨 (吨)	Synthetic Ammonia (ton)	220198	104.8	213893
农用氮、磷、钾化学肥料总计(折纯)(吨)	Chemical Fertilizer (ton)	96408	100.7	93086
化学农药原药(折有效成分100%)(吨)	Chemical Pesticide (ton)	79884	76.2	13573
涂料(油漆) (吨)	Paint (ton)	140621	107.2	77122
合成洗涤剂 (吨)	Synthetic Detergent (ton)	135149	100.5	105046
化学药品原药(化学原料药) (吨)	Original Drug Chemicals (ton)	12048	108.3	11660
中成药 (吨)	Traditional Chinese Medicine (ton)	7330	43.7	6046
橡胶轮胎外胎(轮胎外胎) (万条)	Rubber Tires (10000 units)	5978	111.0	5966
水泥 (万吨)	Cement (10000 tons)	1583	99.2	812
铁合金 (万吨)	Iron Alloy (10000 tons)	3	58.4	
钢材 (万吨)	Steel Products (10000 tons)	441	104.5	435
精炼铜(电解铜) (吨)	Refined Copper (ton)	276438	126.6	276438
工业锅炉 (蒸发量吨)	Industry Boiler (ton)	7247	90.9	7247
金属切削机床 (台)	Metal－cutting Machine Tools (unit)	19560	117.7	17306

4－20 续表 2 continued 2

产品名称	Item	全市 Whole City 2017 年	为上年(%) As Compared with the Preceding Year(%)	市区 Urban District
金属成形机床(锻压设备)(台)	Metal Forming Machine(Forge Equipment) (Tai)	7853	133.3	7853
泵(液体泵) (万台)	Pump (10000 sets)	959426	106.4	950595
滚动轴承(轴承) (万套)	Bearings (10000 units)	14031	107.5	14031
汽车 (辆)	Motor Vehicles (unit)	64463	70.3	64463
叉车 (台)	Forklift (unit)	89381	124.6	9043
两轮自行车(自行车) (万辆)	Bicycles (10000 units)	192	98.5	191
交流电动机 (万千瓦)	AC Motor (10000 kw)	182	130.3	169
钢绞线 (吨)	Strand (ton)	56537	78.8	56396
通信及电子网络用电缆 (万对千米)	Communication Cable (10000 km)	4060412	87.4	1214828
光缆(光纤通讯电缆)(万芯千米)	Electric Power Cable (10000 km)	3455	95.2	3285
家用电冰箱 (万台)	Household Refrigerators (10000 units)	76	68.3	76
家用洗衣机 (万台)	Household Washing Machines (10000 units)	289	96.9	289
吸排油烟机 (万台)	Smoke Absorbers (10000 units)	373	123.0	373
移动通信手持机(手机)(万部)	Mobile Telephone Sets (10000 units)	42	5.9	42
电工仪器仪表 (万台)	Electric Instrument and Apparatus (10000 units)	3833	124.6	3833
工业自动调节仪表与控制系统 (万台)	Industrial Automatic Adjustment Meter and Control System (10000 units)	193	116.7	193
电光源(灯泡) (亿只)	Light Bulbs (100 million units)	6	86.8	3
彩色电视机 (万部)	Color－Television Sets (10000 units)	2	371.4	2
微型计算机设备 (万台)	Micro－computer Equipment (10000 units)	143	108.1	143

4－21　分地区节能降耗情况(2017 年)

Energy Efficency and Energy Consumption Reduction by Region(2017)

地　区	Region	单位 GDP 能耗降低率(%) Decrease Rate of Energy Consumption Per Unit of GDP (±%)	单位 GDP 电耗降低率(%) Decrease Rate of Energy Consumption Per Unit of GDP (±%)	单位工业增加值能耗降低率 Decrease Rate of Energy Consumption Per Unit of Industriul Value－Added (±%)
杭州市	Hangzhou	3.4	－0.7	4.1
#上城区	Shangcheng	－	1.7	5.0
下城区	Xiacheng	－	－3.8	5.4
江干区	Jianggan	－	－1.1	0.5
拱墅区	Gongshu	－	10.6	33.0
西湖区	Xihu	－	－2.1	4.4
高新(滨江)区	Hi－Tech(Binjiang)	－	－0.6	4.4
萧山区	Xiaoshan	1.8	－1.0	－2.0
大江东产业集聚区	Dajiangdong Industry Cluster District	－	－15.0	－6.4
余杭区	Yuhang	4.7	－0.2	6.6
富阳区	Fuyang	0.3	－4.1	2.3
临安区	Lin′an	0.0	2.3	－5.8
经济技术开发区	Economic and Technological Development Zone	－	－12.9	2.0
桐庐县	Tonglu	9.0	8.3	15.1
淳安县	Chun′an	1.6	2.0	1.4
建德市	Jiande	5.1	5.4	6.1

注:若降低率为负数,说明本期的指标值与去年同期相比没有降低,反而上升。

a)If the Decrease Rate was a negative number,it means the indicator was increased compared to last year.

4－22 全市规模以上工业能源购进消费与库存(2017 年)

Purchasing,Consuming and Stocking of Energy in Industrial Enterprises Above Designated Size(2017)

能源名称	Item	购进量 Purchasing	消费量合计 Total Consumption	工业生产消费 Industry
原煤 （吨）	Raw Coal （Ton）	11046413	11041450	11028644
洗精煤 （吨）	Washing Coal （Ton）	－	－	－
煤制品 （吨）	Coal Puoducts （Ton）	750283	754162	754162
焦炭 （吨）	Coke （Ton）	38481	32848	32848
天然气(气态) （万立方米）	Natural Gas(Gas)(10000 cu. m)	168612	168650	168148
液化天然气(液态) （吨）	Liquefied Natural Gas(Liquid) (Ton)	45114	45035	44905
汽油 （吨）	Gasoline （Ton）	42333	42056	13317
煤油 （吨）	Kerosene （Ton）	661	672	651
柴油 （吨）	Diesel Oil （Ton）	128620	128728	109961
燃料油 （吨）	Fuel Oil （Ton）	25657	25406	25386
液化石油气 （吨）	Liquefied Petroleum Gas （Ton）	9888	9898	9715
润滑油 （吨）	Lubricating Oil （Ton）	11981	11687	11686
溶剂油 （吨）	Solvent Oil （Ton）	384	381	381
石油沥青 （吨）	Petroleum Asphalt （Ton）	－	－	－
其他石油制品 （吨）	Other Petroleum Products （Ton）	17454	17487	17487
热力 （百万千焦）	Heat (Million kilo－joule)	85049280	96634994	95797410
电力 （万千瓦时）	Electricity (10000 kwh)	3332756	3539786	3465154
煤矸石用于燃料 （吨）	Coal Gangue for Fuel （Ton）	－	－	－
城市垃圾用于燃料 （吨）	Municipal Waste for Fuel （Ton）	－	785184	785184
生物质废料用于燃料 （吨）	Biomass Waste for Fuel （Ton）	153010	150842	150738
余热余压 （百万千焦）	Residual Heat and Pressure (Million kilo－joule)	3308053	8987468	8987468
其它工业废料用于燃料 （吨）	Other Industrial Waste for Fuel (Ton)	46571	59830	59830
其它燃料 （吨标准煤）	Other Fuel (Tons of SCE)	19373	34471	34471

4－23 工业企业主要能源

Energy Consumption of Industrial

行 业	Sector	原煤(吨) Raw Coal(Ton)	洗精煤(吨) Washing Coal(Ton)	焦炭(吨) Coke(Ton)	汽油(吨) Gasoline(Ton)	煤油(吨) Kerosene(Ton)
总 计	**Total**	**11041450**	**–**	**32848**	**42056**	**672**
煤炭开采和洗选业	Coal Mining and Dressing	–	–	–	–	–
黑色金属矿采选业	Ferrous Metals Mining and Dressing	–	–	–	–	–
有色金属矿采选业	Nonferrous Minerals Mining and Dressing	–	–	–	42	–
非金属矿采选业	Nonmetal Minerals Mining and Dressing	13669	–	–	25	–
农副食品加工业	Agricultural Products Processing	862	–	–	320	–
食品制造业	Food Manufacturing	6996	–	–	1045	15
酒、饮料和精制茶制造业	Wine, Beverage and Tea Manufacturing	–	–	–	59	–
烟草制品业	Tobacco Processing	–	–	–	23	–
纺织业	Textile Processing	442939	–	–	3765	–
纺织服装、服饰业	Textile Products and Costume Industry	317	–	–	1626	–
皮革、毛皮、羽毛及其制品和制鞋业	Leather. Furs. Downand Related and Shoes Products	–	–	–	1211	–
木材加工和木、竹、藤、棕、草制品业	Timber Processing, Bamboo, Cane, Plam Fiber and Straw Products	–	–	–	120	–
家具制造业	Furniture Manufacturing	–	–	–	507	10
造纸和纸制品业	Paper Making and Paper Products	28356	–	–	2328	6
印刷和记录媒介复制业	Printing	–	–	–	568	–
文教、工美、体育和娱乐用品制造业	Cultural, Educational. Industrial Arts. Sports and Entertainment Goods	116	–	70	673	–
石油、煤炭和其他燃料加工业	Petroleum, Coal and Other Fuel Processing	68	–	–	214	–

注：上述数据统计范围为规上工业企业。石油、煤炭及其他燃料加工业仍为 2011 行业代码所含企业。

消费量按行业分(2017 年)
Enterprises by Sector(2017)

柴油(吨) Diesel oil(Ton)	燃料油(吨) Fuel Oil(Ton)	液化石油气(吨) Liquefied Petroleum Gas(Ton)	天然气(万立方米) Natural Gas (10000 cu. m)	其他石油制品(吨) Other Petroleum Products(Ton)	热力(百万千焦) Heat(Million kilo - joule)	电力(万千瓦时) Electricity (10000 kwh)
128729	**25406**	**9898**	**168650**	**17487**	**96634994**	**3539786**
–	–	–	–	–	–	193
–	–	–	–	–	–	–
15	–	–	–	–	–	2012
3355	–	–	–	–	–	7659
1315	48	55	1280	–	309208	14233
1468	976	54	1674	–	1354307	28483
856	95	5	1823	–	1398314	59043
186	–	–	727	–	151050	7099
3390	1404	93	10436	209	28063816	459941
1164	–	5	602	–	556502	25502
440	–	4	690	–	94970	11768
201	–	–	19	–	2217	3845
698	37	–	624	–	61114	12142
2863	11	150	1676	–	31729415	279807
653	–	24	230	–	31965	15612
351	–	18	92	–	133947	14963
365	201	–	28	55	46903	463

a) Data in the table refer to industrial enterprises above designated Size Petroleam, coal and other Fuel Processing refer to the enterprises which included in Industrial Class fication 2011.

4-23 续表

行业	Sector	原煤(吨) Raw Coal(Ton)	洗精煤(吨) Washing Coal(Ton)	焦炭(吨) Coke(Ton)	汽油(吨) Gasoline(Ton)	煤油(吨) Kerosene(Ton)
化学原料和化学制品制造业	Raw Chemical Materials and Chemical Products	1413344	–	–	2663	1
医药制造业	Medical and Pharmaceutical Products	49990	–	–	547	–
化学纤维制造业	Chemical Fiber	135934	–	–	484	–
橡胶和塑料制品业	Rubber and Plastic Products	210690	–	–	2285	10
非金属矿物制品业	Nonmetal Minerals Products	2520950	–	–	1466	–
黑色金属冶炼和压延加工业	Smelting and Processing of Ferrous Metals	2354	–	552	571	–
有色金属冶炼和压延加工业	Smelting and Processing of Nonferrous Metals	274	–	32153	165	–
金属制品业	Metal Products	2220	–	38	1786	5
通用设备制造业	Ordinary Machinery	10384	–	35	4988	314
专用设备制造业	Special Purpose Equipment	108	–	–	1452	1
汽车制造业	Automobile Manufacturing	201	–	–	2766	293
铁路、船舶、航空航天和其他运输设备制造业	Railway. watercraft. Avigation spaceflight and other Equipment Manufacturing	169	–	–	392	–
电气机械和器材制造业	Electric Equipment and Machinery	534	–	–	3266	15
计算机、通信和其他电子设备制造业	Computers. Telecommunications and Other Electronic Equipment Manufacturing	–	–	–	2849	–
仪器仪表制造业	Instruments and Meters Manufacturing	–	–	–	1327	1
其他制造业	Other Manufacturing	201856	–	–	116	–
废弃资源综合利用业	Multiple Utilization of Waste Resouces	14528	–	–	48	–
金属制品、机械和设备修理业	Metal Products, Machinery and Equipment Repair	–	–	–	–	–
电力、热力生产和供应业	Production and Supply of Electric Power and Hot Water	5984593	–	–	1724	–
燃气生产和供应业	Production and Supply of Gas	–	–	–	296	–
水的生产和供应业	Production and Supply of Tap Water	–	–	–	339	–

continued

柴油(吨) Diesel oil(Ton)	燃料油(吨) Fuel Oil(Ton)	液化石油气(吨) Liquefied Petroleum Gas(Ton)	天然气(万立方米) Natural Gas (10000 cu. m)	其他石油制品(吨) Other Petroleum Products(Ton)	热力(百万千焦) Heat(Million kilo – joule)	电力(万千瓦时) Electricity (10000 kwh)
6980	14414	130	2261	14403	18550215	493025
1461	197	30	2190	–	1010614	65208
653	–	–	981	–	5454719	357746
2685	1306	3434	734	2	4582750	220423
72122	2478	147	4820	1661	327730	212556
552	–	308	4687	73	298521	76108
1090	1974	108	3204	–	207287	84055
3105	2044	466	6888	4	421600	98191
7111	176	268	1025	601	71380	122904
908	–	463	529	–	172424	25917
4649	45	48	2213	431	145445	98966
205	–	265	240	34	–	7856
2770	–	3160	2164	4	434602	145194
4128	–	648	718	–	346409	132031
348	–	1	90	–	9078	20175
730	–	1	138	–	–	3333
69	–	–	–	8	85817	14115
–	–	–	–	–	–	16
1563	–	–	115833	3	582677	340145
117	–	–	33	–	–	638
163	–	12	3	–	–	78420

4-24 全市分行业电力消费量(2017年)
Electricity Consumption by Sector(2017)

单位:万千瓦时 (10000 kwh)

项目	Item	2017年	2016年	增长% Growth %
总计	**Total**	**7380288**	**6782940**	**8.81**
#线路损失电量	#Losses in Transmission	233242	221290	5.40
农林牧渔业	Farming, Forestry, Animal Husbandry and Fishery Conservancy	50657	47780	6.02
工业	Industry	4322669	4015466	7.65
#轻工业	Light Industry	2172442	2025716	7.24
重工业	Heavy Industry	2150227	1989750	8.07
#采矿业	#Mining and Quarrying	25644	26099	-1.74
制造业	Manufacturing Industry	3848308	3566582	7.90
电力、燃气及水的生产和供应业	Produotion and supply of electricity, gas & water	448718	422785	6.13
建筑业	Construction	137453	131661	4.40
交通运输、仓储及邮政业	Transportation, Storage, Post & Telecommunications	156387	141035	10.89
信息传输、计算机服务和软件业	Information Transmission, Computer Services and Software	198414	181098	9.56
商业、住宿和餐饮业	Commerce, Catering and lodging	443229	396025	11.92
金融、房地产、商务及居民服务业	Finance, Real Estate Commerce and Service for the Residents	470610	383163	22.82
公共管理和社会组织	Public Management and Social Organizations	452293	413742	9.32
城乡居民生活用电	Residential Consumption	1148575	1072970	7.05
#城市	Cities	724906	676120	7.22
乡村	#Rural Areas	423669	396850	6.76

4-25 水资源量和总用水量(2007-2017年)

Total Water Resources and Water Consumption(2007-2017)

单位:亿立方米 (100 million Cubic Meters)

		全市 Whole City	市区 Urban District	萧山区 Xiaoshan	余杭区 Yuhang	富阳区 Fuyang	临安区 Lin'an	桐庐县 Tonglu	淳安县 Chan'an	建德市 Jiangde
2007年	水资源量 Water Resources	104.13	20.28	6.94	7.52	11.76	20.36	10.12	29.88	11.72
	用水量 Water Consumption	49.56	32.57	13.27	6.87	6.45	3.39	2.53	1.53	3.09
2008年	水资源量 Water Resources	154.38	24.58	8.31	9.75	14.20	32.92	14.95	49.22	18.52
	用水量 Water Consumption	56.70	39.57	14.71	7.44	6.49	3.70	2.90	1.32	2.69
2009年	水资源量 Water Resources	141.50	23.38	7.86	8.51	16.33	32.03	16.67	37.46	15.63
	用水量 Water Consumption	54.28	39.24	8.34	6.47	5.18	3.07	2.52	1.46	2.81
2010年	水资源量 Water Resources	190.40	29.58	9.91	10.08	17.92	29.91	19.03	63.61	30.36
	用水量 Water Consumption	54.95	39.00	9.18	6.20	4.80	3.87	2.79	1.61	2.88
2011年	水资源量 Water Resources	136.70	20.21	6.57	9.95	13.43	27.13	15.81	41.00	19.11
	用水量 Water Consumption	57.71	40.40	9.88	6.21	5.83	4.21	2.98	1.37	2.92
2012年	水资源量 Water Resources	221.26	36.20	13.43	13.14	23.57	38.83	24.89	66.73	31.08
	用水量 Water Consumption	56.45	39.69	10.48	6.00	5.75	4.10	2.67	1.40	2.84
2013年	水资源量 Water Resources	141.15	28.82	9.82	9.24	15.33	26.87	15.63	35.29	19.21
	用水量 Water Consumption	57.77	41.07	10.14	6.07	6.22	3.79	2.53	1.42	2.74
2014年	水资源量 Water Resources	163.00	20.48	7.85	8.14	14.39	27.36	18.37	58.11	24.30
	用水量 Water Consumption	37.14	22.77	9.38	5.32	4.27	3.37	2.57	1.40	2.76
2015年	水资源量 Water Resources	239.06	61.09	14.57	13.84	23.93	44.33	26.68	73.79	33.17
	用水量 Water Consumption	34.79	25.29	8.44	5.06	3.98	3.23	2.44	1.32	2.51
2016年	水资源量 Water Resources	213.10	56.58	7.50	17.00	20.44	43.25	22.86	63.56	26.85
	用水量 Water Consumption	34.24	25.13	5.84	5.00	3.93	3.16	2.28	1.31	3.16
2017年	水资源量 Water Resources	146.87	38.56	9.15	9.80	13.99	26.39	14.67	47.21	20.04
	用水量 Water Consumption	33.47	27.78	7.92	4.93	3.84	3.04	2.15	1.30	2.24

4-26 规模以下工业主要指标(2016-2017年)
Main Indicators of Industrial Enterprises Below Designated Size(2016-2017)

指标名称		Item		2017年	2016年
企业数	(万家)	Number of Enterprises	(10,000 Homes)	3.38	3.39
年末从业人数	(万人)	Total Number of Employed Persons at Year End	(10,000 persons)	35.07	36.38
资产总计	(亿元)	Total Assets	(100 million yuan)	2041.22	1940.72
主营业务收入	(亿元)	Revenues in Main Business	(100 million yuan)	1238.92	1142.00
主营业务成本	(亿元)	Costs in Main Business	(100 million yuan)	1042.97	948.39
税金总额	(亿元)	Total taxes	(100 million yuan)	50.23	41.65
利润总额	(亿元)	Total Profits	(100 million yuan)	15.09	17.20
应付职工薪酬	(亿元)	Employee benefits Payable	(100 million yuan)	143.11	134.53

主要统计指标解释

工业总产值 是以货币表现的工业企业在报告期内生产的已出售或可供出售工业产品总量,它反映一定时间内工业生产的总规模和总水平,它包括:在本企业内不再进行加工,经检验、包装入库(规定不需包装的产品除外)的成品价值,对外加工费收入,自制半成品,在产品期末初差额价值。工业总产值采用"工厂法"计算,即以工业企业作为一个整体,按企业工业生产活动的最终成果来计算,企业内部不允许重复计算,不能把企业内部各个车间(分厂)生产的成果相加。

工业销售产值 是以货币表现的工业企业在一定时期内销售的本企业生产的工业产品总量。包括已销售的成品、半成品价值,对外提供的工业性作业和对本单位基本建设部门、生活福利部门等提供的产品和工业性作业及自制设备的价值。已销售的成品、半成品不论是本期生产的、还是上期生产的,只要是本期销售出去的均包括在内。对外提供的工业性作业是指企业按合同对外提供的工业性劳务。企业为本单位基本建设部门、生活福利部门等提供的产品和工业性作业及自制设备也应视同销售,这部分也作为销售统计。工业销售产值的计算范围、计算价格和计算方法与工业总产值一致,但两者计算的基础不同;工业销售产值计算的基础是产品销售总量,工业总产值计算的基础是工业产品生产总量。

工业增加值 是指工业行业在报告期内以货币表现的工业生产活动的最终成果。

固定资产原价 固定资产原值指企业在建造、购置、安装、改建、扩建、技术改造某项固定资产时所支出的全部货币总额。它一般包括买价、包装费、运杂费和安装费等。

固定资产净值 是指固定资产原价减去历年已提折旧额后的净额。

利税总额 指企业利润总额、产品销售税金及附加和应交增值税之和。

主营业务收入 指企业销售产品的销售收入和提供劳务等主要经营业务取得的收入总额。

主营业务成本 指企业销售产品和提供劳务等主要经营业务的实际成本。

主营业务税金及附加 指企业销售产品和提供工业性劳务等主要经营业务应负担的城市维护建设税、消费税、资源税和教育费附加。

主营业务利润 指企业销售产品和提供工业性劳务等主要经营业务收入和除其成本、费用、税金后的利润。

利润总额 指企业实现的利润。

应交增值税 指企业在报告期内应交纳的增值税额。

总资产 指企业拥有或控制的全部资产。包括流动资产、长期投资、固定资产、无形及递延资产、其他长期资产、递延税项等,即为企业资产负债表的资产总计项。

(1)流动资产指企业可以在一年内或者超过一年的一个生产周期内变现或耗用的资产合计。包括现金及各种存款、短期投资、应收及预付款项、存货等。

(2)固定资产指企业固定资产净值、固定资产清理、在建工程、待处理固定资产损失所占用的资金合计。

(3)无形资产指企业长期使用而没有实物形态的资产。包括专利权、非专利技术、商标权、著作权、土地使用权、商誉等。

总负债 指企业承担并需要偿还的全部债务。包括流动负债和长期负债、递延税项等,即为企业资产负债表的负债合计项。

(1)流动负债指企业在一年内或者超过一年的一个营业周期内需要偿还的债务合计,其中包括短期借款、应付及预收款项、应付工资、应交税金和应交利润等。

(2)长期负债指企业在一年以上或者超过一年的一个生产周期以上需要偿还的债务合计,其中包括长期借款、应付债务、长期应付款项等。

所有者权益 指企业投资人对企业净资产的所有权。企业净资产等于企业全部资产减去全部负债后的余额。其中包括投资者对企业的最初投入,以及资本公积金、盈余公积金和未分配利润,对股份制企业即为股东权益。

Explanatory Notes on Main Statistical Indicators

Gross Industrial Output Value is the total volume of industrial products sold or available for sale in value terms which reflects the total achievements and overall scale of industrial production during a given period. It includes the value of the finished products, which are not to be further processed in the enterprises and have been inspected, packed and put in storage, the value of industrial services rendered to other units, and the changes in the value of the semi – finished products and products in process between the beginning and closing of the period. The gross industrial output value is calculated with "factory method". No double calculations are to be made within the same enterprise. However, double counting does occur among different enterprises.

Industrial Sales Output Value is the total volume of industrial products sold in value term of an industrial enterprise during a given period. It includes the value of finished products, semi – finished products, industrial operations rendered to other units, products industrial operations & self – made equipment provided to the basic construction department, welfare department, etc. of the enterprise. For finished products & semi – finished products, whether produced in this calculation period or the previous one, if they are sold in this calculation period, they should be included. Industrial operations are industrial services rendered to other units according to contracts. Products, industrial operations & self – made equipment provided to basic construction department, welfare department, etc. of the enterprise should be regarded as act of sale, and included in sales statistics.

The scope , price and method of calculation of industrial sales output value are the same as those for gross industrial output value. But the calculation bases are different: the base for sales output value is the total volume of products sold; the base for gross industrial output value is total volume of production of industrial products.

Value – added of Industry refers to the final results of industrial production of the industrial trade in money terms during the reference period.

Original Value of Fixed Assets refers to the original value of all assets owned by industrial enterprises, calculated at the cost paid at the time of purchase, installation, reconstruction, expansion, and technical innovation and transformation of the said assets, which includes expenses on purchase, package, transportation, and installation, etc.

Net Value of Fixed Assets is obtained by deducting depreciation over years from the original value of fixed assets.

Total Pre – tax Profits refers to the sum of sales tax and extra charges adding total profits.

Sales Revenue of Industrial Products refers to the revenue from the sales of products by industrial enterprises and the revenue from services provided and etc.

Sales Cost of Industrial Products refers to the actual cost of products of industrial enterprises and industrial services provided, etc.

Tax and Extra Charges on Sales of Products refer to the tax on city maintenance and construction, consumption tax, resources tax and extra charges for education, which should be borne by the enterprises in selling products and providing industrial services.

Sales Profit of Products refers to the profit gained by the enterprises by deducting cost, charges and taxes from the business income of the enterprises obtained in selling products and providing industrial services.

Total Profits refer to the profits gained by the enterprises.

Value – added Tax Payable refers to the amount of the value added tax which should be paid by the enterprises in the reporting period.

Total Assets refer to all assets which are owned or controlled by enterprises, including circulating assets, long term investment, fixed assets, intangible assets and deferred assets, other long term assets, and deferred taxes, etc. The summation of above items is equal to total assets shown in the balance sheets of the enterprises.

(1) Circulating assets (working capital) refer to assets which can be cashed in or spent or consumed in an operating cycle of one year or over one year, including cash, all kinds of deposits, short term investment, receivables, advance payment, stock, etc.

(2) Fixed assets refer to the net value of fixed assets, clearance of fixed assets, project under construction, fixed assets losses in suspense. These are corporations' fund holdings.

(3) Intangible assets refer to assets without material form used by enterprises over a lone time, such as patents, non – patent technologies, trade marks, copyright, land use right, business reputation, etc.

Total Liabilities refer to the debts that enterprises are responsible for repayment, including liquid liabilities, long – term liabilities and deferred taxes, etc. Total liabilities correspond to the summation item of liabilities shown in the balance sheets of the enterprises.

(1) Liquid liabilities (also called quick liabilities or immediate liabilities) refer to enterprises' total debt payable within an operating cycle of one year or over one year, including short term loans, payables and advance payments, wages payable, taxes payable and profit payable, etc.

(2) Long term liabilities refers to total debt payable within an operating cycle of one year or over one year, including long – term loans, payable liabilities, long – term payables, etc.

Creditors' Equity refers to investors' ownership of net assets of the enterprise. It is equal to the total assets of the enterprise minus its total liabilities, including the primary input from investors, capital accumulation fund, surplus accumulation fund and undistributed profit. It is the shareholder's equity in share – holding companies.

五、建筑业

CONSTRUCTION

5

建筑业
Construction

主 要 统 计 指 标
Major Statistical Indicators

建筑业总产值	Gross Output Value of Construction	4323.73	亿元	(100 million yuan)
为上年	As Compared with the Preceding Year	105.3	%	(%)
房屋建筑施工面积	Floor Space of Buildings Under Construction	25617	万平方米	(10, 000 sq.m)
为上年	As Compared with the Preceding Year	94.1	%	(%)
房屋建筑竣工面积	Floor Space of Buildings Completed	8108	万平方米	(10, 000 sq.m)
为上年	As Compared with the Preceding Year	83.1	%	(%)

5－01 全市分地区建筑业总产值(2017 年)
Gross Output Value of Construction by Region(2017)

单位:万元 (10000 yuan)

地 区	Region	建筑企业单位数(个) Number of Construction Enterprises (unit)	建筑业总产值 Gross Output Value of Construction	建筑工程产值 Output Value of Construction Projects	安装工程产值 Output value of Installation Projects	其他产值 Other Output Values
全 市	**Total**	**1410**	**43237256**	**37584752**	**4599347**	**1053157**
市 区	Urban District	1268	41820369	36331834	4471327	1017208
#上城区	Shangcheng	75	2517625	1409190	1060970	47465
下城区	Xiacheng	63	1716738	1414348	244129	58261
江干区	Jianggan	106	3031710	2616789	345564	69357
拱墅区	Gongshu	142	2932125	2252368	623268	56489
西湖区	Xihu	132	9556735	8824003	524217	208516
高新(滨江)区	Hi－Tech (Binjiang)	57	5551066	5336967	84832	129268
萧山区	Xiaoshan	274	10939286	9616098	990156	333033
大江东产业集聚区	Dajiangdong Industry Cluster District	33	716821	642230	56940	17651
余杭区	Yuhang	189	2192979	1909275	281328	2377
富阳区	Fuyang	113	1232326	1043280	149534	39513
临安区	Lin'an	62	917209	776871	95896	44443
经济技术开发区	Economic and Technological Development Zone	18	209913	184582	14495	10836
西湖风景名胜区	The West Lake Scenic Zone	4	305835	305835	－	－
桐庐县	Tonglu	54	746028	684159	49588	12282
淳安县	Chun'an	47	323948	265458	38500	19990
建德市	Jiande	41	346912	303301	39933	3678

5－02 建筑总专包

Financial Indicators on Construction Enterprises of

单位：万元

指标名称	Item	年末资产 Asset and Liabilities		
		流动资产合计 Circulating Funds	固定资产合计 Fixed Assets	资产合计 Total Assets
总 计	**Total**	**27695056**	**2292476**	**34263560**
#特、一、二级企业	of Which：Special Grade，First Grade，Second Grade	25468961	1965452	31501229
#国有及国有控股企业	of Which：State－owned and State Holding Enterprises	7369432	351218	9010596
一、按登记注册类型分组	**Grouped by Registration Status**			
内资企业	Domestic Funded	27695056	2292476	34263560
国有企业	State－owned	178729	17935	204211
集体企业	Collective－owned	34420	1950	36780
股份合作企业	Share－holding Cooperative Enterprises	16859	10808	35530
联营企业	Joint Venture			
有限责任公司	Limited Liability Corporations	13566982	998726	16412689
股份有限公司	Share－holding Corporations Ltd.	3933608	288165	5484207
私营企业	Private Enterprises	9759594	946356	11841972
其他企业	Other Enterprises	2349	91	2440
港、澳、台商投资企业	Funded from Hong Kong，Macao and Taiwan	181767	26693	221734
外商投资企业	Foreign Funded	20749	1751	23998
二、按国民经济行业分组	**Grouped by Sector**			
房屋建筑业	Housing Construction	14493897	1100055	18305557
土木工程建筑业	Civil Engineering Construction	9773879	871295	11926243
建筑安装业	Installation of Lines，Pipelines and Equipment	1523687	139316	1773614
建筑装饰和其他建筑业	Fitting、Decoration of Building and Others Construction	1903594	181811	2258146

企业财务指标(2017 年)

General Contractors and Specialist Contractors(2017)

(10000 yuan)

负债 at Year - end		所有者权益合计 Owners´Equity		
流动负债合计 Current Liabilities	负债合计 Total Liabilities		实收资本 Paid - in Capitals	国家资本 State Capital
20579766	**22067499**	**12196062**	**6364528**	**417427**
19282834	20725143	10776087	5304445	406095
6827833	7292438	1718158	862476	401467
20579766	22067499	12196062	6364528	417427
150090	150119	54093	17626	16626
29436	29762	7019	3738	2550
26438	26438	9092	5000	–
10795520	11780389	4632299	2211918	318251
3186124	3406514	2077693	696240	80000
6237289	6514185	5327787	3384810	–
614	614	1825	1000	–
141061	146284	75449	38705	–
13193	13193	10804	5490	–
10810208	11637647	6667910	3142457	4444
7292254	7851969	4074274	2386926	358538
1103209	1141284	632330	317612	12233
1374096	1436599	821547	517532	42212

单位：万元　　5－02　续表

指标名称	Item	损益 Expenditure，Income 工程结算收入 Revenue of Project Settlement Accounts	工程结算成本 Costs of Project Settlement Accounts
总　计	**Total**	**36710604**	**34035852**
#特、一、二级企业	of Which：Special Grade，First Grade，Second Grade	34051222	31690129
#国有及国有控股企业	of Which：State－owned and State Holding Enterprises	8659006	8126890
一、按登记注册类型分组	**Grouped by Registration Status**		
内资企业	Domestic Funded	36710604	34035852
国有企业	State－owned	252589	230848
集体企业	Collective－owned	26585	22741
股份合作企业	Share－holding Cooperative Enterprises	19559	15542
联营企业	Joint Venture		
有限责任公司	Limited Liability Corporations	18253068	17121455
股份有限公司	Share－holding Corporations Ltd.	4356293	3904597
私营企业	Private Enterprises	13661509	12612797
其他企业	Other Enterprises	2635	2104
港、澳、台商投资企业	Funded from Hong Kong，Macao and Taiwan	106359	96726
外商投资企业	Foreign Funded	32007	29042
二、按国民经济行业分组	**Grouped by Sector**		
房屋建筑业	Housing Construction	20547384	19357575
土木工程建筑业	Civil Engineering Construction	11133451	10153712
建筑安装业	Installation of Lines，Pipelines and Equipment	2144565	1926782
建筑装饰和其他建筑业	Fitting Decoration of Building and Others Construction	2885205	2597782

continued (10000 yuan)

及分配 and Distribution					
工程结算税金及附加 Taxes and Extra Charges Project Settlement Accounts	销售费用 Sales Expenses	管理费用 Management Expenditure	财务费用 Financial Expenditure	利润总额 Total Profits	应交所得税 Income Taxes Payable
186867	**90820**	**1163506**	**271466**	**1075459**	**223835**
167380	74377	974632	255274	1000906	203003
26002	12502	262120	55077	233913	44644
186867	90820	1163506	271466	1075459	223835
1193	698	8667	334	12408	3216
160	550	2074	-48	1065	264
143	927	1941	681	430	108
83315	28995	523024	115692	413835	90087
17083	13936	155232	40944	281113	43816
84151	43950	465009	109156	367253	86051
9	19	474	0	28	6
694	1525	5392	4508	-1423	77
119	219	1695	198	749	211
112507	29504	446325	172306	513034	99701
55010	37805	474038	72247	358435	80161
7614	11203	123439	8816	78112	14454
11735	12307	119704	18097	125879	29519

5－03　建筑业企业生产情况（2014－2017年）
Statistics on Production of Construction Enterprises（2014－2017）

指标名称	Item	2014	2015	2016	2017
一、建筑业合同情况	**Contract of Construction**				
签订的合同额（万元）	Total Value of Contracts (10000 yuan)	69933228	70729328	72311485	80872710
上年结转合同额（万元）	Value from Contracts Signed in 2016 (10000 yuan)	28874679	31220942	31413457	30503869
本年新签合同额（万元）	Value from New Contracts Signed in 2017 (10000 yuan)	41058549	39509226	40898029	50368841
二、承包工程完成情况	**Completion of Contracted Projects**				
直接从建设单位承揽工程完成的产值（万元）	Complete Output Value of Projects Contacted Directly from Investors (10000 yuan)	39364500	40695653	40898836	42804635
自行完成施工产值（万元）	Own－completed Output Value (10000 yuan)	38129851	39318980	39270784	41202046
分包出去工程的产值（万元）	Output Value of Out－sourced Projects (10000 yuan)	1234649	1377814	1628052	1602590
从建设单位以外承揽工程完成的产值（万元）	Completed Output Value of Projects Contacted from Non－investors (10000 yuan)	1584025	1657315	1782188	2035210
建筑业总产值（万元）	Gross Output Value (10000 yuan)	39713876	40975734	41052972	43237256
#装饰装修产值（万元）	of Which: Output Value of Fitting and Decoration of Buildings (10000 yuan)	3469325	3486860	3642482	4800059
#在外省完成的产值（万元）	of Which: Completed Output Value outside of Zhejiang Province (10000 yuan)	12425411	12018157	11675079	12005017
按构成分	by Structure				
建筑工程产值（万元）	Output Value of Construction Projects (10000 yuan)	34894095	36080625	36106015	37584752
安装工程产值（万元）	Output value of Installation Projects (10000 yuan)	3735431	3942809	3978388	4599347
其他产值（万元）	Other Output Values (10000 yuan)	1084350	951857	968569	1053157
竣工产值（万元）	Output Value of Buildings Completed (10000 yuan)	21665909	25994238	23746502	21888828
房屋建筑施工面积（万平方米）	Floor Space of Buildings Under Construction (10000 sq. m)	29581	28124	27221	25617
#本年新开工面积（万平方米）	of Which: Beginning Projects in this Year (10000 sq. m)	11156	9596	8583	8869
#实行投标承包面积（万平方米）	of Which: Floor Space of Biding System (10000 sq. m)	26927	23653	22615	-
房屋建筑竣工面积（万平方米）	Floor space of Buildings Completed (10000 sq. m)	9514	10137	9754	8108
三、年末自有施工机械设备	**Machinery and Equipment Owned (year－end)**				
年末自有施工机械设备净值（万元）	Net Value of Machinery and Equipment Owned (10000 yuan)	796789	837565	782395	822402
年末自有施工机械设备总台数（台）	Number of Machinery and Equipment Owned (set)	175738	173850	162491	162507
年末自有施工机械设备总功率（千瓦）	Total Power of Machinery and Equipment Owned (1000 kw)	4076303	3279495	3301850	3264229
四、就业人员情况	**Number of Employed Persons**				
计算劳动生产率的平均人数（人）	Average Employed Persons Overall Labor Productivity (person)	1293740	1310577	1237441	1239143
年末就业人员数（人）	Employed Persons (year－end) (person)	-	1268020	1203999	1224693

5-04 全市具有资质等级建筑业企业主要生产经营指标(2011-2017年)

Major Economic Indicators of Qualified Construction Enterprises(2011-2017)

单位:万元 (10000 yuan)

指标名称 Item	2011	2012	2013	2014	2015	2016	2017
企业个数(个) Nomber of Enterprises (unit)	1373	1430	1515	1476	1480	1474	1410
亏损企业个数(个) Loss Making Enterprises (unit)	200	216	252	224	236	256	253
建筑业总产值 Gross Output Value of Construction	30324975	33073420	37554704	39713876	40975734	41052972	43237256
竣工产值 Output Value of Buildings Completed	16286512	17557004	21021307	21665909	25994238	23746502	21888828
房屋建筑施工面积(万平方米) Floor Space of Buildings Under Construction (10,000 sq. m)	26104	26420	29538	29581	28124	27221	25617
房屋建筑竣工面积(万平方米) Floor Space of Buildings Completed (10,000 sq. m)	8556	8404	9613	9514	10137	9754	8108
固定资产原价 Orginal Value of Fixed Assets	2846687	2967321	3293095	3393624	3488088	3239557	3552611
实收资本合计 Total Capital Hold	3888171	4394124	5019389	5493120	5799067	5932301	6364527
流动资产合计 Circulating Funds	16267419	17809148	19959672	22168981	23867659	25412440	27695056
其中:存货 Stock	3758947	4034742	4934518	5900549	6360774	6751318	7530374
在建工程 Projects wnder Construction	198636	235510	320533	313490	211195	175075	216619
固定资产合计 Fixed Assets	2199708	2233648	2371260	2826312	2829483	2067226	2292476
年末负债合计 Total Liabilities at Year-end	13868500	14970479	17591701	18186469	19365824	20274680	22067498
流动负债合计 Circulating Funds	13311213	17809148	16473990	16894050	17964478	18752593	20579766
所有者权益合计 Crediors´Equity	6634943	7381024	8559878	9656533	10453107	10883382	12196061
营业收入 Revenue of Business	27251719	29552959	33709184	34704862	35568492	36069232	36965857
营业成本 Operating Costs	24719576	27047034	30614028	31501139	32365477	33270805	34248463
营业税金及附加 Main Sales Tax and Extra Charges	842437	880051	996370	1029405	1020437	541967	199457
管理费用 Management Expenditure	720238	853136	905194	918904	965161	1042943	1163505
财务费用 Financial Expenditure	256538	295135	318198	330680	301313	258903	271466
营业利润 Management Profits	723488	759792	850362	888932	883320	917779	1043476
利润总额 Total Profits	731358	791175	883887	913117	895484	950047	1075458

主要统计指标解释

建筑业总产值　建筑业总产值是以货币表现的建筑业企业在一定时期内生产的建筑业产品和服务的总和。建筑业总产值包括建筑工程产值、安装工程产值和其他产值三部分内容。

房屋建筑施工面积　指报告期内施过工的全部房屋建筑面积，它包括本期新开工的面积、上期跨入本期继续施工的房屋面积、上期停缓建在本期恢复施工的房屋面积、本期竣工的房屋面积以及本期施工后又停缓建的房屋面积。

房屋建筑竣工面积　指在报告期内房屋建筑按照设计要求已全部完工，达到了使用条件，经检查验收鉴定合格的房屋建筑面积。

工程结算收入（主营业务收入）　指本企业承包工程实现的工程价款结算收入以及向发包单位收取的除工程价款以外按规定列作营业收入的各种款项，如临时设施费、劳动保险费、施工机构调迁费等以及向发包单位收取的各种索赔款。

工程结算成本（主营业务成本）　指在报告期内与发包单位办理工程价款结算的已完工程实际成本。

Explanatory Notes on Main Statistical Indicators

Gross Output Value of Construction refers to total of construction products and services, expressed in money terms, produced or rendered by construction and installation enterprises during a given period of time. It includes: output value of construction projects, output value of installation projects and other output values.

Floor Space of Buildings Under Construction refers to floor space of buildings under construction during the reference period, including the floor space of buildings for which construction has newly started; buildings for which construction has started earlier and is continuing during the reference period; and buildings for which construction has been suspended earlier but has restarted during the reference period; buildings completed during the reference period; and buildings under construction but construction has subsequently been during the reference period.

Floor Space of Buildings Completed refers to the floor space of buildings that are completed in the reference period in accordance with the requirements of the design, up to the standard for being put into use, and having been checked and accepted by departments concerned as qualified ones.

Income from Settlement of Projects refers to the income received by the construction enterprise from the contracted project through settlement procedures, and other charges to the contractor as operational costs in addition to the value of the project, such as temporary facility fee, labor insurance premium, moving cost of construction equipment, as well as various types of claims to the contractor.

Project Settlement Costs refers to the contracting process works price of the actual settlement costs of projects have been completed during the reporting period.

六、交通运输邮电

TRANSPORTATION, POST AND TELECOMMUNICATIONS

6 交通运输、邮电
Transportation, Post and Telecommunications

主要统计指标
Major Statistical Indicators

客运量	Passenger Traffic	22289	万人次	(10, 000 person-times)
为上年	As Compared with the Preceding Year	108.5	%	(%)
货运量	Freight Traffic	34785	万吨	(10, 000 tons)
为上年	As Compared with the Preceding Year	115.3	%	(%)
邮电业务收入	Business Income of Post & Telecommunication Service	467.77	亿元	(100 million yuan)
为上年	As Compared with the Preceding Year	115.2	%	(%)
年末固定电话用户数	Number of Local Telephone Subscribers(year-end)	259.37	万户	(10, 000 subscribers)
为上年	As Compared with the Preceding Year	97.6	%	(%)
年末移动电话用户数	Number of Mobile Telephone Subscribers(year-end)	1724.17	万户	(10, 000 subscribers)
为上年	As Compared with the Preceding Year	99.4	%	(%)
年末宽带业务户数	Broadband Subscribers of Internet(year-end)	508.69	万户	(10, 000 subscribers)
为上年	As Compared with the Preceding Year	114.7	%	(%)

6-01 全市客运量(1978-2017年)
Total Passenger Traffic (1978-2017)

单位:万人次 (10,000 person-times)

年 份 Year	合 计 Total	铁 路 Railways	公 路 Highways	水 路 Waterways	民 航 Civil Aviation
1978	2878	485	-	-	3
1979	3122	560	1829	729	4
1980	3905	672	2358	870	5
1981	4484	769	2857	850	8
1982	5263	813	3377	1064	9
1983	5451	878	3530	1035	8
1984	6056	983	3912	1151	10
1985	6724	1004	4595	1111	14
1986	6765	1034	4768	941	22
1987	6905	1127	4852	896	30
1988	6593	1237	4445	877	34
1989	7493	1182	5488	801	22
1990	8119	1056	6350	691	22
1991	10701	1062	8876	710	53
1992	13358	1083	11538	670	67
1993	13070	1139	11403	454	74
1994	13373	1230	11669	390	84
1995	16620	1242	14921	339	118
1996	16714	1112	15184	273	145
1997	17034	1040	15623	260	111
1998	17395	1120	15925	235	115
1999	17882	1168	16369	235	110
2000	18607	1202	17102	179	124
2001	20342	1342	18707	148	145
2002	21089	1574	19213	108	194
2003	21348	1534	19510	89	215
2004	22833	1908	20372	237	316
2005	24124	2011	21431	304	378
2006	25810	2124	22961	267	458
2007	28026	2255	24836	306	629
2008	29084	2498	25630	277	679
2009	30116	2494	26454	372	796
2010	33772	2741	29671	456	904
2011	34778	2962	30305	595	916
2012	35819	3112	31126	592	989
2013	36409	3717	30994	547	1151
2014	24070	4689	17431	616	1334
2015	23942	5282	16591	597	1472
2016	20541	6053	12282	584	1622
2017	22289	6807	13019	638	1825

注:1990年以前为交通系统数,1990年起为全社会数(后同)。2014年起运输量统计方法调整。

a) The data in the table only included transportation department before 1990, while extended to the whole society after 1990 (the same below). The statistical method has been adjusted since 2014.

6－02　全市货运量(1978－2017年)
Total Freight Traffic（1978－2017）

单位:万吨　　(10000 tons)

年　份 Year	合　计 Total	铁　路 Railways	公　路 Highways	水　路 Waterways	民　航 Civil Aviation
1978	1706	418	633	655	
1979	1983	440	771	772	
1980	2070	444	762	864	
1981	1972	449	886	637	
1982	2261	485	795	981	
1983	2299	488	838	973	
1984	2385	510	888	987	
1985	2488	524	890	1074	
1986	2558	551	874	1133	
1987	2515	574	899	1041	1
1988	2416	555	823	1037	1
1989	7377	539	5095	1743	
1990	6522	449	4479	1594	
1991	7017	451	4891	1675	
1992	8434	534	6063	1836	1
1993	9082	580	6353	2148	1
1994	8962	491	6563	1907	1
1995	10347	482	7021	2842	2
1996	10962	445	7735	2780	2
1997	11015	406	7932	2676	1
1998	11329	418	8196	2713	2
1999	11684	403	8037	3241	3
2000	11459	417	7865	3173	4
2001	12443	452	8588	3398	5
2002	14347	446	10391	3504	6
2003	16815	438	12118	4253	6
2004	18895	480	13117	5289	9
2005	19909	525	13539	5833	12
2006	20924	569	14588	5754	13
2007	22569	573	16484	5500	12
2008	22550	483	16822	5232	13
2009	22372	427	16536	5396	13
2010	25915	379	19148	6371	17
2011	28831	331	21755	6727	18
2012	30089	322	23243	6503	20
2013	30734	284	23884	6545	22
2014	29335	312	23202	5797	24
2015	29384	307	23800	5251	25
2016	30170	274	25194	4673	29
2017	34785	328	29378	5044	35

6-03 客货运输量(2012-2017年)
Total Passenger and Freight Traffic(2012-2017)

项 目 Item	2012	2013	2014	2015	2016	2017
一、客运量合计(万人次) Passenger Traffic(10000 person-times)	**35819**	**36409**	**24070**	**23942**	**20541**	**22289**
铁路客运量 Passenger Railways	3112	3717	4689	5282	6053	6807
民航客运量 Passenger Civil Aviation	989	1151	1334	1472	1622	1825
公路客运量 Passenger Highways	31126	30994	17431	16591	12282	13019
水路客运量 Passenger Waterways	592	547	616	597	584	638
二、旅客周转量合计(万人公里) Total Passenger-kilometers(10000 passenger-km)	**1598527**	**1573289**	**1151642**	**1085769**	**943874**	**905008**
公路旅客周转量 Passenger-kilometers Highways	1590435	1566046	1143750	1078054	936574	897116
水路旅客周转量 Passenger-kilometers Waterways	8092	7243	7892	7715	7300	7892
三、货运量合计(万吨) Total Freight Traffic(10000 tons)	**30089**	**30734**	**29335**	**29384**	**30170**	**34785**
铁路货运量 Freight Railways	322	284	312	307	274	328
民航货运量 Freight Civil Aviation	20	22	24	25	29	35
公路货运量 Freight Highways	23243	23884	23202	23800	25194	29378
水路货运量 Freight Waterways	6503	6545	5797	5251	4673	5044
四、货运周转量合计(万吨公里) Total Freight Ton-kilometers(10000 ton-km)	**4563560**	**4724588**	**4550550**	**4629814**	**4796677**	**5304007**
公路货物周转量 Freight Ton-kilometers Highways	2643428	2719204	2760873	3003728	3217983	3615581
水路货物周转量 Freight Ton-kilometers Waterways	1920132	2005384	1789677	1626086	1578694	1688426

6－04 分地区交通

Statistics on Traffic and

项　目		Item		全市 Whole City	市区 Urban District
铁路旅客运量	（万人）	Passenger Railways	（10,000 Persons）	6807	6708
铁路货物运量	（万吨）	Freight Railways	（10,000 tons）	328	183
公路客运量	（万人）	Passenger Highways	（10,000 Persons）	13019	8180
公路货运量	（万吨）	Freight Highways	（10,000 tons）	29378	19348
民用航空客运量	（万人）	Passenger Civil Aviation	（10,000 Persons）	1825	1825
民用航空货邮运量	（万吨）	Freight Civil Aviation	（10,000 tons）	35	35
水路客运量	（万人）	Passenger Waterways	（10,000 Persons）	638	295
水路货运量	（万吨）	Freight Waterways	（10,000 tons）	5044	1121
非营运汽车拥有量	（辆）	Possession of Non－Business Vehicles(year－end)	（Unit）	2638992	2398178
#私人汽车拥有量	（辆）	in which:Possession of Private Vehicles	（Unit）	1998520	1863630

运输情况(2017 年)

Transport by Region(2017)

萧山区 Xiaoshan	余杭区 Yuhang	富阳区 Fuyang	临安区 Lin'an	桐庐县 Tonglu	淳安县 Chun'an	建德市 Jiande
–	100	–	–	–	–	–
58	118				84	61
549	242	1055	384	838	719	1052
4211	1663	1116	499	1062	710	769
1825	–	–	–	–	–	–
35	–	–	–	–	–	–
17	–	–	36	26	241	23
1908	1137	524	104	147	7	96
507265	376812	152943	148564	89646	66159	83925
350147	285149	108354	91352	56550	31615	46167

6-05 全市运输线路长度(2012-2017年)
Length of Transportation Routes(2012-2017)

单位:公里 (km)

项　目 Item	2012	2013	2014	2015	2016	2017
公路通车里程 (公里) Length of Highways (km)	15747	15900	16024	16210	16306	16424
#高速公路 (公里) Expressway (km)	550	550	582	615	632	632
一级公路 (公里) First Class Highways (km)	768	791	803	836	832	835
二级公路 (公里) Second Class Highways (km)	1542	1526	1570	1616	1615	1631
内河通航里程 (公里) Length of Navigable Inland Waterways (km)	2006	2006	2006	2006	2006	2006
民用航空航线 (条) Number of Civil Aviation Routes (line)	144	185	222	235	240	286
国内航线 (条) Domestic Routes (line)	117	156	186	196	195	229
国际航线 (条) International Routes (line)	20	22	28	32	38	49
地区航线 (条) Regional Routes (line)	7	7	8	7	7	8
民用航空通航城市 (个) Number of Cities Can Arrive by Civil Aviation	87	103	119	129	138	160
国内城市 (个) Domestic Cities	68	82	92	99	103	117
港澳台城市 (个) Hongkong,Macau and Taiwan	6	6	6	5	5	5
国际城市 (个) International Cities	19	21	27	30	35	43

6-06 民用机动车辆年末拥有量(2012-2017年末)

Total Number of Motor Vehicles End of the Year(End of 2012-2017)

单位:辆 (unit)

项目	Item	2012	2013	2014	2015	2016	2017
全市合计	**Total**	**2267027**	**2542976**	**2696340**	**2733537**	**2633541**	**2793595**
一、汽车	Vehicles	1761001	2045618	2184000	2244767	2341536	2451226
1. 载客汽车	Passenger Vehicles	1570099	1860794	1992112	2056143	2127393	2210376
其中:大型	Large	16118	17078	17485	18657	20017	20880
中型	Medium	18096	17849	14411	10797	10035	9365
小型	Small	1499444	1794017	1936836	2002730	2076098	2157089
微型	Mini	36441	31850	23380	23959	21243	23042
其中:轿车	Car	-	1678453	1799442	1773864	1483128	1530805
2. 载货汽车	Trucks	179399	173227	180475	177674	202775	229038
其中:重型	Heavy	31154	35917	39998	41999	49480	57794
中型	Medium	25242	17530	14444	8851	9422	9213
轻型	Light	122316	119205	125508	126321	143441	161703
微型	Mini	687	575	525	503	432	328
3. 其他汽车	Vehicles	11503	11597	11413	10950	11368	11812
其中:三轮汽车	Vehicles	-	385	182	179	139	102
低速货车	Low Speed Trucks	-	384	416	549	806	792
二、摩托车	Motorcycles	500080	490884	505360	481230	282477	329905
1. 普通	Genera	470779	466625	481027	463722	277238	324469
2. 轻便	Light	29301	24259	24333	17508	5239	5436
三、挂车	Trailer	-	6433	6939	7464	9457	12396
四、其他类型	Other	-	41	41	76	71	68

6-07 邮政、电信主要指标(2012-2017年)
Main Indicators of Post and Telecommunications(2012-2017)

项 目 Item	2012	2013	2014	2015	2016	2017
邮政业务总收入 (万元) Total Business Income of Postal Service (10,000 yuan)	533059	702664	1176704	1596884	2151732	2750911
#快递业务收入 (万元) Business Income of Express Mail Service (10,000 yuan)	427356	563459	1022279	1437542	1956944	2510479
电信业务收入 (万元) Total Business Income of Telecommunications Services (10,000 yuan)	1597344	1752286	1700825	1736600	1908315	1926800
函件 (万件) Number of Letters (10,000 pcs)	21226	20133	17412	13256	9634	11656
包裹 (万件) Number of Parcels (10,000 pcs)	129	133	113	81	49	51
快递 (万份) Pieces of Express Mail Service (10,000 copies)	25536	46852	84563	125707	180473	232630
#国际及港澳台快递 (万份) Pieces of Express to overseas and HongKong,macao,Taiwan (10,000 copies)	525	738	1731	2046	2495	4065
纪特邮票 (万枚) Stamps for Collettion (10,000 pcs)	1744	1412	1151	1231	1295	969
年末固定电话用户数 (万户) Number of Local Telephone Subscribers(year-end) (10,000 subscribers)	346.22	334.87	311.14	293.44	265.70	259.37
年末移动电话用户数 (万户) Number of Subscribers of Mobile Telephone(year-end) (10,000 subscribers)	1438.67	1546.83	1561.71	1726.76	1734.41	1724.17
年末宽带业务户数 (万户) Number of Wide Band Subscribers (10,000 subscribers)	275.91	338.63	278.78	294.96	443.57	508.69

注:邮政业务总收入含规模以上快递企业。

a) The total business income of postal services included the express enterprises above designated sice.

主要统计指标解释

货(客)运量 指在一定时期内,各种运输工具实际运送的货物(旅客)数量。是反映运输业为国民经济和人民生活服务的数量指标,也是制定和检查运输生产计划、研究运输发展规模和速度的重要指标。货运按吨计算,客运按人计算。货物不论运输距离长短、货物类别,均按实际重量统计。旅客不论行程远近或票价多少,均按一人一次作为客运量统计;半价票、小孩票也按一人统计。

货物(旅客)周转量 指在一定时期内,由各种运输工具运送的货物(旅客)数量与其相应运输距离的乘积之总和。是反映运输业生产总成果的重要指标,也是编制和检查运输生产计划,计算运输效率、劳动生产率以及核算运输单位成本的主要基础资料。通常以吨公里和人公里为计算单位。计算货物周转量通常按发出站与到达站之间的最短距离,也就是计费距离计算。

移动电话用户 指在邮电部门登记,通过移动电话交换机进入移动电话网,占有移动电话号码的电话用户。用户数量以实际办理登记手续进入邮电部门移动电话网的户数进行计算,一部或一台移动电话统计为一户。

Explanatory Notes on Main Statistical Indicators

Freight(passenger) Traffic refers to the volume of freight (passenger) transported with various means. Freight transport is calculated in tons and passenger traffic is calculated in the number of persons. Despite the type of freight and traveling distance, the freight transport is calculated in the actual weight of the goods; and despite the traveling distance and ticket price, the passenger traffic is calculated by the principle that one person can be counted only once in one travel. The passenger who travel with a half – price ticket or a child ticket is also calculated as one person. The freight (passenger) traffic provides a quantitative measure to show how the transport industry serves the national economy and people, and is also an important indicator for plan the transport industry and for studying the development scale and speed of the transport industry.

Freight Ton – kilometers(Passenger – kilometers) refers to the sum of the products of the volume of transported cargo (passengers) multiplying by the transport distance, usually using ton – kilometer and passenger – kilometer as units for measurement . Normally, the shortest distance between the departure station and the terminal station (i. e. , the payable distance) is the basis to calculate the freight ton – kilometers. This is an important indicator to show the total results of the transport industry, to prepare and examine the transport plan and to measure the efficiency, the labour productivity and the unit cost of transport.

Mobile Telephone Subscribers refer to the persons who own mobile telephone number connected with the mobile telephone communication network and registered by post and telecommunications organization. The number of subscribers is calculated only when the subscribers who have gone through all the register formalities and entered into the mobile telephone network. One mobile telephone is treated as a subscriber.

七、固定资产投资

INVESTMENT IN FIXED ASSETS

7 固定资产投资
Investment in Fixed Assets

主要统计指标
Major Statistical Indicators

固定资产投资额	Investment in Fixed Assets	5856.65	亿元	(100 million yuan)
为上年	As Compared with the Preceding Year	101.4	%	(%)
第一产业	Primary Industry	33.67	亿元	(100 million yuan)
为上年	As Compared with the Preceding Year	111.2	%	(%)
第二产业	Secondary Industry	866.55	亿元	(100 million yuan)
为上年	As Compared with the Preceding Year	100.9	%	(%)
第三产业	Tertiary Industry	4956.43	亿元	(100 million yuan)
为上年	As Compared with the Preceding Year	101.5	%	(%)
房地产企业营业收入	Operating Revenue of Real Estate Enterprise	3631.06	亿元	(100 million yuan)
为上年	As Compared with the Preceding Year	137.0	%	(%)
房地产企业单位数	Number of Enterprises for Real Estate Developement	1651	个	(unit)
为上年	As Compared with the Preceding Year	100.7	%	(%)

7-01 全市固定资产投资总额(1978-2017年)

Investment in Fixed Assets (1978-2017)

单位:万元 (10000 yuan)

年 份 Year	固定资产投资 Investment in Fixed Assets	房地产开发投资 Investment in Real Estate Development	项目投资 Projects Investment	基础设施投资 Investment in Infrastructure	工业投资 Industrial Investment	民间投资 Nongovernment Investment
1978	23941					
1979	34407					
1980	45752					
1981	51538					
1982	66123					
1983	68306					
1984	93244					
1985	141889					
1986	182398					
1987	200516					
1988	205967					
1989	202131					
1990	229214	20409				
1991	255696	25247				
1992	384136	41886				
1993	825382	218006				
1994	1059437	320532				
1995	1566280	527985				
1996	1819333	572749				
1997	2139012	572686				
1998	2681740	666244				
1999	3233609	848441				
2000	3766473	1015347				
2001	4634929	1409132				
2002	5623366	1982517				
2003	8952090	2588452	6363638	2907234	3194960	4192567
2004	11081993	3285409	7796584	3254648	4357950	5761350
2005	12777972	4105706	8672266	3715525	4438723	6723758
2006	13734482	4426534	9307948	3871462	4640261	7551249
2007	15837775	5187904	10649871	4056241	5271141	8215570
2008	18822936	6154060	12668876	5410313	5693385	9450542
2009	21951706	7046752	14904954	6018416	6091653	11127373
2010	26518839	9561970	16956869	6452236	6855587	13680327
2011	31000218	13027234	17972984	6437025	7474806	17507040
2012	37227544	15973611	21253933	7785196	8518653	20595909
2013	42638732	18532841	24105891	8524663	9104614	22536325
2014	49527010	23010823	26516187	10055306	9133973	28438054
2015	55563183	24720743	30842440	13551793	9300133	29768831
2016	58424194	26064090	32360104	16305335	8839451	30067802
2017	58566453	27340047	31226406	15970399	8614761	33005389

注:2011 年起固定资产投资口径由计划总投资 500 万元以上项目投资及房地产开发投资构成。

a) Since 2011, the date of investment in fixed Assets was composed by investment projects of which each is over 5 million yuan and investment in real estate.

7－02 市区固定资产投资总额(1990－2017年)

Investment in Fixed Assets of Urban District (1990－2017)

单位:万元 (10000 yuan)

年 份 Year	固定资产投资 Investment in Fixed Assets	房地产开发投资 Investment in Real Estate Development	项目投资 Projects Investment	基础设施投资 Investment in Infrastructure	工业投资 Industrial Investment	民间投资 Nongovernment Investment
1990		12750				
1991		16509				
1992		29784				
1993		115116				
1994		189357				
1995		375816				
1996		439245				
1997		445316				
1998		538499				
1999		636705				
2000		737950				
2001		1255605				
2002		1724128				
2003	7409538	2176433	5233105	2535843	2424383	3316886
2004	8963515	3088508	6153009	2624214	3299235	5238005
2005	10358519	3485810	6872709	3071506	3247399	5802542
2006	10944075	3653393	7290682	3150192	3289532	5559199
2007	12630099	4298687	8331412	3396807	3617512	6218211
2008	15184281	5269947	9914334	4726734	3676567	7076219
2009	17797778	6261562	11536216	5070500	3821313	8632900
2010	21437496	8486495	12951001	5438685	4293707	10332997
2011	25202394	11409566	13792828	5451654	4801419	13302115
2012	30160782	13749412	16411370	6495070	5554286	15669790
2013	34029665	15978470	18051195	6728552	5787728	16735292
2014	42572154	21128840	21443314	8010162	7100359	24220917
2015	47507571	22981761	24525810	10960519	6835700	25114041
2016	49572744	24325359	25247385	13229143	6173050	24924679
2017	52395657	26449190	25946467	13447972	6718135	29402238

7－03 全市固定资产投资总额发展指数(2011－2017 年)

Indices of Investment in Fixed Assets(2011－2017)

(上年＝100) (Preceding Year＝100)

年份 Year	固定资产投资 Investment in Fixed Assets	第一产业 Primary Industry	第二产业 Secondary Industry	第三产业 Primary Industry	民间投资 Nongovernment Investment	房地产开发投资 Investment in Real Estate Development	基础设施 Investment in Infrastructure	工业投资 Industrial Investment
2011	116.9	183.3	108.9	119.6	128.0	136.2	99.8	109.0
2012	120.1	55.5	114.0	122.3	117.6	122.6	120.9	114.0
2013	114.5	196.9	107.0	116.7	109.4	116.0	109.5	106.9
2014	116.2	227.0	100.3	120.2	126.2	124.2	118.0	100.3
2015	112.2	165.0	101.8	114.3	104.7	107.4	134.8	101.8
2016	105.1	125.1	95.2	107.0	101.0	105.4	120.3	95.0
2017	101.4	111.2	100.9	101.5	110.4	104.9	100.1	100.5

注:按第三次农业普查结果对 2016 年固定资产投资基数进行调整,2017 年指数按可比口径计算。

a) The data of investment in fixed assets were adjusted according to the results of the 3rd agricultural census, and the indices in 2017 were calculated on a comparable basis.

7-04 分地区固定资产投资发展指数(2011-2017年)

Indices of Investment in Fixed Assets by Region(2011-2017)

(上年=100) (Preceding Year=100)

年份 Year	全市 Whole City	上城区 Shangcheng	下城区 Xiacheng	江干区 Jianggan	拱墅区 Gongshu	西湖区 Xihu	高新(滨江)区 Hi-Tech (Binjiang)	萧山区 Xiaoshan
2011	116.9	67.8	101.3	119.1	135.3	120.6	115.9	115.0
2012	120.1	109.4	116.6	129.8	120.7	121.5	118.9	118.9
2013	114.5	107.2	125.6	92.2	125.1	124.5	111.7	118.4
2014	116.2	121.6	66.5	118.7	124.6	118.4	118.9	116.4
2015	112.2	114.1	112.5	118.5	118.9	107.2	76.5	113.2
2016	105.1	123.1	129.3	101.3	97.8	80.1	126.5	112.0
2017	101.4	111.3	102.0	87.4	75.2	120.5	79.8	104.3

(上年=100) 7-04 续表 continued (Preceding Year=100)

年份 Year	大江东产业集聚区 Dajiangdong Industry Cluster District	余杭区 Yuhang	富阳区 Fuyang	临安区 Lin'an	经济技术开发区 Economic and Technological Development Zone	西湖风景名胜区 The West Lake Scenic Zone	桐庐县 Tonglu	淳安县 Chun'an	建德市 Jiande
2011		118.8	106.5	118.6	116.5	46.7	115.7	118.9	120.9
2012		123.9	122.5	121.6	120.7	74.2	121.9	122.0	120.8
2013		123.3	122.4	119.2	118.7	712.7	122.2	123.1	122.3
2014		124.5	122.0	120.1	106.3	125.3	121.5	121.5	121.8
2015	115.6	117.0	115.3	117.1	68.2	136.9	117.9	104.3	122.7
2016	108.0	113.1	100.2	115.0	101.2	176.4	102.5	106.0	116.7
2017	84.5	108.0	87.4	109.2	111.2	28.8	89.5	108.8	115.1

注:按第三次农业普查结果对2016年固定资产投资基数进行调整,2017年指数按可比口径计算。

a) The data of investment in fixed assets were adjusted according to the results of the 3rd agricultural census, and the indices in 2017 were calculated on a comparable basis.

7-05 三次产业固定资产投资(1978-2017年)

Investment in Fixed Assets Grouped by Three Industries (1978-2017)

单位:万元 (10000 yuan)

年份 Year	绝对数(万元) Absolute Figure(10000 yuan)				比重(以投资总额为100) Proportion(%)		
	合计 Total	第一产业 Primary Industry	第二产业 Secondary Industry	第三产业 Tertiary Industry	第一产业 Primary Industry	第二产业 Secondary Industry	第三产业 Tertiary Industry
1978	23941	2174	14455	7312	9.1	60.4	30.5
1979	34407	2454	19927	12026	7.1	57.9	35.0
1980	45752	1608	26211	17933	3.5	57.3	39.2
1981	51538	850	29176	21512	1.6	56.6	41.8
1982	66123	1352	37648	27123	2.0	57.0	41.0
1983	68306	1297	37823	29186	1.9	55.4	42.7
1984	93244	2831	46619	43794	3.0	50.0	47.0
1985	141889	3207	71608	67074	2.3	50.5	47.2
1986	182398	2265	94394	85739	1.2	51.8	47.0
1987	200516	2994	106600	90922	1.5	53.2	45.3
1988	205967	4746	118736	82485	2.3	57.6	40.1
1989	202131	3038	117651	81442	1.5	58.2	40.3
1990	229214	2181	126263	100770	1.0	55.1	43.9
1991	255696	3204	132303	120189	1.3	51.7	47.0
1992	384136	4424	206659	173053	1.2	53.8	45.0
1993	825382	5650	346416	473316	0.7	42.0	57.3
1994	1059437	3905	354672	700860	0.4	33.5	66.1
1995	1566280	5821	534687	1025772	0.4	34.1	65.5
1996	1819333	3100	640273	1175960	0.2	35.2	64.6
1997	2139012	1712	595966	1541334	-	27.9	72.1
1998	2681740	4053	706948	1970739	0.2	26.4	73.4
1999	3233609	23546	764309	2445754	0.7	23.6	75.7
2000	3766473	774	844334	2921365	-	22.4	77.6
2001	4634929	595	953494	3680840	-	20.6	79.4
2002	5623366	6514	1104212	4512640	0.1	19.6	80.3
2003	8952090	10489	3208885	5732716	0.1	35.9	64.0
2004	11081993	15992	4369015	6696986	0.1	39.4	60.5
2005	12777972	13982	4451936	8312054	0.1	34.8	65.1
2006	13734482	17892	4651420	9065170	0.1	33.9	66.0
2007	15837775	23278	5286340	10528157	0.1	33.4	66.5
2008	18822936	30810	5705736	13086390	0.2	30.3	69.5
2009	21951706	31335	6115482	15804889	0.1	27.9	72.0
2010	26518839	41959	6875840	19601040	0.2	25.9	73.9
2011	31000218	76931	7486832	23436455	0.2	24.2	75.6
2012	37227544	42668	8531598	28653278	0.1	22.9	77.0
2013	42638732	84018	9125316	33429398	0.2	21.4	78.4
2014	49527010	190748	9152477	40183785	0.4	18.5	81.1
2015	55563183	314688	9317825	45930670	0.6	16.8	82.6
2016	58424194	393625	8869013	49161556	0.7	15.2	84.1
2017	58566453	336686	8665510	49564257	0.6	14.8	84.6

7-06 全市固定资产投资房屋建筑面积及造价(1978-2017年)

Floor Space of Buildings and Their Cost (1978-2017)

年份 Year	施工面积(万平方米) Floor Space of Buildings Under Construction (10000sq. m)	住宅 Residential Buildings	竣工面积(万平方米) Floor Space of Buildings Completed (10000 sq. m)	住宅 Residential Buildings	竣工房屋价值(万元) Value of Buildings Completed (10000 yuan)	住宅 Residential Buildings	每平方米造价(元) Cost Per Square (yuan)	住宅 Residential Buildings
1978			101.95	39.58	8869	2810	87	71
1979			150.26	68.01	13223	4965	88	73
1980	456.54		202.58	104.44	19448	8564	96	82
1981	507.94		232.25	120.35	26709	12396	115	103
1982	554.89	258.09	281.63	148.66	34095	16470	121	111
1983	531.79	244.36	247.07	125.86	33938	15494	137	123
1984	620.71	293.21	267.85	138.71	42740	18398	160	133
1985	741.47	333.72	327.75	157.85	56561	22825	173	145
1986	674.58	278.19	338.19	160.19	50561	27338	238	170
1987	544.64	149.07	254.73	73.16	68801	14944	270	204
1988	526.70	156.92	230.21	75.44	68407	17820	297	236
1989	420.81	116.12	202.15	64.15	69750	18200	345	284
1990	472.59	209.50	236.44	112.77	93557	34266	396	304
1991	459.00	205.41	226.84	92.72	93158	28599	411	308
1992	604.85	301.21	262.11	114.97	116169	39834	452	350
1993	958.91	533.01	380.29	199.96	224251	105107	589	525
1994	1069.68	613.62	460.20	274.19	375211	212705	815	776
1995	1320.68	737.79	524.58	319.41	491705	274314	937	859
1996	1399.70	758.00	582.70	354.50	688569	370485	1182	1045
1997	1363.80	660.70	642.10	338.00	871361	449235	1357	1329
1998	1456.02	743.59	515.16	271.91	709730	390624	1378	1437
1999	1681.71	956.15	709.10	411.44	1119141	641717	1578	1560
2000	1721.58	949.32	744.42	419.80	1207767	709044	1622	1689
2001	2318.95	1251.92	830.05	402.46	1310380	679449	1579	1688
2002	2713.02	1586.28	890.05	492.95	1623662	956643	1820	1941
2003	4392.79	2083.58	1618.01	651.58	2732763	1353422	1689	2077
2004	5731.48	2909.03	1865.83	717.46	2791115	1313596	1496	1831
2005	6671.39	3628.34	1856.34	801.34	3265491	1865538	1759	2328
2006	7260.08	3747.60	1737.51	706.13	2900836	1580689	1670	2239
2007	7942.07	4040.54	1849.24	858.99	3750264	2329184	2028	2712
2008	9471.42	4160.27	2057.86	846.34	4113211	2171525	1999	2566
2009	10308.45	4441.84	2009.90	700.63	3626421	1684092	1804	2404
2010	12971.81	5534.10	2695.90	902.57	5274936	2285285	1957	2532
2011	15982.64	6442.52	3108.57	991.72	6209320	2498468	1997	2519
2012	17329.23	6938.29	2952.06	1048.95	6015778	2485123	2038	2369
2013	19226.78	7392.23	3666.67	1308.83	7744168	3530744	2112	2698
2014	20877.58	7757.60	4274.87	1350.19	9613177	3951202	2249	2926
2015	21686.34	8163.82	4877.76	1600.80	-	-	-	-
2016	17896.18	7370.57	3937.72	1443.96	12561050	5092235	3190	3527
2017	18807.44	6910.48	4953.34	1470.84	15291293	6139823	3087	4174

注:2015年竣工房屋价值相关指标取消。

a) Since 2015, the indicators related to floor space of buildings completed have been cancelled.

7-07 市区固定资产投资房屋建筑面积及造价(1978-2017年)
Urban District Floor Space of Buildings and Their Cost (1978-2017)

年份 Year	施工面积(万平方米) Floor Space of Buildings Under Construction (10000 sq. m)	住宅 Residential Buildings	竣工面积(万平方米) Floor Space of Buildings Completed (10000sq. m)	住宅 Residential Buildings	竣工房屋价值(万元) Value of Buildings Completed (10000 yuan)	住宅 Residential Buildings	每平方米造价(元) Cost Per Square (yuan)	住宅 Residential Buildings
1978			71.56	29.06	6941	2237	97	77
1979			109.23	53.37	10267	4056	94	76
1980			137.11	76.73	14396	6752	105	88
1981			163.36	90.12	20093	9643	123	107
1982	378.88	172.11	189.92	100.07	25200	11980	133	120
1983	376.32	169.17	157.14	81.68	24029	11045	153	135
1984	465.27	221.72	191.13	104.55	33863	14658	177	140
1985	532.66	258.19	219.79	114.26	40344	17489	184	153
1986	465.75	203.22	219.33	116.70	58619	21149	267	181
1987	336.85	86.05	150.59	41.72	46530	9513	309	228
1988	315.80	90.98	117.71	37.63	38501	10117	330	269
1989	253.41	56.39	99.86	28.89	38680	9087	387	315
1990	301.82	128.50	137.88	62.47	60551	20361	439	326
1991	265.61	118.99	114.19	42.31	53819	12892	471	305
1992	329.16	190.55	115.59	57.36	55758	19706	483	344
1993	500.08	266.80	175.22	104.83	101528	53540	579	511
1994	618.91	352.16	212.06	123.74	182730	102924	862	832
1995	821.03	463.98	244.94	152.10	250073	139666	1021	918
1996	969.10	538.50	350.10	229.00	437239	274244	1249	1196
1997	1017.30	485.20	442.00	232.70	675762	357624	1529	1537
1998	1055.24	541.41	321.17	184.18	516400	317402	1608	1723
1999	1204.30	656.07	489.23	294.85	908844	533675	1858	1810
2000	1176.29	617.80	497.64	269.94	916212	528385	1841	1957
2001	2053.02	1085.30	698.29	325.64	1193818	615802	1710	1891
2002	2330.97	1335.78	744.48	404.35	1483862	869969	1993	2152
2003	3637.82	1699.61	1325.48	516.33	2395039	1174735	1807	2275
2004	4740.42	2453.87	1389.30	528.26	2257386	1068708	1625	2023
2005	5533.58	3039.08	1478.07	661.56	2804402	1626514	1897	2459
2006	5898.15	3114.45	1327.37	580.22	2365342	1357671	1782	2340
2007	6496.01	3357.18	1355.43	674.97	3063585	1992874	2260	2953
2008	7812.71	3466.88	1537.69	668.13	3372465	1827426	2193	2735
2009	8558.17	3807.67	1398.49	537.39	2725150	1321357	1949	2459
2010	10738.49	4759.75	1983.33	732.55	4255543	1927150	2146	2631
2011	13259.13	5451.45	2091.12	797.96	4736356	2122126	2265	2659
2012	14385.57	5680.08	2169.11	889.73	4966296	2207085	2290	2481
2013	15693.30	5910.71	2637.83	986.35	6074353	2822878	2303	2862
2014	18219.47	6591.75	3516.92	1132.80	8406996	3536426	2390	3122
2015	18872.19	6972.04	3868.26	1269.66	-	-	-	-
2016	15655.38	6338.80	3192.00	1205.44	10907502	4524544	3417	3753
2017	17404.30	6305.16	4454.20	1332.41	14156506	5784449	3178	4341

注:2015年竣工房屋价值相关指标取消。

a) Since 2015, the indicators related to floor space of buildings completed have been cancelled.

7－08 分地区

Investment in Fixed Assets

单位:万元

年份 Year	全市 Whole City	上城区 Shangcheng	下城区 Xiacheng	江干区 Jianggan	拱墅区 Gongshu	西湖区 Xihu	高新(滨江)区 Hi－Tech (Binjiang)
2003	8952090						
2004	11081993						
2005	12777972						
2006	13734482						
2007	15837775						
2008	18822936						
2009	21951706						
2010	26518839	802793	1030077	2901447	1508325	2188293	1609857
2011	31000218	544686	1043891	3456831	2041130	2638752	1866605
2012	37227544	595996	1217244	4486541	2463963	3205079	2220183
2013	42638732	638625	1528423	4138372	3081999	3991415	2480827
2014	49527010	776441	1017029	4914073	3838785	4723858	2948885
2015	55563183	885811	1144348	5823773	4565672	5064510	2254688
2016	58424194	1090808	1479399	5899757	4467059	4058658	2851746
2017	58566453	1214556	1509493	5158741	3327270	4889773	2274389

固定资产投资(2003－2017 年)

by Region(2003－2017)

(10000 yuan)

萧山区 Xiaoshan	大江东产业集聚区 Dajiangdong Industry Cluster District	余杭区 Yuhang	富阳区 Fuyang	临安区 Lin'an	经济技术开发区 Economic and Technological Development Zone	西湖风景名胜区 The West Lake Scenic Zone	桐庐县 Tonglu	淳安县 Chun'an	建德市 Jiande
1835889		1162453	563603	346980			250100	135275	246594
2246807		1478151	767880	479669			352987	218730	299212
2161067		1718028	896329	525840			424962	275543	316779
2424763		1758656	1017368	600270			470450	324444	377875
2745133		1929019	1155871	673495			542615	403119	432576
3184947		2317510	1334619	665978			653234	475340	509484
3769557		2823192	1534401	763725			738391	542037	575374
4515095		3480147	1796500	956408	1732557	18393	1001737	668168	658530
5190805		4134743	1913712	1134746	2018316	8594	1158682	794383	796301
6169275		5121242	2343812	1379851	2436859	6378	1412038	969471	961590
7307304		6312261	2868320	1644498	2891767	45458	1725986	1193796	1176467
8508518	2226738	7861506	3500717	1975132	3074966	56971	2096371	1450503	1432850
9631238	2574129	9200016	4037889	2312053	2098220	77986	2472662	1512184	1758713
10783163	2780042	10403247	4043949	2659669	2123585	137576	2534994	1603624	2053163
11042552	2180400	11232991	3406491	2904328	2162102	39564	2133136	1744157	2293503

7-09 分地区分类型固定

Investment in Fixed Assets

单位:万元

指　　标	Item	全　市 Total	市　区 Urban District
固定资产投资额	**Investment in Fixed Assets**	**58566453**	**52395657**
#民间投资	#Private Investment	33005389	29402238
#工业投资	Industrial Investment	8614761	6718135
#基础设施投资	Investment in Infrastructure	15970399	13447972
一、按投资类型分	**Grouped by Sector**		
投资项目完成额	Investment Projects	31226406	25946467
房地产开发投资完成额	Real Estate	27340047	26449190
二、按登记注册类型分	**Grouped by Status of Registration**		
内资	Domestic - funded	53936865	48101809
国有	State - owned	7020738	6209669
集体	Collective - owned	495118	351167
股份合作	Cooperative	43093	37569
联营企业	State Joint Ownership	3504	3504
国有独资公司	State - owned Corporations	4336573	3837176
其他有限责任公司	Other Limited Liability Corporations	22545477	20686359
股份有限公司	Share - holding Corporations Ltd.	1260055	1105714
私营	Private	17872048	15567466
其他	Other	360259	303185
港、澳、台商投资	Investment from Hong Kong, Macao and Taiwan	3505486	3286387
外商投资	Foreign Investment	1107719	1000974
个体经营	Individual	16383	6487

资产投资(2017 年)
by Region(2017)

(10000 yuan)

萧山区 Xiaoshan	余杭区 Yuhang	富阳区 Fuyang	临安区 Lin'an	桐庐县 Tonglu	淳安县 Chun'an	建德市 Jiande
11042552	**11232991**	**3406491**	**2904328**	**2133136**	**1744157**	**2293503**
7696823	6477096	2107709	1661309	1267054	1070579	1265518
1956406	1152906	1277569	779318	591225	373381	932020
1891273	2391237	888142	939462	928274	550367	1043786
5075185	5363125	2345814	2026837	1841120	1308233	2130586
5967367	5869866	1060677	877491	292016	435924	162917
10372582	9458909	3181858	2766842	2058010	1603045	2174001
906880	780348	164317	195017	339760	151730	319579
44735	54343	90937	2043	69898	–	74053
–	2013	15315	–	331	–	5193
–	–	–	–	–	–	–
634675	720714	455308	625732	262460	226583	10354
3209809	3990763	1176100	576695	431627	385738	1041753
136211	308755	88969	98394	18185	53864	82292
5438766	3591066	1151475	1118771	888100	779940	636542
1506	10907	39437	150190	47649	5190	4235
440060	1453053	92366	118960	59325	93500	66274
228543	321029	131707	13966	15469	45623	45653
1367	–	560	4560	332	1989	7575

单位:万元　　　　7-09 续表

指　标	Item	全　市 Total	市　区 Urban District
三、按行业分	**Grouped by Sector**		
农林牧渔业	Agricultare, Forestry, Animal Husbandry and Fishery	402999	153110
采矿业	Mining	60101	25307
制造业	Manufacturing	7052114	5444804
电力、热力、燃气及水的生产和供应业	Production and Supply of Electric Power, Heat Power, Gas and Tap Water	1502546	1248024
建筑业	Construction	75530	63471
批发和零售业	Wholesale & Retail Trades	319776	246213
交通运输、仓储和邮政业	Transportation, Storage and Post	5058477	4357397
住宿和餐饮业	Hotels and Catering Services	600357	236398
信息传输、软件和信息技术服务业	Information Transmission, Softuare and Information Technology	1609346	1554066
金融业	Financial Intertnediation	188058	180610
房地产业	Real Estate	31357609	30234979
租赁和商务服务业	Leasing and Business Services	560366	548970
科学研究和技术服务业	Scientific Research and Technical Service	286835	260695
水利、环境和公共设施管理业	Management of Water Conservancy, Environment and Public Facilities	6596611	5228968
居民服务、修理和其他服务业	Residentid Service, Repairs and Other Service	28957	22465
教育	Education	1627072	1566611
卫生和社会工作	Health Care and Social Welfare	497843	389195
文化、体育和娱乐业	Culture, Sports and Entertainment	578314	513108
公共管理、社会保障和社会组织	Public Management, Social Security and Social Organizations	163542	121266

continued (10000 yuan)

萧山区 Xiaoshan	余杭区 Yuhang	富阳区 Fuyang	临安区 Lin'an	桐庐县 Tonglu	淳安县 Chun'an	建德市 Jiande
–	–	29189	123215	114474	85733	49682
–	–	4822	20485	1518	10786	22490
1811940	952302	1163422	656441	533987	309146	764177
144466	200604	109325	102392	55720	53449	145353
–	7680	–	1783	4653	450	6956
18154	66917	10669	15953	13786	40456	19321
438441	498823	121898	167075	159524	329872	211684
72100	49613	4293	37520	94823	228588	40548
65590	908501	70271	–	–	26787	28493
3041	2647	–	–	2255	–	5193
7111662	6685635	1187695	1011822	367481	459935	295214
73090	76077	6326	767	7765	699	2932
1095	53114	290	59383	5588	3867	16685
1029763	1077352	519254	624407	660853	125258	581532
–	728	941	9434	3619	–	2873
224745	392653	110205	33938	14914	16037	29510
23577	81566	33492	4008	56206	11774	40668
19038	150413	5151	10073	9214	37786	18206
5850	28366	29248	25632	26756	3534	11986

7－10 分地区分类型

Investment in Industrial

单位:万元

指标	Item	全市 Total	市区 Urban District 合计 Total
总计	**Total**	**8614761**	**6718135**
#技术改造投资	**Investment in Technique Innovation**	**6432256**	**5037608**
一、按登记注册类型分	**Grouped by Status of Registration**		
内资	Domestic－funded	7612191	5842328
国有	State－owned	727182	663596
集体	Collective－owned	10916	4697
股份合作	Cooperative	625	625
联营企业	State Joint Ownership	3504	3504
国有独资公司	State－funded Corporations	330554	277734
其他有限责任公司	Other Limited Liability Corporations	2695788	2228205
股份有限公司	Share－holding Corporations Ltd.	426050	328708
私营	Private	3415231	2334603
其他	Other	2341	656
港、澳、台商投资	Investment from Hong Kong,Macao and Taiwan	456080	401755
外商投资	Foreign Investment	535551	470409
个体经营	Individual	10939	3643
二、按行业分	**Grouped by Sector**		
采矿业	Mining	60101	25307
制造业	Manufacturing	7052114	5444804
#农副食品加工业	Processing of Food from Agricultural Products Processing	84314	57794
食品制造业	Food Manufacturing	110691	49333
酒、饮料和精制茶制造业	Wine,Beverage and Tea Manufacturing	207415	45409
烟草制品业	Tobacco Processing	41729	41729
纺织业	Textile Processing	316485	258825
纺织服装、服饰业	Textile Products and Costume Industry	127424	69759

工业投资(2017 年)
Sector by Region(2017)

(10000 yuan)

萧山区 Xiaoshan	余杭区 Yuhang	富阳区 Fuyang	临安区 Lin'an	桐庐县 Tonglu	淳安县 Chun'an	建德市 Jiande
1956406	**1152906**	**1277569**	**779318**	**591225**	**373381**	**932020**
1606297	**659506**	**1070391**	**509570**	**447773**	**282569**	**664306**
1749166	911627	1165188	761480	559490	344459	865914
28542	24014	2352	8888	7550	10285	45751
–	3201	–	1496	2479	–	3740
–	625	–	–	–	–	–
–	–	–	–	–	–	–
46362	30004	55142	36640	44479	8341	–
995216	273580	430448	137908	114739	23790	329054
77993	50392	88233	86585	6674	27576	63092
601053	529811	589013	489307	381884	274467	424277
–	–	–	656	1685	–	–
92295	157839	31589	12979	23941	16895	13489
113578	83440	80232	3143	7462	12027	45653
1367	–	560	1716	332	–	6964
–	–	4822	20485	1518	10786	22490
1811940	952302	1163422	656441	533987	309146	764177
18156	9132	11103	19403	4224	6913	15383
9952	8930	18459	7799	6639	40442	14277
13372	11452	–	–	34556	58513	68937
–						
196258	48395	2150	10853	7758	25215	24687
31434	15063	–	–	54492	–	3173

单位:万元　　7－10　续表

指　　标	Item	全　　市 Total	市　　区 Urban District 合　计 Total
皮革、毛皮、羽毛及其制品和制造业	Leather, Furs, Down and Related Products	26491	14246
木材加工和木、竹、藤、棕、草制品业	Timber Processing, Bamboo, Cane, Palm Fiber and Straw Products	26905	10269
家具制造业	Furniture Manufacturing	48399	29855
造纸和纸制品业	Paper Making and Paper Products	140914	126828
印刷业和记录媒介复制业	Printing and Reproduction of Recording media	83683	54751
文教、工美、体育和娱乐用品制造业	Cultural, Educational and Sports Goods	102520	52112
石油加工、炼焦和核燃料加工业	Petroleum and Nuclear Fuel Processing	11104	3350
化学原料和化学制品制造业	Raw Chemical Material and Chemical Products	510323	341922
医药制造业	Medical and Pharmaceutical Products	461194	421145
化学纤维制造业	Chemical Fiber	177335	177335
橡胶和塑料制品业	Rubber and Plastic Products	302000	194667
非金属矿物制品业	Nonmetal Mineral Products	381437	159360
黑色金属冶炼和压延加工业	Ferrous Metals Smelting and Pressing	14722	6817
有色金属冶炼和压延加工业	Nonferrous Metal Smelting and Pressing	120879	112460
金属制品业	Metal Products	240773	172866
通用设备制造业	General Purpose Machinery	503929	416060
专用设备制造业	Special Purpose Machinery	244544	201186
汽车制造业	Automobile Manufacturing	918425	866611
铁路、船舶、航空航天和其他运输设备制造业	Railway, Watercraft, Avigation Spaceflight and other Equipment Manufacturing	39105	24422
电气机械和器材制造业	Electric Equipment and Machinery	623345	536007
计算机、通信和其他电子设备制造业	Computers, Telecommunications and other Electronic Equipment Manufacturing	718162	617983
仪器仪表制造业	Instruments and Meters Manufacturing	164849	160415
其他制造业	Other Manufacturing	181826	135618
废弃资源综合利用业	Multiple Utilization of Waste Resouces	96411	77740
金属制品、机械和设备修理业	Metal Products, Machinery and Equipment Repair	24781	7930
电力、燃气及水的生产和供应业	Production and Supply of Electric Power, Heat Power, Gas and Tap Water	1502546	1248024

continued (10000 yuan)

萧山区 Xiaoshan	余杭区 Yuhang	富阳区 Fuyang	临安区 Lin'an	桐庐县 Tonglu	淳安县 Chun'an	建德市 Jiande
6542	1691	4855	–	545	–	11700
950	5171	3634	514	–	14766	1870
18400	8074	1192	1224	5798	–	12746
4572	31323	34783	56150	10439	–	3647
9209	5366	14432	3114	19556	4899	4477
17505	21636	7944	2871	41663	2309	6436
–	3350	–	–	–	–	7754
233342	16908	25972	65594	5624	14545	148232
30754	46331	158147	9265	17900	5744	16405
157825	325	3434	3239	–	–	–
32636	13945	105376	35634	28650	8935	69748
21582	39466	63481	25089	33216	22289	166572
5448	1369	–	–	–	–	7905
769	42212	69347	132	4856	–	3563
47053	38525	57865	19928	16810	6817	44280
110785	127281	66373	51652	51253	8268	28348
30965	72093	51183	9409	28048	7793	7517
588693	111476	47281	71100	17375	20307	14132
11212	8380	4455	–	48	6084	8551
123525	110450	140260	128207	21449	35525	30364
28669	64357	125478	95078	91323	2590	6266
14454	33732	54170	32734	400	4034	–
25152	47818	44607	–	27339	13158	5711
22726	121	47441	7452	3046	–	15625
–	7930	–	–	980	–	15871
144466	200604	109325	102392	55720	53449	145353

7－11　分地区房地产
Investment in Real Estate

指　　标	Item	全市 Total	市区 Urban District 合计 Total
房地产开发投资额　（万元）	**Investment in Real Estate Development　(10000 yuan)**	**27340047**	**26449190**
住宅　（万元）	Residential Buildings　(10000 yuan)	17129297	16634861
办公楼　（万元）	Office Buildings　(10000 yuan)	2455681	2433138
商业营业用房　（万元）	Buildings for Business Use　(10000 yuan)	3286295	3130891
其他　（万元）	Others　(10000 yuan)	4468774	4250300
房屋建筑面积	**Floor space of Buildings**		
施工面积　（万平方米）	Under Construction　(10000 sq. m)	11523	10633
#住宅　（万平方米）	#Residential Buildings　(10000 sq. m)	5939	5366
新开工面积　（万平方米）	Started This Year　(10000 sq. m)	2177	1984
#住宅　（万平方米）	#Residential Buildings　(10000 sq. m)	1244	1116
竣工面积　（万平方米）	Construction Completed　(10000 sq. m)	2086	1897
#住宅　（万平方米）	#Residential Buildings　(10000 sq. m)	1171	1053
商品房销售情况	**Selling of Commercialized Buildings**		
销售金额　（万元）	Total Sales of Buildings　(10000 yuan)	41801134	40319243
#住宅　（万元）	#Residential Buildings　(10000 yuan)	32257549	30946501
现房销售额　（万元）	Sales of Completed Buildings　(10000 yuan)	8527802	8020832
#住宅　（万元）	#Residential Buildings　(10000 yuan)	5296119	4858245
期房销售金额　（万元）	Sales of Future Buildings　(10000 yuan)	33273332	32298411
#住宅　（万元）	#Residential Buildings　(10000 yuan)	26961430	26088256
销售面积　（万平方米）	Floor Space of Buildings Sold　(10000 sq. m)	20536743	18744008
#住宅　（万平方米）	#Residential Buildings　(10000 sq. m)	15197292	13575695
现房销售面积　（万平方米）	Floor Space of Completed Buildings Sold　(10000 sq. m)	4885769	4227491
#住宅　（万平方米）	#Residential Buildings　(10000 sq. m)	2965631	2382312
期房销售面积　（万平方米）	Floor Space of Futures Buildings Sold　(10000 sq. m)	15650974	14516517
#住宅　（万平方米）	#Residential Buildings　(10000 sq. m)	12231661	11193383

开发投资(2017 年)
Development by Region(2017)

萧山区 Xiaoshan	余杭区 Yuhang	富阳区 Fuyang	临安区 Lin'an	桐庐县 Tonglu	淳安县 Chun'an	建德市 Jiande
5967367	**5869866**	**1060677**	**877491**	**292016**	**435924**	**162917**
4051744	3984045	782650	629762	174764	222537	97135
441723	380259	35283	24492	17210	265	5068
413940	677677	79567	88814	85757	53178	16469
1059960	827885	163177	134423	14285	159944	44245
2284	3031	531	557	316	366	207
1220	1795	332	399	212	230	132
659	418	138	184	50	85	57
368	300	98	137	38	57	32
336	469	136	92	63	83	42
192	321	85	57	43	52	23
9923767	8950103	1473764	1620168	605666	382462	493763
8340043	7428685	1113250	1510161	521015	353347	436686
1152767	1607479	410507	256138	228242	126957	151771
652323	1387320	254780	204987	200431	117603	119840
8771000	7342624	1063257	1364030	377424	255505	341992
7687720	6041365	858470	1305174	320584	235744	316846
4387015	5252349	1106885	1393705	817999	442152	532584
3516240	4020511	837070	1280770	724135	411980	485482
618679	1048478	328536	267020	302021	187906	168351
304576	834537	189298	210469	265579	177105	140635
3768336	4203871	778349	1126685	515978	254246	364233
3211664	3185974	647772	1070301	458556	234875	344847

7－12 房屋建筑面积及造价(2017 年)
Floor Space of Buildings and Their Cost(2017)

指　　标	Item	施工面积(万平方米) Floor Space of Buildings Under Construction (10000 sq. m)	竣工面积(万平方米) Floor Space of Buildings Completed (10000 sq. m)	竣工房屋的价值(万元) Value of Buildings Completed (10000 yuan)	每平方米造价(元) Cost Per Square Meter (yuan)
全　市	**Total**				
房屋建筑面积合计	**Floor Space of Buildings**	**18807**	**4953**	**15291293**	**3087**
#住宅	#Residential Buildings	6910	1471	6139823	4174
房地产开发	Real Estate Development	11523	2086	8841612	4239
#住宅	#Residential Buildings	5939	1171	5119365	4373
市　区	**Urban District**				
房屋建筑面积合计	**Floor Space of Buildings**	**17404**	**4454**	**14156506**	**3178**
#住宅	#Residential Buildings	6305	1332	5784449	4341
房地产开发	Real Estate Development	10633	1897	8314592	4384
#住宅	#Residential Buildings	5366	1053	4810538	4568
#萧 山 区	**Xiaoshan**				
房屋建筑面积合计	**Total Floor Space of Buildings**	**3437**	**595**	**1964965**	**3300**
#住宅	#Residential Buildings	1486	240	1018519	4236
房地产开发	Real Estate Development	2284	336	1339983	3986
#住宅	#Residential Buildings	1220	192	860331	4481
余 杭 区	**Yuhang**				
房屋建筑面积合计	**Total Floor Space of Buildings**	**4252**	**1033**	**3366514**	**3258**
#住宅	#Residential Buildings	1876	358	1541516	4302
房地产开发	Real Estate Development	3031	469	1817361	3879
#住宅	#Residential Buildings	1795	321	1372481	4277

7－12　续表　continued

指　　标	Item	施工面积（万平方米）Floor Space of Buildings Under Construction（10000 sq. m）	竣工面积（万平方米）Floor Space of Buildings Completed（10000 sq. m）	竣工房屋的价值（万元）Value of Buildings Completed（10000 yuan）	每平方米造价（元）Cost Per Square Meter（yuan）
富阳区	**Fuyang**				
房屋建筑面积合计	**Total Floor Space of Buildings**	**979**	**432**	**901635**	**2087**
#住宅	#Residential Buildings	376	122	345017	2830
房地产开发	Real Estate Development	531	136	349780	2565
#住宅	#Residential Buildings	332	85	247802	2929
临安区	**Lin'an**				
房屋建筑面积合计	**Total Floor Space of Buildings**	**862**	**211**	**621428**	**2941**
#住宅	#Residential Buildings	411	64	266731	4151
房地产开发	Real Estate Development	557	92	414885	4515
#住宅	#Residential Buildings	399	57	253749	4422
桐庐县	**Tonglu**				
房屋建筑面积合计	**Total Floor Space of Buildings**	**462**	**126**	**376136**	**2983**
#住宅	#Residential Buildings	213	43	178219	4165
房地产开发	Real Estate Development	316	63	267840	4234
#住宅	#Residential Buildings	212	43	178219	4165
淳安县	**Chun'an**				
房屋建筑面积合计	**Total Floor Space of Buildings**	**463**	**157**	**344384**	**2189**
#住宅	#Residential Buildings	238	54	109284	2012
房地产开发	Real Estate Development	366	83	181058	2170
#住宅	#Residential Buildings	230	52	98299	1877
建德市	**Jiande**				
房屋建筑面积合计	**Total Floor Space of Buildings**	**477**	**216**	**414267**	**1920**
#住宅	#Residential Buildings	154	41	67871	1643
房地产开发	Real Estate Development	207	42	78122	1855
#住宅	#Residential Buildings	132	23	32309	1429

7－13 分注册类型和资质等级

Financial Statistics on Enterprises for Real Estate Development

单位:万元

项　　目	Item	法人企业数(个) Number of Enterprises (unit)	年末 Asset and		
			流动资产合计 Circulating Funds	应收账款 Account Receivable	固定资产合计 Fixed Assets
总计	**Total**	**1651**	**163220669**	**2536186**	**3084454**
一、按登记注册类型分组	**Grouped by Registration Status**				
内资企业	Domestic Funded	1512	139929338	2330748	1951912
国有企业	State－owned	7	1225476	20424	34435
集体企业	Collective－owned	–	–	–	–
股份合作企业	Share－holding Cooperative Enterprises	–	–	–	–
联营企业	Joint Venture	1	61846	343	510
有限责任公司	Limited Liability Corporations	904	91424013	1617980	1374305
股份有限公司	Share－holding Corporations Ltd.	27	5327679	6846	159163
私营企业	Private Enterprises	573	41890324	685156	383499
其他企业	Other Enterprises	–	–	–	–
港澳台商投资企业	Funded from Hong Kong, Macao and Taiwan	106	14391374	120312	699508
外商投资企业	Foreign Funded	33	8899957	85126	433035
二、按企业资质等级分	**Grouped by Qualification Grade**				
一级	Grade Ⅰ	45	15413206	62321	232872
二级	Grade Ⅱ	107	9310068	168779	210613
三级	Grade Ⅲ	181	11353257	229639	519953
四级	Grade Ⅳ	60	2832275	43506	22584
暂定	Tentative	830	75741441	1429706	1484660
其他	Others	428	48570423	602237	613774

房地产开发企业财务状况(2017 年)

Grouped by Registration Status and Qualification Grade(2017)

(10000 yuan)

资产负债 Liabilities at Year－end						所有者权益合计 Creditors′ Equity	
固定资产原价 Orginal Value of Fixed Assets	累计折旧 Accumulated Depreciation	#本年折旧 Depreciation This Year	在建工程 Projects wnder Construction	资产合计 Total Assets	负债合计 Total Liabilities		实收资本 Capital Hold
3366254	**685546**	**133931**	**4233927**	**192369338**	**148296522**	**44072816**	**32394150**
2278704	582459	88138	3726527	163419099	130438768	32980331	23766670
26002	2266	43	10757	1270997	1076580	194417	64715
–	–	–	–	–	–	–	–
–	–	–	–	–	–	–	–
1574	1064	6	–	95291	42027	53264	1800
1584929	395949	63086	3576414	109651138	87535051	22116086	16177166
191336	36835	4533	438	7005560	4055952	2949608	1197061
474863	146345	20471	138917	45396114	37729157	7666957	6325929
–	–	–	–	–	–	–	–
774054	75003	36021	359779	17592895	9036139	8556756	7473291
313496	28084	9773	147621	11357345	8821616	2535729	1154189
355604	124270	10189	–	23693258	16590192	7103066	2494999
297015	102596	11445	76598	12099409	8532256	3567153	1563860
555181	131422	20840	3126080	15891735	11557048	4334687	1959614
36596	14349	1815	10447	3030169	2616853	413315	201507
1443017	202172	60517	791898	85355566	66886444	18469122	16577497
678841	110737	29125	228905	52299202	42113729	10185472	9596674

单位:万元 7－13 续表

项　　目	Item	营业收入 Revenue of Business	#主营业务收入 Main Revenue of Business	营业成本 Operating Costs	#主营业务成本 Main Cost of Business
总计	**Total**	**36310618**	**36062128**	**28011595**	**26873256**
一、按登记注册类型分组	**Grouped by Registration Status**				
内资企业	Domestic Funded	31626855	31439934	24438554	23595414
国有企业	State－owned	17785	17785	15343	15343
集体企业	Collective－owned	–	–	–	–
股份合作企业	Share－holding Cooperative Enterprises	–	–	–	–
联营企业	Joint Venture	4604	4604	3043	3043
有限责任公司	Limited Liability Corporations	23701530	23560112	18461313	17757497
股份有限公司	Share－holding Corporations Ltd.	181356	181066	79275	76246
私营企业	Private Enterprises	7721579	7676366	5879581	5743285
其他企业	Other Enterprises	–	–	–	–
港澳台商投资企业	Funded from Hong Kong, Macao and Taiwan	4237554	4198352	3268709	2978879
外商投资企业	Foreign Funded	446210	423843	304332	298964
二、按企业资质等级分	**Grouped by Qualification Grade**				
一级	Grade Ⅰ	1134667	1084038	742843	722827
二级	Grade Ⅱ	1551987	1546111	1280056	1272140
三级	Grade Ⅲ	2217366	2211228	1534156	1436282
四级	Grade Ⅳ	275254	274684	163796	163597
暂定	Tentative	25165878	25029734	19673816	18873272
其他	Others	5965466	5916334	4616929	4405138

continued (10000 yuan)

营业税金及附加 Main Sales Tax and Extra Charges	销售费用 Cost of Sales	管理费用 Administration Cost	财务费用 Financil Cost	#利息支出 Interest Expenditure	营业利润 Management Profits	利润总额 Total Profits	应交所得税 Income Tax
2017188	**1072765**	**888311**	**505898**	**613541**	**4891447**	**4850697**	**901402**
1787486	924931	736913	462406	515414	4089318	4055841	761561
265	675	2059	–	2	–	–	–
–	–	–	–	–	–	–	–
–	–	–	–	–	–	–	–
–	74	2259		216	597	585	73
1383281	571725	499674	389756	433206	2945140	2966607	545922
15786	11081	26266		20373	271518	267854	24710
388526	341378	206656	91370	61617	873152	821880	190856
–	–	–	–	–	–	–	–
217625	100421	89555	24433	39928	601359	596010	111244
12078	47413	61842	19060	58199	200771	198846	28596
130668	32502	136490	78545	198176	739167	741578	39811
85036	47156	81266	57343	36745	165896	173289	23921
178123	51934	98850	73184	67566	339314	331760	73371
12966	8104	9722	536	454	81503	81196	20784
1327135	674405	403525	222065	252870	2952132	2900944	609042
283261	258663	158457	74225	57730	613436	621929	134473

7－14　全市分行业基础设施投资(2010－2017年)

Investment in Infrastructure by Sector(2010－2017)

单位:亿元　　(100 million yuan)

年　份 Year	基础设施投资 Investment in Infrastructure	水利、环境和公共设施 Water, Environment and Public Facilities	电力、燃气及水的生产供应业 Produotion and supply of Electricity, Gas & Water	交通运输、仓储和邮政业 Transportation, Storage and Post	电信和其他信息传输服务业 Telecommunications and Other Information Transmission Services	教育设施 Education Facilities	卫生设施 Sanitary Facilities
2010	6452236	2593603	682482	2415265	162166	339381	165668
2011	6437025	2529677	809813	2193350	142099	382672	167024
2012	7785196	2725934	1275603	2572604	162947	572350	201913
2013	8524663	3486809	1167072	2375342	199444	643681	261722
2014	10055306	3940406	1131323	3129697	180788	959814	241614
2015	13551793	5899889	1616380	3892605	201924	1234331	231015
2016	16305335	8101751	1696715	3887608	231813	1587853	358314
2017	15970399	6596611	1502546	5058477	229410	1627072	396390

主要统计指标解释

固定资产投资额　固定资产投资完成额是以货币表现的建造和购置固定资产的工作量以及与此有关的费用的总称。它是反映固定资产投资规模、速度、比例关系和使用方向的综合性指标。

房地产开发投资　包括各种经济类型的房地产开发公司、商品房建设公司及其他房地产开发单位统一开发的包括统代建、拆迁还建的住宅、厂房、仓库、饭店、宾馆、度假村、写字楼、办公楼等房屋建筑物和配套的服务设施、土地开发工程,如道路、给水、排水、供电、供热、通讯、平整场地等基础设施工程的投资。不包括单纯的土地交易活动。

施工和竣工房屋建筑面积　房屋建筑面积是从房屋外墙线算起的各层平面面积的总和,包括房屋结构(如柱、墙)占用的面积和地下室面积。多层建筑按各自然层面积总和计算,包括房屋内的楼隔层,突出墙面的眺望间、门斗、有柱雨罩的面积。不包括突出墙面结构的构件、艺术装饰等所占的面积,如台阶等。凹阳台、挑阳台按其水平投影面积一半计算建筑面积。

房屋新开工面积　指在报告期内新开工建设的房屋面积。不包括上期跨入报告期继续施工的房屋面积和上期停缓建而在本期恢复施工的房屋面积。房屋的开工应以房屋正式开始破土刨槽(地基处理或打永久桩)的日期为准。

商品房销售面积　指报告期内出售商品房屋的合同总面积(即双方签署的正式买卖合同中所确定的建筑面积)。由现房销售建筑面积和期房销售建筑面积两部分组成。

(1)现房销售面积:是指在报告期内正式签订买卖合同、已经竣工达到入住条件的商品房屋建筑面积。包括以一次性付款方式和分期付款方式销售的现房建筑面积。

(2)期房销售面积:是指在报告期内正式签订买卖合同、正在建设尚未竣工交付使用的商品房屋建筑面积。包括以一次性付款方式和分期付款方式销售的商品房屋建筑面积。期房销售建筑面积竣工后不再转为现房销售建筑面积。

新增固定资产　指通过投资活动所形成的新的固定资产价值。包括已经建成投入生产或交付使用的工程价值和达到固定资产标准的设备、工具、器具的价值及有关应摊入的费用。它是以价值形式表示的固定资产投资成果的综合性指标,可以综合反映不同时期、不同部门、不同地区的固定资产投资成果。

Explanatory Notes on Main Statistical Indicators

Investment in Fixed Assets refer to the volume of activities in construction and purchases of fixed assets in monetary terms and other relative expenses. It is a comprehensive indicator which shows the size, pace, proportional relations and use orientation of investment in fixed assets.

Investment in Real Estate Development include the investment by the real estate development companies, commercial buildings construction companies and other real estate development units of various types of ownership in the construction of house buildings, such as residential buildings, factory buildings, warehouses, hotels, guesthouses, holiday supply, water drainage, power supply, heating, telecommunications, land leveling and other projects of infrastructure, it excludes the activities in simple land transaction.

Floor space of Building Under Construction and Completed refer to total floor space in each story of buildings calculate from the outside line of building walls, including the space occupied by construction like pillars or walls and basements. The floor space of multi – story building includes the total floor space of each story, including area occupied by separating walls, watching rooms, door – ways, and pillars, but excluding protruding wall structures, artistic decoration, etc. (for example, flight of steps). The space of balcony is counted by half of the projection area.

Beginning to Construction Floor Space of Building refer to the area space which constructed in report period, not including the floor whose construction lasted to report period and which stopped in the last period to continue construction in the report period. And the beginning of construction of floor space should base on the date of breaking the earth(disposal the basement or piling).

Selling of the Commercial Building refer to the total area that sold by contract(which reflected in the contract), which include completed and future buildings.

(1) Floor Space of Completed Building: refer to the area which formal contract has been signed and which has been completed and reached the condition of living, including payment in one time and installment payment.

(2) Floor Space of Future Building: refer to the area which signed by formal contract and under constructing, including payment in one time and installment payment. Which can not be turned into completed building's sale when they completed.

Newly Increased Fixed Assets refer to the newly increased value of fixed assets through investment, including the value of projects completed and put into production, the value of equipment, tools, and vessels considered as fixed assets, as well as the relevant expenses as investment in fixed assets. This is a comprehensive indicator of investment in fixed assets, reflecting the achievements of investment in fixed assets in different periods, different sectors, and different regions.

八、国内贸易

DOMESTIC TRADE

8 国 内 贸 易
Domestic Trade

主 要 统 计 指 标
Major Statistical Indicators

社会消费品零售总额	Total Retail Sales of Consumer Goods	5717.43	亿元	(100 million yuan)
为上年	As Compared with the Preceding Year	110.5	%	(%)
商品零售	Commodity Retail	5120.74	亿元	(100 million yuan)
为上年	As Compared with the Preceding Year	110.4	%	(%)
餐费收入	Catering Revenue	596.69	亿元	(100 million yuan)
为上年	As Compared with the Preceding Year	110.7	%	(%)

8－01　社会消费品零售总额(1978－2017年)
Total Retail Sale of Consumer Goods(1978－2017)

单位:万元　　(10,000 yuan)

年　份 Year	全　市 Total	市　区 Urban District	县(市)合计 All Counties
1978	119509	73653	45856
1979	150462	93342	57120
1980	205381	128440	76941
1981	236188	148152	88036
1982	251068	154582	96486
1983	273664	169508	104156
1984	343722	215901	127821
1985	478117	308901	169216
1986	557963	360479	197484
1987	657838	426745	231093
1988	866373	557374	308999
1989	927019	600816	326203
1990	981713	650278	331435
1991	1155476	777559	377917
1992	1408525	928586	479939
1993	1901509	1300037	601472
1994	2616477	1733572	882905
1995	2993250	1930140	1063110
1996	3478156	2310619	1167537
1997	3815537	2537537	1278000
1998	4178013	2794171	1383842
1999	4574924	3053983	1520941
2000	5146789	3436536	1710253
2001	5790138	4993078	797060
2002	6606548	5701707	904841
2003	7425760	6401970	1023790
2004	8554476	7385662	1168814
2005	9784275	8440559	1343716
2006	11191900	9630210	1561690
2007	13082930	11247539	1835391
2008	15775872	13542665	2233207
2009	18378198	15793645	2584553
2010	22250034	19141417	3108616
2011	26902226	23152666	3749561
2012	31651929	27196536	4455393
2013	38648394	33483819	5164575
2014	42014577	37855211	4159366
2015	46864334	42192730	4671604
2016	51762033	46581230	5180803
2017	57174278	53336336	3837942

注:1)根据国家统一规定,2013年经济普查后对2009－2013年度数据作了相应调整。
2)从2013年开始,零售总额口径从“在地口径”调整为“法人口径”。
a)According to the standards by NBS,the data of 2009－2013 are adjusted by the resuct of economic census.
b)The donotation of retail sale has been adjusted to "legal" from "regional".

8－02 分地区社会消费品

Total Retail Sale of Consumer Goods

单位:万元

年份 Year	全市 Whole City		市区 Urban District					
	合计 Total	为上年(%) As Compared with the Preceding Year(%)	合计 Total	上城区 Shangcheng	下城区 Xiacheng	江干区 Jianggan	拱墅区 Gongshu	西湖区 Xihu
2001	5790138	113.6	4993078					
2002	6606548	114.1	5701707					
2003	7425760	112.4	6401970					
2004	8554476	115.2	7385662					
2005	9784275	114.4	8440559	875997	2211413	921149	1214351	973276
2006	11191900	114.4	9630210	1009624	2525806	1037537	1276948	1123397
2007	13082930	116.9	11247539	1187213	2974715	1182818	1462099	1301510
2008	15775872	120.6	13542665	1453850	3481959	1383411	1701815	1566397
2009	18378198	116.5	15793645	1658259	4038155	1613453	2001549	1827286
2010	22250034	121.1	19141417	1835792	4674657	1974898	2457354	2461164
2011	26902226	120.9	23152666	2185077	5626892	2400276	2981552	2984970
2012	31651929	117.7	27196536	2535185	6570798	2830689	3480268	3521955
2013	38648394	115.1	33483819	2846236	7457146	3195632	3982649	4197443
2014	42014577	108.7	37855211	3064010	8184312	3484859	4159942	4606757
2015	46864334	111.8	42192730	3418056	9162747	3887534	4617536	5139067
2016	51762033	110.5	46581230	3794726	10092262	4315163	5080110	5676221
2017	57174278	110.5	53336336	3960577	11114868	4752823	5561885	6274323

零售总额(2001 -2017 年)
by Region(2001 -2017)

(10000 yuan)

高新(滨江)区 Hi -Tech(Binjiang)	萧山区 Xiaoshan	大江东产业集聚区 Dajiangdong Industry Cluster District	余杭区 Yuhang	富阳区 Fuyang	临安区 Lin'an	经济技术开发区 Economic and Technological Development Zone	西湖风景名胜区 The West Lake Scenic Zone	桐庐县 Tonglu	淳安县 Chun'an	建德市 Jiande
	690721		446812	223782	187499			166892	90133	128754
	795711		508919	254887	215437			188087	101581	144849
	929390		584748	289297	247106			209153	114990	163244
	1069728		674799	331534	282936			237598	130974	185772
61378	1234568		778848	382960	326768	99577	70006	272394	149456	212138
71889	1462157		906960	450365	373144	130145	75745	317484	173272	247425
86073	1721511		1064956	526750	446942	168722	97921	371057	201769	288873
220282	2059811		1302135	643169	543759	256127	116877	451356	244069	350854
263639	2425882		1534222	745144	627647	288218	142982	522835	282629	406299
432557	2955860		1849231	895185	751216	336766	163138	624511	338317	499388
537647	3578930		2248637	1081323	904030	415098	193588	752559	409590	602059
656956	4270442		2616486	1285095	1071278	502576	211180	896018	488301	714702
889240	4871438		3077344	1504100	1242715	610530	225115	1030908	563508	823344
928820	5156481		3494348	1707917	1411117	715540	238287	1173697	640460	934093
1066796	5739163	400901	3912097	1980415	1581862	833283	264499	1323402	721510	1044830
1180895	6350442	461386	4331598	2224502	1740840	883476	291033	1478405	808981	1152578
1542862	7012231	518301	4812598	2504521	1923337	993236	323040	1648589	909853	1279500

8－03　社会消费品

Total Retail Sale of

单位:万元

地　区	Region	合　计 Total
全　市	**Total**	**57174278**
市　区	Urban District	53336336
#上城区	Shangcheng	3960577
下城区	Xiacheng	11114868
江干区	Jianggan	4752823
拱墅区	Gongshu	5561885
西湖区	Xihu	6274323
高新(滨江)区	Hi－Tech(Binjiang)	1542862
萧山区	Xiaoshan	7012231
余杭区	Yuhang	4812598
富阳区	Fuyang	2504521
临安区	Lin'an	1923337
桐庐县	Tonglu	1648589
淳安县	Chun'an	909853
建德市	Jiande	1279500

零售总额(2017 年)
Consumer Goods(2017)

(10000 yuan)

按经营地分 By Location		按消费形态分 By Consumption	
城镇 Urban Areas	乡村 Rural Areas	商品零售 Commodity Retail	餐费收入 Catering Revenue
54206051	**2968226**	**51207394**	**5966884**
51735112	1601224	48035164	5301171
3960577	–	3474245	486331
11114868	–	10374506	740361
4752823	–	4318997	433826
5561885	–	5278403	283483
6274323	–	5717455	556868
1542862	–	1437527	105335
7012231	–	6152765	859466
4812598	–	4410911	401687
1713146	791375	2296721	207800
1113488	809849	1647605	275732
1021399	627190	1418241	230348
553400	356453	724426	185427
896140	383360	1029562	249937

8-04 按登记注册类型分限额以上批发零售贸易企业商品销售总额(2017年)

Sales of Wholesale and Retail Trades Above Designated Size by Status of Registration(2017)

单位:万元 (10000 yuan)

项目	Item	法人企业(个) Number of Enterprises (unit)	销售总额 Total Sales	批发额 Wholesale	零售额 Retail
总计	**Total**	**4406**	**207067738**	**179226007**	**27841731**
1. 内资企业	**Domestic - funded Enterprises**	**4270**	**186530738**	**163421540**	**23109198**
国有企业	State - owned Enterprises	14	1999932	1946874	53058
集体企业	Collective - owned Enterprises	7	54805	4033	50772
股份合作企业	Cooperative Enterprises	2	5695	300	5395
联营企业	Joint Ownership Enterprises	5	49019	460	48558
国有联营企业	State Joint Ownership Enterprises	1	-	-	-
国有与集体联营企业	Joint State - collective Enterprises	4	34993	-	34993
有限责任公司	Limited Liability Corporations	1197	93297463	80770496	12526966
国有独资公司	State - funded Corporations	47	10074118	9787831	286287
其他有限责任公司	Other Limited Liability Corporations	1150	83223345	70982665	12240680
股份有限公司	Share - holding Corporations Ltd.	113	32077334	29156154	2921180
私营企业	Private Enterprises	2883	58931774	51464389	7467385
私营独资企业	Private - funded Enterprises	18	31405	6549	24856
私营合伙企业	Private Partnership Enterprises	2	3037	2436	601
私营有限责任公司	Private Limited Liability Corporations	2821	58084604	50681543	7403061
私营股份有限公司	Private Share - holding Corporations Ltd.	42	812728	773861	38867
其他企业	Other Enterprises	49	114718	78833	35884
2. 港、澳、台商投资企业	**Enterprises With Investment from Hong Kong, Macao and Taiwan**	**65**	**6070184**	**3811414**	**2258770**
合资经营企业(港或澳、台资)	Joint - venture Enterprises (With Funds from Hong Kong, Macao and Taiwan)	21	1177383	417896	759487
合作经营企业(港或澳、台资)	Coorperative Enterprises (With Funds from Hong Kong, Macao and Taiwan)	1	-	-	-
港、澳、台商独资经营企业	Enterprises With Sole Investment from Hong Kong, Macao and Taiwan	41	4844650	3384278	1460371
港、澳、台商投资股份有限公司	Share - holding Corporations Ltd. With Investment from Hong Kong, Macao and Taiwan	1	-	-	-
其他港澳台投资企业	Other Enterprises With Investment from Hong Kong, Macao and Taiwan	1	-	-	-
3. 外商投资企业	**Enterprises With Foreign Investment**	**71**	**14466816**	**11993053**	**2473763**
中外合资经营企业	Joint - venture Enterprises	14	11832495	11075189	757306
中外合作经营企业	Cooperation Enterprises	1	-	-	-
外资企业	Enterprises With Sole Foreign Investment	53	2532880	826205	1706675
外商投资股份有限公司	Share - holding Corporations Ltd. With Foreign Investment	3	94644	91660	2984

注:因年报批发零售统计口径调整,数据与2016年不可比较。

Note: due to the adjustment of statistical caliber, the data cannot be compared with previous year.

8－05 按国民经济行业分限额以上批发零售贸易企业商品销售总额(2017年)

Total Sales of Wholesale and Retail Trades Above Designated Size by Sector(2017)

单位:万元 (10000 yuan)

项　目	Item	法人企业(个) Number of Enterprises (unit)	销售总额 Total Sales	批发额 Wholesale	零售额 Retail
总　计	**Total**	**4406**	**207067738**	**179226007**	**27841731**
一、批发业	**Wholesale**	**3029**	**176968917**	**175187779**	**1781138**
农、林、牧产品批发	Wholesale of Farm, Forestry and Animal Husbandry Products	40	802997	795317	7679
食品、饮料及烟草制品批发	Wholesale of Food, Beverages and Tobaccos	254	11664318	11422204	242114
纺织、服装及家庭用品批发	Wholesale of Textile Products, Garments and Household Articles	738	19054081	18644075	410005
文化、体育用品及器材批发	Wholesale of Cultural and Sports Goods	111	4083009	3957067	125943
医药及医疗器材批发	Wholesale of Medicines and Medical Appliances	191	9723944	9503661	220283
矿产品、建材及化工产品批发	Wholesale of Mineral Products, Building and Chemical Materials	1153	106720631	106295424	425207
机械设备、五金产品及电子产品批发	Wholesale of Machinery, Hardware and Electronic Products	510	24449053	24099337	349716
#汽车、摩托车及零配件批发	Wholesale of Automobiles, Motorcycle and Parts	108	12549289	12430079	119210
其他批发业	Other	32	470885	470694	192
二、零售业	**Retail Trade**	**1377**	**30098821**	**4038228**	**26060593**
综合零售	Comprehensive Retail Trade	120	5856503	665450	5191053
食品、饮料及烟草制品专门零售	Specialism Retail of Food, Beverages and Tobaccos	136	401983	56687	345297
纺织、服装及日用品专门零售	Specialism Retail of Textile Products, Garments, Shoes and Caps	104	1259404	120487	1138918
文化、体育用品及器材专门零售	Specialism Retail of Cultural and Sports Goods	54	485246	66998	418248
医药及医疗器材专门零售	Specialism Retail of Medicines and Medical Appliances	83	753703	92905	660798
汽车、摩托车、燃料及零配件专门零售	Specialism Retail of Automobiles, Motorcycle, Fuels and Parts	501	14235174	1996964	12238210
#汽车零售	Specialism Retail of Automobiles	319	10582899	1253813	9329086
家用电器及电子产品专门零售	Specialism Retail of Household Electric Applianes, and Electronic Products	127	1704615	292157	1412458
五金、家具及室内装饰材料专门零售	Specialism Retail of Hardware and Upholstery Materials	55	311630	68792	242838
货摊、无店铺及其他零售业	Stall, Non－shop and Other Retails	197	5090564	677789	4412775

注:因年报批发零售统计口径调整,数据与2016年不可比较。

Note: due to the adjustment of statistical caliber, the data cannot be compared with previous year.

8－06 按登记注册类型分限额以上

Main Financial Indicators of Enterprises Above Designated Size of

单位:万元

项　目	Item	法人企业数(个) Number of Enterprises (unit)	年末资产负债 Assets and Liabilities 流动资产合计 Circulating Funds	存　货 Inventory	固定资产原价 Orginal Value of Fixed Assets
批发零售贸易业企业合计	**Total**	**4406**	**63954944**	**10142331**	**5162782**
1. 内资企业	**Domestic－funded Enterprises**	**4270**	**58129282**	**9124684**	**4598939**
国有企业	State－owned Enterprises	14	862500	71435	121932
集体企业	Collective－owned Enterprises	7	8653	1678	2350
股份合作企业	Cooperative Enterprises	2	7343	1820	3293
联营企业	Joint Ownership Enterprises	5	6906	268	1557
国有联营企业	State Joint Ownership Enterprises	1	－	－	－
国有与集体联营企业	Joint State－collective Enterprises	4	5389	249	1404
有限责任公司	Limited Liability Corporations	1197	27877435	4948420	1621333
国有独资公司	State－funded Corporations	47	3171238	955610	170337
其他有限责任公司	Other Limited Liability Corporations	1150	24706197	3992810	1450996
股份有限公司	Share－holding Corporations Ltd.	113	8502006	1326496	1377839
私营企业	Private Enterprises	2883	20840745	2771913	1461769
私营独资企业	Private－funded Enterprises	18	8779	2807	2550
私营合伙企业	Private Partnership Enterprises	2	1246	197	113
私营有限责任公司	Private Limited Liability Corporations	2821	20526303	2716845	1431357
私营股份有限公司	Private Share－holding Corporations Ltd.	42	304417	52064	27749
其他企业	Other Enterprises	49	23695	2653	8867
2. 港、澳、台商投资企业	**Enterprises With Investment from Hong Kong, Macao and Taiwan**	**65**	**2161803**	**301131**	**247790**
合资经营企业(港或澳、台资)	Joint－venture Enterprises (With Funds from Hong Kong, Macao and Taiwan)	21	540382	34567	151597
合作经营企业(港或澳、台资)	Coorperative Enterprises (With Funds from Hong Kong, Macao and Taiwan)	1	－	－	－
港、澳、台商独资经营企业	Enterprises With Sole Investment from Hong Kong, Macao and Taiwan	41	1601543	265718	80712
港、澳、台商投资股份有限公司	Share－holding Corporations Ltd. With Investment from Hong Kong, Macao and Taiwan	1	－	－	－
其他港澳台投资企业	Other Enterprises With Investment from Hong Kong, Macao and Taiwan	1	－	－	－
3. 外商投资企业	**Enterprises With Foreign Investment**	**71**	**3663859**	**716515**	**316053**
中外合资经营企业	Joint－venture Enterprises	14	1677977	512242	60161
中外合作经营企业	Cooperation Enterprises	1	－	－	－
外资企业	Enterprises With Sole Foreign Investment	53	1908730	202780	246943
外商投资股份有限公司	Share－holding Corporations Ltd. With Foreign Investment	3	70794	603	6016

批发零售贸易企业财务状况(2017 年)
Wholesale and Retail Trades by Status of Registration(2017)

(10000 yuan)

累计折旧 Accumulated Depreciation	本年折旧 Depreciation	资产总计 Total Assets	负债合计 Total Liabilities	所有者权益合计 Creditors´ Equity
2166704	**275064**	**85701194**	**62379374**	**23321820**
1915833	**250172**	**78527292**	**57002463**	**21524829**
72346	8522	938731	192210	746521
1304	114	9712	2311	7401
679	633	14450	11017	3432
805	78	7658	4294	3364
–	–	–	–	–
700	61	6093	3066	3027
663349	84523	36981953	28609992	8371961
62941	5384	4163540	2849225	1314316
600408	79139	32818413	25760768	7057645
580514	60028	14070033	8130541	5939492
595006	95923	26470027	20033387	6436640
782	118	11418	8247	3171
48	15	1401	1124	277
580454	93803	26086469	19824606	6261863
13722	1988	370739	199411	171328
1830	351	34728	18709	16019
116233	**8611**	**3034034**	**2131885**	**902149**
72722	3188	872545	620834	251711
–	–	–	–	–
33567	5567	2129141	1506121	623020
–	–	–	–	–
–	–	–	–	–
134639	**16281**	**4139868**	**3245027**	**894842**
30472	2894	1745042	1633944	111099
–	–	–	–	–
101300	12945	2285828	1573041	712787
845	335	97202	35153	62049

单位:万元　　8－06　续表

项　　目	Item	营业收入 Revenue of Business	主营业务收入 Main Revenue of Business	主营业务成本 Main Cost of Business	主营业务税金及附加 Main Sales Tax and Extra Charges
批发零售贸易业企业合计	**Total**	**181423406**	**179693426**	**169699251**	**420518**
1. 内资企业	**Domestic－funded Enterprises**	**163599087**	**162030427**	**153110091**	**392641**
国有企业	State－owned Enterprises	1726423	1719877	1205966	216828
集体企业	Collective－owned Enterprises	46842	46842	39816	154
股份合作企业	Cooperative Enterprises	5505	5061	4187	126
联营企业	Joint Ownership Enterprises	41896	41896	33723	177
国有联营企业	State Joint Ownership Enterprises	11988	11988	8717	70
国有与集体联营企业	Joint State－collective Enterprises	29909	29909	25006	107
有限责任公司	Limited Liability Corporations	82163579	81405601	77749115	80805
国有独资公司	State－funded Corporations	8855785	8823608	8647460	4931
其他有限责任公司	Other Limited Liability Corporations	73307794	72581993	69101654	75875
股份有限公司	Share－holding Corporations Ltd.	27474808	26921965	25362394	31589
私营企业	Private Enterprises	52030122	51779283	48610670	62885
私营独资企业	Private－funded Enterprises	23671	23659	20829	60
私营合伙企业	Private Partnership Enterprises	2917	2917	2795	1
私营有限责任公司	Private Limited Liability Corporations	51272564	51025707	47937764	62026
私营股份有限公司	Private Share－holding Corporations Ltd.	730970	727000	649282	798
其他企业	Other Enterprises	109912	109902	104220	78
2. 港、澳、台商投资企业	**Enterprises With Investment from Hong Kong, Macao and Taiwan**	**5294730**	**5243433**	**4772780**	**13420**
合资经营企业(港或澳、台资)	Joint－venture Enterprises (With Funds from Hong Kong, Macao and Taiwan)	1037601	1011872	883586	5460
合作经营企业(港或澳、台资)	Coorperative Enterprises (With Funds from Hong Kong, Macao and Taiwan)	31167	31167	24948	444
港、澳、台商独资经营企业	Enterprises With Sole Investment from Hong Kong, Macao and Taiwan	4213921	4188353	3854735	7484
港、澳、台商投资股份有限公司	Share－holding Corporations Ltd. With Investment from Hong Kong, Macao and Taiwan	3690	3690	2565	14
其他港澳台投资企业	Other Enterprises With Investment from Hong Kong, Macao and Taiwan	8351	8351	6945	17
3. 外商投资企业	**Enterprises With Foreign Investment**	**12529589**	**12419566**	**11816380**	**14457**
中外合资经营企业	Joint－venture Enterprises	10171800	10127778	9829273	4101
中外合作经营企业	Cooperation Enterprises	7500	5810	5781	59
外资企业	Enterprises With Sole Foreign Investment	2268843	2204540	1913829	9963
外商投资股份有限公司	Share－holding Corporations Ltd. With Foreign Investment	81446	81438	67497	333

continued (10000 yuan)

销售费用 Cost of Sales	管理费用 Administration Cost	财务费用 Financil Cost	营业利润 Management Profits	利润总额 Total Profits	应交所得税 Income Tax	从业人员平均人数(人) Average Number of Employees (person)
5455834	**2308191**	**835928**	**2953971**	**3110176**	**600673**	**266075**
4657969	**2074246**	**817394**	**2813381**	**2962949**	**546041**	**240695**
27168	40413	-28334	262030	261747	65097	1461
1704	480	-2	4691	4688	1207	130
189	944	-1	76	85	28	48
2229	110	-55	5713	5710	1428	93
1140	36	-17	2042	2041	510	22
1090	74	-38	3671	3669	918	71
1996279	755085	468051	1084575	1197734	256498	98895
76077	63912	21479	165879	192297	12508	3747
1920202	691174	446572	918696	1005437	243990	95148
926267	342946	84926	1002437	1020705	95618	34002
1703019	932631	292545	451286	469639	126043	105461
868	910	68	924	917	57	336
-	82	37	1	12	-	15
1662292	910178	286448	436699	454534	121953	103004
39859	21462	5992	13663	14176	4034	2106
1113	1637	264	2573	2641	122	605
330456	**105024**	**13024**	**42098**	**51871**	**32391**	**11270**
92636	43538	3856	-5202	1431	16200	3539
1555	2813	79	1327	1248	354	284
236013	56909	9077	45513	48734	15596	7366
43	1509	11	-452	-456	-	51
209	255	1	913	914	241	30
467409	**128921**	**5509**	**98492**	**95356**	**22241**	**14110**
295440	23047	-1239	18112	17301	5039	5718
1375	3	9	50	54	43	58
167228	101990	6953	61465	59149	15548	8145
3367	3880	-214	18864	18853	1610	189

8－07 按国民经济行业分限额以上

Main Financial Indicators of Enterprises Above Designated

单位:万元

项　目	Item	法人企业数(个) Number of Enterprises (unit)	年末资产负债 Assets and Liabilities 流动资产合计 Circulating Funds	存　货 Inventory	固定资产原价 Orginal Value of Fixed Assets
总　计	**Total**	**4406**	**63954944**	**10142331**	**5162782**
一、批发业	**Wholesale**	**3030**	**53624709**	**7819013**	**3268120**
农、林、牧产品批发	Wholesale of Farm, Forestry and Animal Husbandry Products	40	349923	76760	40217
食品、饮料及烟草制品批发	Wholesale of Food, Beverages and Tobaccos	254	5680806	798443	502448
纺织、服装及家庭用品批发	Wholesale of Textile Products, Garments and Household Articles	738	7031323	1070348	411374
文化、体育用品及器材批发	Wholesale of Cultural and Sports Goods	111	1600104	509974	78311
医药及医疗器材批发	Wholesale of Medicines and Medical Appliances	191	3784407	788687	218893
矿产品、建材及化工产品批发	Wholesale of Mineral Products, Building and Chemical Materials	1154	28187801	3413770	1724253
机械设备、五金产品及电子产品批发	Wholesale of Machinery, Hardware and Electronic Products	510	6830524	1147912	284934
#汽车、摩托车及零配件批发	Wholesale of Automobiles, Motorcycle and Parts	108	2833901	554676	61192
其他批发业	Other	32	159822	13120	7691
二、零售业	**Retail Trade**	**1376**	**10330235**	**2323317**	**1894662**
综合零售	Comprehensive Retail Trade	120	2960324	239333	808735
食品、饮料及烟草制品专门零售	Specialism Retail of Food, Beverages and Tobaccos	136	170893	39337	52047
纺织、服装及日用品专门零售	Specialism Retail of Textile Products, Garments, Shoes and Caps	104	564069	240869	66602
文化、体育用品及器材专门零售	Specialism Retail of Cultural and Sports Goods	54	325348	141542	84528
医药及医疗器材专门零售	Specialism Retail of Medicines and Medical Appliances	83	387442	77671	58406
汽车、摩托车、燃料及零配件专门零售	Specialism Retail of Automobiles, Motorcycle, Fuels and Parts	500	3314518	724438	569234
#汽车零售	Specialism Retail of Automobiles	319	3025870	688382	462397
家用电器及电子产品专门零售	Specialism Retail of Household Electric Applianes, and Electronic Products	127	653551	170210	64745
五金、家具及室内装饰材料专门零售	Specialism Retail of Hardware and Upholstery Materials	55	104383	19644	84958
货摊、无店铺及其他零售业	Stall, Non－shop and Other Retails	197	1849707	670274	105406

批发零售贸易企业财务状况(2017 年)
Size in Wholesale and Retail Trades by Sector(2017)

(10000 yuan)

累计折旧 Accumulated Depreciation	本年折旧 Depreciation	资产总计 Total Assets	负债合计 Total Liabilities	所有者权益合计 Creditors´ Equity
2166704	**275064**	**85701194**	**62379374**	**23321820**
1386377	**168028**	**71716159**	**52139765**	**19576394**
15240	2198	637667	451181	186486
212398	33940	7590315	4336581	3253734
182987	22375	8859203	6708680	2150523
35409	2949	1925530	1314723	610807
88087	19013	4747751	2983340	1764411
722667	73156	39540300	29861429	9678872
126683	13982	8212986	6343781	1869205
27647	564	3012103	2862824	149279
2905	416	202406	140050	62355
780327	**107036**	**13985035**	**10239609**	**3745426**
382625	39870	4226650	2790145	1436504
18876	3476	237318	153606	83712
28048	5124	665003	481601	183402
33152	2534	403407	303349	100058
16601	5205	895943	630044	265899
225921	36865	4333775	3365346	968429
177354	31224	3835794	3124058	711736
26914	3487	816843	568819	248024
19038	1457	200012	128617	71395
29154	9018	2206083	1818081	388003

项 目	Item	营业收入 Revenue of Business	主营业务收入 Main Revenue of Business	主营业务成本 Main Cost of Business	主营业务税金及附加 Main Sales Tax and Extra Charges
总 计	**Total**	**181423406**	**179693426**	**169699251**	**420518**
一、批发业	**Wholesale**	**156086248**	**154902072**	**148139478**	**340682**
农、林、牧产品批发业	Wholesale of Farm , Forestry and Animal Husbandry Products	783156	752267	719672	847
食品、饮料、烟草制品批发	Wholesale of Food, Beverages and Tobaccos	10482190	10255531	8648670	237071
纺织、服装及家庭用品批发	Wholesale of Textile Products, Garments and Household Articles	17181982	17021627	15842602	15586
文化、体育用品及器材批发	Wholesale of Cultural and Sports Goods	3699407	3669479	3473251	3957
医药及医疗器材批发	Wholesale of Medicines and Medical Appliances	8461912	8413686	7733824	13368
矿产品、建材及化工产品批发	Wholesale of Mineral Products, Building and Chemical Materials	93578872	92944710	90828064	54183
机械设备、五金产品及电子产品批发	Wholesale of Machinery, Hardware and Electronic Products	21486945	21365674	20436929	14826
#汽车、摩托车及零配件批发	Wholesale of Automobiles, Motorcycle and Parts	10767773	10752231	10459538	4203
其他批发业	Other	411783	411039	390638	845
二、零售业	**Retail Trade**	**25337158**	**24791354**	**21559772**	**79836**
综合零售	Comprehensive Retail Trade	5411202	5124450	4395463	21929
食品、饮料及烟草制品专门零售	Specialism Retail of Food, Beverages and Tobaccos	365651	359831	277648	1676
纺织、服装及日用品专门零售	Specialism Retail of Textile Products, Garments, Shoes and Caps	1110196	1096843	701808	6394
文化、体育用品及器材专门零售	Specialism Retail of Cultural and Sports Goods	431579	427328	360916	4108
医药及医疗器材专门零售	Specialism Retail of Medicines and Medical Appliances	668107	662363	530097	2414
汽车、摩托车、燃料及零配件专门零售	Specialism Retail of Automobiles, Motorcycle, Fuels and Parts	10958825	10793059	10033979	29911
#汽车零售	Specialism Retail of Automobiles	9354915	9236058	8642800	26272
家用电器及电子产品专门零售	Specialism Retail of Household Electric Appliances, and Electronic Products	1546288	1524243	1377210	2871
五金、家具及室内装饰材料专门零售	Specialism Retail of Hardware and Upholstery Materials	276758	271034	198264	1414
货摊、无店铺及其他零售业	Stall, Non - shop and Other Retails	4568553	4498473	3652850	9122

continued (10000 yuan)

销售费用 Cost of Sales	管理费用 Administration Cost	财务费用 Financil Cost	营业利润 Management Profits	利润总额 Total Profits	应交所得税 Income Tax	从业人员平均人数(人) Average Number of Employees (person)
5455834	**2308191**	**835928**	**2953971**	**3110176**	**600673**	**266075**
3224728	**1554440**	**724636**	**2389313**	**2519168**	**442418**	**140500**
13475	17806	12755	2433	8375	324	1147
818076	221921	-3190	717419	747918	118480	31078
584136	334743	115121	210538	216241	57328	34966
75352	51778	12391	104981	106839	6892	4910
312286	171170	44768	210447	209222	47381	14633
887516	525340	479128	941073	1040657	162455	31554
523376	225793	55054	203995	191843	49128	21763
301169	45183	1830	-40429	-37754	7979	5253
10512	5890	8608	-1573	-1926	430	449
2231106	**753750**	**111292**	**564658**	**591009**	**158255**	**125575**
620489	173063	-7064	199718	200246	58842	36653
54583	21314	2011	8634	7685	1315	5576
287984	77457	4106	34324	43635	10095	13614
40404	21002	2722	3803	3998	734	3709
79018	43680	9634	40027	40580	5942	8562
359607	219333	60806	211769	216160	57011	28270
285158	199066	57801	142165	147096	37816	23868
97288	47194	8772	10059	13699	3457	10273
48612	21857	2267	497	101	-213	2306
643122	128850	28038	55826	64905	21072	16612

8－08 分地区限额以上

Main Indicators of Wholesale

单位:万元

地　区	Region	企业法人数(个) Number of Enterprises (unit)	商品销售总额 Total Sales of Commodities	主营业务收入 Main Revenue of Business	主营业务成本 Main Cost of Business	主营业务税金及附加 Main Sales Tax and Extra Charges
全　市	**Total**	**4406**	**207067738**	**179693426**	**169699251**	**420518**
市　区	Urban District	4097	204716784	177632227	167851843	416456
#上城区	Shangcheng	406	33508173	29718123	27899108	249055
下城区	Xiacheng	471	38522876	33670298	32273250	34215
江干区	Jianggan	410	26215868	22847800	21664663	19127
拱墅区	Gongshu	359	23041229	19951781	19296163	18936
西湖区	Xihu	333	14798453	11473351	10250070	21927
高新(滨江)区	Hi－Tech(Binjiang)	253	24224931	21173480	20267572	17531
萧山区	Xiaoshan	762	22350979	19574948	18499966	27328
大江东产业集聚区	Dajiangdong Industry Cluster District	78	2207318	1961570	1835987	2385
余杭区	Yuhang	598	11184528	9722298	8955505	13222
富阳区	Fuyang	210	6106130	5276345	4994116	6421
临安区	Lin'an	182	1334621	1234453	1167255	1730
经济技术开发区	Economic and Technological Development Zone	100	3379759	2945353	2549853	6770
西湖风景名胜区	The West Lake Scenic Zone	13	49239	43998	34323	193
桐庐县	Tonglu	147	970954	848925	791200	1274
淳安县	Chun'an	95	950617	810612	696664	1862
建德市	Jiande	67	429385	401662	359543	926

批发零售业主要指标(2017 年)

and Retail Trades by Region(2017)

(10000 yuan)

销售费用 Cost of Sales	管理费用 Administration Cost	财务费用 Financil Cost	利润总额 Total Profits	本年应交增值税 Value Added Tax Payable	从业人员平均人数(人) Average Number of Employees (person)
5455834	**2308191**	**835928**	**3110176**	**1990360**	**266075**
5343413	2257135	822291	3058690	1962828	256458
679279	348050	85210	852399	277170	30319
714205	380028	172233	465582	142786	34131
655686	280268	46073	326568	138881	31815
353134	191675	158867	206614	606707	26447
835513	274996	48872	526845	172713	35826
629630	171162	90990	213462	235343	18650
559089	218928	91386	206010	211284	28593
120962	25950	5114	-10925	14404	2365
401135	229647	95530	115567	75689	26030
202322	65025	20794	17230	47676	8614
27861	25889	8193	37512	10760	4082
282448	67463	4038	88035	42331	11428
3112	4005	106	2867	1489	523
21682	21465	8621	7285	7516	3217
67086	19924	2301	35316	15027	4524
23654	9666	2714	8885	4989	1876

8－09 按注册类型、行业分限额以上

Main Financial Indicators of Hotels and Catering Services

单位:万元

项　目	Item	法人企业数(个) Number of Enterprises (unit)	年末资产负债 Assets and Liabilities		
			流动资产合计 Circulating Funds	存　货 Inventory	固定资产原价 Orginal Value of Fixed Assets
总　计	**Total**	**952**	**1899435**	**122167**	**2915545**
(一)按登记注册类型分组	**Grouped By Registered Type**				
内资企业	**Domestic－funded Enterprises**	**918**	**1584697**	**99977**	**2330903**
国有企业	State－owned Enterprises	41	155201	2559	288190
集体企业	Collective－owned Enterprises	9	11962	891	43705
股份合作企业	Cooperative Enterprises	1	268	2	240
联营企业	Joint Ownership Enterprises	1	5258	53	4916
有限责任公司	Limited Liability Corporations	259	755065	71487	1270907
股份有限公司	Share－holding Corporations Ltd.	9	57865	1341	96941
私营企业	Private Enterprises	596	597610	23617	623223
其他企业	Other Enterprises	2	1468	27	2780
港、澳、台商投资企业	**Enterprises With Investment from Hong Kong, Macao and Taiwan**	**22**	**215762**	**17262**	**363061**
外商投资企业	**Enterprises With Foreign Investment**	**12**	**98977**	**4928**	**221582**
(二)按国民经济行业分组	**Grouped By Sector**				
1.住宿业	**Lodging**	**446**	**1346104**	**93701**	**2179805**
旅游饭店	Restaurants for Junketing	259	1230282	91231	2041656
一般旅馆	General Hotel	184	115211	2358	135964
民宿服务	Homestay Service	3	611	112	2186
露营地服务	Campgralad Service	－	－	－	－
其他住宿业	Others Lodging	－	－	－	－
2.餐饮业	**Catering Services**	**506**	**553331**	**28466**	**735740**
正餐服务	Dinner Services	458	451316	21333	608661
快餐服务	Short Order Services	22	78806	6154	115842
饮料及冷饮服务	Beverages and Services	14	5124	620	2093
餐饮配送及外卖送餐服务	Catering Distribution and Delivery Service	6	9197	94	4629
其他餐饮业	Others Catering Services	6	8889	265	4515

住宿业和餐饮业财务状况(2017 年)
Enterprises Above Designated Size by Status of Registration and Sector(2017)

(10000 yuan)

累计折旧 Accumulated Depreciation	本年折旧 Depreciation	资产总计 Total Assets	负债合计 Total Liabilities	所有者权益合计 Creditors´ Equity
1290742	**149468**	**4489397**	**3176597**	**1312799**
998140	**108457**	**3767475**	**2620320**	**1147155**
128384	17237	370979	106323	264656
27333	1912	35458	24982	10476
127	39	380	316	64
3726	157	6451	1059	5392
529424	57495	1927117	1416865	510252
49761	3081	205266	51215	154051
259303	28504	1217598	1019277	198321
83	32	4225	282	3943
186223	**13474**	**447010**	**355528**	**91482**
106379	**27537**	**274912**	**200749**	**74162**
1012684	**95844**	**3198960**	**2178846**	**1020114**
948658	87049	2949817	1991912	957905
63983	8751	244256	184320	59936
43	43	4888	2615	2274
–	–	–	–	–
–	–	–	–	–
278059	**53624**	**1290436**	**997752**	**292685**
211587	32277	1038473	812111	226362
59483	20456	220532	177264	43268
1518	176	6785	5041	1744
2717	238	11181	3471	7710
2753	478	13466	–135	13601

单位:万元

8-09 续表

项　　目	Item	营业收入 Revenue of Business	主营业务收入 Main Revenue of Business	主营业务税金及附加 Business Tax and Extra Charges
总　　计	**Total**	**2639367**	**2605306**	**16022**
(一)按登记注册类型分组	**Grouped By Registered Type**			
内资企业	**Domestic - funded Enterprises**	**1859449**	**1837194**	**13276**
国有企业	State - owned Enterprises	156602	152864	2349
集体企业	Collective - owned Enterprises	16372	16312	183
股份合作企业	Cooperative Enterprises	1472	1472	1
联营企业	Joint Ownership Enterprises	4676	4676	40
有限责任公司	Limited Liability Corporations	705524	694324	5872
股份有限公司	Share - holding Corporations Ltd.	114856	114535	726
私营企业	Private Enterprises	858625	851688	4027
其他企业	Other Enterprises	1323	1323	79
港、澳、台商投资企业	**Enterprises With Investment from Hong Kong, Macao and Taiwan**	**266565**	**260888**	**2045**
外商投资企业	**Enterprises With Foreign Investment**	**513354**	**507224**	**701**
(二)按国民经济行业分组	**Grouped By Sector**			
1.住宿业	**Lodging**	**1125131**	**1103083**	**12427**
旅游饭店	Restaurants for Junketing	951194	931779	10738
一般旅馆	General Hotel	172440	169807	1689
民宿服务	Homestay Service	1497	1497	1
露营地服务	Campgralad Service	-	-	-
其他住宿业	Others Lodging	-	-	-
2.餐饮	**Catering Services**	**1514236**	**1502222**	**3595**
正餐服务	Dinner Services	841763	833279	3009
快餐服务	Short Order Services	605062	602033	315
饮料及冷饮服务	Beverages and Services	13460	13460	69
餐饮配送及外卖送餐服务	Catering Distribution and Delivery Service	18805	18577	154
其他餐饮业	Others Catering Services	35146	34874	49

continued (10000 yuan)

销售费用 Cost of Sales	管理费用 Administration Cost	财务费用 Financil Cost	营业利润 Management Profits	利润总额 Total Profits	应交所得税 Income Taxes Payable	从业人员平均人数(人) Average Number of Employees (person)
874559	**570478**	**70214**	**128526**	**148312**	**39173**	**98167**
612168	**471083**	**55911**	**35622**	**51678**	**16833**	**69311**
55099	51492	582	8044	6785	2811	5034
5993	5366	26	104	120	57	662
10	206	–	–142	14	1	60
1958	1528	–69	153	161	40	97
238935	210855	32856	–2813	3270	5762	28469
46076	20116	294	29104	30734	1099	3843
263767	181439	22224	1217	10620	7062	31028
330	81	–	–45	–27	–	118
120836	**38503**	**13182**	**18266**	**18700**	**2615**	**11932**
141556	**60892**	**1121**	**74638**	**77935**	**19725**	**16924**
399013	**377514**	**51418**	**–2084**	**12022**	**9801**	**41395**
345452	320848	49353	–3528	11035	8260	34924
52888	56513	2038	1589	1117	1537	6398
673	154	27	–145	–130	4	73
–	–	–	–	–	–	–
–	–	–	–	–	–	–
475547	**192964**	**18796**	**130610**	**136290**	**29372**	**56772**
259100	130482	15954	48965	54172	8570	31264
197236	52819	2794	77463	77652	19424	22945
1733	5005	6	234	255	177	393
732	2056	–57	1427	1442	423	417
16746	2602	97	2521	2769	779	1753

8-10 按登记注册类型和国民经济行业分限额以上住宿业和餐饮业经营情况(2017年)

Management Conditions of Hotels and Catering Services Enterprises Above Designated Size by Status of Registration and Sector(2017)

单位:万元 (10000 yuan)

项目	Item	法人企业(个) Number of Enterprises (unit)	营业额 Revenue of Business	客房收入 Revenue of Guest Rooms	餐饮收入 Revenue of Catering Services	商品销售收入 Revenue of Goods Sales
一、按登记注册类型分	**Grouped By Registered Type**					
总计	**Total**	**952**	**2755771**	**697381**	**1894642**	**13106**
1. 内资企业	**Domestic - funded Enterprises**	**918**	**1941964**	**628178**	**1165032**	**12881**
国有企业	State - owned Enterprises	41	164436	75221	70262	1394
集体企业	Collective - owned Enterprises	9	17322	11093	3476	54
股份合作企业	Cooperative Enterprises	1	-	-	-	-
联营企业	Joint Ownership Enterprises	1	-	-	-	-
国有与集体联营企业	Joint State - collective Enterprises	1	-	-	-	-
有限责任公司	Limited Liability Corporations	259	726749	292533	347312	3063
国有独资公司	State - funded Corporations	17	75545	23068	26102	174
其他有限责任公司	Other Limited Liability Corporations	242	651204	269465	321211	2888
股份有限公司	Share - holding Corporations Ltd.	9	123345	15593	104068	1100
私营企业	Private Enterprises	596	902211	230880	635246	7208
私营独资企业	Private - funded Enterprises	16	13203	1214	11498	376
私营合伙企业	Private Partnership Enterprises	4	3558	-	3525	-
私营有限责任公司	Private Limited Liability Corporations	567	875311	226424	613567	6822
私营股份有限公司	Private Share - holding Corporations Ltd.	9	10140	3242	6656	10
其他企业	Other Enterprises	2	1402	196	1173	-

项　目	Item	法人企业(个) Number of Enterprises (unit)	营业额 Revenue of Business	客房收入 Revenue of Guest Rooms	餐饮收入 Revenue of Catering Services	商品销售收入 Revenue of Goods Sales
2.港、澳、台商投资企业	**Enterprises With Investment from Hong Kong, Macao and Taiwan**	**22**	**274117**	**54415**	**209359**	**145**
合资经营企业(港或澳、台资)	Joint－venture Enterprises (With Funds from Hong Kong, Macao and Taiwan)	12	101864	39567	54136	－
合作经营企业(港或澳、台资)	Coorperative Enterprises (With Funds from Hong Kong, Macao and Taiwan)	1	－	－	－	－
港、澳、台商独资经营企业	Enterprises With Sole Investment from Hong Kong, Macao and Taiwan	7	145026	4375	140129	－
港、澳、台商投资股份有限公司	Share－holding Corporations Ltd. With Investment from Hong Kong, Macao and Taiwan	2	26748	10018	15094	145
3.外商投资企业	**Enterprises With Foreign Investment**	**12**	**539690**	**14789**	**520252**	**81**
中外合资经营企业	Joint－venture Enterprises	2	491124	8391	481642	－
中外合作经营企业	Cooperation Enterprises	－	－	－	－	－
外资企业	Enterprises With Sole Foreign Investment	9	47401	6397	37444	81
外商投资股份有限公司	Share－holding Corporations Ltd. With Foreign Investment	1	－	－	－	－
二、按国民经济行业分	**Grouped By Sector**					
总　计	**Total**	**952**	**2755771**	**697381**	**1894642**	**13106**
1.住宿业	**Lodging**	**446**	**1156972**	**642022**	**391799**	**4675**
旅游饭店	Restaurants for Junketing	259	974568	500072	365362	4054
一般旅馆	General Hotel	184	180829	140778	26041	615
民宿服务	Homestay Service	3	1575	1172	396	6
露营地服务	Campground Service	－	－	－	－	－
其他住宿业	Others Lodging	－	－	－	－	－
2.餐饮业	**Catering Services**	**506**	**1598799**	**55358**	**1502843**	**8432**
正餐服务	Dinner Services	458	886490	55358	798050	7657
快餐服务	Short Order Services	22	639335	－	634901	150
饮料及冷饮服务	Beverages and Services	14	14115	－	13496	602
餐饮配送及外卖送餐服务	Catering Distribution and Delivery Service	6	21379	－	19205	22
其他餐饮业	Others Catering Services	6	37480	－	37191	－

8－11 分地区限额以上

Main Indicators of Lodging

单位:万元

地　区　Region	企业法人数（个）Number of Enterprises（unit）	营业额 Revenue of Business	客房收入 Revenue of Guest Rooms	餐饮收入 Revenue of Catering Services	主营业务收入 Main Revenue of Business
全　市　Total	**952**	**2755771**	**697381**	**1894642**	**2605306**
市　区　Urban District	850	2607901	625174	1826456	2460149
#上城区　Shangcheng	151	461744	137353	301538	437531
下城区　Xiacheng	93	324390	76852	231380	304945
江干区　Jianggan	83	167963	52402	100072	164306
拱墅区　Gongshu	63	141387	37328	92402	132304
西湖区　Xihu	135	779636	90055	635152	731621
高新(滨江)区　Hi－Tech(Binjiang)	42	73781	25746	46569	70038
萧山区　Xiaoshan	65	230961	64141	157013	216405
大江东产业集聚区　Dajiangdong Industry Cluster District	3	10866	3085	7500	10251
余杭区　Yuhang	55	75903	24360	45793	71802
富阳区　Fuyang	32	35177	10701	21826	33078
临安区　Lin'an	34	42147	15029	23306	39828
经济技术开发区　Economic and Technological Development Zone	43	50900	11559	38431	47949
西湖风景名胜区　The West Lake Scenic Zone	54	223912	79649	132975	210343
桐庐县　Tonglu	22	32628	13590	17461	29918
淳安县　Chun'an	59	97620	53723	38244	98542
建德市　Jiande	21	17622	4894	12482	16696

住宿餐饮业主要指标(2017 年)
and Catering by Region(2017)

(10000 yuan)

主营业务税金及附加 Business Tax and Extra Charges	销售费用 Cost of Sales	管理费用 Administration Cost	财务费用 Financil Cost	利润总额 Total Profits	从业人员平均人数(人) Average Number of Employees (person)
16022	**874559**	**570478**	**70214**	**148312**	**98167**
14677	824765	527372	64016	154496	91275
3444	156895	96650	20333	47721	14271
2031	140170	53026	8636	9524	13824
477	53037	36293	1223	6205	4964
1125	48501	34035	1767	858	4584
1797	205695	113031	3524	84988	27256
256	19734	23571	1597	-1769	2849
1154	77469	38883	18845	6033	8610
13	3074	2908	31	-667	387
237	16516	26822	1638	-3980	3411
408	8283	10851	1960	352	1964
679	8964	9815	2645	408	1893
117	16638	12407	654	-2793	1614
2951	72863	71988	1195	6950	6035
352	9595	8640	3621	-3809	1510
901	35789	30220	2153	-1677	4475
92	4411	4245	423	-699	907

8－12 个体工商业登记注册情况(2017 年末)

Statistics on Individual Business Registration(End of 2017)

项目	Item	全市 Whole City		市区 Urban District	
		合计 Total	#城镇 Urban	合计 Total	#城镇 Urban
户数(户)	**Number of Households (household)**	**471374**	**349112**	**403078**	**315801**
农、林、牧、渔业	Farming, Forestry, Animal Husbandry and Fishery	7828	2804	5852	2330
农、林、牧、渔专业及辅助性活动	Service for Farming, Forestry, Animal Husbandry and Fishery	508	219	392	186
采矿业	Mining and Quarrying	42	11	30	7
开采专业及辅助性活动	Support Activity for Mining and Quarrying	–	–	–	–
制造业	Manufacturing	21461	8194	15039	6166
金属制品、机械和设备修理业	Metal Products, Machinery and Equipment Repair	157	82	129	70
电力、热力、燃气及水的生产和供应业	Production and Supply of Electricity, Gas and Water	45	23	31	21
建筑业	Construction	2284	1487	1964	1333
批发和零售业	Wholesale and Retail Trade & Catering Services	293282	221308	255157	202754
交通运输、仓储和邮政业	Transportation, Storage and Post	6763	3922	5609	3508
住宿和餐饮业	Lodging and Catering	71310	58239	61230	52414
信息传输、软件和信息技术服务业	Information Transmission, Computer Services and Software	1166	938	870	761
金融业	Banking and Insurance	18	14	13	10
房地产业	Real Estate	152	137	87	82
租赁和商务服务业	Renting and Business Service	10576	8323	8782	7209
科学研究和技术服务业	Scientific Research and Technical Service	1496	1118	1139	955
水利、环境和公共设施管理业	Water Conservancy, Environment and Public Utility	74	45	68	43
居民服务、修理和其他服务业	Service for the Residents and Other Service Sector	51069	39446	44010	35474
教育	Education	545	447	488	405
卫生和社会工作	Health Care, Sports & Social Welfare	587	425	449	346
文化、体育和娱乐业	Culture, Sports and Entertainment	2644	2218	2237	1971
其他	Others	32	13	23	12

8－12　续表1　continued 1

项　　目	Item	全　市 Whole City		市　区 Urban District	
		合　计 Total	#城　镇 Urban	合　计 Total	#城　镇 Urban
从业人员(人)	**Employed Persons(person)**	**924064**	**672896**	**770454**	**597934**
农、林、牧、渔业	Farming, Forestry, Animal Husbandry and Fishery	20376	6536	13958	5009
农、林、牧、渔专业及辅助性活动	Service for Farming, Forestry, Animal Husbandry and Fishery	1241	545	853	424
采矿业	Mining and Quarrying	178	35	136	28
开采专业及辅助性活动	Support Activity for Mining and Quarrying	－	－	－	－
制造业	Manufacturing	77358	25655	43562	16400
金属制品、机械和设备修理业	Metal Products, Machinery and Equipment Repair	355	169	293	140
电力、热力、燃气及水的生产和供应业	Production and Supply of Electricity, Gas and Water	92	51	58	46
建筑业	Construction	6778	3459	5277	2791
批发和零售业	Wholesale and Retail Trade & Catering Services	477724	363765	415531	330951
交通运输、仓储和邮政业	Transportation, Storage and Post	11109	6338	8837	5476
住宿和餐饮业	Lodging and Catering	172315	143554	148462	128575
信息传输、软件和信息技术服务业	Information Transmission, Computer Services and Software	2128	1742	1550	1372
金融业	Banking and Insurance	59	50	21	14
房地产业	Real Estate	228	206	145	137
租赁和商务服务业	Renting and Business Service	19328	14994	15442	12366
科学研究和技术服务业	Scientific Research and Technical Service	3110	2504	2406	2095
水利、环境和公共设施管理业	Water Conservancy, Environment and Public Utility	237	102	227	99
居民服务、修理和其他服务业	Service for the Residents and Other Service Sector	123051	95961	106665	85809
教育	Education	1510	1199	1359	1076
卫生和社会工作	Health Care, Sports & Social Welfare	1455	1076	1126	875
文化、体育和娱乐业	Culture, Sports and Entertainment	7001	5642	5671	4794
其他	Others	27	27	21	21

8－12 续表2 continued 2

项目	Item	全市 Whole City		市区 Urban District	
		合计 Total	#城镇 Urban	合计 Total	#城镇 Urban
注册资金(万元)	**Capital Registered(10000 yuan)**	**4498107**	**3176820**	**3546662**	**2664262**
农、林、牧、渔业	Farming, Forestry, Animal Husbandry and Fishery	270766	95403	178949	71323
农、林、牧、渔专业及辅助性活动	Service for Farming, Forestry, Animal Husbandry and Fishery	19531	6339	16586	5404
采矿业	Mining and Quarrying	2110	543	1355	231
开采专业及辅助性活动	Support Activity for Mining and Quarrying	–	–	–	–
制造业	Manufacturing	265350	104184	159546	70998
金属制品、机械和设备修理业	Metal Products, Machinery and Equipment Repair	1624	1017	1123	675
电力、热力、燃气及水的生产和供应业	Production and Supply of Electricity, Gas and Water	283	98	152	80
建筑业	Construction	44466	22121	36138	18452
批发和零售业	Wholesale and Retail Trade & Catering Services	2175545	1662151	1797400	1437452
交通运输、仓储和邮政业	Transportation, Storage and Post	88899	51100	70436	44673
住宿和餐饮业	Lodging and Catering	926663	707122	729434	580037
信息传输、软件和信息技术服务业	Information Transmission, Computer Services and Software	8650	6855	6440	5588
金融业	Banking and Insurance	164	93	129	68
房地产业	Real Estate	964	780	378	282
租赁和商务服务业	Renting and Business Service	146722	92786	92294	65493
科学研究和技术服务业	Scientific Research and Technical Service	12090	9656	8192	7378
水利、环境和公共设施管理业	Water Conservancy, Environment and Public Utility	1561	672	1238	661
居民服务、修理和其他服务业	Service for the Residents and Other Service Sector	493162	372540	417780	321524
教育	Education	5552	4016	4883	3495
卫生和社会工作	Health Care, Sports & Social Welfare	9709	7606	6903	5711
文化、体育和娱乐业	Culture, Sports and Entertainment	44164	38510	34273	30242
其他	Others	1287	584	742	574

8－13　私营企业登记注册情况(2017年末)

Statistics on Private Enterprises Registration(End of 2017)

项　目	Item	全市 Whole City		市区 Urban District	
		合计 Total	#城镇 Urban	合计 Total	#城镇 Urban
户数(户)	**Number of Households (household)**	**480986**	**390257**	**450061**	**373644**
农、林、牧、渔业	Farming, Forestry, Animal Husbandry and Fishery	6751	2897	4930	2352
农、林、牧、渔专业及辅助性活动	Service for Farming, Forestry, Animal Husbandry and Fishery	984	568	807	499
采矿业	Mining and Quarrying	164	41	91	23
开采专业及辅助性活动	Support Activity for Mining and Quarrying	5	3	5	3
制造业	Manufacturing	51125	20098	44178	18085
金属制品、机械和设备修理业	Metal Products, Machinery and Equipment Repair	329	243	319	236
电力、热力、燃气及水的生产和供应业	Production and Supply of Electricity, Gas and Water	743	385	456	305
建筑业	Construction	22097	17320	20672	16461
批发和零售业	Wholesale and Retail Trade & Catering Services	159405	135129	150700	130134
交通运输、仓储和邮政业	Transportation, Storage and Post	6687	4924	5499	4078
住宿和餐饮业	Lodging and Catering	8675	6978	7984	6546
信息传输、软件和信息技术服务业	Information Transmission, Computer Services and Software	46729	43153	44780	41744
金融业	Banking and Insurance	6030	5277	5782	5139
房地产业	Real Estate	11226	9121	10428	8577
租赁和商务服务业	Renting and Business Service	78277	71557	75143	69266
科学研究和技术服务业	Scientific Research and Technical Service	45378	41583	44120	40821
水利、环境和公共设施管理业	Water Conservancy, Environment and Public Utility	1544	1131	1295	995
居民服务、修理和其他服务业	Service for the Residents and Other Service Sector	19152	15377	17976	14534
教育	Education	2541	2312	2464	2251
卫生和社会工作	Health Care, Sports & Social Welfare	1645	1068	1532	1007
文化、体育和娱乐业	Culture, Sports and Entertainment	12733	11856	11969	11287
其他	Others	84	50	62	39

8－13 续表1 continued 1

项 目	Item	全 市 Whole City		市 区 Urban District	
		合 计 Total	#城 镇 Urban	合 计 Total	#城 镇 Urban
从业人员(人)	**Employed Persons(person)**	**3122535**	**2205600**	**2856977**	**2087802**
农、林、牧、渔业	Farming, Forestry, Animal Husbandry and Fishery	40587	17190	27742	13395
农、林、牧、渔专业及辅助性活动	Service for Farming, Forestry, Animal Husbandry and Fishery	5805	3246	4568	2742
采矿业	Mining and Quarrying	2457	537	1490	190
开采专业及辅助性活动	Support Activity for Mining and Quarrying	34	27	34	27
制造业	Manufacturing	449469	143205	336364	121842
金属制品、机械和设备修理业	Metal Products, Machinery and Equipment Repair	1824	1290	1752	1245
电力、热力、燃气及水的生产和供应业	Production and Supply of Electricity, Gas and Water	4916	2369	3216	1847
建筑业	Construction	142685	99090	130783	91521
批发和零售业	Wholesale and Retail Trade & Catering Services	944634	694791	899648	666937
交通运输、仓储和邮政业	Transportation, Storage and Post	43485	30445	34545	23820
住宿和餐饮业	Lodging and Catering	56411	45043	50725	40852
信息传输、软件和信息技术服务业	Information Transmission, Computer Services and Software	281644	242444	270594	233956
金融业	Banking and Insurance	47713	40714	45304	39600
房地产业	Real Estate	64730	51525	58523	46727
租赁和商务服务业	Renting and Business Service	419837			
科学研究和技术服务业	Scientific Research and Technical Service	284172	229644	273921	224449
水利、环境和公共设施管理业	Water Conservancy, Environment and Public Utility	8797	6284	7427	5439
居民服务、修理和其他服务业	Service for the Residents and Other Service Sector	113126	80524	106647	76275
教育	Education	14324	12298	13797	11845
卫生和社会工作	Health Care, Sports & Social Welfare	9226	6778	8412	6264
文化、体育和娱乐业	Culture, Sports and Entertainment	74116	66615	69019	62818
其他	Others	466	274	351	188

8－13 续表2 continued 2

项 目	Item	全 市 Whole City		市 区 Urban District	
		合 计 Total	#城 镇 Urban	合 计 Total	#城 镇 Urban
注册资金(万元)	**Capital Registered(10000 yuan)**	**417947655**	**372387552**	**399628362**	**360349315**
农、林、牧、渔业	Farming, Forestry, Animal Husbandry and Fishery	2567139	1329425	1741461	1029088
农、林、牧、渔专业及辅助性活动	Service for Farming, Forestry, Animal Husbandry and Fishery	615740	409842	482037	359943
采矿业	Mining and Quarrying	154086	55591	97425	39154
开采专业及辅助性活动	Support Activity for Mining and Quarrying	21600	21100	21600	21100
制造业	Manufacturing	23542229	10305179	21200987	9332889
金属制品、机械和设备修理业	Metal Products, Machinery and Equipment Repair	115458	93250	112928	91050
电力、热力、燃气及水的生产和供应业	Production and Supply of Electricity, Gas and Water	832979	647686	676896	569401
建筑业	Construction	17384432	14333604	16068241	13373808
批发和零售业	Wholesale and Retail Trade & Catering Services	46580650	41307307	44167132	39633608
交通运输、仓储和邮政业	Transportation, Storage and Post	2896339	2263225	2256165	1756477
住宿和餐饮业	Lodging and Catering	1915244	1582184	1635701	1400339
信息传输、软件和信息技术服务业	Information Transmission, Computer Services and Software	26796999	24850736	25761772	23991789
金融业	Banking and Insurance	20993443	19327056	19481462	18322366
房地产业	Real Estate	16797089	14220193	16001879	13617290
租赁和商务服务业	Renting and Business Service	214988297	203372393	209892202	199827957
科学研究和技术服务业	Scientific Research and Technical Service	27082203	24783389	26100383	24089361
水利、环境和公共设施管理业	Water Conservancy, Environment and Public Utility	1239019	1030178	1061851	922678
居民服务、修理和其他服务业	Service for the Residents and Other Service Sector	6556518	5791805	6269843	5568155
教育	Education	578746	541716	538313	512618
卫生和社会工作	Health Care, Sports & Social Welfare	811259	725175	748163	678062
文化、体育和娱乐业	Culture, Sports and Entertainment	6187928	5892251	5896029	5658159
其他	Others	43056	28459	32457	26116

8－14　分行业、类型规模以上
Main Indicators of Service Enterprises

单位:亿元

项　　目	Item	单位数(个) Number of Enterprise (Unit)	资产总计 Total Assets	固定资产原价 Orginal Value of Fixed Assets
总　计	**Total**	**3744**	**20198**	**3657**
按登记注册类型分	**Grouped By Registered Type**			
国有企业	State－owned Enterprises	88	1245	217
集体企业	Collective－owned Enterprises	66	363	120
股份合作企业	Cooperative Enterprises	12	71	44
联营企业	Joint Ownership Enterprises	2	1	－
有限责任公司	Limited Liability Corporations	1302	9758	1805
股份有限公司	Share－holding Corporations Ltd.	202	1932	317
私营企业	Private Enterprises	1873	2361	376
其他企业	Other Enterprises	27	35	7
港澳台商投资企业	Enterprises With Investment from Hong Kong, Macao and Taiwan	96	3982	618
外商投资企业	Enterprises With Foreign Investment	76	450	153
按国民经济行业分	**Grouped by Sector**			
交通运输、仓储和邮政业	Transportation, Storage and Post	642	1598	834
信息传输、软件和信息技术服务业	Information Transmission, Softuare and Information Technology	808	6256	1045
房地产业(除房地产开发经营)	Real Estate	277	1065	149
租赁和商务服务业	Leasing and Business Services	868	8524	1194
科学研究和技术服务业	Scientific Research and Technical Service	581	1438	193
水利、环境和公共设施管理业	Water Conservancy, Environment and Public Utility	126	506	128
居民服务、修理和其他服务业	Service for the Residents and Other Service Sector	114	41	11
教育	Education	53	26	6
卫生和社会工作	Health Care and Social Welfare	118	53	17
文化、体育和娱乐业	Culture, Sports and Entertainment	157	700	80

服务业企业主要经济指标(2017 年)
Above Designated Size by Sector and Type(2017)

(100 million yuan)

本年折旧 Depreciation	负债合计 Total Liabilities	所有者权益合计 Total Owners′ Equities	营业收入 Revenue of Business	主营业务收入 Main Revenue of Business	营业成本 Operating Costs	主营业务成本 Main Cost of Business	营业税金及附加 Sales Taxes and Extra Charges in Main Business
234	**10063**	**10135**	**8557**	**8445**	**5410**	**5368**	**47**
16	363	882	382	378	268	266	2
3	156	207	35	34	13	13	3
1	20	51	7	7	1	1	1
–	1	–	2	2	1	1	–
81	5496	4263	2175	2134	1649	1630	14
24	734	1198	584	576	422	416	3
30	1399	962	1820	1800	1344	1336	7
–	21	14	24	23	15	15	–
71	1583	2399	2331	2292	539	533	16
7	291	159	1199	1198	1159	1158	3
49	828	770	889	879	787	780	3
111	2743	3513	5088	5032	2779	2765	22
7	620	436	210	203	135	131	4
43	4495	4029	1054	1033	758	750	11
11	814	625	825	819	628	625	4
6	309	198	153	147	117	112	1
1	25	16	39	39	24	24	–
1	17	8	26	26	15	15	–
2	34	18	75	74	44	44	–
5	178	522	197	194	122	121	2

单位:亿元　　8-14 续表

项　目	Item	主营业务税金及附加 Main Sales Tax and Extra Charges	销售费用 Cost of Sales	管理费用 Administration Cost
总　计	**Total**	**45**	**457**	**1223**
按登记注册类型分	**Grouped By Registered Type**			
国有企业	State - owned Enterprises	1	14	33
集体企业	Collective - owned Enterprises	3	2	10
股份合作企业	Cooperative Enterprises	1	-	2
联营企业	Joint Ownership Enterprises	-	-	-
有限责任公司	Limited Liability Corporations	13	102	269
股份有限公司	Share - holding Corporations Ltd.	3	43	81
私营企业	Private Enterprises	7	95	279
其他企业	Other Enterprises	-	3	5
港澳台商投资企业	Enterprises With Investment from Hong Kong, Macao and Taiwan	16	183	523
外商投资企业	Enterprises With Foreign Investment	3	16	18
按国民经济行业分	**Grouped by Sector**			
交通运输、仓储和邮政业	Transportation, Storage and Post	3	16	52
信息传输、软件和信息技术服务业	Information Transmission, Softuare and Information Technology	21	315	854
房地产业(除房地产开发经营)	Real Estate	4	18	29
租赁和商务服务业	Leasing and Business Services	10	57	122
科学研究和技术服务业	Scientific Research and Technical Service	4	20	102
水利、环境和公共设施管理业	Water Conservancy, Environment and Public Utility	1	5	17
居民服务、修理和其他服务业	Service for the Residents and Other Service Sector	-	6	6
教育	Education	-	3	5
卫生和社会工作	Health Care and Social Welfare	-	9	14
文化、体育和娱乐业	Culture, Sports and Entertainment	2	9	22

continued (100 million yuan)

财务费用 Financil Cost	营业利润 Management Profits	利润总额 Total Profits	所得税费用 Income Tax	应付职工薪酬 Payroll Payable	应交增值税 Value Added Tax Payable	平均用工人数（万人）Average Number of Employed Persons (10000 Persons)
53	**1636**	**1689**	**196**	**1123**	**194**	**76.24**
-8	97	100	3	59	13	3.69
1	13	13	1	6	2	0.42
-	3	2	-	-	-	0.06
-	-	-	-	-	-	0.01
67	218	246	35	365	49	31.51
-	66	73	10	122	15	10.66
18	122	127	23	183	34	21.37
-	1	1	-	6	1	0.55
-29	1115	1119	122	351	76	6.17
4	2	7	3	29	4	1.79
17	57	87	21	133	14	11.71
-32	1211	1226	127	588	114	23.06
7	26	27	5	62	9	10.36
55	179	178	23	123	23	13.81
6	76	79	13	135	21	8.68
3	13	15	3	16	4	2.11
-	2	2	-	12	1	2.41
-	3	3	1	8	1	0.86
-	7	6	1	17	-	1.60
-3	61	65	2	28	7	1.63

8-15 规模以上服务业企业主要经济指标(2012-2017年)
Main Indicators of Service Enterprises Above Designated Size(2012-2017)

单位:亿元 (100 million yuan)

项目	Item	2012	2013	2014	2015	2016	2017
单位数(个)	Number of Enterprises(Unit)	4571	4770	4393	3238	3486	3744
资产总计	Total Assets	10826	13208	14340	15412	18951	20198
固定资产原价	Orginal Value of Fixed Assets	2195	2399	2716	2847	3129	3657
本年折旧	Depreciation	120	138	156	177	207	234
负债合计	Total Liabilities	5657	6789	7181	7463	9134	10063
所有者权益合计	Total Owners´Equities	5169	6418	7160	7949	9816	10135
营业收入	Revenue of Business	3014	3719	4353	5236	6639	8557
主营业务收入	Main Revenue of Business	2909	3609	4247	5111	6512	8445
营业成本	Main Cost of Business	1918	2335	2650	3215	4111	5410
主营业务成本	Main Cost of Business	1863	2288	2609	3170	4039	5368
营业税金及附加	Sales Taxes and Extra Charges in Main Business	82	59	58	59	47	47
主营业务税金及附加	Main Sales Tax and Extra Charges	79	56	54	57	46	45
销售费用	Cost of Sales	196	221	257	314	341	457
管理费用	Administration Cost	379	468	621	765	932	1223
财务费用	Financil Cost	70	70	62	65	43	53
营业利润	Management Profits	484	725	858	1020	1352	1636
利润总额	Total Profits	560	795	934	1110	1443	1689
所得税费用	Income Tax Costs	65	76	123	110	174	196
应付职工薪酬	Employee benefits Payable	377	486	588	718	904	1123
应交增值税	Value Added Tax Payable	19	61	107	106	153	194
平均用工人数(万人)	Average Number of Employed Persons	48.70	57.74	60.29	63.22	68.92	76.24

注:1.2016年及以前为“应交所得税”,2017年改为“所得税费用”。

2.2016年及以前为“从事服务业活动的从业人员平均人数”,2017年改为“平均用工人数”。

a) Since 2017, the indicator was changed to "Income Tax Costs", which was "Income Tax Payable" at past.

b) Since 2017, the indicator was changed to "Average Number of Employed Persons", which was "Average Number of Employed Persons in service activities" at past.

8－16　规模以上服务业非企业单位主要经济指标(2011－2017年)
Main Indicators of Service Non－Enterprise Units Above Designated Size(2011－2017)

单位:亿元　　(100 million yuan)

年　份 Year	单位数 (个) Number of Enterprise (Unit)	从业人员平均人数 (万人) Average Number of Employees(10000 person)	年末资产 Total Assets at the End of Year	固定资产原价 Orginal Value of Fixed Assets
2011	4141	36.72	3414	1306
2012	2321	32.39	5531	1211
2013	2356	34.10	6058	1346
2014	2367	35.14	6401	1499
2015	2382	35.69	6497	1628
2016	2376	36.26	7263	1708
2017	2369	36.55	8964	1823

单位:亿元　　8－16　续表　continued　　(100 million yuan)

年　份 Year	收入合计 Total Revenue	支出合计 Total Expenditure	工资福利支出 Wages and Welfare Expenses	商品和服务支出 Goods and Services Spending	对个人和家庭的补助 For Individual and Family Allowance
2011	1557	1481	316	604	133
2012	1497	1439	314	577	140
2013	1610	1527	352	594	138
2014	1672	1601	391	638	156
2015	1814	1787	469	699	172
2016	2027	1975	572	768	165
2017	2372	2371	646	819	158

8-17 分行业规模以上服务业非企业
Main Indicators of Service Non - Enterprise Units

单位:亿元

项　目	Item	单位数(个) Number of Units(Unit)	从业人员平均人数(万人) Average Number of Employees(10000 person)	年末资产 Total Assets at the End of Year
总　计	**Total**	**2369**	**36.55**	**8964**
按国民经济行业分	**Grouped by Sector**			
交通运输、仓储和邮政业	Transportation, Storage and Post	16	0.24	24
信息传输、软件和信息技术服务业	Information Transmission, Softuare and Information Technology	19	0.13	12
房地产业(除房地产开发经营)	Real Estate	9	0.04	8
租赁和商务服务业	Leasing and Business Services	65	0.25	198
科学研究和技术服务业	Scientific Research and Technical Service	136	1.34	730
水利、环境和公共设施管理业	Water Conservancy, Environment and Public Utility	84	0.97	78
居民服务、修理和其他服务业	Service for the Residents and Other Service Sector	18	0.08	8
教育	Education	733	13.07	1420
卫生和社会工作	Health Care and Social Welfare	319	9.66	625
文化、体育和娱乐业	Culture, Sports and Entertainment	118	0.68	92
公共管理、社会保障和社会组织	Public Management, Social Security and Social Organizations	847	9.97	1294

注:1. 有5家金融业单位,因此分类项相加与总计不一致。

2. 本表行业分类标准为2011《国民经济行业分类》。

单位主要经济指标(2017 年)
Above Designated Size by Sector(2017)

(100 million yuan)

固定资产原价 Orginal Value of Fixed Assets	收入合计 Total Revenue	支出合计 Total Expenditure	工资福利支出 Wages and Welfare Expenses	商品和服务支出 Goods and Services Spending	对个人和家庭的补助 For Individual and Family Allowance
1823	**2372**	**2371**	**646**	**819**	**158**
13	20	19	3	1	1
6	6	6	1	2	–
1	1	1	1	1	–
30	18	14	3	5	1
87	122	102	22	30	5
58	36	36	8	14	2
3	3	3	1	1	–
738	494	487	221	148	55
351	638	616	194	359	22
62	38	38	10	11	3
461	985	991	178	242	69

a) The sum of all sectors is not equal to total, because the includes 5 Financial units.
b) This table uses《Industrial classification for national economic activitles》2011.

主要统计指标解释

社会消费品零售额 指各种经济类型的批发零售贸易业、住宿餐饮业对城乡居民和社会集团的消费品零售额总和。这个指标反映通过各种商品流通渠道向居民和社会集团供应的生活消费品来满足他们生活需要，是研究人民生活、社会消费品购买力、货币流通等问题的重要指标。社会消费品零售额包括：(1)售给城乡居民作为生活用的商品和修建房屋用的建筑材料；(2)售给机关、团体、学校、部队、企业、事业单位的职工食堂各种食品、燃料；(3)售给部队干部、战士生活用的粮食、副食品、衣着品、日用品、燃料；(4)售给来华的外国人、华侨、港澳台同胞的消费品；(5)售给社会集团的办公用品、纸张、帐册、文印用品、计算工具、书刊杂志和奖品；公共用品和纺织品、针织品；学校用的教学用具；文体用品；非专用的劳动保护用品，如工作服、套袖、围裙、手套、毛巾、肥皂等；日用百货和杂品，包括职工食堂用的餐具、炊具、设备和清洁卫生工具等；家具、设备、日用电器、电讯设备、电影器材和照相器材等；取暖用的设备和燃料、防暑、降温的饮料；非生产经营用的交通工具，如小轿车、面包车、工具车、卡车和油料；零星修理的各种零配件、材料、工具、建筑材料等；举办各种招待会、茶话会、宴会用的烟酒茶和各种食品及馈赠的礼品；从公费医疗经费中开支的中、西药品、中药材和医疗器材以及其他非生产性设备和用品。

限额以上批发零售业 指批发业年主营业务收入在2000万元及以上，零售业年主营业务收入在500万元及以上的各种经济类型商贸企业。

商品销售总额 指对本企业(单位)以外的单位和个人出售(包括对国(境)外直接出口)的商品金额。这个指标反映批发零售贸易业在国内市场上销售商品以及出口商品的总量。商品销售总额包括：(1)售给城乡居民和社会集团消费用的商品；(2)售给工业、农业、建筑业、运输邮电业、批发零售贸易业、餐饮业、服务业等作为生产、经营使用的商品；(3)售给批发零售贸易业作为转卖或加工后转卖的商品；(4)对国(境)外直接出口的商品，不包括：出售本企业(单位)自用的废旧包装用品，未通过买卖行为付出的商品，经本单位介绍，由买卖双方直接结算，本单位只收取手续费的业务，购货退出的商品以及商品损耗和损失等。

Explanatory Notes on Main Statistical Indicators

Total Retail Sales of Consumer Goods referring to the sum of retail sales of consumer goods sold by wholesale and retail, catering and lodging to urban and rural residents and social groups. This indicator is used to show the supply of consumer goods through various channels to households and institutions, and is very important for the study on people's livelihood, on the purchasing power of consumer goods and on the circulation of money. The retail sales of consumer goods include: (1) commodities sold to urban and rural residents for their daily use and building materials sold to them for the construction or repair of houses; (2) food and fuels sold to canteens of institutions, enterprises, schools and military units; (3) grains and non – staple food, clothing, daily articles and fuels sold to military personnel; (4) consumer goods sold to foreigners, overseas Chinese, and Chinese compatriots form Taiwan, Hong Kong and Macao during their stay in the mainland of China; (5) commodities sold to social groups. included under this heading are : office appliances, paper, account books, printing articles, calculaters, newspapers, magazines and prizes; public articles, textiles and knitgoods; realias for schools; cultural and sports articles; working articles for unspecial use i. e. working clothes, raglan sleeves, gloves, towels and soaps; commidities and miscellaneous goods for daily use i. e. dishwares, cookers and cleaning articles for canteens of institutions, enterprises, schools; furnishings, appliances, communications facilities , film and photograph equipments and materials; heating facilities, fuels and beverages; vehicles (exclude for business use) such as cars, microbuses, trucks and oils; parts , fittings, instruments and building materials, tobaccoes, alcohols, teas, foods for all kinds of reception meetings and banquets and prizes for presenting; Chinese and Western medicines, herbs and medical facilities expenditured by medical insurance fund and other non – production goods and equipments.

Wholesale And Retail Trade Above Designated Size wholesale trade, with year main business revenue over 20 million yuan of different status of registration; retail sale trade, with year main business revenue over 5 million yuan of different status of registration.

Total Sales of Commodities refer to selling of commodities by the establishments to other establishments and individuals (including direct export). This indictor is used to show the total value of sales of commodities at domestic markets and export. The total sales include: (1) commodities sold to urban and rural residents and social groups for their consumption; (2) commodities sold to establishments in industry, agriculture, construction, transportation, post and telecommunications, wholesale and retail trades, catering trade and public utility for their production and operation; (3) commodities sold to wholesale and retail establishment for re – selling, with or without further processing; and (4) commodities for direct export to other countries. Excluded are selling of waste packaging materials used by the establishments(units) themselves, commodities transferred without buying or selling procedures, commission income from brokerage in transactions whose settlement is directly handled by buyers and sellers, rejected commodities in the purchase, loss in commodities, etc.

九、对外经济旅游

FOREIGN ECONOMIC COOPERATION AND TOURISM

9 对外经济、旅游
Foreign Economic Cooperation and Tourism

主要统计指标
Major Statistical Indicators

实际利用外资金额	Foreign Investments Actually Utilized	66.10	亿美元	(USD 100 million)
为上年	As Compared with the Preceding Year	91.7	%	(%)
进出口总额	Total Imports and Exports	750.65	亿美元	(USD 100 million)
为上年	As Compared with the Preceding Year	110.4	%	(%)
# 出口总额	Total Exports	509.95	亿美元	(USD 100 million)
为上年	As Compared with the Preceding Year	101.5	%	(%)
进出口总额	Total Imports and Exports	5085.08	亿元	(100 million yuan)
为上年	As Compared with the Preceding Year	113.3	%	(%)
# 出口总额	Total Exports	3456.62	亿元	(100 million yuan)
为上年	As Compared with the Preceding Year	104.3	%	(%)
接待境外旅游者人数	Number of Oversea Visitor Arrivals	402.23	万人次	(10000 person-times)
为上年	As Compared with the Preceding Year	110.7	%	(%)
旅游外汇收入	Total Foreign Exchange Earnings from International Tourism	35.43	亿美元	(USD 100 million)
为上年	As Compared with the Preceding Year	112.5	%	(%)

9-01 外商直接投资情况(1978-2017年)
Foreign Direct Investment(1978-2017)

单位:万美元 (USD 10000)

年 份 Year	项目个数(个) Number of Projects (unit)	协议总投资额 Total Investments of Agreements	协议利用外资金额 Contracted Foreign Investment	实际利用外资金额 Foreign Investments Actually Utilized
1978				
1979				
1980	3	153	128	
1981				
1982				
1983	2	356	100	
1984	9	6932	2697	
1985	21	6638	1731	907
1986	9	5722	2017	683
1987	10	2685	1256	1470
1988	23	6781	2734	696
1989	34	3897	1569	1860
1990	68	7817	3951	751
1991	121	11107	5551	2129
1992	583	125224	60915	9678
1993	1078	222325	121947	35713
1994	624	174406	110541	41098
1995	427	136662	90207	42659
1996	221	108150	70982	53651
1997	174	51682	27888	41187
1998	216	98219	51400	38425
1999	212	83416	56742	42025
2000	315	89781	64548	43093
2001	483	154447	103023	50324
2002	587	247888	96720	52186
2003	869	432660	200104	100850
2004	802	629727	307746	140982
2005	756	770941	400503	171274
2006	747	1080602	537986	225536
2007	574	854907	558059	280181
2008	483	862523	622788	331154
2009	554	948323	696486	401370
2010	545	1188055	770911	435627
2011	500	1291015	817108	472230
2012	510	1342616	826516	496061
2013	415	1419926	913144	527633
2014	408	1329217	723838	633460
2015	475	1649709	1038042	711253
2016	462	1503411	847841	720915
2017	575	1877119	1069651	661001

9－02 分行业外商直接投资情况(2017 年)
Foreign Direct Investment by Sector(2017)

单位:万美元 (USD 10,000)

行 业 Sector	项目数(个) Projects(unit)	占总数% Proportion(%)	实际利用外资金额 Foreign Investments Actually Utilized	占总数(%) Proportion(%)
合 计 Total	**575**	**100**	**661001**	**100**
农 业 Agriculture	1	0.17	145	0.02
采矿业 Mining				
制造业 Manufacturing	54	9.39	77738	11.76
电力、燃气及水生产和供应业 Production & Supply of Electricity, Gas & Water	4	0.7	–	–
建筑业 Construction	6	1.04	12026	1.82
交通运输、仓储和邮政业 Transportation, Storage and Post	8	1.39	21091	3.19
信息传输、软件和信息技术服务业 Information Transmission, Softuare and Information Technology	97	16.87	131737	19.93
批发和零售贸易、餐饮业 Whole sale and Retail Tvade. Catering Services	122	21.22	78114	11.82
金融业 Banking and Insurance	72	12.52	34824	5.27
房地产业 Real Estate	11	1.91	94157	14.24
租赁和商务服务业 Leasing and Business Services	90	15.65	112802	17.07
科学研究和技术服务业 Scientific Research and Technical Service	98	17.04	95032	14.38
其他行业 Others	12	2.09	3335	0.5
第一产业 Primary Industry	**1**	**0.17**	**145**	**0.02**
第二产业 Secondary Industry	**64**	**11.13**	**89764**	**13.58**
第三产业 Tertiary Industry	**510**	**88.7**	**571092**	**86.4**

9-03 分国别(地区)外商直接投资情况(2017年)

Foreign Direct Investment by Region or Territory(2017)

单位:万美元 (USD 10000)

国别(地区)	Country (territory)	历年累计 Accumulated 项目(个) Projects (unit)	总投资额 Total Investments	协议外资金额 Total Contracted Foreign Investments	2017年 In Year 2017 项目(个) Projects (unit)	总投资额 Total Investments	协议外资金额 Total Contracted Foreign Investments	实际利用外资 Foreign Investments Actually Utilized
合　计	**Total**	**13926**	**18731551**	**11210635**	**575**	**1877119**	**1069651**	**661001**
#中国香港	#Hong Kong	6099	12632209	7502383	267	1480295	784345	518924
中国澳门	Macao	76	82948	47999	3	6479	2430	-
中国台湾	Taiwan	1565	450524	253797	34	26929	21270	7461
日本	Japan	780	593174	255432	12	61888	23212	6715
泰国	Thailand	44	13375	3696	2	497	194	39
马来西亚	Malaysia	84	50660	34095	2	9086	11277	-
新加坡	Singapore	337	474940	298910	7	-9843	-209	16476
印度	India	29	5932	5352	5	77	77	15
韩国	Republic of Korea	376	141862	80712	24	31258	9946	8186
德国	Germany	222	114469	67581	7	4011	1200	1847
法国	France	133	74015	44140	6	957	3529	3085
意大利	Italy	231	154064	72580	6	1487	1565	1227
荷兰	Netherlands	90	103479	23899	1	1749	1284	909
英国	Britain	210	199816	133303	7	8992	2693	99
西班牙	Spain	75	68014	26621	3	254	124	2467
奥地利	Austria	25	31334	22513	1	1637	1169	2807
俄罗斯联邦	The Russion Federation	19	3310	1572				
英属维尔京群岛	The British Virgin Islands	582	1495137	718799	3	56106	29981	16034
加拿大	Canada	245	110096	73053	15	1098	782	118
美国	U.S.A	1747	1203819	602761	61	38690	14555	1278
澳大利亚	Australia	205	102495	79206	7	936	396	102
新西兰	New Zealand	44	13671	9425	3	1084	751	-

9－04 分地区外商直接投资情况(2017年)
Foreign Direct Investment by Region(2017)

单位:万美元 (USD 10000)

区 域 Region		批准项目个数(个) Number of Projects(unit)		实际利用外资金额 Foreign Investments Actually Utilized	
		2017年 In Year 2017	历年累计 Accumulated Until the End of 2017	2017年 In Year 2017	历年累计 Accumulated Until the End of 2017
全 市	**Total**	**575**	**13926**	**661001**	**6768323**
市 区	Urban District	555	12897	630607	6407688
#上城区	Shangcheng	39	758	21700	274080
下城区	Xiacheng	22	789	40225	106897
江干区	Jianggan	28	765	32100	309290
拱墅区	Gongshu	21	992	38270	414173
西湖区	Xihu	65	1154	64110	532252
高新(滨江)区	Hi－Tech(Binjiang)	83	1189	73600	804498
萧山区	Xiaoshan	133	1891	147823	1042848
大江东产业集聚区	Dajiangdong Industry Cluster District	18	18	60016	60016
余杭区	Yuhang	91	1658	103975	727149
富阳区	Fuyang	16	746	27762	290412
临安区	Lin'an	11	444	23107	188054
经济技术开发区	Economic and Technological Development Zone	42	42	57935	57935
桐庐县	Tonglu	7	564	16500	165090
淳安县	Chun'an	2	200	3375	97585
建德市	Jiande	11	265	13500	97960

9-05 分地区国内招商引资情况(2016-2017年)
Domestic Investment by Region(2016-2017)

单位:亿元 (100 million yuan)

区域 Region		批准项目个数(个) Number of Projects(unit)		实际利用资金 Investments Actually Utilized	
		2017年 In Year 2017	2016年 In Year 2016	2017年 In Year 2017	2016年 In Year 2016
全 市	**Total**	**2772**	**2733**	**1562.80**	**1397.07**
市 区	Urban District	2453	2149	1430.07	1231.03
#上城区	Shangcheng	205	125	103.05	94.81
下城区	Xiacheng	412	206	183.30	165.14
江干区	Jianggan	138	240	180.81	161.03
拱墅区	Gongshu	739	595	193.10	172.27
西湖区	Xihu	313	304	201.62	186.27
高新(滨江)区	Hi-Tech(Binjiang)	40	86	95.85	85.26
萧山区	Xiaoshan	260	330	191.03	167.1
大江东产业集聚区	Dajiangdong Industry Cluster District	73	252	69.80	105.97
余杭区	Yuhang	96	108	123.82	111.21
富阳区	Fuyang	68	77	60.83	52.69
临安区	Lin'an	128	126	56.09	48.62
经济技术开发区	Economic and Technological Development Zone	54	78	40.57	35.25
桐庐县	Tonglu	98	110	50.47	45.29
淳安县	Chun'an	80	147	31.38	28.17
建德市	Jiande	141	201	50.88	43.96

9 - 06 国家级开发区

The Construction of National -

项　目	Item	合计 Total	杭州经济技术开发区 Hangzhou Economic and Technological Development Zone
规划面积　（平方公里）	Area of planning (sq. km)	844.45	64.25
已开发面积　（平方公里）	Area of Development (sq. km)	222.66	49.89
历年累计基础设施投资额（亿元）	Accumulative Total Investments in Infrastructure (100 million yuan)	2481.27	557.88
历年累计批准进区企业（个）	Accumulative Number of Enterprises Approved (unit)	107585	21835
#三资企业　（个）	Foreign Investments Enter - prises (unit)	3347	878
历年累计协议利用外资（亿美元）	Accumulative Total Foreign Investments of Agreements (USD 100 million)	350.71	135.85
历年累计实际利用外资（亿美元）	Accumulative Total Foreign Investments Actually Used (USD 100 million)	296.36	85.47
年末实有投产企业个数（个）	Number of Enterprises in Production or Operation at the Year - end (unit)	83590	15464
#三资企业　（个）	Foreign Investments Enter - prises (unit)	2337	636
当年规模以上工业总产值（亿元）	Gross Industrial Output Value of the Year (100 million yuan)	8407.34	1926.21
当年规模以上企业主营业务收入（亿元）	Fulfilled Profits and Tax of the Year (100 million yuan)	11157.80	2532.48
当年规模以上企业实现利润（亿元）	Fulfilled Profits of the Enterprises above the Designated Size of the Year (100 million yuan)	817.01	217.94
当年出口创汇（亿美元）	Foreign Exchange Earmings of Export of the Year (USD 100 million)	205.22	49.75
当年财政总收入　（亿元）	Total Financial Revenue of the Year (100 million yuan)	886.25	178.86
# 税收收入　（亿元）	Tax Revenue (unit)	770.62	168.98

建设发展情况(2017 年)

Class Development Zones(2017)

杭州高新技术开发区 Hangzhou High - tech Development Zone	萧山经济技术开发区 Xiaoshan Economic and Technological Development Zone	富阳经济技术开发区 Fuyang Economic and Technological Development Zone	余杭经济技术开发区 Yuhang Economic and Technological Development Zone	临江国家高新区 Linjiang National High - Tech Zone
12.64	105.20	126.10	109.26	427.00
12.64	38.65	25.09	44.20	52.19
374.49	255.10	600.40	434.40	259.00
35845	10122	14202	18304	7277
624	682	524	456	183
–	93.05	31.64	37.54	52.63
82.00	49.03	24.07	23.58	32.21
28158	8723	5964	18304	6977
624	339	168	456	114
1773.90	1264.00	1104.02	1178.49	1160.72
1762.10	2466.70	1875.33	1177.48	1343.71
216.23	120.40	92.12	96.88	73.44
58.45	30.03	16.76	37.92	12.31
287.28	98.14	82.60	152.19	87.18
279.29	98.14	68.00	120.05	36.16

9-07 省级产业集聚区建设发展情况(2016-2017 年末)
Statistics on Provincial-level Industry Cluster Districts Development (End of 2016-2017)

项　　目	Item	大江东产业集聚区 Dajiangdong Industry Cluster District		城西科创产业集聚区 Chengxi Technological and Creative Industry Cluster District	
		2017 年末 End of 2017	2016 年末 End of 2016	2017 年末 End of 2017	2016 年末 End of 2016
入区企业数(个)	Proposed Enterprises (unit)	1190	1034	13956	12506
投产企业数(个)	Operating Enterprises (unit)	285	261	594	543
已开发建设面积(平方千米)	Land Space under Construction (sq. km)	23.88	23.88	36.70	36.70
已建成投产面积(平方千米)	Land Space Completed (sq. km)	22.69	22.69	34.2	34.20
当年产业增加值(亿元)	Current year's Value-added (100 million yuan)	220.98	202.16	1341.31	1013.70
#工业增加值(亿元)	Value-added of Industry (100 million yuan)	211.90	195.00	129.97	111.06
#服务业增加值(亿元)	Value-added of the Tertiary Industry (100 million yuan)	9.08	7.16	1211.34	902.64
当年实际引进内资(亿元)	Current Year's Amount of Domestic Investment (100 million yuan)	68.54	66.89	51.7	44.80
当年实际利用外资(亿美元)	Current Year's Amount of Foreign Investment Actually Utilized (100 million USD)	6.00	6.58	2.9	2.40
当年科技活动经费支出(亿元)	Current Year's S & T Expenditure (100 million yuan)	18.11	15.27	179.07	164.74
科技活动人员数(人)	S & T Personnel (person)	4401	4174	20316	16261
当年财政预算总收入(亿元)	Current Year's Total Financial Revenue (100 million yuan)	71.85	69.15	233.7	169.10
当年固定资产投资完成额(亿元)	Current Year's Investment in Fixed Asset's (100 million yuan)	160.47	228.40	430.72	366.90
当年工业总产值(亿元)	Current Year's Gross Industrial Output Value (100 million yuan)	1030.53	1013.40	588.25	494.78
当年服务业营业收入(亿元)	Current Year's Operating Revenue of the Tertiary Industry (100 million yuan)	193.69	170.96	3307.8	2226.81
当年出口交货值(亿元)	Current Year's Export Delivery Value (100 million yuan)	54.32	49.00	94.0	83.08
当年利税总额(亿元)	Current Year's Total Taxes and Profits (100 million yuan)	105.55	107.00	1107.27	811.90
#利润总额(亿元)	Total Profits (100 million yuan)	67.67	64.80	1016.08	732.80

注:2017 年城西科创产业集聚区统计口径有调整,2016 年数据已调整成同口径;城西科创产业集聚区的财政预算总收入为企业税收收入。

a) The statistical method of Chengxi Technological and Creative Industry Cluster District was adjusted in 2017, and the data of 2016 were adjusted by the same way. The total financial revenue of Chengxi Technological and Creative Industry Cluster District refers to enterperises'tax revenue.

9-08 特色小镇发展情况(2017年)
Statistics on Characteristic Towns(2017)

	企业数(家) Number of Enterprises (unit)	本年新入驻企业数(家) Number of new Enterprises to enter this year (unit)	"新四军"人数(个) Number of XinSiJun (unit)	固定资产投资(不包括商业住宅和商业综合体项目)(亿元) Investment in Fixed Assets (Excluding commercial housing and commercial complex projects) (100 million yuan)
合 计 Total	**38740**	**10918**	**12183**	**595**
省级特色小镇创建对象 Provincial Characteristic Towns to Create Objects	22031	7581	8571	330
省级特色小镇培育对象 Provincial Characteristic Towns to Cultivate Objects	11110	2308	2210	125
市级特色小镇 Municipal Characteristic Towns	5599	1029	1402	140

注:"新四军"创业人员数:包括大学生创业者、大企业高管及其他连续创业者、科技人员创业者、留学归国人员创业者等创业人员数。包括个体工商户和企业中有技术、资本入股的人员。

a) "New Fourth Army" Entrepreneurs: including college student entrepreneurs, big business executives and other serial entrepreneurs, tech entrepreneurs, overseas returnees entrepreneurs and so on. Also including people with technical capital and equity of individual industrial and commercial businesses or enterprises.

9-08 续表 continued

	特色产业投资(亿元) Characteristic Industry Investment (100 million yuan)	工业企业主营业务收入(亿元) Industrial Enterprise Revenues in Main Business (100 million yuan)	服务业营业收入(亿元) Service Revenues (100 million yuan)	税收收入(亿元) Tax Revenues (100 million yuan)
合 计 Total	**434**	**2293**	**5592**	**372**
省级特色小镇创建对象 Provincial Characteristic Towns to Create Objects	257	1251	1767	230
省级特色小镇培育对象 Provincial Characteristic Towns to Cultivate Objects	80	649	3529	96
市级特色小镇 Municipal Characteristic Towns	97	392	296	47

9-09 进出口情况(1990-2017年)

Imports and Exports (1990-2017)

年 份 Year	亿美元 USD 100 million						亿元 100 million yuan					
	进出口 Exports And Imports		出口 Exports		进口 Imports		进出口 Exports And Imports		出口 Exports		进口 Imports	
	总值 Total Value	为上年% As Compared with the Preceding Year(%)	总值 Total Value	为上年% As Compared with the Preceding Year(%)	总值 Total Value	为上年% As Compared with the Preceding Year(%)	总值 Total Value	为上年% As Compared with the Preceding Year(%)	总值 Total Value	为上年% As Compared with the Preceding Year(%)	总值 Total Value	为上年% As Compared with the Preceding Year(%)
1990	1.45	172.6	0.99	198.0	0.46	135.3						
1991	2.18	150.3	1.48	149.5	0.70	152.2						
1992	3.42	156.9	2.16	146.0	1.26	180.0						
1993	8.73	255.3	4.92	227.8	3.81	302.4						
1994	34.96	400.5	26.11	530.7	8.85	232.3						
1995	45.18	129.2	33.18	127.1	12.00	135.6						
1996	43.52	96.3	31.11	93.8	12.41	103.4						
1997	48.83	112.2	37.43	120.3	11.40	91.8						
1998	59.73	122.3	44.16	118.0	15.57	136.6						
1999	73.40	122.9	50.79	115.0	22.61	145.3						
2000	104.76	142.7	69.65	137.1	35.11	155.3						
2001	112.98	107.9	72.84	104.6	40.14	114.3						
2002	131.07	116.0	84.81	116.4	46.26	115.3						
2003	182.38	139.2	109.55	129.2	72.83	157.4						
2004	244.96	134.3	151.75	138.6	93.21	128.0						
2005	298.70	121.9	198.04	130.5	100.66	108.0						
2006	389.09	130.3	262.28	132.4	126.81	126.0						
2007	434.26	111.7	299.66	114.3	134.60	106.2						
2008	480.65	110.7	336.14	112.2	144.51	107.4						
2009	404.20	84.1	271.80	80.9	132.40	91.6						
2010	523.55	129.5	353.37	130.0	170.18	128.6	3551.87		2397.67		1154.20	
2011	639.72	122.2	415.21	117.5	224.50	131.9	4152.76	116.9	2696.47	112.5	1456.28	126.2
2012	616.83	96.4	412.62	99.4	204.22	91.0	3893.23	93.8	2604.88	96.6	1288.35	88.5
2013	650.71	105.5	447.66	108.5	203.05	99.5	4037.01	103.7	2777.31	106.6	1259.70	97.8
2014	679.98	104.5	491.66	109.8	188.32	92.8	4177.24	103.5	3020.29	108.7	1156.95	91.8
2015	665.66	97.9	500.67	101.8	165.00	87.7	4132.43	99.0	3108.03	102.9	1024.40	88.7
2016	679.92	102.2	502.59	100.5	177.34	107.6	4485.97	108.7	3313.80	106.7	1172.17	114.6
2017	750.65	110.4	509.95	101.5	240.70	135.7	5085.08	113.3	3455.61	104.3	1629.46	138.8

9-10 分经济类型进出口情况(2016-2017年)

Statistics on Imports and Exports by Econimic Type(2016-2017)

单位:亿美元 (USD 100 million)

项　目	Item	2017年 In Year 2017	2016年 In Year 2016	为上年(%) As Compared with year 2016 (%)
全市进出口总值(海关口径)	Total Exports And Imports	750.65	679.92	110.4
一、出口总额	Exports	509.95	502.59	101.5
1. 国有企业	State-owned Enterprises	63.13	64.30	98.2
2. 三资企业	Foreign Investment Enterprises	103.61	108.27	95.7
(1)中外合作企业	Cooperation Enterprises	0.75	0.63	119.0
(2)中外合资企业	Joint-Venture Enterprises	46.61	51.25	90.9
(3)外商独资企业	Enterprises With Sole Foreign Investment	56.25	56.39	99.8
3. 集体企业	Collective-owned Enterprises	16.47	16.53	99.6
4. 私营企业	Private Enterprises	326.50	312.17	104.6
二、进口总额	Imports	240.70	177.34	135.7

9－11 分地区外贸进出口情况(2017年)

Imports and Exports by Region(2017)

单位:万美元 (USD 10000)

区 域	Region	进出口总值 Total Imports and Exports	为上年(%) As Compared with the Preceding Year(%)	出口总值 Exports of This Year	为上年(%) As Compared with the Preceding Year(%)	进口总值 Imports of This Year	为上年(%) As Compared with the Preceding Year(%)
全市合计	**Total**	**7506524**	**110.4**	**5099533**	**101.5**	**2406990**	**135.7**
#不含省属	#Non－provincial	6901288	110.8	4678070	102.2	2223218	134.6
#上城区	Shangcheng	263919	114.6	140960	105.6	122958	127.2
下城区	Xiacheng	366274	118.6	230466	107.0	135809	145.1
江干区	Jianggan	299399	116.6	203351	107.6	96048	141.9
拱墅区	Gongshu	171407	79.5	146713	81.8	24693	68.4
西湖区	Xihu	337875	119.1	274854	115.8	63020	135.8
高新(滨江)区	Hi－Tech(Binjiang)	784620	116.5	584528	110.6	200091	137.9
萧山区	Xiaoshan	1079155	112.0	804078	102.9	275078	150.7
大江东产业集聚区	Dajiangdong Industry Cluster District	168657	108.1	123064	106.4	45593	113.2
余杭区	Yuhang	577771	111.0	533943	111.8	43827	102.0
富阳区	Fuyang	372442	135.6	170135	121.2	202307	150.7
临安区	Lin'an	274535	123.0	229465	123.7	45070	120.0
经济技术开发区	Economic and Technological Development Zone	948120	117.7	488943	107.0	459176	131.6
桐庐县	Tonglu	110464	79.4	104085	78.6	6379	94.1
淳安县	Chun'an	16843	91.7	15120	91.6	1722	92.4
建德市	Jiande	84169	79.2	77602	77.3	6567	111.0

9-12 分地区外贸进出口总值(2004-2017年)
Total Value of Imports and Exports by Region(2004-2017)

单位:万美元 (USD 10000)

年份 Year	全市 Whole City	市区 Urban District					桐庐县 Tonglu	淳安县 Chun'an	建德市 Jiande
		合计 Total	#萧山区 Xiaoshan	余杭区 Yuhang	富阳区 Fuyang	临安区 Lin'an			
2004	2449671	2364434	414374	88538	52399	28918	32333	4461	19525
2005	2986993	2892191	510950	128999	72357	33262	30489	5211	25841
2006	3890853	3769910	610201	183930	81616	41492	38522	6797	34132
2007	4342666	4181699	795487	255534	105765	55542	48811	8319	48295
2008	4806503	4545719	953377	324421	126829	74862	71753	12478	101692
2009	4041991	3821965	829827	285496	116158	70454	60064	12039	77470
2010	5235549	4946409	1135326	385736	166652	101387	73919	17183	96651
2011	6397180	6044765	1432742	484903	216575	132729	93464	20459	105763
2012	6168325	5814547	1367290	512531	224446	142340	103153	21604	86681
2013	6507102	6115754	1408929	555640	265788	165094	119539	19692	87023
2014	6799775	6355378	1384823	601220	284980	193001	133392	23802	94202
2015	6656636	6178381	1189039	537405	285540	209150	147326	20814	100965
2016	6799241	6313076	1120689	520195	273306	223014	139150	18377	105623
2017	7506524	7295048	1079155	577771	372442	274535	110464	16843	84169

9-13 外贸出口分国别(地区)情况(2016-2017年)
Export by Country or Region(2016-2017)

单位:万美元 (USD 10000)

国别(地区)	Country (territory)	2017年 In Year 2017	2016年 In Year 2016	为上年(%) As Compared with the Preceding Year(%)
合 计	**Total**	**5099533**	**5025852**	**101.5**
#中国香港	Hong Kong China	78632	91265	86.2
中国台湾	Taiwan China	56417	56240	100.3
美国	U.S.A	1005123	1015565	99.0
日本	Japan	335547	317434	105.7
德国	Germany	204677	205134	99.8
英国	Britain	194689	201912	96.4
印度	India	225536	196021	115.1
越南	Vietnam	139846	150220	93.1
韩国	Republic of Korea	158727	140446	113.0
荷兰	Netherlands	146274	140270	104.3
意大利	Italy	111032	110896	100.1
法国	France	113966	108550	105.0
俄罗斯	Russia	114679	104824	109.4
澳大利亚	Australia	108105	120960	89.4
印度尼西亚	Indonesia	95065	97796	97.2
西班牙	Spain	90227	89138	101.2
加拿大	Canada	95105	88312	107.7
巴西	Brazil	102855	85670	120.1
墨西哥	Mexico	89105	80960	110.1
泰国	Thailand	80672	80829	99.8
"一带一路"国家	Countries along the Belt and Road	1548327	1546011	100.1

9-14 旅游发展情况(1995-2017年)

Statistics on Tourism(1995-2017)

年 份 Year	旅游总收入(亿元) Total Tourism Revenue (100 million yuan)	国内旅游收入(亿元) Domestic Earnings (100 million yuan)	旅游外汇收入(亿美元) Foreign Exchange Earnings from International Tourism (USD 100 million)	旅游总人数(万人次) Total Tourists (10000 person-times)	国内游客人数(万人次) Domestic Tourists (10000 person-times)
1995	106.0	94.3	1.45	2148	2104
1996	136.5	122.6	1.67	2055	2009
1997	158.8	142.1	2.01	2150	2100
1998	163.4	146.0	2.10	2172	2121
1999	186.0	166.7	2.37	2266	2207
2000	214.3	190.0	2.92	2376	2305
2001	249.7	218.9	3.37	2592	2510
2002	294.4	254.8	4.77	2758	2652
2003	325.9	290.9	4.22	2862	2776
2004	410.1	361.2	5.97	3139	3016
2005	465.1	403.6	7.58	3417	3266
2006	543.7	471.2	9.09	3864	3682
2007	630.1	548.6	11.19	4320	4112
2008	707.2	617.2	12.96	4773	4552
2009	803.1	708.9	13.80	5324	5094
2010	1025.7	910.9	16.90	6581	6305
2011	1191.0	1063.8	19.60	7487	7181
2012	1392.3	1253.2	22.02	8568	8237
2013	1603.7	1469.9	21.60	9725	9409
2014	1886.3	1743.9	23.18	10933	10606
2015	2200.7	2019.7	29.31	12382	12040
2016	2571.8	2362.6	31.49	14059	13696
2017	3041.3	2802.1	35.43	16287	15884

9－15　境外旅游者人数(1978－2017年)
Number of International Tourists (1978－2017)

单位:人次　　　(person－times)

年　份 Year	合　计 Total	#外国人 Foreigners	港澳台同胞 Compatriots from Hong Kong, Macao and Taiwan	平均逗留天数 Average days of Staying
1978	53475	728	26648	
1979	84914	44714	39131	2.59
1980	124960	61710	61382	2.70
1981	154745	87727	65014	2.71
1982	152897	89100	61314	2.49
1983	160564	97803	59625	2.18
1984	179200	105771	70915	2.12
1985	238385	156311	75063	2.18
1986	266370	170960	87092	2.38
1987	300603	183477	100078	2.38
1988	349246	149512	159745	2.08
1989	248502	66094	163589	2.08
1990	388345	86621	268131	2.09
1991	390197	136809	229690	2.00
1992	489578	183781	267256	2.03
1993	459620	199796	234640	2.06
1994	337362	201692	124346	2.10
1995	441262	249418	177236	2.06
1996	462313	273477	178845	2.07
1997	504276	288949	205267	2.20
1998	507243	261353	231609	2.20
1999	591853	324625	257978	2.09
2000	707148	400906	306242	2.15
2001	819438	447689	371749	2.41
2002	1056266	631576	424690	2.50
2003	861163	482073	379090	2.72
2004	1234063	791616	442447	2.59
2005	1513585	1020840	492745	2.63
2006	1820171	1236792	583379	2.57
2007	2085997	1453650	632347	2.67
2008	2213329	1543665	669654	2.73
2009	2304045	1572838	731207	2.87
2010	2757147	1878528	878619	2.94
2011	3063140	2108263	954877	2.96
2012	3311225	2298763	1012462	2.95
2013	3160058	2198187	961871	2.93
2014	3261337	2254866	1006471	2.93
2015	3415619	2378461	1037158	2.99
2016	3632252	2556247	1076005	3.14
2017	4022309	2849993	1172316	3.25

注:从1995年起为全市数。

a) Data in this table has included the tourists of whole municipality since 1995.

9－16 接待境外游客及居民出境旅游情况(2016－2017 年)

Number of International Tourists and Outbound Tourists(2016－2017)

项　目	Item	2017 年 In Year 2017	2016 年 In Year 2016	为上年(%) As Compared with the preceding year(%)
一、接待境外游客	**International Tourists**			
全年接待人数(人次)	**Number of Foreign Tourists(person－times)**	**4022309**	**3632252**	**110.7**
#外国人	#Foreigners	2849993	2556247	111.5
港澳台同胞	Compatriots From Hong Kong, Macao and Taiwan	1172316	1076005	109.0
全年接待人天数(人天)	**Total Person－days (person－days)**	**13092273**	**11414114**	**114.7**
#外国人	#Foreigners	9545816	8409339	113.5
港澳台同胞	Compatriots From Hong Kong, Macao and Taiwan	3545457	3004775	118.0
平均逗留天数(天)	**Average Days of Staying (days)**	**3.25**	**3.14**	**103.5**
#外国人	#Foreigners	3.35	3.29	101.8
港澳台同胞	Compatriots From Hong Kong, Macao and Taiwan	3.02	2.79	108.2
旅游外汇总收入(万美元)	**Total Foreign Exchange Earnings From International Tourism (USD 10000)**	**354286**	**314944**	**112.5**
二、居民出境旅游	**Outbound Tourism**			
居民出境旅游人数(人次)	**Outbound Tourists(Person－time)**	**1730474**	**1598969**	**108.2**

注:2015 年旅游外汇总收入统计口径调整,同比增速按可比口径计算。

a) Since 2015, the date of the total foreign exchange earnings from international tourism were adjusted, the growth rate were calculated at comparable prices.

9－17　接待境外游客分国别(地区)情况(2016－2017年)

Number of International Tourists by Country or Territory(2016－2017)

单位:人次　(person－times)

国别(地区)	Country (territory)	2017年 In Year 2017	2016年 In Year 2016	为上年(%) As Compared with the Preceding Year(%)
合　计	**Total**	**4022309**	**3632252**	**110.7**
#中国香港	#Hong Kong China	442832	409723	108.1
中国澳门	Macao China	66158	60785	108.8
中国台湾	Taiwan China	663326	605479	109.6
日本	Japan	216044	206004	104.9
美国	U.S.A	275707	243223	113.4
新加坡	Singapore	127261	103915	122.5
澳大利亚	Australia	55661	49705	112.0
泰国	Thailand	112922	96103	117.5
意大利	Italy	35655	31834	112.0
荷兰	Netherlands	31803	26047	122.1
西班牙	Spain	23253	21274	109.3
马来西亚	Malaysia	122671	106738	114.9
韩国	Republic of Korea	636392	649096	98.0
法国	France	73583	63951	115.1
德国	Germany	91776	80463	114.1
加拿大	Canada	62324	49906	124.9
英国	Britain	79276	69216	114.5
印度尼西亚	Indonesia	26004	24665	105.4
印度	India	34940	31786	109.9
菲律宾	Filipine	16545	16138	102.5

主要统计指标解释

利用外资 指我市政府部门，企业和其他经济组织通过对外借款，吸收外商直接投资以及用其他方式筹措的境外现汇、设备、技术等。

外商直接投资 是指外国企业和经济组织或个人（包括华侨、港澳台胞以及我国在境外注册的企业）按我国有关政策、法规，用现汇、实物、技术等在我市境内开办外商独资企业、与我市境内的企业或经济组织共同举办中外合资经营企业、合作经营企业或者合作开发资源的投资（包括外商投资收益的再投资）以及经政府有关部门批准的项目投资总额内，企业从境外借入的资金。

进出口总额 海关进出口总额指实际进出我国国境的货物总金额。包括对外贸易实际进出口货物，来料加工装配进出口货物，国家间、联合国及国际组织无偿援助物资和赠送品，华侨、港澳台同胞和外籍华人捐赠品，租赁期满归承租人所有的租赁货物，进料加工进出口货物，边境地方贸易及边境地区小额贸易进出口货物（边民互市贸易除外），中外合资经营企业、中外合作经营企业、外商独资经营企业进出口货物和公用物品，到、离岸价格在规定限额以上的进出口货样和广告品（无商业价值、无使用价值和免费提供出口的除外），从保税仓库提取在中国境内销售的进口货物，以及其他进出口货物。进出口总额以观察一个国家在对外贸易方面的总规模。我国规定出口货物按离岸价格统计，进口货物按到岸价格统计。

境外旅游者人数 指来我市参观、访问、旅行、探亲、访友、休养、考察、参加会议和从事经济、科技、文化、教育、体育、宗教等活动的外国人、华侨、港澳和台湾同胞的人数。不包括外国在我市的常驻机构，如使领馆、通讯社、企业办事处的工作人员；来我市常住的外国专家、留学生以及在岸逗留不过夜人员。

境外旅游（外汇）收入 指入境旅游的外国人、华侨、港澳台同胞在杭州旅游过程中发生的一切旅游支出，对我市来说就是境外旅游（外汇）收入。

Explanatory Notes on Main Statistical Indicators

Utilization of Foreign Capital refers to remittance, equipment and technology financed from abroad, by loans, foreign direct investment and other forms undertaken by the government units of Hangzhou, by various departments, enterprises and other economic units.

Foreign Direct Investment refers to the investments inside China by foreign enterprises and economic organizations or individuals (including overseas Chinese, compatriots from Hong Kong, Macao and Taiwan, and Chinese enterprises registered abroad), following the relevant policies and laws of China, for the establishment of ventures exclusively with foreign own investment, Sino – foreign joint ventures and cooperative enterprises or for co – operative exploration of resources with enterprises or economic organizations in Hangzhou. It includes the re – investment of the foreign entrepreneurs with the profits gained from the investment and the funds that enterprises borrow from abroad in the total investment of projects which are approved by the relevant department of the government.

Total Imports and Exports refer to the value of commodities imported into and exported from the boundary of China. They include the actual imports and exports through foreign trade, imported and exported goods under the processing and assembling trades and materials, supplies and gifts as aid given gratis between governments and by the United Nations and other international organizations, and contributions donated by overseas Chinese, compatriots in Hong Kong, Macao and Chinese foreign citizenship, leasing commodities owned by tenant at the expiration of leasing period, the imported and exported commodities processed with imported materials, commodities trading in border areas (excluding mutual exchange goods), the imported and exported commodities and articles for public use of the Sino – foreign joint ventures, cooperative enterprises and ventures exclusively with foreign own investment. Also included are import or export of samples and advertising goods for whose CIF or FOB value are beyond the permitted ceiling (excluding goods of no trading or use value and free commodities for export), imported goods sold in China from bonded warehouses and other imported or exported goods. The indicator of the total imports and exports at customs can be used to observe the total size of external trade in a country. In accordance with the stipulation of Chinese government, imports are calculated at CIF, while exports are calculated at FOB.

Number of International Tourists refer to foreigners, overseas Chinese compatriots from Hong Kong, Macao and Taiwan coming to Hangzhou for sightseeing, visits, tours, family reunions, vacations, study tours, conferences and other activities of a business, scientific and technological, cultural, educational and religious nature. It does not include representatives and employees of resident institutions of foreign countries in China such as embassies, consulates, news agencies and offices of foreign companies and organizations, nor does it include long – term foreign experts or students residing in Hangzhou, or persons in transition without spending a night in China.

Foreign Exchange Earnings from International Tourism refer to the total expenditures of foreigners, overseas Chinese, Chinese compatriots from Hong Kong, Macao and Taiwan during their stay in the mainland of China, which are earnings of foreign exchange form international tourism from the point of vies from China.

十、财政、金融保险

FINANCE,BANKING AND INSURANCE

10 财政、金融、保险
Finance, Banking and Insurance

主要统计指标
Major Statistical Indicators

财政总收入	Total Financial Revenue	2921.30	亿元	(100 million yuan)
为上年	As Compared with the Preceding Year	114.2	%	(%)
一般公共预算收入	General Public Budget Revenue	1567.42	亿元	(100 million yuan)
为上年	As Compared with the Preceding Year	117.4	%	(%)
一般公共预算支出	General Public Financial Budgetary Expenditure	1540.92	亿元	(100 million yuan)
为上年	As Compared with the Preceding Year	109.7	%	(%)
年末金融机构各项存款余额	Balance of Deposits of Financial Institutions at Year-end	36483.24	亿元	(100 million yuan)
为上年	As Compared with the Preceding Year	109.3	%	(%)
# 住户存款余额	The Increased Amount of Household Deposits	8670.60	亿元	(100 million yuan)
为上年	As Compared with the Preceding Year	102.1	%	(%)
年末金融机构各项贷款余额	Balance of Loans of Financial Institutions at Year-end	29270.94	亿元	(100 million yuan)
为上年	As Compared with the Preceding Year	111.9	%	(%)

10-01 财政收入及支出(1978-2017年)
Financial Revenue and Expenditure (1978-2017)

单位:万元 (10000 yuan)

年份 Year	财政总收入 Financial Revenue		一般公共预算收入 General Public Budget Revenue		一般公共预算支出 General Public Budget Expenditure	
	全市 Total	市区 Urban District	全市 Total	市区 Urban District	全市 Total	市区 Urban District
1978	94102	73396	-	-	16170	7779
1979	103259	81885	-	-	20334	11289
1980	118529	94015	-	-	21726	11867
1981	128564	100645	-	-	23964	13891
1982	140510	107298	-	-	24945	13687
1983	153941	116559	-	-	32765	17822
1984	172996	130757	-	-	46937	28710
1985	186472	131923	-	-	57710	35435
1986	205952	141943	-	-	73213	43959
1987	226262	152268	-	-	70717	41011
1988	246961	161208	-	-	95655	53031
1989	255003	156649	-	-	113571	61534
1990	252503	149904	-	-	118167	62587
1991	267597	158130	-	-	123134	62403
1992	286394	168341	-	-	132814	65984
1993	394946	233670	-	-	185168	90545
1994	484597	300014	197292	116733	215415	102430
1995	551262	339828	230431	135041	249050	120084
1996	635334	414557	268438	169987	302390	151016
1997	740725	485650	312797	196885	363834	197054
1998	869824	585615	368484	236269	424478	237221
1999	1026577	689394	449593	288002	563524	335243
2000	1428519	970937	691891	599910	734328	445698
2001	1884608	1612225	1042789	884738	1049330	849479
2002	2571408	2235021	1183153	1022964	1410199	1166298
2003	3297091	2861459	1503888	1290778	1635948	1340463
2004	3957516	3488744	1974523	1712813	1956282	1602303
2005	5207930	4584112	2504565	2172575	2383344	1957619
2006	6244906	5484645	3013888	2616084	2754809	2254347
2007	7884237	6929667	3916195	3421403	3357153	2747060
2008	9105489	7991043	4553531	3972842	4196674	3454599
2009	10194264	8965758	5207899	4535191	4903983	4000324
2010	12454323	10988265	6713413	5894414	6165836	4988197
2011	14889206	13009046	7851524	6822765	7475004	5971740
2012	16278879	14244888	8599875	7475989	7862800	6222930
2013	17349750	15157584	9452020	8207264	8557370	6662314
2014	19201076	17750305	10273169	9426504	9611771	8077961
2015	22387456	20738698	12338820	11360166	12054777	10235061
2016	25584128	23844189	14023826	12988095	14043065	12019355
2017	29212996	28010839	15674169	14979182	15409156	13968866

10－02 分地区财政
Local Financial

单位:万元

指标	Item	全市 Total	市区 Urban District	上城区 Shangcheng
财政总收入合计	**Total**	**29212996**	**28010839**	**1445598**
一、一般公共预算收入	General Public Budget Revenue	15674169	14979182	731869
(一)税收收入	Tax Revenue	14171594	13544326	699607
1.国内增值税	Domestic Value－added Tax	2969672	2787387	103674
2.改征增值税	Newly Changed Value－added Tax	2693559	2570218	137811
3.营业税	Business Tax	5288	5479	393
4.企业所得税	Corporate Income Tax	2702212	2608841	170581
5.个人所得税	Individual Income Tax	1461998	1425823	141541
6.城市维护建设税	City Construction and Maintenance Tax	984315	949566	37436
7.房产税	Real Estate Tax	557952	532777	42498
8.城镇土地使用税	Urban Land Use Tax	205548	185080	1915
9.土地增值税	Land Appreciation Tax	975587	937254	48751
10.耕地占用税	Tax on the Use of Arable Land	37784	33998	－
11.契税	Contract Tax	1205784	1157440	－
12.其他税收	Others Tax	371895	350463	15007
(二)非税收入	Non－tax Revenue	1502575	1434856	32262
1.专项收入	Special Revenue	1180199	1133144	29388
#教育费附加	Revenue from Extra－Charges for Education	366329	348683	13536
地方教育附加收入	Local Education Additional Revenue	244273	232514	9012
水利建设专项收入	Special Revenue of Water Coservancy Construction	116103	111633	7013
残疾人就业保障金收入	Employment Security for The Disabled Revenue	272842	266905	－
教育资金收入	Educational Fund Revenue	174619	170820	－
农田水利建设资金收入	Fund in The Farmland Irrigation Construction Revenue	48079	43862	－
2.行政事业性收费收入	Income from Administrative Fees	218482	203424	2429
3.罚没收入	Penalty and Confiscatory Income	－174529	－169829	－
4.国有企业计划亏损补贴	Subsides to Loss－making of state－owned Enterprises	－175381	－170681	－
5.国有资源(资产)有偿使用收入	Compensation for the Use of Seate－owned Assets Income	101288	95445	445
6.政府住房基金收入	Government Housing Fund Income	128247	128001	－
7.其他收入	Others Revenue	809	809	－
二、上划中央"六税"小计	Subtotal Revenue of Central Government	13538827	13031657	713729
1.消费税	Consumption Tax	1623984	1616568	3667
2.国内增值税	Domestic Value－added Tax	2969673	2787388	103674
3.企业所得税	Corporate Income Tax	4053324	3913267	255872
4.个人所得税	Individual Income Tax	2192999	2138737	212312
5.改征增值税	Newly Changed Value－added Tax	2693559	2570218	137811
6.营业税	Business Tax	5288	5479	393

总收入(2017 年)
Revenue by Region(2017)

(10000 yuan)

下城区 Xiacheng	江干区 Jianggan	拱墅区 Gongshu	西湖区 Xihu	高新(滨江)区 Hi - Tech (Binjiang)	萧山区 Xiaoshan
1512467	**1594783**	**1408367**	**2452283**	**2872830**	**4053685**
820368	880088	781355	1259835	1428138	2274820
778689	841616	733277	1193551	1348223	1995581
144272	135936	167386	171149	214442	644817
159160	225870	178477	346051	234847	309924
228	1168	846	833	619	139
150227	161463	131677	217828	370140	332950
105358	71511	53215	230350	292736	105043
42081	50482	49201	69073	109328	146618
47458	47612	34140	49296	46946	96300
2972	3673	6075	6711	5715	61975
36169	129356	96345	80534	49502	135520
-	-	-	-	-	8928
-	-	-	-	-	99046
90764	14545	15915	21726	23948	54321
41679	38472	48078	66284	79915	279239
34413	36501	38260	53064	76691	233805
15325	17913	18692	25018	39607	56150
10212	11948	12462	16664	26457	37457
9082	7166	6944	11923	11282	14169
-	-	-	-	-	77490
-	-	-	-	-	49594
254	-	213	746	-	5597
5129	6556	8646	9551	2935	24433
-	-5131	-	-	-	-7000
-	-5131	-	-	-	-7000
1883	546	959	2923	289	21627
-	-	-	-	-	327
-	-	-	-	-	450
692099	714695	627012	1192448	1444692	1778865
5061	2259	2964	2148	469	166995
144272	135936	167386	171149	214442	644817
225341	242195	197516	326742	555210	499425
158037	107267	79823	345525	439105	157565
159160	225870	178477	346051	234847	309924
228	1168	846	833	619	139

指　标	Item	大江东产业集聚区 Dajiangdong Industry Cluster District	余杭区 Yuhang	富阳区 Fuyang
财政总收入合计	**Total**	**871777**	**5038019**	**1068942**
一、一般公共预算收入	General Public Budget Revenue	394132	2800053	637020
(一)税收收入	Tax Revenue	361590	2603836	572580
1. 国内增值税	Domestic Value－added Tax	162431	362540	205050
2. 改征增值税	Newly Changed Value－added Tax	31759	579707	78319
3. 营业税	Business Tax	8	878	－79
4. 企业所得税	Corporate Income Tax	74796	547914	65375
5. 个人所得税	Individual Income Tax	12112	307699	32796
6. 城市维护建设税	City Construction and Maintenance Tax	39513	150820	45177
7. 房产税	Real Estate Tax	12022	90255	25662
8. 城镇土地使用税	Urban Land Use Tax	8116	48965	23938
9. 土地增值税	Land Appreciation Tax	12582	255267	29289
10. 耕地占用税	Tax on the Use of Arable Land	－	15455	2169
11. 契税	Contract Tax	－	201083	40869
12. 其他税收	Others Tax	8251	43253	24015
(二)非税收入	Non－tax Revenue	32542	196217	64440
1. 专项收入	Special Revenue	26341	184881	37947
#教育费附加	Revenue from Extra－Charges for Education	15175	51344	19297
地方教育附加收入	Local Education Additional Revenue	10117	34232	12864
水利建设专项收入	Special Revenue of Water Coservancy Construction	1585	12595	4380
残疾人就业保障金收入	Employment Security for The Disabled Revenue	－	53330	－
教育资金收入	Educational Fund Revenue	－	34131	－
农田水利建设资金收入	Fund in The Farmland Irrigation Construction Revenue	1628	3794	3832
2. 行政事业性收费收入	Income from Administrative Fees	2199	11024	15502
3. 罚没收入	Penalty and Confiscatory Income	－	－7000	－3000
4. 国有企业计划亏损补贴	Subsides to Loss－making of state－owned Enterprises	－	－7000	－3000
5. 国有资源(资产)有偿使用收入	Compensation for the Use of Seate－owned Assets Income	2374	3465	10159
6. 政府住房基金收入	Government Housing Fund Income	－	36	－
7. 其他收入	Others Revenue	－	17	－
二、上划中央"六税"小计	Subtotal Revenue of Central Government	477645	2237966	431922
1. 消费税	Consumption Tax	153085	11422	1375
2. 国内增值税	Domestic Value－added Tax	162431	362540	205050
3. 企业所得税	Corporate Income Tax	112194	821871	98063
4. 个人所得税	Individual Income Tax	18168	461548	49194
5. 改征增值税	Newly Changed Value－added Tax	31759	579707	78319
6. 营业税	Business Tax	8	878	－79

continued (10000 yuan)

临安区 Lin'an	经济技术开发区 Economic and Technological Development Zone	西湖风景名胜区 The West Lake Scenic Zone	桐庐县 Tonglu	淳安县 Chun'an	建德市 Jiande
749114	**1343749**	**108728**	**465922**	**309065**	**427170**
433009	703084	57417	278292	172688	244007
401473	655484	54975	247949	158826	220493
127244	303510	5010	70757	37350	74178
59871	54148	13349	47840	39107	36394
-384	796	10	68	-69	-190
60837	146821	15528	31401	27248	34722
22643	38150	6433	14535	9799	11841
28600	57816	2370	13031	7688	14030
15902	23107	10492	9342	6485	9348
18084	3037	1164	10114	2389	7965
35466	18113	-	19388	10322	8623
813	-	-	81	1442	2263
19666	-	-	23584	13459	11301
12731	9986	619	7808	3606	10018
31536	47600	2442	30343	13862	23514
43285	40311	2031	19630	9334	18091
11517	20958	838	7025	4207	6414
7687	13969	558	4684	2802	4273
3811	5443	663	1626	1154	1690
10421	-	-	3619	486	1832
6670	-	-	2316	311	1172
3024	758	-	2910	128	1179
8747	1770	397	5512	2009	7537
-27150	852	-	-	-	-4700
-27150	-	-	-	-	-4700
2297	3900	14	2291	2241	1311
1000	-	-	-	150	96
333	9	-	-	-	-
316105	640665	51311	187630	136377	183163
4153	4754	-	61	4419	2936
127244	303510	5010	70757	37350	74178
91256	220232	23292	47102	40872	52083
33965	57225	9650	21802	14698	17762
59871	54148	13349	47840	39107	36394
-384	796	10	68	-69	-190

10－03 分地区公共

General Public

单位:万元

指　　标	Item	全　市 Total	市　区 Urban District	上城区 Shangcheng
一般公共预算支出	**General Public Budget Expenditure**	**15409156**	**13968866**	**400841**
一、一般公共服务	Expenditure for General Public Services	1311829	1170390	39680
二、国防	Expenditure for National Defense	9311	8252	31
三、公共安全	Expenditure for Public Security	944310	865343	37831
四、教育	Expenditure for Education	2792968	2519759	89952
#教育费附加支出	Expenditure on Extra－Charges for Educations	257958	241584	12210
五、科学技术	Expenditure for Science and Technology	923236	877184	14198
六、文化体育与传媒	Expenditure for Culture,Sports and Media	309282	276736	3579
七、社会保障和就业	Expenditure for Social Safety Net and Employment Effort	1731704	1551299	81974
八、医疗卫生与计划生育	Expenditure for Medical and Health Care and Birth Control	1123291	986817	18521
九、节能环保	Expenditure for Energy Conservation Environmental Protection	377904	321171	166
#排污费支出	Sewage Expenses	－	－	－
十、城乡社区	Expenditure for Urban and Rural Community	2736428	2654982	60658
十一、农林水	Expenditure for Agriculture,Forestry and Water Conservancy	896205	710142	8140
十二、交通运输	Expenditure for Trarssportation	515070	433292	－
十三、资源勘探信息等	Resources Exploration Information,etc	515593	494326	11959
十四、商业服务业等	Expenditure for Commercial Service Industry	353454	336005	9686
十五、金融支出	Expenditure for Financial Supervision	18524	18197	12646
十六、援助其他地区	Expenditure for Aiding Other Territories	59400	57294	1516
十七、国土海洋气象等	Expenditure for Land, Ocean and Meteorological Services	86786	72713	830
十八、住房保障	Expenditure on Housing Support	286287	250046	1316
十九、粮油物资储备	Expenditure for Grain and Oil Reservation and other Materials Services	9802	5706	－
二十、债务付息	Expenditure for Interest Payment of Government debt	271186	225551	2566
二十一、其他	Other Expenditure	136586	133661	5592

预算支出(2017 年)
Expenditure by Region(2017)

(10000 yuan)

下城区 Xiacheng	江干区 Jianggan	拱墅区 Gongshu	西湖区 Xihu	高新(滨江)区 Hi - Tech (Binjiang)	萧山区 Xiaoshan
351552	**649888**	**409437**	**741268**	**1134859**	**2408393**
38357	60218	49027	70279	32489	202032
387	–	43	1048	–	1873
38694	47002	44786	58303	33897	124086
70488	109144	105362	140104	171994	441252
6736	12908	18030	14792	35391	32964
12430	67395	17261	37799	139707	84536
6206	9612	3774	9361	25394	23885
64070	73919	45109	104887	105238	181244
22220	33036	24199	46217	27240	215702
1	12026	4137	612	6664	57097
–	–	–	–	–	–
65828	175148	94228	181009	445675	330856
1144	16109	1627	16863	20488	191645
–	60	90	40	20	140432
5624	5495	2710	41099	76100	109635
9205	2832	6554	5615	15178	47673
240	291	509	600	288	182
–	–	1340	7826	7378	10673
831	1236	1110	2824	1939	24240
11033	6325	6182	12120	12034	138348
–	–	–	–	–	2462
4794	8743	489	4647	9352	48031
–	21297	900	15	3784	32509

指　　标	Item	大江东产业集聚区 Dajiangdong Industry Cluster District	余杭区 Yuhang	富阳区 Fuyang
一般公共预算支出	**General Public Budget Expenditure**	**345489**	**2703850**	**662997**
一、一般公共服务	Expenditure for General Public Services	42875	221067	76487
二、国防	Expenditure for National Defense	74	2430	－
三、公共安全	Expenditure for Public Security	15089	98414	39714
四、教育	Expenditure for Education	47887	464331	186091
#教育费附加支出	Expenditure on Extra－Charges for Educations	1450	53140	8977
五、科学技术	Expenditure for Science and Technology	1446	150308	34822
六、文化体育与传媒	Expenditure for Culture,Sports and Media	2307	49877	15712
七、社会保障和就业	Expenditure for Social Safety Net and Employment Effort	13729	218531	36026
八、医疗卫生与计划生育	Expenditure for Medical and Health Care and Birth Control	30392	236656	55462
九、节能环保	Expenditure for Energy Conservation Environmental Protection	14853	88212	27622
#排污费支出	Sewage Expenses	－	－	－
十、城乡社区	Expenditure for Urban and Rural Community	40070	519633	37865
十一、农林水	Expenditure for Agriculture,Forestry and Water Conservancy	23852	144891	75457
十二、交通运输	Expenditure for Trarssportation	2876	84089	16767
十三、资源勘探信息等	Resources Exploration Information,etc	62613	144693	5974
十四、商业服务业等	Expenditure for Commercial Service Industry	3348	204127	2813
十五、金融支出	Expenditure for Financial Supervision	75	326	95
十六、援助其他地区	Expenditure for Aiding Other Territories	－	7669	2721
十七、国土海洋气象等	Expenditure for Land,Ocean and Meteorological Services	1839	8743	5667
十八、住房保障	Expenditure on Housing Support	887	18520	13638
十九、粮油物资储备	Expenditure for Grain and Oil Reservation and other Materials Services	－	115	281
二十、债务付息	Expenditure for Interest Payment of Government debt	11008	37838	29783
二十一、其他	Other Expenditure	30269	3380	－

continued (10000 yuan)

临安区 Lin'an	经济技术开发区 Economic and Technological Development Zone	西湖风景名胜区 The West Lake Scenic Zone	桐庐县 Tonglu	淳安县 Chun'an	建德市 Jiande
647766	**500412**	**135591**	**416717**	**573686**	**449887**
55916	54761	6257	32200	60887	48352
279	69	–	327	255	477
36435	25095	14133	26337	27448	25182
141183	85603	3190	104576	79450	89183
3802	20000	562	5847	8977	1550
38311	59433	386	19163	10678	16211
11293	776	12544	11959	11140	9447
72835	19721	10875	54441	75355	50609
57887	5810	1635	47053	51426	37995
17941	37035	–	14706	25572	16455
–	–	–	–	–	–
62720	126650	83977	15311	41780	24355
66545	3001	1418	37512	78111	70440
37052	–	20	19011	44468	18299
8480	56855	201	2871	16065	2331
5331	9047	484	4171	9286	3992
86	159	75	196	30	101
1324	2436	184	1149	–	957
4246	3440	212	5932	4163	3978
12574	5142	–	11983	14643	9615
1011	–	–	1538	2534	24
16151	5379		6206	20278	19151
166	–	–	75	117	2733

10－04 全市分税种、支出科目财政收支情况(2012－2017年)

Local Public Financial Budgetary Expenditure by Tax and Expenditure Account(2012－2017)

单位:万元 (10000 yuan)

指标 Item	2012	2013	2014	2015	2016	2017
财政总收入合计 Total	**16278879**	**17349750**	**19201076**	**22387456**	**25584128**	**29212996**
一、一般公共预算收入 General Public Budget Revenue	8599875	9452020	10273169	12338820	14023826	15674169
(一)税收收入 Tax Revenue	8302478	9106690	9952111	11259532	12892210	14171594
1. 国内增值税 Domestic Value－added Tax	1094696	1122297	1224336	1301043	2097640	2969672
2. 改征增值税 Newly Changed Value－added Tax		593744	837724	1000427	1705813	2693559
3. 营业税 Business Tax	2970123	2670660	2650471	3094627	1988053	5288
4. 企业所得税 Corporate Income Tax	1448553	1518112	1723639	1928567	2215439	2702212
5. 个人所得税 Individual Income Tax	498726	573227	681449	920917	1155176	1461998
6. 城市维护建设税 City Construction and Maintenance Tax	604523	658593	693932	792815	890160	984315
7. 房产税 Real Estate Tax	317711	323897	378171	398528	443407	557952
8. 城镇土地使用税 Urban Land Use Tax				155914	147437	205548
9. 土地增值税 Land Appreciation Tax				551468	851760	975587
10. 耕地占用税 Tax on the Use of Arable Land	102820	91622	72117	64426	40610	37784
11. 契税 Contract Tax	465946	674188	805656	761861	1056441	1205784
12. 其他税收 Others Tax	799380	880350	884616	288939	300274	371895
(二)非税收入 Non－tax Revenue	297397	345330	321058	1079288	1131616	1502575
1. 专项收入 Special Revenue	245863	267287	278423	1073893	1102959	1180199

指　　标 Item	2012	2013	2014	2015	2016	2017
2. 行政事业性收费收入 Income from Administrative Fees	19137	19738	13988	12213	10968	48079
3. 罚没收入 Penalty and Confiscatory Income	128549	148738	148190	149897	160147	218482
4. 国有企业计划亏损补贴 Subsides to Loss－making of state－owned Enterprises	－105032	－105699	－147887	－197823	－250873	－174529
5. 国有资源(资产)有偿使用收入 Compensation for the Use of Seate－owned Assets Income	8870	14314	27927	38904	58175	101288
6. 政府住房基金收入 Government Housing Fund Income	－	－	－	－	47.46	128247
7. 其他收入 Others Revenue	10	952	417	2204	47146	809
二、一般公共预算支出 General Public Budget Expenditure	7862800	8557370	9611771	12054777	14043065	15409156
1. 一般公共服务 Expenditure for General Public Services	893776	915881	892027	1011605	1125425	1311829
2. 教育 Expenditure for Education	1469266	1624445	1826924	2234425	2530114	2792968
3. 科学技术 Expenditure for Science and Technology	401878	462600	524082	701490	749190	923236
4. 文化体育与传媒 Expenditure for Culture, Sports and Media	207869	223604	242375	449192	283936	309282
5. 社会保障和就业 Expenditure for Social Safety Net and Employment Effort	871431	946033	1082564	1309862	1492895	1731704
6. 医疗卫生与计划生育 Expenditure for Medical and Health Care and Birth Control	559225	621518	716754	766328	970504	1123291
7. 节能环保 Expenditure for Energy Conservation Environmental Protection	161518	197392	300159	445749	408576	377904
8. 城乡社区 Expenditure for Urban and Rural Community	1042885	1064358	1143602	1586419	2338331	2736428
9. 农林水 Expenditure for Agriculture, Forestry and Water Conservancy	448764	506246	562286	880440	914373	896205
10. 交通运输 Expenditure for Trarssportation	253757	305919	306032	389625	518178	515070
11. 住房保障 Expenditure on Housing Support	65066	77290	93521	122825	219590	286287

10－05 全市金融机构存、贷款余额(1978－2017年)

Balance of Deposits and Loans of Financial Institutions (1978－2017)

单位:万元 (10000 yuan)

年份 Year \ 项目 Item	各项存款 Deposits	住户存款 Household Deposits	城镇住户存款 Urban Household Deposits	各项贷款 Loans
1978	86824	20714	17056	136759
1979	108998	28937	22640	135713
1980	180707	40447	30896	174153
1981	226949	51440	38889	236678
1982	262156	67192	50113	216040
1983	303130	86635	64736	236203
1984	388305	115766	85439	329195
1985	484999	159596	115592	580180
1986	635514	222110	153572	769841
1987	776105	302762	207505	967477
1988	839680	351943	241839	1145989
1989	1017087	501592	346318	1338984
1990	1646165	697515	479031	1803266
1991	2036334	904490	616308	2136903
1992	2652966	1144737	763309	2651983
1993	3469954	1563328	1048413	3415527
1994	5061345	2394370	1642498	4450932
1995	7079650	3423379	2448787	5672105
1996	9619291	4638458	3459439	7434243
1997	12251840	5583306	4229591	9388500
1998	14948225	6701158	5155548	11620537
1999	17886717	7425967	5760527	14937506
2000	20884723	7885579	6151084	16866431
2001	26215100	9418400	7396800	20877000
2002	33731500	11834000	9492300	27523800
2003	46527300	15899600	13079600	38187000
2004	57072000	18351700	15016100	48000400
2005	67487200	21916600	17960100	55453000
2006	78555500	25552400	20789600	66038600
2007	93109600	26348300	21154300	84306800
2008	113333500	34765900	27584600	100690500
2009	142842104	42869189	34027871	131133023
2010	170843548	49909744	39352353	150787269
2011	183965719	55474824	43464332	165737441
2012	201487672	60899841	46965391	180908011
2013	221747107	64085856	47733077	193504605
2014	244505093	67672009	49107745	213168315
2015	298638294	76177515	55659016	233279520
2016	333860429	84932733	62521938	261689982
2017	364832373	86705977	63076960	292709406

注:1. 1989年以前数据均为银行机构存贷款,1990年及以后年份数据为调整后金融机构存贷款。2003年起金融机构存贷款为本外币合并数据。

2. 2015年起,各项存款和各项贷款分类调整。

a) Data before 1989 belonged to banking system, data after 1990 adjusted for deposits and loans of financial institutions, data of 2003 included both RMB and foreign currency.

b) Since 2015, the classification in deposits and Loans has been adjusted.

10-06 市区金融机构存、贷款余额(1978-2017 年)

Balance of Deposits and Loans of Financial Institutions of Urban District(1978-2017)

单位:万元 (10000 yuan)

年份 Year \ 项目 Item	各项存款 Deposits	住户存款 Household Deposits	城镇住户存款 Urban Household Deposits	各项贷款 Loans
1978	58372	13774	13246	101144
1979	73720	18055	17241	98792
1980	134275	24702	23282	121231
1981	172721	31358	29345	170539
1982	198350	39756	37047	142091
1983	226160	50439	46833	155297
1984	293145	66108	61934	194977
1985	359825	89114	82868	418214
1986	458142	115818	106703	557763
1987	565429	156704	142642	714313
1988	610601	180341	163466	846998
1989	737388	256238	229518	1000731
1990	1062574	354316	297390	1271779
1991	1309462	451756	397322	1469671
1992	1695011	572660	479248	1774158
1993	2263969	762234	662234	2298124
1994	3383877	1242379	1085363	3033010
1995	4851774	1853512	1639875	3907199
1996	6828786	2734904	2371657	5350499
1997	8831147	3287475	2873638	6772221
1998	10785066	3905602	3440607	8615412
1999	13051806	4336058	3835542	11462505
2000	15436286	4620235	4101716	13105849
2001	23765400	7976400	6460200	19237800
2002	30638400	10139800	8370100	25476700
2003	42522000	13834200	11693000	30297500
2004	52542100	16014700	13479900	44517600
2005	62249500	19231800	16208400	51455900
2006	72269600	22391800	18737800	61190700
2007	86197300	23124600	19132300	78456200
2008	104930100	30665200	24996500	93838100
2009	131800234	37837816	30801878	121473548
2010	156776515	43676938	35370599	138671334
2011	168052916	48263525	38996516	151756838
2012	183719227	52347969	41789531	156426086
2013	201596137	54488059	42142666	175670366
2014	222558892	57202595	43243610	191888081
2015	284321331	68516344	51360093	222078475
2016	317723682	76306727	57718389	249684325
2017	345461303	77416526	57941703	278049912

10－07　全市金融机构本外币

Balance of Deposits and Loans(RMB and Foreign Currency)

单位:万元

指　标	Item	全　市 Total 绝对值 Absolute Value	全　市 Total 为上年(%) As Compared with the Preceding Year(%)	市　区 Urban District 小计 Subtotal
一、各项存款	**Deposits**	**364832373**	**109.28**	**345461303**
(一)境内存款	Domestic Deposits	362239821	108.93	342916282
1.住户存款	Household Deposits	86705977	102.09	77416526
(1)活期存款	Current Deposits	39013968	105.34	35103068
(2)定期及其他存款	Term and Other Deposits	47692009	99.57	42313458
2.非金融企业存款	Non－financial Enterprise Deposits	163131816	112.69	156595830
(1)活期存款	Current Deposits	61674844	123.22	57827037 5
(2)定期及其他存款	Term and Other Deposits	101456972	107.12	98768793
3.广义政府存款	General Government Deposits	71626072	123.70	68189426
(1)财政性存款	Treasury Deposits	14224147	275.04	13803648
(2)机关团体存款	Organization Deposits	57401925	108.85	54385778
4.非银行业金融机构存款	Non－banking Financial Institutions Deposits	40775955	90.73	40714500
(二)境外存款	Overseas Deposits	2592552	197.01	2545021
二、各项贷款	**Loans**	**292709406**	**111.85**	**278049912**
(一)境内贷款	Domestic Loans	290112705	111.82	275453714
1.住户贷款	Household Loans	96536824	123.75	89406416
(1)短期贷款	Short－term Loans	23511896	117.60	21268390
(2)中长期贷款	Medium and Long term Loans	73024929	125.87	68138026
2.非金融企业及机关团体贷款	Non－financial Enterprise and Organization Loans	193259376	106.63	185730794
(1)短期贷款	Short－term Loans	74378581	100.54	71393062
(2)中长期贷款	Medium and Long term Loans	101724743	123.76	97253860
(3)票据融资	Note Financing	8188995	48.77	8123128
(4)融资租赁	Finance lease	8651227	110.43	8651227
(5)各项垫款	Advance Money	315830	69.07	309516
3.非银行业金融机构贷款	Non－banking Financial Institutions Loans	316505	172.57	316505
(二)境外贷款	Overseas Loans	2596700	115.45	2596198

存、贷款余额(2017 年末)

of Financial Institutions(End of 2017)

(10000 yuan)

				桐庐县 Tonglu	淳安县 Chun'an	建德市 Jiande
萧山区 Xiaoshan	余杭区 Yuhang	富阳区 Fuyang	临安区 Lin'an			
38200623	**27154743**	**9873461**	**7868598**	**4309599**	**3152080**	**4040794**
38136451	27128182	9835193	7866046	4266906	3151406	4039182
14959776	10660493	4185190	3024585	2319809	1586480	2358577
5444547	3896255	1896440	1408842	938838	683005	880216
9515229	6764238	2288750	1615743	1380971	903475	1478361
15656486	9233430	3913574	3314921	1314350	807294	1099421
6953424	4784864	1736491	1788558	807210	526550	725489
8703063	4448566	2177083	1526363	507140	280744	373932
7199803	7206752	1625033	1507287	614653	756605	558101
912042	1363278	117593	241746	46362	65997	66395
6287761	5843474	1507440	1265541	568291	690608	491707
320385	27508	111397	19252	18094	1026	23083
64172	26560	38268	2552	42693	674	1612
33216506	**18262193**	**11391789**	**5411950**	**4036096**	**2149134**	**3062314**
33211628	18259182	11391789	5411547	4036096	2149048	3062300
10261559	7512470	4086529	2545803	1914208	1297598	1372800
2842340	1729504	1129108	895478	486246	387160	474621
7419219	5782966	2957421	1650325	1427962	910437	898179
22940069	10746712	7305260	2865744	2121888	851450	1689500
14144123	4470271	4590712	1013153	971339	320232	680795
8333771	5710924	2610223	1817981	1135773	527779	989350
406205	561625	90022	32589	14178	3440	15660
–	–	–	–	–	–	–
55970	3892	14303	2021	598	–	3695
10000	–	–	–	–	–	–
4878	3010	–	403	–	86	13

10－08 全市金融机构人民币
Balance of RMB Deposits and Loans

单位:万元

指 标	Item	全 市 Total 绝对值 Absolute Value	全 市 Total 为上年(%) As Compared with the Preceding Year(%)	市 区 Urban District 小计 Subtotal
一、各项存款	**Deposits**	**353219355**	**108.63**	**334162440**
(一)境内存款	Domestic Deposits	352707882	108.72	333662281
1.住户存款	Household Deposits	85029613	102.28	75798738
(1)活期存款	Current Deposits	38094186	105.92	34216614
(2)定期及其他存款	Term and Other Deposits	46935427	99.51	41582123
2.非金融企业存款	Non－financial Enterprise Deposits	155566076	112.29	149249348
(1)活期存款	Current Deposits	58292531	123.61	54584364
(2)定期及其他存款	Term and Other Deposits	97273545	106.45	94664984
3.广义政府存款	General Government Deposits	71618075	123.72	68181481
(1)财政性存款	Treasury Deposits	14224147	275.04	13803648
(2)机关团体存款	Organization Deposits	57393928	108.87	54377833
4.非银行业金融机构存款	Non－banking Financial Institutions Deposits	40494118	90.28	40432715
(二)境外存款	Overseas Deposits	511472	69.43	500159
二、各项贷款	**Loans**	**285736311**	**112.21**	**271086025**
(一)境内贷款	Domestic Loans	285524620	112.27	270874836
1.住户贷款	Household Loans	96530246	123.76	89400138
(1)短期贷款	Short－term Loans	23505546	117.63	21262340
(2)中长期贷款	Medium and Long term Loans	73024700	125.87	68137797
2.非金融企业及机关团体贷款	Non－financial Enterprise and Organization Loans	188677869	107.12	181158194
(1)短期贷款	Short－term Loans	71826913	101.41	68850302
(2)中长期贷款	Medium and Long term Loans	99698922	124.26	95228039
(3)票据融资	Note Financing	8188995	48.77	8123128
(4)融资租赁	Finance lease	8651227	110.43	8651227
(5)各项垫款	Advance Money	311812	69.12	305498
3.非银行业金融机构贷款	Non－banking Financial Institutions Loans	316505	172.57	316505
(二)境外贷款	Overseas Loans	211691	63.04	211189

存、贷款余额(2017 年末)
of Financial Institutions(End of 2017)

(10000 yuan)

萧山区 Xiaoshan	余杭区 Yuhang	富阳区 Fuyang	临安区 Lin'an	桐庐县 Tonglu	淳安县 Chun'an	建德市 Jiande
36988854	**26678573**	**9489622**	**7740871**	**4176021**	**3137254**	**4002769**
36941403	26654114	9486679	7738514	4169123	3136587	4001378
14854580	10607564	4163571	3010806	2288806	1582181	2349083
5389054	3858307	1883093	1400193	922010	679977	875391
9465526	6749257	2280478	1610613	1366796	902204	1473691
14567315	8812915	3586841	3201217	1247570	796776	1071165
6466107	4542985	1508506	1716959	775702	517222	698283
8101208	4269930	2078334	1484258	471868	279554	372881
7199498	7206130	1624871	1507238	614653	756604	558099
912042	1363278	117593	241746	46362	65997	66395
6287456	5842852	1507278	1265492	568291	690607	491705
320010	27504	111397	19252	18094	1026	23031
47451	24460	2943	2358	6898	666	1392
32930901	**18218808**	**11345559**	**5410456**	**4035360**	**2148436**	**3056034**
32926023	18215797	11345559	5410053	4035360	2148350	3056021
10261057	7512263	4086328	2545680	1914129	1297559	1372740
2841838	1729297	1128961	895355	486168	387122	474561
7419219	5782966	2957368	1650325	1427962	910437	898179
22654966	10703534	7259231	2864373	2121231	850791	1683280
13862243	4427093	4544682	1011782	970682	319572	674575
8333771	5710924	2610223	1817981	1135773	527779	989350
406205	561625	90022	32589	14178	3440	15660
–	–	–	–	–	–	–
52746	3892	14303	2021	598	–	3695
10000	–	–	–	–	–	–
4878	3010	–	403	–	86	13

10-09 住户(本外币)存款余额(2017年末)

Balance of Savings Deposits(RMB and Foreign Currency) of Rural and Urban Residents(End of 2017)

单位:万元 (10000 yuan)

地区	Region	总计 Total		城镇住户 Urban Residents		农村住户 Rural Residents	
		2017年末 At the End of Year 2017	为上年(%) As Compared with the Preceding Year(%)	2017年末 At the End of Year 2017	为上年(%) As Compared with the Preceding Year(%)	2017年末 At the End of Year 2017	为上年(%) As Compared with the Preceding Year(%)
全　市	**Total**	**86705977**	**102.09**	**63076960**	**100.89**	**23629017**	**105.44**
市　区	Urban District	77416526	101.45	57941703	100.39	19474823	104.77
#萧山区	Xiaoshan	14959776	103.12	8111048	100.65	6848728	106.20
余杭区	Yuhang	10660493	107.10	5586094	106.24	5074399	108.07
富阳区	Fuyang	4185190	101.59	2293086	100.25	1892104	103.26
临安区	Lin'an	3024585	113.23	1674879	116.23	1349706	109.71
桐庐县	Tonglu	2319809	103.59	1219326	101.10	1100483	106.51
淳安县	Chun'an	1586480	105.31	817912	100.77	768568	110.61
建德市	Jiande	2358577	106.77	1423140	105.82	935438	108.25

10－10 金融机构人民币信贷收支表(资金来源,2012－2017年)

Credit Funds Balance Sheet of Financial Institutions (RMB,Sources of Funds,2012－2017)

单位:亿元 (100 million yuan)

项　目	Item	2012	2013	2014	2015	2016	2017
资金来源合计	**All Sources**	**19629.31**	**22028.95**	**25403.81**	**30190.21**	**36881.85**	**38680.06**
一、各项存款	Deposits	19857.46	22386.39	25721.84	29003.07	32514.64	35321.94
(一)境内存款	Domestic Deposits	19795.13	22322.27	25642.26	28945.99	32440.97	35270.79
1.住户存款	Household Deposits	6198.63	6831.58	7223.78	7507.09	8313.13	8502.96
2.非金融企业存款	Non－financial Enterprise Deposits	9842.96	10733.60	11508.67	12437.24	13853.66	15556.61
3.广义政府存款	General Government Deposits	2784.09	3476.44	4218.53	4674.92	5788.91	7161.81
4.非银行业金融机构存款	Non－banking Financial Institutions Deposits	969.45	1280.64	2691.28	4326.75	4485.28	4049.41
(二)境外存款	Overseas Deposits	62.33	64.12	79.58	57.08	73.67	51.15
二、金融债券	Bonds	137.57	130.65	168.43	239.84	342.64	439.42
三、卖出回购资产	Sell Repurchase Assets	7.18	27.11	－	－	－	4.72
四、借款及非银行业金融机构拆入	Borrowing and Non Banking Financial Institutions Borrowing	178.71	216.25	258.90	0.30	15.35	3.00
五、联行往来(净)	Interbank Transactions (net)						
六、应付及暂收款	Accounts Payable and Temporary Collection of Money	549.14	699.24	907.61	935.16	1008.12	1101.74
七、各项准备	All Reserves	456.58	399.37	480.22	600.05	733.19	850.04
八、所有者权益	Creditor's Equity	660.01	828.71	929.92	967.10	1104.44	1491.11
其中:实收资本	Paid－in Capital	152.95	180.29	201.14	283.48	315.27	475.22
九、其他	Others	－2217.33	－2658.76	－3063.11	－1555.31	1163.46	－531.90

10-11 金融机构人民币信贷收支表(资金运用,2012-2017年)

Credit Funds Balance Sheet of Financial Institutions (RMB, Use of Funds, 2012-2017)

单位:亿元 (100 million yuan)

项 目	Item	2012	2013	2014	2015	2016	2017
资金运用合计		**19629.31**	**22028.95**	**25403.81**	**30190.21**	**36881.85**	**38680.06**
一、各项存款	**Deposits**	**17106.54**	**18426.94**	**20388.37**	**22395.29**	**25464.83**	**28573.63**
(一)境内贷款	**Domestic Loans**	**17099.47**	**18420.12**	**20382.37**	**22373.03**	**25431.25**	**28552.46**
1.住户贷款	**Household Loans**	**3778.53**	**4372.82**	**4918.01**	**5858.42**	**7799.69**	**9653.02**
(1)短期贷款	Short-term Loans	1290.02	1481.46	1770.03	1874.03	1998.31	2350.55
(2)中长期贷款	Medium and Long term Loans	2488.51	2891.37	3147.99	3984.39	5801.38	7302.47
2.非金融企业及机关团体贷款	**Non-financial Enterprise and Organization Loans**	**13266.48**	**14019.88**	**15432.16**	**16502.18**	**17613.23**	**18867.79**
(1)短期贷款	Short-term Loans	6884.25	7074.96	6909.51	6943.84	7082.51	7182.69
(2)中长期贷款	Medium and Long term Loans	5477.42	5958.28	7145.36	7539.38	8023.23	9969.89
(3)票据融资	Note Financing	421.60	441.08	731.55	1311.28	1678.99	818.90
(4)融资租赁	Finance lease	416.64	484.62	589.24	663.57	783.39	865.12
(5)各项垫款	Advance Money	66.57	60.95	56.49	44.11	45.11	31.18
3.非银行业金融机构贷款	**Non-banking Financial Institutions Deposits**	**54.46**	**27.41**	**32.20**	**12.44**	**18.34**	**31.65**
(二)境外贷款	**Overseas Loans**	**7.06**	**6.82**	**6.00**	**22.26**	**33.58**	**21.17**
二、债券投资	**Bond Investment**	**802.06**	**1021.41**	**1667.86**	**2005.65**	**2032.81**	**2694.21**
三、股权及其他投资	**Equity and other Investment**	**224.96**	**814.64**	**1076.84**	**1738.10**	**2642.37**	**2804.86**
四、买入返售资产	**Bug Assets Repurchased**	**79.28**	**589.67**	**336.63**	**62.63**	**48.35**	**87.36**
五、存放非银行业金融机构款项	**Deposit of non Banking Financial Institutions**	**0.34**	**0.11**	**0.27**	**0.97**	**1.11**	**1.36**
六、联行往来(净)	**Interbank Transactions (net)**	**927.52**	**410.23**	**1315.59**	**3374.29**	**5960.97**	**3831.49**
七、金银占款	**Funds Outstanding for Gold and Silver**						
八、外汇买卖	**Foreign Exchange Trading**	**11.33**	**68.01**	**-33.91**	**-7.34**	**-**	**-**
九、应收及预付款	**Collectable Account and Advance Payment**	**262.68**	**475.07**	**420.79**	**391.61**	**488.74**	**430.88**
十、投资性房地产	**Investment Property**	**1.10**	**2.77**	**2.75**	**2.63**	**5.74**	**6.49**
十一、固定资产	**Fitness Assets**	**213.50**	**220.11**	**228.62**	**226.38**	**236.93**	**249.78**

10－12 保险业务情况(2015－2017年)

Statistics on Insurance Business(2015－2017)

单位:万元　　　　(10000 yuan)

指　标	Item	保险费收入 Premium			赔付金额 Indemnity Expenditure		
		2015	2016	2017	2015	2016	2017
全市总计	**Total**	**3743769**	**5183992**	**6337034**	**1396924**	**1588847**	**1696354**
为上年%	As Compared with the Preceding Year(%)	116.8	138.5	122.2	117.4	113.7	106.8
一、财产保险	Property Insurance	1569067	1724886	1939978	937229	1000353	1059642
企业财产险	Enterprise Property Insurance	90317	93299	93949	42398	40793	37715
家庭财产险	Family Property Insurance	10012	9084	9003	4641	6606	4668
机动车辆险	Transportation Equipment Insurance	1153742	1212797	1330482	702258	734273	762543
工程险	Project Insurance	19167	20089	21736	7798	6579	8251
责任险	Responsibilihty Insurance	42734	62457	91555	15975	29742	43768
信用险	Export Credit Insurance	130809	148168	162086	101830	95939	89346
保证险	Guarantee Insurance	39963	66594	70729	13759	17314	12146
船舶险	Shipping Insurance	4326	4538	4474	4078	3795	4238
货运险	Cargo Insurance	21933	39567	72197	10172	23571	45655
特殊风险保险	Special Pisks Insurance	5455	7014	7184	320	174	2183
农业保险	Agriculture Insurance	17775	18038	21903	9312	12479	13793
其他险	Other	32834	43242	54679	24688	29088	35337
二、人身险	Personal Insurance	2174702	3459106	4397056	459695	588494	636712
寿险	Life Insurance	1612350	2300127	3291187	370520	470950	471748
意外伤害险	Accidental Insurance	125954	178268	204765	23802	32600	44147
健康险	Health Insurance	436398	980711	901104	65373	84944	120817

主要统计指标解释

财政收入 包括:(1)各项税收。主要有增值税、营业税、土地增值税、城市维护建设税、资源税、城市土地使用税、印花税、个人所得税、企业所得税、关税和耕地占用税等。

(2)专项收入包括征收排污费、征收城市水资源费收入,教育费附加收入等。

存款 企业、机关、团体或居民根据可以收回的原则,把货币资金存入银行或其他信用机构保管并取得一定利息的一种信用活动形式。根据存款对象的不同可划分为企业存款、财政存款、机关团体存款、基本建设存款、城镇储蓄存款、农村存款等科目。它是银行信贷资金的主要来源。

贷款 银行或其他信用机构根据必须归还的原则,按一定利率,为企业、个人等提供资金的一种信用活动形式。我国银行贷款分为流动资金贷款、固定资产贷款、城乡个体工商户贷款、城乡个体工商户贷款以及农业贷款等科目。

Explanatory Notes on Main Statistical Indicators

Financial Revenue It includes the following main items: (1) various tax revenues, including value added tax, business tax, land value added tax, tax on city maintenance and construction, resources tax, tax on use of urban land, stamp tax, personal income tax, enterprise income tax and tax on occupancy of cultivated land, etc. (2) Special revenues, including revenue collected from imposing fee on sewage treatment, revenue collected from imposing fee on urban water resources, and extra – charges for education, etc.

Deposit is a form of credit by which enterprises, institutions, organizations or households can put money into banks and other credit institutions for safekeeping and interest earning under the principle of free withdrawal. According to different depositors, deposits are divided into enterprise deposits, treasury deposits, deposits of government agencies and organizations, capital construction deposits, urban savings deposits, rural deposits and other deposits. Deposits are major sources of the credit funds of banks.

Loan is a form of credit by which banks and other credit institutions provide funds at certain interest rate to enterprises and individuals in the light of the principle of unconditional repayment. Loans from Chinese banks include circulating capital loans, fixed assets loans, loans to urban and rural individuals engaged in industrial and commercial business and agricultural loans.

十一、城市建设环境保护

URBAN CONSTRUCTION AND ENVIRONMENTAL PROTECTION

11 城市建设、环境保护
Urban Construction and Environmental Protection

主要统计指标
Major Statistical Indicators

市区建成区面积	Developed Area in Urban District	591.08	平方千米	(sq.km)
市区实有道路面积	Area of Roads in Urban District at Year-end	8291	万平方米	(10, 000 sq.m)
市区用电量	Electricity Consumption of Urban District	673.73	亿千瓦时	(100 million kw/h)
# 工业用电	Industrial Electricity Consumption	389.00	亿千瓦时	(100 million kw/h)
生活用电	Electricity Consumption for Residential Use	105.29	亿千瓦时	(100 million kw/h)
市区供水能力	Water-supply Capacity of Urban District	421	万吨/日	(10, 000 tons/day)
市区供水总量	Annual Volume of Tap Water Supplied in Urban District	83192	万吨	(10, 000 tons)
市区气化率	Percentage of Population with Access to Gas in Urban District	100	%	(%)
市区公园绿地面积	Park Green Area in Urban District	8770	公顷	(hectare)
市区空气质量达标(AQI＜100)天数	The Number of Days of Air Quality Reaching(AQI＜100) the Standards	271	天	(day)

11-01 市区公共交通情况(2010-2017年)
Public Transportation in Urban Districts(2010-2017)

指 标	Item	2010	2011	2012	2013	2014	2015	2016	2017
一、轨道交通	**Rail Transit**								
年末运营线路总长度（千米）	Length of Operating Routes (year-end) (km)	-	-	47.97	47.97	66.30	81.50	81.50	117.60
客运总量（万人次）	Passenger Traffic (10,000 person-times)	-	-	561	9237	14521	22348	26877	33986
二、公共汽车	**Bus**								
年末运营线路条数（条）	Number of Operating Routes (year-end) (unit)	548	611	620	645	703	756	758	937
年末运营线路总长度（千米）	Length of Operating Routes (year-end) (km)	8594	11106	11351	11445	12032	12791	13866	16819
#BRT线路长度（千米）	BRT line length (km)				122	113	128	151	151
年末运营公共汽车（辆）	Number of Public Transportation Vehicles(year-end) (unit)	7209	7543	7450	8249	8656	8555	8770	9672
#无轨电车（辆）	Number of Operating Trolleys (unit)	65	54	51	101	115	150	150	150
客运总量（万人次）	Passenger Traffic (10,000 person-times)	127967	126999	131901	132221	140928	142312	141441	151263
三、出租汽车	**Tax**								
年末实有出租汽车数（辆）	Number of Taxis(year-end) (unit)	9362	10905	10344	10904	11913	11963	12209	13233

11－02 市区城市供电、供水情况(2010－2017年)

Electricity and Water Supply in Urban Districts(2010－2017)

指标	Item	2010	2011	2012	2013	2014	2015	2016	2017
一、城市供电	**Urban Electricity Supply**								
全年用电总量（亿千瓦时）	Total Electricity Consumption (100 million kwh)	392.64	432.57	444.95	484.05	552.71	559.54	583.96	673.73
#工业（亿千瓦时）	Industrial Electricity Consumption (100 million kwh)	258.35	282.95	278.93	296.08	355.06	345.23	337.04	389.00
生活（亿千瓦时）	Electricity Consumption for Residential Use (100 million kwh)	50.74	55.49	63.62	71.52	72.56	78.27	93.03	105.29
二、城市供水（自来水）	**Urban Water Supply**								
总售水量（万吨）	Total Annual Volume of Tap Water Saled (10,000 tons)	45666	44335	49549	51709	56401	56478	55566	71076
平均日供水（万吨）	Per Capita Daily Consumption of Tap Water (10,000 tons)	147	144	159	166	181	183	178	228
供水能力（万吨/日）	Capacity of Water Supply (10,000 tons/day)	320	320	320	350	380	380	384	421
供水总量（万吨）	Total Annual Volume of Tap Water Supplied (10,000 tons)	53565	52660	58183	60747	66172	66760	65087	83192
#生产用水（万吨）	For Productive Use (10,000 tons)	11479	11884	12478	13005	14792	14902	14161	16157
生活用水（万吨）	For Residential Use (10,000 tons)	30978	22384	22861	23733	26894	26162	25078	33960
用水普及率（%）	Percentage of Population with Access to Tap Water (%)	100	100	100	100	100	100	100	100

11－03 市区市政建设情况(主要年份)

Public Utilities in Urban Districts(Main Years)

指 标	Item	2010	2011	2012	2013	2014	2015	2016	2017
一、市政建设	**Urban Infrastructure**								
建成区面积(平方公里)	Constructed Area (sq. m)	412.59	432.98	452.62	462.48	495.22	506.09	541.38	591.08
年末实有道路面积(万平方米)	Area of Roads (year－end) (10,000 sq. m)	4754	4900	5284	5426	6145	6540	6932	8291
年末实有道路长度(公里)	Length of Roads(year－end) (km)	2194	2255	2458	2479	2748	2991	3075	3550
年末实有桥梁数(座)	Number of Bridges(year－end) (unit)	1021	1059	1129	1165	1235	1337	1353	1443
排水管道长度(公里)	Length of Drainage Pipelines (km)	3904	4056	4280	4455	5012	5370	5944	8614
城市污水排放量(万立方米)	Volume of Sewage Drained (10,000 cu. m)	43746	44809	47330	48432	53111	56974	57916	69834
城市污水处理总量(万立方米)	the Total Volume of Urban Sewage Treatment (10,000 cu. m)	41733	42781	45197	46251	50318	54137	55061	66516
二、城市液化气	**Urban Liquefied Petroleum Gas**								
供气总量 (万吨)	Total Volume of Liquefied Petroleum Gas Supply (10,000 tons)	11.44	11.19	11.17	11.92	9.87	12.38	13.14	12.86
#家庭用气(万吨)	Supply for Residential Use (10,000 tons)	5.77	5.93	5.90	4.70	5.08	6.08	5.90	6.48
三、人工煤气及天然气	**Coal Gas and Natural Gas**								
家庭用气总量(万立方米)	Total Volume of Coal Gas Consumed (10,000 cu. m)	10053	11365	13397	13869	18019	20659	21878	23614
家庭用气户数(万户)	Residential Households with Access to Gas (10,000 households)	62.85	72.50	81.72	91.08	111.30	130.69	139.03	153.17
四、全社会气化率 %	**Percentage of Population with Access to Gas** (%)	**100**	**100**	**100**	**100**	**100**	**100**	**100**	**100**

11－04　市区园林绿化情况（2010－2017年）
Urban Forestation（2010－2017）

指　标	Item	2010	2011	2012	2013	2014	2015	2016	2017
建城区绿化覆盖面积（公顷）	The Green Areas Coveraged in Constructed Areas (hectare)	16483	17336	18135	18606	20031	20464	22035	23620
建城区园林绿地面积（公顷）	Total Area of Parks, Gardens and Green Areas in Constructed Areas (hectare)	15118	15898	16647	17071	18386	18949	20118	21726
#公园绿地（公顷）	Public Green Area (hectare)	5017	5287	5635	5820	6304	7640	8118	8770
建城区绿化覆盖率（%）	Rate of the Green Areas Coveraged in Constructed Areas (%)	39.95	40.00	40.07	40.23	40.57	40.43	40.70	39.96
公园景点个数（个）	Number of Parks and Scenic Resorts (unit)	176	181	185	190	207	217	222	245
公园景点面积（公顷）	Area of Parks and Scenic Resorts (hectare)	1906	2047	2065	2094	2298	2488	2754	3074

11－05 环境保护情况（2017年）

Statistics on Environmental Protection（2017）

指标名称		Item		全市 Whole City	市区 Urban District
工业废水排放量	（万吨）	Industrial Wastewater Emissions	（10,000 tons）	24559	23331
工业废水中COD排放量	（吨）	COD Emissions in Industrial Wastewater	（tons）	12639	12212
工业废水中氨氮排放量	（吨）	Ammonia emissions in Industrial wastewater	（tons）	507	482
工业二氧化硫产生量	（吨）	Industrial Sulfur Dioxide Produced	（tons）	106895	83069
工业二氧化硫排放量	（吨）	Industrial Emissions of Sulfur Dioxide	（tons）	26497	21136
工业氮氧化物排放量	（吨）	Industrial Nitrogen Oxide Emissions	（tons）	31123	21581
工业烟（粉）产生量	（吨）	Industrial Smoke（Powder）Production	（tons）	11719689	10601667
工业烟（粉）尘排放量	（吨）	Industrial Smoke, Powder and Dust Emissions	（tons）	16343	11579
一般工业固体废物综合利用率	（%）	Comprehensive Utilization Rate of General Industrial Solid Waste	（%）	77.06	77.36
城市污水集中处理率	（%）	Centralized Treatment Rate of Urban Sewage	（%）	95.1	95.25
城市生活垃圾无害化处理率	（%）	Harmless Treatment Rate of City's Living Garbage	（%）	100	100
空气质量优良天数	（天）	Air Quality Days	（days）	-	271
集中式饮用水源地水质达标率	（%）	Compliance Rate of Centralized Sources of Drinking Water	（%）	100	-

注：2016年起环境统计方法有调整。

a）The environmental statistical method has been adjusted since 2016.

主要统计指标解释

自来水生产能力　指年底城建部门管理的自来水厂实际生产能力。

生活用水量　指居民日常生活与公共福利设施的用水量。包括居民、饮食店、旅馆、医院、理发店、浴池、洗衣店、游泳池、商店、学校、机关、部队等单位的用水量。

供气总量　指全年售给各类用户的全部煤气量。包括工业用量、家庭用量和其他用量。

年末实有道路长度　指除土路外，路面经过铺装宽度在3.5米以上的道路，包括高级、次高级道路和普通道路。

城市桥梁　指城市范围内，修建在河道上的桥梁和道路与道路立交、道路跨越铁路的立交桥，以及人行天桥。包括永久性桥和半永久性桥，不包括临时性桥、铁路桥、涵洞。

营运线路长度　指设置的固定营运线路的长度，包括郊区营运线路长度。不包括临时行驶的线路长度。

用水普及率　指城市用水的非农业人口数(不包括临时人口和流动人口)与城市非农业人口总数之比。计算公式为：

$$用水普及率=\frac{城市用水非农业人口数}{城市非农业人口数}\times 100\%$$

城市园林绿地面积　指城市公共绿地、专用绿地、生产绿地、防护绿地、郊区风景名胜区的全部面积。

公园绿地面积　指供游览休息的各种公园、动物园、植物园、陵园以及花园、游园和供游览休息用的林荫道绿地、广场绿地。不包括一般栽植的行道树及林荫道的面积。

Explanatory Notes on Main Statistical Indicators

Production Capacity of Tap Water refers to the actual comprehensive production capacity of the waterworks administered by the urban construction department.

Consumption of water for Residential Use refers to the water consumption of households for daily life and the water consumption of public welfare facilities, including the consumption of restaurants, hotels, hospitals, barber shops, public bathhouses, laundries, swimming pools, shops, schools, institutions, army units and other units.

Volume of Gas Supply refers to the total volume of gas Sold to users in a year, including the volume for industrial use, residential use and other uses.

Length of Roads at the Year – end refers to the length of roads with a paved surface, and with a width of more than 3 – 5 meters, including high quality, medium quality and ordinary roads.

Urban Bridges refers to bridges over river courses, great separated junctions and overpasses in urban areas. Permanent bridges and semi – permanent bridges are included. Temporary bridges, railway bridges and culverts are excluded.

Length in Operation refers to the length of the roads in fixed operation, including the suburb one, but excluding the tomporary ones.

Percentage of Urban Population with Access to Tap Water refers to the ratio of the urban non – agricultural population (excluding temporary and mobile population) with access to tap water to the tolal urban non – agricultural population. The formula is:

$$\text{Percentage of Poputalion with Access to Tap Water} = \frac{\text{Urban Non – agricultural Population with Access to Tap Water}}{\text{Urban Non – agricultural Population}} \times 100\%$$

Area of Urban Gardens and Green Areas refers to the total area of urban public green land, special green land, production green land, protection green land and suburban scenic spots.

Park Green Area refers to green area of various parks, zoos, botanical gardens, cemeteries, amusement parks, tree – flanked boulevards Greenland squares for tourism and relaxing. Areas with trees planted along – side the streets and boulevards are excluded.

十二、科技、教育 文化、卫生、体育

SCIENCE AND TECHNOLOGY,EDUCATION,
CULTURE,PUBLIC HEALTH AND SPORTS

12

科技、教育、文化、卫生、体育
Science and Technology, Education, Culture, Public Health and Sports

主要统计指标
Major Statistical Indicators

高等学校数	Number of Regular Institution of Higher Education	39	个	(unit)
高等学校在校学生数	Number of Students in Regular Institution of Higher Education	48.41	万人	(10, 000 person)
高中在校学生数	Number of Students in Senior High Schools	11.31	万人	(10, 000 person)
初中在校学生数	Number of Students in Junior High Schools	22.48	万人	(10, 000 person)
小学在校学生数	Number of Students in Primary Schools	56.04	万人	(10, 000 person)
医疗病床数	Number of Beds in Health Institutions	7.59	万张	(10, 000 bed)
# 医院	Number of Beds in Hospitals	7.02	万张	(10, 000 bed)
卫生技术人员数	Number of Medical Technical Personnel	11.04	万人	(10, 000 person)
# 执业(助理)医师	Number of Licensed (Assistant) Doctors	4.18	万人	(10, 000 person)
公共图书馆	Public Library	15	个	(unit)

12－01　全市科技活动情况(2013－2017年)

Statistics on Scientific and Technological Activities(2013－2017)

指　标　　Item	2013	2014	2015	2016	2017
一、全社会科技活动 **The Scientific and Technological Activities in whole Society**					
研究与试验发展活动折合全时人员 (人年) Full－time Equivalent of R&D Personnel	81617	90193	94323	94696	103245
研究与试验发展经费支出 (亿元) R&D Financial Expenditure (0.1 billion yuan)	248.73	274.00	302.19	346.36	396.82
研究与试验发展经费支出与GDP之比 (%) The Proportion of R&D Financial Expenditure in GDP (%)	2.96	2.98	3.01	3.06	3.15
二、规模以上工业科技活动 **The Scientific and Technological Activities of Industrial Enterprises Above Designated Size**					
有研究与试验发展活动企业数 (个) The Number of Scientific and Technological Activities Enterprises (Unit)	1453	1518	1671	1753	1819
研究与试验发展项目数 (个) Projeet on R&D (Unit)	7342	7383	8265	8943	10000
企业有科技机构 (个) Scientific and Technological Institutions of Enterprises (Unit)	1273	1346	1354	1410	1611
科技机构仪器和设备原价 (亿元) Original Value of Machines of Scientlfic and Technological (0.1 billion yuan)	87.06	99.61	100.73	126.23	142.78
研究与试验发展人员 (万人) R&D Personnel (10,000)	6.88	7.41	8.01	7.92	8.39
每万名从业人员中研究与试验发展活动人员数 (人) The Number of R&D Activities Personnel per 10,000 Employees (Person)	578	644	725	743	794
研究与试验发展经费支出 (亿元) R&D Financial Expenditure (0.1 billion yuan)	160.21	177.39	198.06	215.03	241.93
研究与试验发展经费支出占主营业务收入的比例 (%) The Proportion of R&D Financial Expenditure in Main Business Income (%)	1.33	1.42	1.66	1.79	1.88

12－02　全社会 R&D 经费投入情况（2012－2017 年）
Basic Statistics on R&D Activities Funds（2012－2017）

单位：亿元　　　　(100 million yuan)

年份 Year	总计 Total	按执行部门分 By Sector			
		研究机构 Research and Development Institutions	高等院校 Colleges and Universties	规模以工业 Industrial Enterprises above Designated Size	其他部门 Others
2012	228.00	14.96	38.12	143.47	31.44
2013	248.73	15.91	39.78	160.21	32.83
2014	274.00	17.34	42.06	177.39	37.21
2015	302.19	20.88	46.04	198.06	37.21
2016	346.36	16.55	40.79	215.03	73.99
2017	396.82	18.04	44.56	241.93	92.29

12－03　规模以上工业企业 R&D 经费投入情况（2012－2017 年）
Basic Statistics on R&D Activities of Industrial Enterprises above Designated Size（2012－2017）

单位：亿元　　　　(100 million yuan)

年份 Year	总计 Total	按经费来源分 By Source			
		政府资金 Government Appropriation Funds	企业资金 Self－raised Funds by Enterprise	境外资金 Overseas Capital	其他资金 Other
2012	143.47	4.63	137.73	0.41	0.70
2013	160.21	4.35	154.42	0.26	1.19
2014	177.39	5.24	171.18	0.10	0.89
2015	198.06	5.35	191.03	0.24	1.43
2016	215.03	3.88	209.98	0.08	1.09
2017	241.93	7.73	233.04	0.22	0.94

12－04 分地区、行业非私营及规上私营单位年末人才资源(2017 年)

Trained Personnel Resource of Non－Private and Private Units above Designated Size by Region(2017)

单位:人 (person)

项 目	Item	合计 Total	非私营单位 Non－Private	#专业技术人员 Technical Personnel	非私营单位 Non－Private	#技术工人 Technical Workers	非私营单位 Non－Private
全市	**Whole City**	**2904284**	**1872606**	**961857**	**703962**	**1310807**	**736586**
市区	Urban District	2711225	1778505	904930	668562	1224552	704561
#上城区	Shangcheng	157860	124833	63277	53783	51259	38783
下城区	Xiacheng	173823	150677	79950	71268	48563	43175
江干区	Jianggan	276098	116219	70999	42444	149958	39019
拱墅区	Gongshu	193682	100481	51519	31220	107743	47275
西湖区	Xihu	368794	297222	132808	107003	157126	125809
高新(滨江)区	Hi－Tech(Binjiang)	241743	183113	134010	111422	50506	28322
萧山区	Xiaoshan	563830	340623	142381	89044	324573	192113
大江东产业集聚区	Dajiangdong Industry Cluster District	73768	39506	19754	8670	41941	24227
余杭区	Yuhang	313653	185712	103167	69626	137873	68829
富阳区	Fuyang	182239	100096	52306	33048	92449	46051
临安区	Lin'an	97991	55263	31628	21816	41454	18008
经济技术开发区	Economic and Technological Development Zone	128446	112124	37997	33314	58996	53332
西湖风景名胜区	The West Lake Scenic Zone	13066	12142	4888	4574	4052	3845
桐庐县	Tonglu	86815	33919	22096	12080	48155	12392
淳安县	Chun'an	47865	26899	14815	11175	13930	7387
建德市	Jiande	58379	33283	20016	12145	24170	12246

单位:人　　12－04　续表 continued　　(person)

项　目	Item	合计 Total	非私营单位 Non－Private	#专业技术人员 Technical Personnel	非私营单位 Non－Private	#技术工人 Technical Workers	非私营单位 Non－Private
按国民经济行业分组	**Total**						
农、林、牧、渔业	Farming, Forestry, Animal Husbandry and Fishery	859	747	149	138	452	380
采矿业	Mining	1225	516	193	78	752	324
制造业	Manufacturing	712660	453131	170118	120139	412564	258441
电力、热力、燃气及水生产和供应业	Production & Supply of Electricity, Heat, Gas & Water	16764	15656	3521	3297	9934	9272
建筑业	Construction	1020209	465459	214999	91253	729611	341724
批发和零售业	Wholesale & Retail Trades	124715	73591	33139	20829	26341	20655
交通运输、仓储和邮政业	Transportation, Storage and Posts	91226	70141	14115	8783	58622	50359
住宿和餐饮业	Hotels and Catering Services	29277	18972	6146	3244	7897	5914
信息传输、软件和信息技术服务业	Information Transmission, Software and Information Technology	168383	123280	103056	82343	6988	5704
金融业	Financial Intermediation	66854	65812	42645	42413	2455	2451
房地产业	Real Estate	59365	45689	19283	15267	5495	4191
租赁和商务服务业	Leasing and Business Services	82419	53507	25278	13715	18919	12557
科学研究、技术服务业	Scientific Research, Technical Services	100205	77673	75778	59016	5901	4663
水利、环境和公共设施管理业	Management of Water Conservancy, Environment and Public Facilities	17728	11776	6189	3867	6191	3984
居民服务、修理和其他服务业	Service to Households, Repair and Other Services	9584	4019	2558	824	3091	1151
教育	Education	154776	151877	125333	124154	6728	6128
卫生和社会工作	Health Care and Social Work	110501	104526	95246	90836	4979	4916
文化、体育和娱乐业	Culture, Sports and Entertainment	19102	17802	13603	13258	770	655
公共管理、社会保障和社会组织	Public Management, Social Security and Social Organizations	118432	118432	10508	10508	3117	3117

12－05　专利申请与授权情况(2007－2017 年)
Patent Application and Authorization(2007－2017)

单位:件 (item)

年份 Year	专利申请合计 Patent Applications	发明 Inventions	实用新型 Utility Models	外观设计 Designs	专利授权合计 Patent Applications Granted	发明 Inventions	实用新型 Utility Models	外观设计 Designs
2007	13295	4592	4332	4371	7563	1320	3638	2605
2008	18549	5130	5796	7623	9831	1923	4637	3271
2009	26077	6703	9806	9568	15507	2535	5806	7166
2010	29732	7766	13108	8858	26483	3238	11888	11357
2011	40890	9717	18783	12390	29249	4511	14556	10182
2012	53785	11960	25313	16512	40651	5526	20400	14725
2013	58280	14031	25523	18726	41518	4903	23159	13456
2014	48569	14779	21711	12079	33548	5552	18147	9849
2015	60839	17777	29048	14014	46245	8296	24764	13185
2016	73546	24951	32187	16408	41052	8647	21763	10642
2017	75709	25578	35096	15035	42227	9872	21282	11073

12－06　全市分地区专利申请与授权情况(2017 年)

Patent Application and Authorization by Region(2017)

单位:件　　(item)

地　区	Region	专利申请合计 Patent Applications	发明 Inventions	实用新型 Utility Models	外观设计 Designs	专利授权合计 Patent Applications Granted	发明 Inventions	实用新型 Utility Models	外观设计 Designs
全市	**Whole City**	**75709**	**25578**	**35096**	**15035**	**42227**	**9872**	**21282**	**11073**
市区	Urban District	71675	25089	33497	13089	39908	9700	20434	9774
#上城区	Shangcheng	2035	578	906	551	1080	207	485	388
下城区	Xiacheng	5077	2214	1902	961	2753	1025	1279	449
江干区	Jianggan	12074	4593	5349	2132	6741	1965	3119	1657
拱墅区	Gongshu	2588	609	1446	533	1619	228	957	434
西湖区	Xihu	10002	5450	3539	1013	5975	2690	2393	892
高新(滨江)区	Hi－Tech(Binjiang)	14010	5894	5340	2776	7474	1893	3268	2313
萧山区	Xiaoshan	6802	1523	4345	934	3907	486	2670	751
大江东产业集聚区	Dajiangdong Industry Cluster District	802	179	596	27	603	78	487	38
余杭区	Yuhang	13277	2808	6993	3476	7010	732	4163	2115
富阳区	Fuyang	3354	850	2097	407	1698	248	1195	255
临安区	Lin'an	2456	570	1580	306	1651	226	905	520
桐庐县	Tonglu	2161	212	663	1286	1404	98	420	886
淳安县	Chun'an	520	150	262	108	278	24	148	106
建德市	Jiande	1353	127	674	552	637	50	280	307

注:江干区含经济技术开发区、西湖区含风景名胜区。

a) Figures of Jianggan include Economic and Technological Development Zone, figures of Xihu include the West Lake Scenic Zone.

12－07 全市文化事业单位数(2000－2017年)
Number of Culture Institutions(2000－2017)

单位:个　　(unit)

年 份 Year	电影院 Cinemas	剧场 Theaters	剧团 Opera Troupes	文化馆 Cultural Centers	文化站 Cultural Stations	图书馆 Libraries	博物馆 Museums	展览馆 Exhibition Buildings
2000	16	9	18	13	268	10	9	1
2001	16	15	18	13	226	10	11	1
2002	18	13	18	13	221	10	11	1
2003	20	11	18	13	220	10	11	1
2004	18	16	18	13	165	10	12	1
2005	22	12	19	13	204	12	12	1
2006	22	12	19	13	197	13	12	1
2007	22	12	19	13	195	14	12	1
2008	23	12	19	13	195	14	13	1
2009	22	12	20	13	198	16	35	1
2010	31	12	21	13	199	16	65	1
2011	30	11	21	15	190	15	65	1
2012	40	11	21	15	192	15	65	1
2013	48	11	21	15	189	15	65	1
2014	66	12	21	15	189	15	65	1
2015	90	11	20	15	189	15	67	1
2016	90	11	20	15	189	15	68	1
2017	158	11	20	15	189	15	68	1

12－08 全市分地区文化部门机构数(2017 年末)

Number of Culture Institutions by Region(End of 2017)

单位:个 (unit)

指　标	Item	剧场 Theaters	剧团 Opera Troupes	文化馆 Cultural Centers	文化站 Cultural Stations	图书馆 Libraries	博物馆 Museums	展览馆 Exhibition Buildings
全市	**Total**	**11**	**20**	**15**	**189**	**15**	**68**	**1**
市区	Urban District	11	18	12	136	12	61	1
#萧山区	Xiaoshan	–	1	1	27	1	9	–
余杭区	Yuhang	2	1	1	19	1	5	–
富阳区	Fuyang	–	1	1	24	1	3	–
临安区	Lin'an	–	–	1	18	1	1	–
桐庐县	Tonglu	–	1	1	14	1	2	–
淳安县	Chun'an	–	–	1	23	1	1	–
建德市	Jiande	–	1	1	16	1	4	–

12－09　市区文化事业单位数(1978－2017年)
Culture Institutions of Urban District (1978－2017)

单位:个　　　　　　　　　　　　　　　　　　　　　　　　　　　　　　　　　　　　　　　(unit)

年　份 Year	电影院 Cinemas	剧　团 Opera Troupes	剧　场 Theaters	文化馆 Cultural Centers	文化站 Cultural Stations	图书馆 Libraries	博物馆 Museums
1978	7	13	6	5	–	2	1
1979	8	14	7	5	27	2	1
1980	8	15	7	5	37	2	1
1981	8	17	7	6	40	2	1
1982	9	17	7	6	45	3	1
1983	9	15	3	6	46	3	1
1984	9	15	4	6	49	3	1
1985	8	16	9	6	47	3	2
1986	8	15	8	6	48	3	2
1987	8	15	9	6	38	3	2
1988	7	14	9	6	50	3	2
1989	7	14	9	6	48	2	2
1990	9	14	9	5	48	3	2
1991	10	14	8	5	48	3	2
1992	11	14	8	5	48	3	6
1993	10	14	9	5	42	3	6
1994	11	13	9	5	48	3	6
1995	11	13	9	5	67	3	6
1996	10	13	8	5	55	3	6
1997	10	13	8	5	52	3	6
1998	9	13	8	6	55	3	7
1999	9	13	6	6	52	3	8
2000	8	12	6	6	52	3	9
2001	49	14	11	8	89	5	11
2002	–	14	10	8	90	4	11
2003	19	14	11	13	92	4	11
2004	18	14	14	8	93	5	12
2005	16	15	10	8	94	7	12
2006	16	15	10	8	94	8	12
2007	16	15	10	8	92	9	12
2008	18	15	11	8	92	9	13
2009	15	16	11	8	95	11	34
2010	25	17	11	8	96	11	54
2011	23	17	10	10	94	10	54
2012	31	17	10	10	96	10	54
2013	31	17	11	10	94	10	54
2014	55	18	11	11	118	11	57
2015	78	18	11	11	118	11	59
2016	78	18	11	11	118	11	60
2017	146	18	11	12	136	12	61

12-10 分地区艺术表演团体演出情况(2017年)
Basic Statistics on Performance of Art Troupes by Region(2017)

指标	Item	艺术表演场所演出场次(场) Number of Performances in Artistic Performance Place (scene)	艺术表演场所演出收入(万元) Income of Performances in Artistic Performance Place (10000 yuan)	剧团演出场次(场) Number of Performances of Opera Troupes (scene)	农村(场) Rural Areas (scene)	剧团演出观众人数(万人次) Number of Spectators of Opera Troupes (10000 person-times)	剧团演出收入(万元) Income of Performances of Opera Troupes (10000 yuan)
全市	**Total**	**1197**	**2840**	**5665**	**2550**	**505.42**	**11721.5**
为上年(%)	As Compared with the Preceding Year (%)	76.7	121.8	100.8	126.4	98.1	133
市区	Urban District	1197	2840	5154	2117	401.82	11442.5
#萧山区	Xiaoshan	-	-	56	30	4.48	94.4
余杭区	Yuhang	50	-	193	172	32	320
富阳区	Fuyang	-	-	171	149	34.2	217
临安区	Lin'an	-	-	-	-	-	-
桐庐县	Tonglu	-	-	183	133	33.6	159
淳安县	Chun'an	-	-	-	-	-	-
建德市	Jiande	-	-	328	300	70	120

12－11　图书出版数量(2016－2017 年)
Number of Books Published(2016－2017)

项　目　Item	本版图书种数(种) Number of Publications (kind)		租型图书种数(种) Number of Publications for Lease (kind)		总印数(万册、万份) Total Printed Copies (1000 copies)		总印张(千印张) Total Printed Sheets (1000 sheets)	
	2016	2017	2016	2017	2016	2017	2016	2017
图书总计 Total	**13412**	**13822**	**485**	**453**	**39309.53**	**39392.74**	**2868085.62**	**2886863.09**
使用《中国标准书号》部分合计 Publication wirh " China Standard Book Number"	13331	13770	485	453	39241.25	39303.03	2865370.71	2878336.46
#哲学 Philosophy	118	148	–	–	96.23	94.58	13064.65	12830.97
社会科学总论 General Social Science	229	190	–	–	100.22	115.35	14094.11	15272.48
文化、科学、教育、体育 Culture, Science, Education and Sports	6895	7029	445	449	30259.10	28979.42	2054432.06	1968945.61
文学 Literature	1891	2053	–	–	5167.45	5372.14	440667.42	470642.58
艺术 Arts	1535	1698	36	–	735.51	725.87	68303.78	77296.37
自然科学总论 General Natural Science	44	17	–	–	30.27	16.41	4017.93	3685.84
不使用《中国标准书号》部分合计 Publications without " China Standard Book Number"	81	52	–	–	68.28	89.71	2714.91	8526.63

12－12　幼儿园基本情况(1978－2017年)

Basic Statistics on Kindergartens(1978－2017)

单位:人 (person)

年　份 Year	园　数(个) Kindergartens(unit)	在园幼儿数 Number of Children	教职员工数 Teachers and Staff	教　师 Number of Full－time Teachers
1978	266	37597	2570	1439
1979	216	59245	3731	2201
1980	518	82182	4763	3398
1981	676	82808	5275	3691
1982	853	95733	6357	4269
1983	1034	95676	6271	4135
1984	1749	112095	7238	4900
1985	1743	115766	7360	5278
1986	1607	118792	7898	5659
1987	1678	133773	8622	6335
1988	1541	139883	9221	6608
1989	1397	132947	9595	6849
1990	1526	136277	9808	7167
1991	1422	150982	10472	7388
1992	1431	133773	9240	6487
1993	1328	171005	10779	7886
1994	1470	165860	10718	7891
1995	1493	149497	10102	7943
1996	1437	150587	10203	7625
1997	1504	146530	10480	7743
1998	1695	153035	10691	7956
1999	1787	156372	10719	8107
2000	2037	168414	11740	8770
2001	1249	174204	11447	7880
2002	1268	175891	11988	8086
2003	1285	176862	13702	9076
2004	1098	186472	14991	9544
2005	1188	188991	16161	10288
2006	1188	195552	17550	11053
2007	1071	212754	19330	12168
2008	1037	235867	21193	12917
2009	972	246336	22970	14211
2010	969	267352	25525	15203
2011	970	271128	27458	16023
2012	914	283421	29843	17811
2013	860	285406	32037	18945
2014	881	295036	35212	20088
2015	910	313385	38238	21404
2016	930	325495	40833	22955
2017	960	336343	43692	24628

12－13 小学基本情况(1978－2017年)

Basic Statistics on Primary Schools(1978－2017)

单位:人 (person)

年份 Year	学校数(个) Number of Schools (unit)	在校学生数 Enrolment	毕业生数 Graduates	教职员工数 Number of Teachers and Staff	专职教师数 Number of Full－time Teachers
1978	4959	605137	－	24103	22291
1979	4850	577811	－	25089	23220
1980	4781	560244	－	25388	22902
1981	4668	525503	－	22468	20832
1982	4528	479264	－	22213	20289
1983	4417	444301	－	20842	18945
1984	4345	427763	－	20496	18500
1985	4286	414839	－	20945	18415
1986	4250	413507	－	20796	18464
1987	4205	405856	－	21067	18751
1988	4137	426842	－	21658	19236
1989	4106	459162	－	22660	20177
1990	4077	460514	－	20542	18099
1991	3972	453055	－	20781	18369
1992	3654	450496	－	21452	19067
1993	3473	477026	－	22141	19775
1994	3352	504867	－	22751	20462
1995	3172	513988	－	23743	21380
1996	3006	525674	－	24553	22197
1997	2762	538390	－	25269	23022
1998	2395	532845	－	25718	23499
1999	1996	512874	－	26350	24120
2000	1659	485679	100405	25938	23876
2001	1354	467982	93365	25535	23179
2002	1197	456535	89752	25425	23138
2003	1044	448969	84051	25304	22955
2004	897	447971	74872	25396	23066
2005	791	458942	75337	25793	23541
2006	605	459529	79070	26040	23848
2007	437	456152	81767	26455	24251
2008	418	452143	82620	26894	24743
2009	417	445132	80441	27445	25424
2010	408	453897	76126	27881	25709
2011	409	465289	73465	27862	26395
2012	415	472613	74547	25620	27777
2013	419	483489	73682	30373	28949
2014	421	502688	73244	31490	30139
2015	443	524513	71398	32815	31280
2016	447	543038	77726	33873	32549
2017	458	560411	84615	35510	34150

12－14 初中基本情况(1978－2017年)

Basic Statistics on Junior Middle Schools(1978－2017)

单位:人 (person)

年 份 Year	学校数(个) Number of Schools (unit)	在校学生数 Enrolment	毕业生数 Graduates	专职教师数 Number of Full－time Teachers
1978	254	247209	–	11978
1979	363	208484	–	11020
1980	369	204073	–	10695
1981	359	194024	–	10015
1982	367	193135	–	10107
1983	370	190221	–	9948
1984	368	192971	–	9679
1985	361	196889	–	9799
1986	376	199638	–	9821
1987	385	195426	–	10264
1988	380	170079	–	10055
1989	376	151223	–	9825
1990	382	160111	–	9564
1991	387	185590	–	10020
1992	367	212022	–	10603
1993	365	203896	–	10876
1994	371	205388	–	11495
1995	373	216300	–	12058
1996	374	229466	–	12810
1997	368	227809	–	13370
1998	359	222191	–	13493
1999	339	239174	–	13723
2000	330	269484	68347	14529
2001	314	285203	75722	15685
2002	315	282951	91056	15758
2003	316	268824	98412	15836
2004	303	252291	93042	16042
2005	289	241374	90094	16205
2006	263	235527	85436	16374
2007	262	238252	76194	16591
2008	260	244464	74827	16965
2009	252	241899	77268	17317
2010	245	236014	78379	17795
2011	246	223545	78431	17652
2012	244	215701	75489	17992
2013	241	213452	71006	18260
2014	241	213936	67988	18671
2015	243	211323	69200	18909
2016	249	215756	69674	19469
2017	251	224797	69084	20144

12-15 高中基本情况(1978-2017年)

Basic Statistics on Senior High Schools(1978-2017)

单位:人 (person)

年份 Year	学校数(个) Number of Schools (unit)	在校学生数 Enrolment	毕业生数 Graduates	专职教师数 Number of Full-time Teachers
1978	352	102815	-	5235
1979	182	58866	-	3471
1980	151	43661	-	3173
1981	118	34606	-	2825
1982	113	35136	-	2740
1983	111	38580	-	2740
1984	105	43167	-	2781
1985	104	47510	-	3016
1986	95	46379	-	2972
1987	92	44697	-	3006
1988	89	42196	-	2947
1989	88	39994	-	2898
1990	86	39829	-	2922
1991	82	37809	-	2896
1992	74	34620	-	2791
1993	72	32483	-	2641
1994	75	35720	-	2673
1995	72	40771	-	2880
1996	70	43692	-	3135
1997	69	47975	-	3388
1998	75	55688	-	3693
1999	82	64459	-	4172
2000	85	73049	17484	4745
2001	88	79632	22012	5262
2002	81	91635	22630	6126
2003	77	108116	25429	6879
2004	81	115303	30630	7510
2005	80	120883	34486	8041
2006	82	124177	39484	8421
2007	80	122939	39805	8542
2008	76	120294	40551	8646
2009	75	118057	41408	8751
2010	72	116983	39319	8871
2011	71	117089	38579	9061
2012	70	115652	38623	9069
2013	70	113894	37810	9125
2014	72	110478	38489	9378
2015	75	109983	37303	9630
2016	77	110431	36022	10016
2017	80	113054	34860	10430

12－16　中等专业学校基本情况（1978－2017年）
Basic Statistics on Specialized Secondary Schools（1978－2017）

单位：人　　(person)

年　份 Year	学校数(个) Number of Schools (unit)	在校学生数 Enrolment	毕业生数 Graduates	教职员工数 Teachers and Staff	专职教师数 Number of Full－time Teachers
1978	26	8711	－	3044	1080
1979	27	11093	－	2601	1124
1980	26	9453	－	2450	1101
1981	35	7309	－	3122	1276
1982	37	8284	－	3694	1529
1983	37	10516	－	3716	1604
1984	42	13419	－	4194	1758
1985	46	16527	－	5095	1959
1986	50	19114	－	5641	2336
1987	52	20929	－	6081	2623
1988	51	22117	－	6144	2741
1989	54	23302	－	6602	2888
1990	55	23564	－	6679	2948
1991	55	23331	－	6584	2770
1992	55	26373	－	6786	2825
1993	56	30336	－	6732	2780
1994	57	36079	－	6881	2840
1995	57	42784	－	6851	2888
1996	58	49593	－	6789	2904
1997	57	51752	－	6731	2896
1998	56	55796	－	6554	2746
1999	50	52272	－	5023	2272
2000	28	45238	15674	2950	1421
2001	26	32763	15202	2053	1051
2002	14	26255	13355	1251	566
2003	13	21735	11866	1058	457
2004	11	21262	6399	869	416
2005	10	20344	6661	893	443
2006	8	12540	5830	410	184
2007	8	8927	4849	414	194
2008	8	5514	4130	345	152
2009	8	4016	2025	233	65
2010	6	3999	1092	348	151
2011	5	4071	934	369	154
2012	5	3909	1252	376	150
2013	5	3656	1215	390	158
2014	7	3974	1077	469	226
2015	7	3968	1134	494	244
2016	7	4402	982	504	262
2017	7	4566	1348	386	177

12－17 高等学校基本情况(1978－2017年)

Basic Statistics on Regular Institutions of Higher Education(1978－2017)

单位:人 (person)

年份 Year	学校数(个) Number of Schools (unit)	招生数 Entrants	在校学生数 Enrolment	毕业生数 Graduates	教职员工数 Teachers and Staff	专职教师数 Number of Full－time Teachers
1978	9	－	13319	－	8966	3946
1979	12	－	17518	－	10182	4458
1980	13	－	23545	－	12400	5278
1981	13	－	28936	－	13090	5359
1982	13	－	25821	－	14363	6067
1983	14	－	27443	－	15267	6172
1984	16	－	31384	－	15889	6387
1985	20	－	36996	－	17507	7247
1986	22	－	40051	－	18968	7845
1987	21	－	39922	－	18965	7876
1988	21	－	40787	－	19582	8133
1989	21	－	40330	－	19680	8107
1990	21	－	39866	－	19495	8075
1991	21	－	42192	－	19489	7737
1992	19	－	43787	－	19841	7561
1993	19	－	51063	－	19787	7561
1994	19	－	59109	－	19903	7703
1995	20	－	63124	－	19883	7799
1996	20	－	66023	－	19693	7824
1997	20	－	69391	－	19540	7793
1998	17	－	76546	－	19320	7723
1999	18	－	89109	－	20136	8135
2000	32	46070	122386	17004	23791	10477
2001	33	63001	174894	22756	25805	11866
2002	34	74656	224048	27213	27307	13605
2003	35	85865	269798	41192	34508	18141
2004	36	96810	313599	53288	33325	18445
2005	36	101374	351918	63989	34816	19583
2006	36	103885	373563	80069	36929	21375
2007	36	110371	392770	90944	38843	23197
2008	36	114714	409559	97778	39762	24017
2009	36	114568	429774	96101	40420	24765
2010	37	113529	434811	101681	41582	25003
2011	38	117892	446721	104486	42222	25735
2012	38	121331	459181	107484	43216	26689
2013	38	123046	471820	108688	43992	27544
2014	38	122099	474652	110512	44710	28265
2015	39	139002	475558	125013	44825	28868
2016	39	138819	480953	128434	45512	29222
2017	39	143784	484070	128880	46337	29843

注:在校学生数包括各高校研究生。

a) Number of students include graduate students in all colleges and universities.

12－18　小学、幼儿园及特殊
Basic Statistics on Primary Schools,

单位：人

指　标	Item	全　市 Total	市　区 Urban District	萧山区 Xiaoshan
小　　学	**Primary Schools**			
学校数（所）	Number of Schools（unit）	458	364	74
班数（班）	Number of Classes（unit）	14850	13049	2412
在校学生数	Number of Students	560411	500308	93299
本年招生数	Number of New Students Enrollment	106381	96264	17662
本年毕业生数	Number of Graduates	84615	74269	15523
专职教师数	Full－time Teachers	34150	29786	5436
2018 年预计毕业生数	Number of Students Will Graduate in 2018	80589	70466	13769
幼儿园	**Kindergartens**			
园数（个）	Number of Kindergartens（unit）	960	836	182
班数（班）	Number of Classes（unit）	11523	10307	1803
在园幼儿数	Number of Children	336343	301489	51032
教师数	Full－time Teachers	24628	22344	3747
盲聋哑学校	**Schools for the Blind，Deaf and Deaf－mute**			
学校数（个）	Number of Schools（unit）	2	2	－
在校学生数	Number of Students	392	392	－
本年招生数	Number of New Students Enrollment	84	84	－
本年毕业生数	Number of Graduates	104	104	－
专职教师数	Number of Full－time Teachers	156	156	－
弱智学校	**Schools for Weaken in Intelligence**			
学校数（个）	Number of Schools（unit）	12	9	1
在校学生数	Number of Students	1172	1034	243
本年招生数	Number of New Students Enrollment	158	147	55
本年毕业生数	Number of Graduates	167	164	68
专职教师数	Number of Full－time Teachers	358	332	67
工读学校	**Reformatory Schools**			
学校数（个）	Number of Schools（unit）	1	1	－
在校学生数	Number of Students	315	315	－
本年招生数	Number of New Students Enrollment	171	171	－
本年毕业生数	Number of Graduates	144	144	－
专任教师数	Number of Full－time Teachers	63	63	－

教育基本情况(2017 年)
Kindergartens and Special Education(2017)

(person)

余杭区 Yuhang	富阳区 Fuyang	临安区 Lin'an	桐庐县 Tonglu	淳安县 Chun'an	建德市 Jiande
50	44	40	28	38	28
2435	1224	825	642	591	568
96870	44385	30196	24107	15254	20742
19421	7667	5387	4163	2399	3555
13835	7667	4850	3975	2904	3467
5428	2639	1812	1461	1623	1280
13226	7161	4568	4099	2661	3363
122	81	75	47	38	39
2000	838	650	429	319	468
61037	24171	18090	13747	8087	13020
4462	1807	1337	852	531	901
–	1	–	–	–	–
–	182	–	–	–	–
–	17	–	–	–	–
–	40	–	–	–	–
–	66	–	–	–	–
1	1	1	1	1	1
112	76	84	48	35	55
17	9	5	5	1	5
–	4	13	2	1	–
28	21	23	10	7	9
–	–	–	–	–	–
–	–	–	–	–	–
–	–	–	–	–	–
–	–	–	–	–	–
–	–	–	–	–	–

12－19 普通中学、职业中学

Basic Statistics on Senior, Junior High

单位:人

指 标	Item	全 市 Total	市 区 Urban District	萧山区 Xiaoshan
高 中	**Senior High Schools**			
学校数(所)	Number of Schools(unit)	80	64	10
在校学生数	Number of Students	113054	94270	19240
本年招生数	Number of New Students Enrollment	38493	32342	6535
本年毕业生数	Number of Graduates	34860	28314	6178
专职教师数	Full－time Teachers	10430	8590	1714
2018 年预计毕业生数	Number of Students Will Graduate in 2018	37155	30572	6307
初 中	**Junior High Schools**			
学校数(所)	Number of Schools(unit)	251	207	38
在校学生数	Number of Students	224797	195522	40016
本年招生数	Number of New Students Enrollment	81588	71453	14389
本年毕业生数	Number of Graduates	69084	59243	12254
专职教师数	Full－time Teachers	20144	17038	3219
2018 年预计毕业生数	Number of Students Will Graduate in 2018			
职业中学	**Vocational Schools**			
学校数(所)	Number of Schools(unit)	30	25	4
在校学生数	Number of Students	58902	51530	10441
本年招生数	Number of New Students Enrollment	19427	17081	3502
本年毕业生数	Number of Graduates	19793	17064	3902
专职教师数	Full－time Teachers	4436	3862	748
2018 年预计毕业生数	Number of Students Will Graduate in 2018	19594	16985	3474
技工学校	**Technical Schools**			
学校数(所)	Number of schools(unit)	17	16	1
在校学生数	Number of Students	24120	22829	2139
专职教师数	Full－time Teachers	1767	1656	239

和技工学校基本情况(2017 年)

Schools and Vacational, Technical Schools(2017)

(person)

余杭区 Yuhang	富阳区 Fuyang	临安区 Lin'an	桐庐县 Tonglu	淳安县 Chun'an	建德市 Jiande
12	7	5	5	5	6
13838	12193	7014	5115	5796	7873
4787	4141	2372	1756	1842	2553
4236	3997	2493	1710	2038	2798
1254	1090	636	551	557	732
4505	4080	2384	1691	2103	2789
35	17	18	12	15	17
36014	21196	13329	10344	8952	9979
13328	7666	4730	3725	3010	3400
10467	6350	4257	3245	3113	3483
2956	1637	1061	961	1009	1136
5	2	2	2	2	1
10617	6828	3590	2801	3264	1307
3620	2190	1172	871	1027	448
3310	2461	1115	849	1114	766
741	563	312	221	243	110
3395	2248	1180	1040	1098	471
–	1	1	–	–	1
–	495	820	–	–	1291
–	42	53	–	–	111

12 - 20 高等学校

Basic Statistics on Regular

单位:人

单位名称	Item	在校学生数 Enrolment	
		2017	为上年(%) As Compared with the Preceding Year(%)
全　　市	**Total**	**425769**	**100.8**
#市　　区	**Urban District**	**403745**	**100.9**
浙江大学	Zhejiang University	24897	103.2
杭州电子科技大学	Hangzhou Dianzi University	15822	97.84
浙江工业大学	Zhejiang Univesity of Technology	19159	95.36
浙江理工大学	Zhejiang Sci - Tech University	17687	100.2
浙江农林大学	Zhejiang Forestry University	14501	100.6
浙江中医药大学	Zhejiang University of Traditional Chinese Medicine	7947	110.2
杭州师范大学	Hangzhou Normal University	16709	94.51
浙江工商大学	Zhejiang Gongshang University	15294	100.1
中国美术学院	China Academy of Art	7069	95.76
中国计量大学	China JiLiang University	15172	100.4
浙江科技学院	Hangzhou Application Engineering and Technology College	16967	102
浙江广播电视大学	Zhejiang Radio & TV University	9152	91
浙江水利水电专科学校	Zhejiang Water Conservancy and Hydroelectricity College	9220	101.2
浙江财经大学	Zhejiang University of Finance and Economics	13489	101.7
浙江警察学院	Zhejiang Police College	4163	101.8
浙江传媒学院	Zhejiang Institute of Media and Communications	13678	99.96
浙江树人大学	Zhejiang Shuren University	15606	101.2
浙江大学城市学院	Zhejiang University City College	13154	100

注:本表不含在校研究生。

基本情况(2017 年)
Institutions of Higher Education(2017)

(person)

本年招生数 Entrants	本年毕业生数 Graduates	教职员工数 Number of Teachers and Staff 合 计 Total	其中:专职教师 Full - time Teachers
122720	**114590**	**46337**	**29843**
116969	**109086**	**44268**	**28371**
6326	5381	8523	3571
3945	4058	2169	1572
4557	5219	3068	2132
4492	4352	1999	1494
3790	3581	1586	1058
2258	1527	1078	724
4199	3842	2229	1550
3986	3885	1827	1405
1812	2035	1094	695
3862	3647	1535	1070
4273	3429	1383	1030
2965	3504	268	78
2769	2578	693	512
3503	3198	1564	1086
846	1002	487	247
3445	3109	1281	768
4136	3945	888	673
3440	3071	1083	745

a) Data in this table does not contain post - graduate students.

12－21 各级成人教育

Basic Statistics on

单位：人

指　标	Item	成人高等学历教育 Higher Education for Adults	成人高校 Adult Institutions of Higher Education	普通高校成人高等学历教育 Adult Higher Education in Ordinary Universities
全　　市	**Total**			
学校数(所)	Number of Schools(unit)	3	3	－
在校学生数	Number of Students	98351	11085	87266
本年招生数	Number of New Students Enrollment	42502	3673	38829
本年毕业生数	Number of Graduates	47642	5320	42322
教职员工数	Number of Teachers and Staff	423	423	－
#专职教师	#Full－time Teachers	167	167	－
市　　区	**Urban District**			
学校数(所)	Number of Schools(unit)	3	3	－
在校学生数	Number of Students	92243	11085	81158
本年招生数	Number of New Students Enrollment	39465	3673	35792
本年毕业生数	Number of Graduates	44932	5320	39612
教职员工数	Number of Teachers and Staff	423	423	－
#专职教师	#Full－time Teachers	167	167	－

基本情况(2017 年)
Various Adult Education(2017)

(person)

成人中等学历教育 Adult Secondary Education	成人中等专业 Adult Secondary Specialized	成人中学 Secondary Schools for Adults
7	5	2
16269	16136	133
7130	7130	-
6240	6123	117
693	684	9
375	336	39
7	5	2
16269	16136	133
7130	7130	-
6240	6123	117
693	684	9
375	336	39

12－22 医疗卫生机构数(1978－2017 年)

Number of Health Institutions(1978－2017)

单位:个 (unit)

年 份 Year	全市合计 Total	医 院 Hospitals	市区合计 Urban District	医 院 Hospitals
1978	1361	421	689	45
1979	1390	426	696	50
1980	1381	425	675	51
1981	1476	424	749	51
1982	1540	432	798	56
1983	1540	435	800	58
1984	1574	437	807	54
1985	1582	404	787	47
1986	1636	407	826	53
1987	1693	420	865	55
1988	1710	438	878	55
1989	1721	443	882	57
1990	1738	440	890	58
1991	1789	441	889	58
1992	1767	436	885	58
1993	1730	403	882	68
1994	1717	416	882	72
1995	1712	414	883	72
1996	1712	416	893	83
1997	1711	411	891	81
1998	1491	419	757	89
1999	1530	400	789	85
2000	1599	396	853	85
2001	1496	391	1072	191
2002	1817	116	1277	88
2003	1901	99	1323	73
2004	1985	114	1396	87
2005	2196	127	1604	97
2006	2570	134	1886	107
2007	2607	138	1872	104
2008	2544	141	1813	108
2009	2687	144	1887	111
2010	2819	151	1906	113
2011	2958	167	1992	122
2012	3017	198	2004	146
2013	4139	208	2233	156
2014	4198	218	2763	173
2015	4428	244	2982	198
2016	4691	277	3214	226
2017	4933	302	3906	273

12－23 医疗病床数(1978－2017年)

Number of Beds in Health Institutions(1978－2017)

单位:张 (bed)

年份 Year	全市 Total	医院 Hospitals	市区 Urban District	医院 Hospitals
1978	14042	11704	6588	5789
1979	15124	12682	7335	6282
1980	16317	13478	8244	6940
1981	17408	13576	9646	7185
1982	17179	14350	9194	7580
1983	17338	14584	9411	7833
1984	17694	14691	9536	7867
1985	19637	15010	11095	7933
1986	20555	16035	11657	8448
1987	21465	16770	12203	8863
1988	23394	17954	13204	9651
1989	24111	18363	13581	9773
1990	24121	18879	13219	10041
1991	24966	19444	13968	10437
1992	25606	20243	14206	10821
1993	25653	20884	14058	10982
1994	25984	20870	14231	11045
1995	26684	21360	14731	11336
1996	28141	22217	15427	12132
1997	26616	22341	15076	12190
1998	27327	23110	15530	12766
1999	26713	22952	14988	12691
2000	27166	23303	15496	13068
2001	27063	23520	20523	17770
2002	27609	22797	21200	18667
2003	29144	22036	22641	18205
2004	31738	24444	25008	20338
2005	33251	25907	26732	21931
2006	33972	27186	27172	23184
2007	36928	29987	29884	25664
2008	38114	31416	30663	26882
2009	40226	33094	32412	28031
2010	42828	36148	34693	30639
2011	45291	39363	36633	33291
2012	49471	44019	40534	37383
2013	52056	46636	42506	39489
2014	55779	50805	48406	44639
2015	63632	58400	55540	51672
2016	69452	63994	60666	56522
2017	75948	70187	69057	64524

12－24 全市

Number of

单位:个

指 标	Item	全 市 Total	市 区 Urban District
总 计	**Total**	**4933**	**3906**
一、医院	**Number of Hospitals**	**302**	**273**
1.综合医院	General Hospitals	141	130
2.中医医院	Hospitals of Chinese Medicine	39	32
3.中西医结合医院	Chinese Therapeutics with Western	6	5
4.专科医院	Specialized Hospitals	99	89
#口腔医院	Hospitals for Mouth	20	19
眼科医院	Hospitals for Eye	8	7
耳鼻喉科医院	ENT Hospitals	－	－
肿瘤医院	Tumor Hospitals	2	2
心血管病医院	Cardiovascular Hospitals	2	2
胸科医院	Chest Hospitals	－	－
血液病医院	Blood Diseases Hospitals	－	－
妇产(科)医院	Hospitals for Pregnant Woman	12	12
儿童医院	Children Hospitals	3	3
精神病医院	Mental Hospitals	7	4
传染病医院	Hospitals for Infectious Diseases	1	1
皮肤病医院	Dermatology Hospital	4	4
结核病医院	Tuberculosis Hospitals	－	－
麻疯病医院	Leprosy Hospitals	－	－
职业病医院	Occupational Disease Hospitals	－	－
骨科医院	Orthopaedics Hospitals	7	6
康复医院	Healing Hospitals	11	9
整型外科医院	Plastic Hospitals	1	1
美容医院	Beauty Hospitals	11	11
其他专科医院	Other Special Hospitals	10	8
5.护理院	Nursing Centers	17	17
二、基层医疗卫生机构	**Community Medical Institutions**	**4528**	**3549**
1.社区卫生服务中心(站)	Health Service Centers for Community	1275	1100
#社区卫生服务中心	Health Service Centers	134	127
社区卫生服务站	Health Service Stations	1141	973
2.卫生院	Health Service Centers	88	35
#街道卫生院	Rural Township Hospitals in Subdistrict	－	－
乡镇卫生院	Rural Township Hospitals in Country	88	35
3.村卫生室	Health Offices in Village	901	381
4.门诊部	Clinics	567	525
5.诊所、卫生所、医务室、护理站	Other Health Care Institutions	1697	1508
三、专业公共卫生机构	**Professional Public Health Institutions**	**60**	**43**
疾病预防控制中心	Centers for Disease Prevention and Control	15	12
专科疾病防治所(所、站)	Specialized Centers for Disease Prevention and Control(stations)	2	－
健康教育所(站、中心)	Education Center for Health(stations)	－	－
妇幼保健院(所、站)	Maternity and Child Care Centers(stations)	9	6
急救中心(站)	First－aid Centers(stations)	10	6
采供血机构	Blood Supplying Agencies	3	2
卫生监督所	Institutions of Public Health Inspection	16	13
计划生育服务机构	Family Planning Service Institutions	5	4
四、其他卫生机构	**Other Health Care Institutions**	**43**	**41**
疗养院	Sanatoriums	8	8
医学科学研究机构	Research Institutions of Medical Science	1	1
医学在职培训机构	Medical Training Organization for Incumbent	4	2
临床检验中心(所、站)	Clinical Laboratory Center	10	10
统计信息中心	Statistical Information Centers	2	2
其他	Other	18	18

医疗卫生机构数(2017 年末)
Health Institutions(End of 2017)

(unit)

萧山区 Xiaoshan	余杭区 Yuhang	富阳区 Fuyang	临安区 Lin'an	桐庐县 Tonglu	淳安县 Chun'an	建德市 Jiande
742	**554**	**455**	**457**	**326**	**315**	**386**
54	**25**	**14**	**28**	**13**	**8**	**8**
42	12	7	11	6	3	2
5	2	4	9	3	2	2
–	–	–	–	–	–	1
7	7	3	7	4	3	3
2	2	1	1	–	1	–
–	1	1	–	–	–	1
–	–	–	–	–	–	–
–	–	–	–	–	–	–
–	–	–	–	–	–	–
–	–	–	–	–	–	–
–	–	–	–	–	–	–
–	1	–	1	–	–	–
–	–	–	–	–	–	–
–	1	1	1	1	1	1
–	–	–	–	–	–	–
1	–	–	–	–	–	–
–	–	–	–	–	–	–
–	–	–	–	–	–	–
–	–	–	–	–	–	–
–	2	–	2	1	–	–
1	–	–	–	–	1	1
–	–	–	–	–	–	–
–	–	–	1	–	–	–
3	–	–	1	2	–	–
–	4	–	1	–	–	–
680	**517**	**433**	**425**	**310**	**298**	**371**
319	181	169	77	107	48	20
29	20	25	5	3	2	2
290	161	144	72	104	46	18
–	–	10	25	10	21	22
–	–	–	–	–	–	–
–	–	10	25	10	21	22
116	–	115	150	122	172	226
55	89	26	12	20	6	16
190	247	113	161	51	51	87
6	**5**	**4**	**4**	**3**	**8**	**6**
1	1	1	1	1	1	1
–	–	–	–	–	1	1
–	–	–	–	–	–	–
–	1	1	1	1	1	1
2	1	1	1	–	3	1
1	–	–	–	–	–	1
1	1	1	1	1	1	1
1	1	–	–	–	1	–
2	**7**	**4**	**–**	**–**	**1**	**1**
1	1	4	–	–	–	–
–	–	–	–	–	–	–
–	1	–	–	–	1	1
1	5	–	–	–	–	–
–	–	–	–	–	–	–
–	–	–	–	–	–	–

12－25 全市

Total Number of

单位:张

指　　标	Item	全　市 Total	市区 Urban District
总　　计	**Total**	**75948**	**69057**
一、医院	**Number of Hospitals**	**70187**	**64524**
1. 综合医院	General Hospitals	38923	35817
2. 中医医院	Hospitals of Chinese Medicine	9502	8056
3. 中西医结合医院	Chinese Therapeutics with Western	4328	4078
4. 专科医院	Specialized Hospitals	15356	14495
#口腔医院	Stomatology Hospitals	316	301
眼科医院	Ophthalmology Hospitals	300	264
耳鼻喉科医院	ENT Hospitals	–	–
肿瘤医院	Tumor Hospitals	2615	2615
心血管病医院	Cardiovascular Hospitals	1048	1048
胸科医院	Chest Hospitals	–	–
血液病医院	Blood Diseases Hospitals	–	–
妇产(科)医院	Hospitals for Pregnant Woman	2006	2006
儿童医院	Children Hospitals	1633	1633
精神病医院	Mental Hospitals	2531	2051
传染病医院	Hospitals for Infectious Diseases	600	600
皮肤病医院	Dermatology Hospital	130	130
结核病医院	Tuberculosis Hospitals	–	–
麻疯病医院	Leprosy Hospitals	–	–
职业病医院	Occupational Disease Hospitals	–	–
骨科医院	Orthopaedics Hospitals	817	779
康复医院	Healing Hospitals	2097	1879
整型外科医院	Plastic Hospitals	120	120
美容医院	Beauty Hospitals	185	185
其他专科医院	Other Special Hospitals	958	884
5. 护理院	Nursing Centers	2078	2078
二、基层医疗卫生机构	**Community Medical Institutions**	**3787**	**3212**
1. 社区卫生服务中心(站)	Health Service Centers for Community	3120	3050
#社区卫生服务中心	Health Service Centers	3100	3050
社区卫生服务站	Health Service Stations	20	–
2. 卫生院	Health Service Centers	649	144
#街道卫生院	Rural Township Hospitals in Subdistrict	–	–
乡镇卫生院	Rural Township Hospitals in Country	649	144
3. 村卫生室	Health Offices in Village	–	–
4. 门诊部	Clinics	18	18
5. 诊所、卫生所、医务室、护理站	Other Health Care Institutions	–	–
三、专业公共卫生机构	**Professional Public Health Institutions**	**1270**	**617**
疾病预防控制中心	Centers for Disease Prevention and Control	–	–
专科疾病防治所(所、站)	Specialized Centers for Disease Prevention and Control(stations)	300	–
健康教育所(站、中心)	Education Center for Health(stations)	–	–
妇幼保健院(所、站)	Maternity and Child Care Centers(stations)	951	608
急救中心(站)	First－aid Centers(stations)	19	9
采供血机构	Blood Supplying Agencies	–	–
卫生监督所(中心)	Institutions of Public Health Inspection	–	–
计划生育服务机构	Family Planning Service Institutions	–	–
四、其他卫生机构	**Other Health Care Institutions**	**704**	**704**
#疗养院	Sanatoriums	704	704
医学科学研究机构	Research Institutions of Medical Science	–	–
医学在职培训机构	Medical Training Organization for Incumbent	–	–
临床检验中心(所、站)	Clinical Laboratory Center	–	–
统计信息中心	Statistical Information Centers	–	–
其他	Other	–	–

医疗病床数(2017 年末)

Beds in Health Institutions(End of 2017)

(bed)

萧山区 Xiaoshan	余杭区 Yuhang	富阳区 Fuyang	临安区 Lin'an	桐庐县 Tonglu	淳安县 Chun'an	建德市 Jiande
10005	**5480**	**4016**	**2981**	**1998**	**1989**	**2904**
9518	**4340**	**2750**	**2868**	**1719**	**1740**	**2204**
7149	2475	1521	1667	1171	965	970
1663	520	917	529	436	540	470
–	–	–	–	–	–	250
706	922	312	622	112	235	514
30	15	15	25	–	15	–
–	30	20	–	–	–	36
–	–	–	–	–	–	–
–	–	–	–	–	–	–
–	–	–	–	–	–	–
–	–	–	–	–	–	–
–	–	–	–	–	–	–
–	35	–	20	–	–	–
–	–	–	–	–	–	–
–	520	277	200	–	120	360
–	–	–	–	–	–	–
40	–	–	–	–	–	–
–	–	–	–	–	–	–
–	–	–	–	–	–	–
–	–	–	–	–	–	–
–	322	–	337	38	–	–
152	–	–	–	–	100	118
–	–	–	–	–	–	–
–	–	–	20	–	–	–
484	–	–	20	74	–	–
–	423	–	50	–	–	–
427	**770**	**594**	**84**	**176**	**99**	**300**
425	770	481	53	22	–	48
425	770	481	53	22	–	28
–	–	–	–	–	–	20
–	–	113	31	154	99	252
–	–	–	–	–	–	–
–	–	113	31	154	99	252
–	–	–	–	–	–	–
2	–	–	–	–	–	–
–	–	–	–	–	–	–
–	**250**	**338**	**29**	**103**	**150**	**400**
–	–	–	–	–	–	–
–	–	–	–	–	–	300
–	–	–	–	–	–	–
–	250	338	20	103	150	90
–	–	–	9	–	–	10
–	–	–	–	–	–	–
–	–	–	–	–	–	–
–	–	–	–	–	–	–
60	**120**	**334**	**–**	**–**	**–**	**–**
60	120	334	–	–	–	–
–	–	–	–	–	–	–
–	–	–	–	–	–	–
–	–	–	–	–	–	–
–	–	–	–	–	–	–
–	–	–	–	–	–	–

12－26 医院诊疗
Number of

指　标	Item	机构数(个) Number of Institutions (unit)	诊疗人次数(万人次) Total Number of Patients Treate (10000 person－times)
总　计	**Total**	**4933**	**12869.87**
一、医院	**Number of Hospitals**	**302**	**6913.05**
1.综合医院	General Hospitals	141	4259.85
2.中医医院	Hospitals of Chinese Medicine	39	1055.40
3.中西医结合医院	Chinese Therapeutics with Western	6	467.66
4.专科医院	Specialized Hospitals	99	1123.30
#口腔医院	Stomatology Hospitals	20	151.55
眼科医院	Ophthalmology Hospitals	8	25.65
耳鼻喉科医院	ENT Hospitals	–	–
肿瘤医院	Tumor Hospitals	2	63.87
心血管病医院	Cardiovascular Hospitals	2	45.55
胸科医院	Chest Hospitals	–	–
血液病医院	Blood Diseases Hospitals	–	–
妇产(科)医院	Hospitals for Pregnant Woman	12	225.35
儿童医院	Children Hospitals	3	366.82
精神病医院	Mental Hospitals	7	47.54
传染病医院	Hospitals for Infectious Diseases	1	73.96
皮肤病医院	Dermatology Hospital	4	21.37
结核病医院	Tuberculosis Hospitals	–	–
麻风病医院	Leprosy Hospitals	–	–
职业病医院	Occupational Disease Hospitals	–	–
骨科医院	Orthopaedics Hospitals	7	34.84
康复医院	Healing Hospitals	11	7.06
整型外科医院	Plastic Hospitals	1	5.67
美容医院	Beauty Hospitals	11	37.66
其他专科医院	Other Special Hospitals	10	16.40
5.护理院	Nursing Centers	17	6.82
二、基层医疗卫生机构	**Community Medical Institutions**	**4528**	**5712.95**
1.社区卫生服务中心(站)	Health Service Centers for Community	1275	3639.23
#社区卫生服务中心	Health Service Centers	134	3545.09
社区卫生服务站	Health Service Stations	1141	94.14
2.卫生院	Health Service Centers	88	459.27
#乡镇卫生院	Rural Township Hospitals in Country	88	459.27
3.村卫生室	Health Offices in Village	901	182.86
4.门诊部	Clinics	567	875.17
5.诊所、卫生所、医务室	Other Health Care Institutions	1697	556.43
三、专业公共卫生机构	**Professional Public Health Institutions**	**60**	**225.58**
专科疾病防治院(所、站)	Specialized Centers for Disease Prevention and Control(stations)	2	7.72
妇幼保健院(所、站)	Maternity and Child Care Centers(stations)	9	205.89
四、其他机构	**Other Institutions**	**43**	**18.29**
疗养院	Sanatoriums	8	18.29

次数和入院人数（2017 年）
Hospital Patients(2017)

门、急诊人次数(万人次) Out - Patients and Emergency Patients (10000 person - times)	入院人数 (万人) Hospital Admissions(10000 person)	每百门急诊次入院人数(人) Hospital Admissions Per 100 Patient - time (person)
12523.99	**2291927**	**2.06**
6893.65	**2171047**	**3.15**
4251.72	1340410	3.15
1047.82	252713	2.41
467.66	121469	2.6
1119.88	444931	3.97
150.59	1540	0.1
25.39	10650	4.19
-	-	-
63.87	120364	18.84
45.55	15407	3.38
-	-	-
-	-	-
224.64	105214	4.68
366.82	88704	2.42
47.52	23287	4.9
73.22	24822	3.39
21.25	610	0.29
-	-	-
-	-	-
-	-	-
34.84	18771	5.39
6.87	12244	17.82
5.67	3790	6.69
37.40	10243	2.74
16.24	9285	5.72
6.56	11524	17.56
5389.30	**21287**	**0.05**
3489.19	12865	0.04
3395.50	12651	0.04
93.69	214	0.02
451.70	8406	0.19
451.70	8406	0.19
178.62	-	-
726.57	16	-
543.22	-	-
225.58	**60276**	**2.82**
7.72	758	0.98
205.89	59518	2.89
15.46	**39317**	**25.43**
15.46	39317	25.43

12－27 全市

Total Number of

单位:人

指　　标	Item	全　市 Total	市　区 Urban District
总　　计	**Total**	**134633**	**122628**
一、卫生技术人员	Number of Medical Technical Personnel	110395	100478
1. 执业(助理)医师	Licensed (Assistant) Doctor	41833	38333
#执业医师	Licensed Doctor	38707	35808
2. 注册护士	Registered Nurse	46343	42580
3. 药剂师	Druggist	6924	6117
4. 技师人员	Checking Member	6183	5664
#检验师	Docimaster	4401	4014
5. 其他	Others	9112	7784
二、其他技术人员	Other Medical Technical Personnel	6259	5943
三、管理人员	Managerial Personnel	5712	5269
四、工勤人员	Logistics Worker	11537	10601

卫生事业人员数(2017 年末)
Medical Technical Personnel(End of 2017)

(person)

萧山区 Xiaoshan	余杭区 Yuhang	富阳区 Fuyang	临安区 Lin'an	桐庐县 Tonglu	淳安县 Chun'an	建德市 Jiande
16266	**11434**	**6627**	**5050**	**4521**	**3074**	**4410**
13342	9458	5398	4136	3753	2553	3611
4729	3626	2226	1683	1233	1043	1224
4112	3202	1893	1439	1022	863	1014
5535	3717	2015	1434	1340	936	1487
976	640	289	330	323	204	280
601	559	259	233	191	132	196
441	401	172	165	143	98	146
1501	916	609	456	666	238	424
522	349	246	355	145	76	95
706	443	271	150	204	74	165
1570	1184	607	303	397	203	336

12－28　卫生技术人员(1978－2017年)

Number of Medical Technical Personnel(1978－2017)

单位:人　　　　(person)

年　份 Year	全　市 Total	执业(助理)医师 Number of Licensed (Assistant) Doctors	注册护士 Registered Nurses	市　区 Urban District	执业(助理)医师 Number of Licensed (Assistant) Doctors	注册护士 Registered Nurses
1978	19059	7375	3483	10867	4346	2510
1979	20060	7539	3536	11779	4733	2632
1980	21110	8311	3885	12376	5179	2804
1981	22737	9284	4139	13697	5946	3032
1982	23558	9883	4369	14221	6204	3193
1983	24914	10833	4562	15213	6990	3352
1984	25648	11291	4817	15807	7393	3487
1985	25593	11503	5071	15840	7644	3705
1986	26489	12623	5391	16543	8239	3940
1987	27663	12369	5805	17361	8329	4156
1988	28676	13674	6938	18022	8710	4801
1989	29791	14177	7348	18619	9146	5085
1990	30990	14483	7822	19231	9374	5397
1991	32169	14858	8153	19630	9494	5610
1992	32628	14842	8417	19690	9373	5736
1993	33172	15181	8643	19708	9499	5797
1994	33964	15465	8979	19907	9472	5940
1995	34245	16465	9531	19943	9607	6249
1996	34946	16789	9794	20695	9889	6508
1997	35423	17112	10019	20728	9902	6571
1998	35857	16022	10577	21035	9452	6788
1999	35256	16668	10587	20519	9610	6856
2000	35487	16317	11186	20344	9050	7300
2001	36643	16994	11576	28293	12968	9343
2002	37193	16092	11922	28818	12332	9653
2003	39019	16614	12460	30299	12731	10161
2004	39816	16770	13248	30886	12894	10840
2005	42353	17833	14514	33206	13802	12034
2006	45375	18831	15557	35904	14689	12986
2007	49780	20701	17455	39860	16290	14601
2008	52379	21223	18702	42015	16747	15556
2009	56270	22753	20997	45219	17996	17530
2010	61117	24345	23418	49232	19414	19481
2011	65869	25773	25231	53008	20566	20949
2012	71618	27369	28382	57971	22004	23760
2013	78340	29686	30996	63359	23886	25808
2014	85614	31977	34724	74064	27675	30528
2015	93036	34832	38182	80799	30316	33672
2016	101194	38172	42011	88076	33344	37154
2017	110395	41833	46343	100478	38333	42580

12－29 体育运动情况(2014－2017 年)

Basic Statistics on Sports Activities(2014－2017)

单位:人 (person)

指　　标	Item	2014 年	2015 年	2016 年	2017 年
一、年末体委工作人员数	**Workers in Sports Commissions at Year－end**	**685**	**695**	**705**	**696**
#教练员	#Full－time Coaches	131	151	152	157
二、等级裁判员发展人数	**Number of Referees in Grades**	**520**	**266**	**78**	**－**
#女	#Female	157	66	44	－
一级裁判员	First Grade Referees	55	34	28	－
二级裁判员	Second Grade Referees	465	232	50	－
三级裁判员	Third Grade Referees	－	－	－	－
三、等级运动员发展人数	**Number of Athletes in Grades**	**425**	**349**	**469**	**509**
#女	#Female	183	149	182	223
一级运动员	First Grade Athlete	124	64	78	113
二级运动员	Second Grade Athlete	301	285	391	396
三级运动员	Third Grade Athlete	－	－	－	－

主要统计指标解释

文化事业机构 指从事专业文化工作和为专业文化工作服务的独立建制的单独核算的单位。不包括这些单位另外举办独立核算的其他机构和各部门的业余文化组织。

艺术表演团体 指从事戏曲、音乐、舞蹈、杂技等专业艺术表演,有独立帐户,实行单独核算的团体。不包括半工半艺、半农半艺和民间职业剧团。

普通高等学校 指按照国家规定的设置标准和审批程序批准举办,通过国家统一招生考试,招收高中毕业生为主要培养对象,实施高等教育的全日制大学、独立设置的学院和高等专科学校、短期职业大学。

成人高等学校 指按照国家有关规定审批,招收通过全国成人高教统一招生考试的具有高中毕业或同等学历的在职从业人员利用脱产、半脱产、业余或函授等多种形式对其实施高等学历教育,培养高等教育专科或本科毕业水平的专门人才,修业年限、课程设置和总学时数均按高等学历教育要求付诸实施的学校。包括广播电视大学、职工高等学校、农民高等学校、管理干部学院、教育学院、独立设置的函授学院等。

小学学龄儿童入学率 指调查范围内已入小学学习的学龄儿童占校内外学龄儿童总数(包括弱智儿童在内,但不包括盲聋哑儿童)的比重。计算公式:

$$小学学龄儿童入学率 = \frac{已入学的小学学龄儿童数}{校内外小学学龄儿童总数} * 100\%$$

等级运动员人数 指经考核正式批准授予等级运动员称号的人数。运动员等级分为国际级运动健将、运动健将、一级运动员、二级运动员、三级运动员、少年级运动员。

等级裁判员人数 指经考核正式批准授予等级裁判员称号的人数。裁判员等级分为国际裁判、国家级裁判、一级裁判、二级裁判、三级裁判。

卫生机构 卫生机构是指从卫生行政部门取得《医疗机构执业许可证》,或从民政、工商行政、机构编制管理部门取得法人单位登记证书,为社会提供医疗保健、疾病控制、卫生监督等服务或从事医学科研、医学教育等卫生单位和卫生社会团体。不包括卫生行政机构、香港和澳门特别行政区以及台湾所属卫生机构。

卫生技术人员 卫生技术人员包括执业(助理)医师、注册护士、药剂人员、检验和影像技师(士、员)等卫生专业人员。

执业(助理)医师、执业(中)药师和注册护士 执业(助理)医师、执业(中)药师和注册护士是指领取医师、药师执业证书和注册护士证书的人员。不包括从事管理工作的医师、药师和护士。

Explanatory Notes on Main Statistical Indicators

Culture Institutions refer to units which have their own organizational system and independent accounting system and specialize in or serve cultural development. They exclude other establishments run by these cultural institutions and amateur cultural groups established by various departments.

Art Troupe refers to the troupe which is engaged in drama, opera, music, dance, acrobatics or other art performance, opens independent accounts with banks and has self – supporting accounting system; excluding the troupes which are engaged partly in industrial or agricultural activities, partly in art performance and the professional troupes organized by the people.

Regular Institutions of Higher Education refer to educational establishments set up according to the government evaluation and approval procedures, enrolling graduates from senior secondary schools and providing higher education courses and training for senior professionals, They include full – time universities, colleges, high professional schools and short – term professional universities.

Institutions of Higher Education for Adults refer to educational establishments, set up in line with relevant rules approved by the government, enrolling staff and workers with senior secondary school or equivalent education, and providing higher education courses in many forms of full – time, part – time, space – time, or correspondence for adults. Professionals thus trained receive a qualification equivalent to graduates studying regular courses at regular universities, colleges and professional colleges. Institutions of higher learning for adults include Radio and TV universities, schools of high education for staff and workers and peasants, colleges for management cadres, pedagogical colleges, independent correspondence colleges.

Enrollment Rate of Primary School – age Children refer to the proportion of school – age children enrolled at schools to the total number of school – age children both in and outside schools (including retarded children, but excluding blind, deaf and mute children). The formula is:

$$\text{Enrollment Rate of Primary School – age Children} = \frac{\text{Total primary School – age Children at Schools}}{\text{Total Primary School – age Children Both at and Outside Schools}}$$

Number of Athletes in Grades refers to the number of athletes who have been given titles through examination. The titles of athletes include international masters of sports, masters of sports, first – grade, second – grade and third – grade sportsmen and young athletes.

Number of Referees in Grades refers to the number of referees who have been given titles after examination. They are classified as international referees, national referees and referees of the first, second and third grades.

Health Institutions refers to the Institutions and Society organization that get the registered license of health and medical institution from the health adiministration department, or get the registered license of units from civil administration department, industry and business administration and organization management department, and offers medical treatment, controlling of disease, supervision of sanitation. Health institution excludes health administration department and Institutions of Hong Kong, Macao, and Taiwan.

Medical Technical Personnel include registered (Assistant) doctor, registered nurse, druggist, checking members and photo artificer.

Licensed(Assistant) Doctor, Licensed Druggist and Licensed Nurse refers to the personnel who get the licence of doctor, druggist and nurse, the management staff excluded.

十三、人民生活 物价、民政

PEOPLE'S LIVELIHOOD, PRICE INDICES AND CIVIL ADMINISTRATION

13 人民生活、物价、民政
People's Livelihood, Price Indices and Civil Administration

主要统计指标
Major Statistical Indicators

非私营单位就业人员工资总额	Total Wages of Employed Persons of Non-private Units	2646.72	亿元	(100 million yuan)
非私营单位就业人员平均工资	Annual Average Wages of Employed Persons of Non-private Units	93891	元	(yuan)
全体居民人均可支配收入	Per Capita Disposable Income of Urban and Rural Residents	49832	元	(yuan)
为上年	As Compared with the Preceding Year	108.1	%	(%)
城镇常住居民人均可支配收入	Per Capita Disposable Income of Permanent Urban Residents	56276	元	(yuan)
为上年	As Compared with the Preceding Year	107.8	%	(%)
农村常住居民人均可支配收入	Per Capita Disposable Income of Permanent Rural Residents	30397	元	(yuan)
为上年	As Compared with the Preceding Year	108.9	%	(%)
市区居民消费价格指数	Consume Price Index of Urban District	102.5	上年=100	(Preceding Year=100)
市区商品零售价格指数	Commodity Retail Price Index of Urban District	101.0	上年=100	(Preceding Year=100)
工业生产者出厂价格指数	Producer Price Indices for Industrial Products	104.4	上年=100	(Preceding Year=100)

13－01 居民家庭人均收入支出(2015－2017年)
Per Capita Income and Expenditure of Households(2015－2017)

单位:元 (yuan)

项目 Item	全体居民 Urban and Rural Residents			城镇常住居民 Permanent Urban Residents			农村常住居民 Permanent Rural Residents		
	2015	2016	2017	2015	2016	2017	2015	2016	2017
一、可支配收入 Disposable Income	42642	46116	49832	48316	52185	56276	25719	27908	30397
工资性收入 Icome from Wages and salaries	25619	26832	28680	28891	30090	32144	15860	17059	18232
经营净收入 Net Buisness Income	5036	5232	5609	4502	4607	4893	6628	7108	7770
财产净收入 Net Income from Property	5377	6214	6574	6851	7906	8329	982	1137	1280
转移净收入 Net Income from Transfer	6610	7838	8969	8072	9582	10910	2249	2604	3115
二、消费支出 Expenditure	30181	31905	34146	33818	35686	38179	19334	20563	21983
食品烟酒 Food, Tobacco and Liquor	8194	8948	9336	9171	9945	10412	5358	5957	6092
衣着 Clothing	1906	2034	1983	2157	2302	2233	1157	1228	1231
居住 Residence	8076	8588	9576	9111	9685	10710	4990	5297	6154
生活用品及服务 Daily Necessities and Services	1468	1646	1765	1622	1841	1963	1008	1062	1170
交通通信 Transportation and Communication	5254	4721	4855	5707	5050	5267	3904	3735	3612
教育文化娱乐 Education, Cultural and Recreation Service	2731	3302	3735	3141	3815	4346	1507	1762	1894
医疗保健 Medicine and Medical Service	1764	1898	2119	2002	2143	2332	1055	1163	1474
其他用品及服务 Other Supplies and Services	788	768	777	907	905	916	355	359	356

13-02 城镇住户调查情况(1978-2017 年)

Basic Conditions of Urban Households (1978-2017)

年份 Year	调查户数(户) Number of Households Surveyed (household)	平均每户人口(人) Average Household Size (person)	平均每户就业人数(人) Average Number of Employed Persons Per Household(person)	年人均可支配收入(元) Per Capita Annual Disposable Income (yuan)	年人均消费支出(元) Per Capita Annual Consumption Expenditure(yuan)	人均住房建筑面积(平方米) Per Capita Living Space in City Areas (sq. m)
1978	28	4.20	2.89	338	301	
1979	28	4.19	2.77	396	365	
1980	28	4.18	2.79	521	491	
1981	100	3.97	2.37	540	513	
1982	100	3.90	2.35	532	532	
1983	100	3.90	2.42	578	535	11.7
1984	100	3.90	2.36	729	679	12.4
1985	150	3.53	2.26	1026	908	12.9
1986	150	3.49	2.27	1169	1072	13.2
1987	150	3.42	2.25	1260	1118	14.1
1988	200	3.41	2.16	1565	1515	14.1
1989	200	3.40	2.15	1764	1615	14.1
1990	200	3.37	2.15	1985	1685	14.5
1991	200	3.40	2.20	2128	1894	14.4
1992	200	3.28	2.14	2580	2296	14.8
1993	200	3.21	2.10	3525	3183	14.9
1994	200	3.31	2.10	5249	4559	15.9
1995	200	3.20	2.05	6301	5559	15.6
1996	200	3.20	2.00	7206	6095	15.9
1997	200	3.14	1.99	7896	6766	16.5
1998	300	3.12	1.93	8465	7235	18.8
1999	300	3.11	1.92	9085	7424	19.5
2000	300	3.10	1.83	9668	7790	19.9
2001	440	2.98	1.72	10896	8968	20.7
2002	500	2.93	1.53	11778	9215	21.7
2003	500	2.92	1.51	12898	9950	22.9
2004	500	2.92	1.48	14565	11213	23.7
2005	600	2.84	1.42	16601	13438	27.6
2006	600	2.81	1.44	19027	14472	28.0
2007	600	2.72	1.45	21689	14896	28.8
2008	600	2.75	1.29	24104	16719	29.9
2009	600	2.68	1.25	26864	18595	30.8
2010	600	2.70	1.25	30035	20219	30.9
2011	600	2.71	1.32	34065	22642	33.7
2012	600	2.69	1.31	37511	22800	34.4
2013	1920	2.79	1.51	40925	30659	34.9
2014	1920	2.79	1.53	44632	32165	35.1
2015	1920	2.79	1.48	48316	33818	35.5
2016	1920	2.80	1.49	52185	35686	35.8
2017	1920	2.91	1.48	56276	38179	36.4

注:2000 年及以前为主城区数据;2001-2012 年为包括萧山区和余杭区在内的市区数据;2013-2017 年为包括所有区、县(市)城乡住户一体化改革后新口径数据。

a) The data on the table include the main urban districts before 2000; The data include Xiaoshan district and Yuhang district in 2001-2012; The date include all districts and counties since 2013; The data in this table are calculated at new rage by the results of integrated survey of urban households and rural households sine 2013.

13－03 城镇居民家庭平均每百户耐用消费品拥有量(2010－2017年)

Number of Major Durable Consumer Goods Owned Per 100 Urban Households(2010－2017)

项目 Item	2010	2011	2012	2013	2014	2015	2016	2017
家用汽车 (辆) Family Car (unit)	22.8	31.2	34.3	40.2	45.4	48.7	52.3	55.8
摩托车 (辆) Motorcycle (unit)	4.5	4.1	4.0	6.6	6.8	5.4	5.0	4.8
电冰箱 (台) Refrigerator (unit)	102.3	102.5	102.5	88.0	92.3	92.2	97.6	99.9
洗衣机 (台) Washing Machine (unit)	96.2	96.3	96.6	82.6	86.8	86.9	92.6	94.6
热水器 (台) Water Heater (unit)	99.4	103.4	105.4	89.4	93.7	95.5	101.4	105.2
空调器 (台) Air Conditioner (unit)	214.6	212.0	214.7	189.6	201.5	207.3	226.6	235.3
彩色电视机 (台) Color TV Set (unit)	179.2	176.9	178.4	166.4	174.0	174.1	183.1	187.3
照相机 (架) Camera (unit)	54.8	62.1	63.5	50.6	54.4	51.5	48.4	49.9
计算机 (台) Computer (unit)	99.0	109.7	112.2	103.7	110.6	110.1	112.0	115.1
#接入互联网的计算机 (台) of which: Internet－connected computer (unit)	78.7	92.3	98.6	92.5	100.2	99.8	100.8	104.9
固定电话 (部) Telephone (set)	89.6	84.7	83.6	51.6	54.2	50.7	47.3	45.9
移动电话 (部) Mobile Phone (set)	193.6	211.0	213.1	217.4	227.9	229.9	242.1	245.4
#接入互联网的移动电话 (部) of which: Internet－connected Mobile Phone (set)				125.1	140.8	155.8	175.3	191.4

注:2010－2012年为包括萧山区和余杭区在内的市区数据;2013－2017年为包括所有区、县(市)城乡住户一体化改革后新口径数据。

a) The data include Xiaoshan district and Yuhang district in 2010－2012; The date include all districts and counties since 2013; The data in this table are calculated at new rage by the results of integrated survey of urban households and rural households sine 2013.

13－04　全市农村住户调查情况（1978－2017 年）

Basic Conditions of Rural Households（1978－2017）

年　份 Year	调查户数（户） Number of Households Surveyed (household)	平均每户人口（人） Average Number of Residents per Household (person)	平均每户就业人数（人） Average Number of Employed Persons Per Household (person)	人均可支配收入（元） Per Capita Annual Disposable Income of Rural Households (yuan)	人均消费支出（元） Per Capita Annual Consumption Expenditure (yuan)	人均住房建筑面积（平方米） Per Capita Floor Space (sq. m)
1978				162		
1979				204		
1980	60	4.72	2.93	250	287	23.3
1981	60	4.60	2.70	333	294	25.2
1982	60	4.43	2.73	405	328	26.3
1983	170	4.55	2.85	395	355	29.9
1984	170	4.44	2.81	510	416	31.7
1985	420	4.40	2.88	624	542	29.9
1986	620	4.39	2.88	675	601	31.3
1987	620	4.34	2.86	820	714	33.1
1988	620	4.26	2.87	996	925	35.5
1989	620	4.17	2.85	1117	1011	36.8
1990	620	4.16	2.89	1171	923	39.6
1991	620	4.03	2.81	1308	1018	38.0
1992	620	4.01	2.81	1493	1129	37.5
1993	540	3.91	2.76	1748	1276	37.1
1994	630	3.85	2.35	2267	1884	37.8
1995	630	3.87	2.30	3012	2373	40.5
1996	630	3.81	2.77	3482	2772	42.2
1997	630	3.87	2.86	3785	2762	42.0
1998	630	3.87	2.88	4006	2858	46.2
1999	630	3.80	2.80	4209	2851	48.0
2000	630	3.61	2.59	4894	3393	49.0
2001	630	3.57	2.53	5330	3909	52.0
2002	630	3.53	2.53	5708	4444	52.7
2003	670	3.48	2.53	6250	5142	54.7
2004	670	3.48	2.54	6950	5608	58.9
2005	1100	3.34	2.34	7655	6004	66.0
2006	1100	3.63	2.52	8515	6901	66.5
2007	1100	3.60	2.61	9549	7568	68.0
2008	1100	3.56	2.58	10692	8446	69.7
2009	1100	3.57	2.59	11822	9065	70.7
2010	1100	3.58	2.59	13186	10267	71.2
2011	1100	3.46	2.49	15245	12125	72.5
2012	1100	3.45	2.50	17017	13612	71.0
2013	1280	3.38	2.03	21208	16021	66.9
2014	1280	3.35	2.05	23555	17816	67.9
2015	1280	3.36	2.02	25719	19334	68.8
2016	1280	3.38	2.04	27908	20563	69.9
2017	1280	3.38	2.03	30397	21983	70.9

注:2013－2017 年为城乡住户一体化改革后新口径数据。

a) The data in this table are calculated at new rage by the results of integrated survey of urban households and rural households sine 2013.

13－05 农村居民家庭平均每百户耐用消费品拥有量(2010－2017年)
Number of Major Durable Consumer Goods Owned Per 100 Rural Households(2010－2017)

项　　目	Item	2010	2011	2012	2013	2014	2015	2016	2017
家用汽车（辆）	Family Car (Unit)	15.7	21.6	27.5	28.8	34.3	38.2	42.4	46.5
摩托车（辆）	Motorcycle (Unit)	66.2	40.8	42.6	33.5	32.7	30.7	26.0	24.5
电冰箱（台）	Refrigerator (Unit)	98.1	93.3	101.8	93.8	99.5	103.9	109.0	112.0
洗衣机（台）	Washing Machine (Unit)	85.1	78.2	87.8	78.3	82.7	86.4	92.5	96.0
热水器（台）	Water Heater (Unit)	84.5	80.7	90.9	79.3	85.9	93.2	103.2	109.9
空调机（台）	Air Conditioner (Unit)	111.2	120.3	143.3	122.9	135.9	147.6	168.2	186.7
彩色电视机（台）	Color TV Set (Unit)	186.3	192.5	210.6	186.0	196.1	202.0	213.5	220.3
照相机（架）	Camera (Unit)	22.6	21.7	26.5	21.1	21.1	19.6	19.8	17.4
计算机（台）	Personal Computer (Unit)	44.2	51.3	60.4	59.3	67.3	69.6	75.0	76.4
#接入互联网的计算机（台）	of which: Internet－connected computer (Unit)		44.6	51.8	51.5	59.8	64.2	68.5	70.2
固定电话（部）	Telephone (Set)				49.6	52.7	46.4	35.0	31.8
移动电话（部）	Mobile Phone (Set)	212.9	230.4	253.1	235.5	244.6	253.8	265.2	274.5
#接入互联网的移动电话（部）	of which: Internet－connect-ed Mobile Phone (Set)				106.0	121.2	141.7	172.2	200.8

注:2013－2017年为城乡住户一体化改革后新口径数据。

a) The data in this table are calculated at new rage by the results of integrated survey of urban households and rural households since 2013.

13－06 全市就业人员工资总额(1978－2017年)

Total Wages of Employed Persons(1978－2017)

单位:万元 (10000 yuan)

年份 Year	全市(非私营及规上私营) Total (includes Non－private Units and private units above designated size)	非私营单位 Non－private	市区(非私营及规上私营) Urban District(includes Non－private Units and private units above designated size)	非私营单位 Non－private
1978		43775		28256
1979		52127		34318
1980		67918		45574
1981		72896		48809
1982		75584		50959
1983		78336		52909
1984		102223		69135
1985		130114		87774
1986		157471		105995
1987		180077		121003
1988		230868		152859
1989		253956		167055
1990		277910		182985
1991		313906		209052
1992		377614		253653
1993		534537		359041
1994		772236		521669
1995		890488		615450
1996		973592		683244
1997		1073862		762957
1998		1112718		803264
1999		1180947		864418
2000		1267524		949872
2001		1481659		1279749
2002		1614676		1398222
2003		1867776		1617504
2004	2844691	2188159	2313930	1859164
2005	3711915	2970200	3112937	2584779
2006	4526841	3811735	3830043	3338568
2007	6233799	4954813	5256791	4317965
2008	8592198	6416424	7338932	5679543
2009	9909330	7549145	8475547	6665279
2010	12305726	9330552	10531483	8238017
2011	15012179	11222834	12934215	9954506
2012	19540005	14839012	17115217	13217453
2013	23604682	17582336	20762852	15820468
2014	26630950	19822713	24629017	18551986
2015	28884146	21523984	26718242	20179320
2016	32370091	24176045	29918514	22617274
2017	35985206	26467155	34266225	25422943

注:口径范围,1997年及以前为全市全部职工,1998－2012为在岗职工,2013年起为就业人员。2004年起包含规模以上私营单位。
a) Data on this table refer to wages of all employees before 1997, that refer to all staff and workers in 1998－2012, and refer to employed persons since 2013. Data on this bill includes Private units above designated size since 2004.

13－07 全市就业人员年平均工资(1978－2017 年)

Average Annual Wages of Employed Persons(1978－2017)

单位:元 (yuan)

年 份 Year	全市(非私营及规上私营) Total (includes Non－private Units and private units above designated size)	非私营单位 Non－private	市区(非私营及规上私营) Urban District(includes Non－private Units and private units above designated size)	非私营单位 Non－private	市区全社会在岗职工 The Fully Employed Persons in Urban Districts
1978		597		642	
1979		643		692	
1980		777		814	
1981		783		810	
1982		791		809	
1983		813		835	
1984		1036		1071	
1985		1266		1316	
1986		1469		1536	
1987		1616		1690	
1988		1986		2073	
1989		2173		2261	
1990		2382		2486	
1991		2586		2706	
1992		3071		3233	
1993		4220		4561	
1994		6118		6597	
1995		7156		7786	
1996		7966		7851	
1997		9108		10048	
1998		10555		11512	
1999		12187		13225	
2000		14257		15454	
2001		18319		18962	18205
2002		21418		22091	19749
2003		24668		25535	20113
2004	21879	28891	24204	30719	22235
2005	24685	31069	26366	32166	22645
2006	27620	32791	29397	33967	23581
2007	29864	36496	31625	37991	25489
2008	32513	40193	34107	41501	27863
2009	35638	43947	37270	45149	30480
2010	39772	48772	41303	49938	34330
2011	45775	54408	47695	55958	38837
2012	51077	56417	52610	57548	42493
2013	55124	63664	56857	64941	46831
2014	60904	69209	61924	70034	51449
2015	66322	76073	67569	77061	55908
2016	73390	85022	74589	85767	61174
2017	80482	93891	81440	94430	67047

注:口径范围,1997 年及以前为全市全部职工,1998－2012 为在岗职工,2013 年起为就业人员。2004 年起包含规模以上私营单位。

a) Data on this table refer to wages of all employees before 1997, that refer to all staff and workers in 1998－2012, and refer to employed persons since 2013. Data on this bill includes Private units above designated size since 2004.

13－08 全市非私营及规上私营单位就业人员工资总额(2017 年)

Total Wages of Employed Persons of Non－private Units and Private Units Above Designated Size(2017)

单位：万元　　　　(10000 yuan)

项 目	Item	就业人员工资总额 Total Wages of Employed Persons	非私营 Non－private	在岗职工工资总额 Total Wages of Fully Employed Staff and Workers	非私营 Non－private	其他就业人员工资总额 Total Wages of Other Employed Persons	非私营 Non－private
全市总计	**Whole city Total**	**35985206**	**26467155**	**34037939**	**25542936**	**1947267**	**924219**
市区总计	Urban District	34266225	25422943	32382580	24531012	1883646	891931
#上城区	Shangcheng	2498761	2121042	2332011	2035337	166750	85704
下城区	Xiacheng	3061900	2756887	2842956	2602545	218943	154342
江干区	Jianggan	3769975	1982955	3041064	1875560	728911	107395
拱墅区	Gongshu	2202155	1235464	2084026	1156663	118130	78800
西湖区	Xihu	5110384	4391515	4869093	4211099	241291	180416
高新(滨江)区	Hi－Tech(Binjiang)	4036673	3423165	4000892	3398940	35781	24225
萧山区	Xiaoshan	5279539	3430621	5150202	3351548	129337	79074
大江东产业集聚区	Dajiangdong Industry Cluster District	728937	439689	713134	431976	15803	7713
余杭区	Yuhang	3963350	2842814	3868790	2776549	94560	66265
富阳区	Fuyang	1397175	877723	1346248	848165	50928	29558
临安区	Lin'an	963573	631729	938627	612603	24946	19126
经济技术开发区	Economic and Technological Development Zone	1773874	1532032	1728973	1493924	44900	38108
西湖风景名胜区	The West Lake Scenic Zone	208867	196997	179699	168079	29168	28918
桐庐县	Tonglu	706971	360136	684305	346749	22667	13387
淳安县	Chun'an	490894	333557	470606	324344	20288	9213
建德市	Jiande	521115	350520	500449	340832	20667	9689

项　目 Item	就业人员工资总额 Total Wages of Employed Persons	非私营 Non－private	在岗职工工资总额 Total Wages of Fully Employed Staff and Workers	非私营 Non－private	其他就业人员工资总额 Total Wages of Other Employed Persons	非私营 Non－private
按国民经济行业分组 Grouped by Sector						
农、林、牧、渔业 Farming, Forestry, Animal Husbandry & Fishery	5913	5418	5668	5172	245	245
采矿业 Mining	11365	3920	11226	3780	140	140
制造业 Manufacturing	7338792	5087564	7231188	5010904	107604	76660
电力、热力、燃气及水生产和供应业 Production & Supply of Electricity, Heat, Gas & Water	250785	241176	248809	239229	1976	1947
建筑业 Construction	8174572	3706222	6980532	3433706	1194040	272516
批发和零售业 Wholesale & Retail Trades	2158814	1498601	2112132	1464365	46682	34236
交通运输、仓储和邮政业 Transportation, Storage and Post	1289615	1042624	1269358	1030986	20257	11638
住宿和餐饮业 Hotels and Catering Services	477155	335981	443529	306132	33625	29849
信息传输、软件和信息技术服务业 Information Transmission, Software and Information Technology	3474399	2906629	3463341	2900754	11058	5875
金融业 Financial Intermediation	2121995	2105938	1971287	1955677	150707	150261
房地产业 Real Estate	1125473	863465	1075111	818663	50362	44802
租赁和商务服务业 Leasing and Business Services	1356437	913637	1303737	872870	52701	40767
科学研究、技术服务业 Scientific Research, Technical Services	1564250	1361095	1521457	1326594	42793	34501
水利、环境和公共设施管理业 Management of Water Conservancy, Environment and Public Facilities	269526	195019	258042	186153	11484	8866
居民服务、修理和其他服务业 Service to Honseholds, Repair and Other Services	135626	61581	127197	59788	8429	1793
教育 Education	2223534	2198050	2159886	2134638	63648	63412
卫生和社会工作 Health Care and Social Work	1759380	1709246	1681724	1635821	77656	73425
文化、体育和娱乐业 Culture, Sports and Entertainment	313703	297119	275648	259636	38055	37483
公共管理、社会保障和社会组织 Public Management, Social Security and Social Organizations	1933872	1933872	1898068	1898068	35805	35805

13－09 全市非私营及规上私营单位就业人员平均工资(2017 年)

Average Annual Wages of Employed Persons of Non－private Units and Private Units Above Designated Size(2017)

单位:元 (yuan)

项目	Item	就业人员 Total employment	非私营单位 Non－private	在岗职工 Staff and Workers	非私营单位 Non－private
全市	**Total**	**80482**	**93891**	**82504**	**96670**
市区	Urban District	81440	94430	83518	97243
#上城区	Shangcheng	104762	119384	107788	122186
下城区	Xiacheng	106106	117468	115584	125638
江干区	Jianggan	76714	99277	78950	102996
拱墅区	Gongshu	68880	80133	70468	84363
西湖区	Xihu	78178	81417	80868	84205
高新(滨江)区	Hi－Tech(Binjiang)	116141	127220	117590	128795
萧山区	Xiaoshan	65921	73862	66357	74480
大江东产业集聚区	Dajiangdong Industry Cluster District	66660	78075	66845	78198
余杭区	Yuhang	85684	109472	87388	112748
富阳区	Fuyang	63021	74981	64414	77609
临安区	Lin'an	66601	79776	67161	81204
经济技术开发区	Economic and Technological Development Zone	84459	89533	85006	89932
西湖风景名胜区	The West Lake Scenic Zone	74061	75774	86656	90258
桐庐县	Tonglu	63395	81300	64289	83476
淳安县	Chun'an	66830	83323	68659	85401
建德市	Jiande	66215	82736	68257	85000

单位:元　　　　13－09　续表　continued　　　　(yuan)

项　目 Item	就业人员 Total employment	非私营单位 Non－private	在岗职工 Staff and Workers	非私营单位 Non－private
按国民经济行业分组 **Grouped by Sector**				
农、林、牧、渔业 Farming, Forestry, Animal Husbandry & Fishery	49071	50024	51107	52404
采矿业 Mining	62688	57816	63030	58515
制造业 Manufacturing	68958	77842	68975	77794
电力、热力、燃气及水生产和供应业 Production & Supply of Electricity, Heat, Gas & Water	125480	129797	126562	130998
建筑业 Construction	53981	54299	53463	55136
批发和零售业 Wholesale & Retail Trades	76725	86569	77708	88261
交通运输、仓储和邮政业 Transportation, Storage and Post	89977	95094	90793	96200
住宿和餐饮业 Hotels and Catering Services	47322	48946	51300	55385
信息传输、软件和信息技术服务业 Information Transmission, Software and Information Technology	164530	188969	165527	189659
金融业 Financial Intermediation	186137	187002	217629	218722
房地产业 Real Estate	75711	76481	77555	78775
租赁和商务服务业 Leasing and Business Services	71049	74542	73275	77775
科学研究、技术服务业 Scientific Research, Technical Services	114257	122124	116180	124048
水利、环境和公共设施管理业 Management of Water Conservancy, Environment and Public Facilities	69668	76731	72024	80225
居民服务、修理和其他服务业 Service to Honseholds, Repair and Other Services	50509	58721	50682	59746
教育 Education	116609	118064	122540	124252
卫生和社会工业 Health Care and Social Work	143563	148327	147498	152476
文化、体育和娱乐业 Culture, Sports and Entertainment	122097	132524	127250	139612
公共管理、社会保障和社会组织 Public Management, Social Security and Social Organizations	140148	140148	145141	145141

13－10 市区消费价格指数(1978－2017年)

Consumer Price Indices in Urban District(1978－2017)

(上年=100)　　(Preceding Year=100)

年 份 Year	居民消费价格指数 Consumer Price Index	商品零售价格指数 Retail Price Index
1978	100.1	100.1
1979	100.4	100.9
1980	100.8	109.3
1981	102.0	102.0
1982	102.0	102.3
1983	102.1	102.3
1984	103.1	103.1
1985	117.2	117.5
1986	106.0	106.1
1987	110.5	111.3
1988	121.9	123.4
1989	117.8	118.2
1990	104.6	104.4
1991	107.5	106.9
1992	110.4	110.2
1993	121.4	117.3
1994	121.5	118.8
1995	116.5	113.3
1996	110.5	107.2
1997	106.7	102.4
1998	101.8	99.8
1999	100.4	98.2
2000	100.8	98.3
2001	99.5	95.3
2002	98.8	97.9
2003	99.5	98.1
2004	102.5	101.6
2005	101.7	100.3
2006	101.2	100.2
2007	103.5	103.1
2008	104.9	106.0
2009	98.6	98.6
2010	103.9	103.7
2011	104.8	104.4
2012	102.5	101.9
2013	102.5	101.5
2014	102.0	100.8
2015	101.8	100.2
2016	102.6	101.5
2017	102.5	101.0

13－11　市区居民消费价格分类指数(2017年)
Consumer Price Indices by Category in Urban District(2017)

(上年=100)　　(Preceding Year=100)

项目	Item	2017
居民消费价格总指数	**Consumer Price Index**	**102.5**
一、食品烟酒	**Food, Tobacco and Liquor**	**100.9**
1.食品	Food	99.4
(1)粮食	Grain	100.5
(2)薯类	Tubers	96.4
(3)豆类	Beans	103.7
(4)食用油	Edible Oil and Fats	100.7
(5)菜	Vegetables	90.2
(6)畜肉类	Meat of Livestock	97.6
(7)禽肉类	Meat of Poultry	98.6
(8)水产品	Aquatic Products	107.9
(9)蛋类	Eggs	97.9
(10)奶类	Milk	100.3
(11)干鲜瓜果类	Dried and Fresh Melons and Fruits	100.9
(12)糖果糕点类	Candy and Cake	103.9
(13)调味品	Flavoring	99.8
(14)其他食品类	Other Foods	104.1
2.茶及饮料	Tea and Beverages	102.7
3.烟酒	Tobacco and Liquor	100.8
4.在外餐饮	Dining Out	104.1
二、衣着	**Clothing**	**100.0**
1.服装	Garments	100.3
2.服装材料	Garments Material	118.2
3.其他衣着及配件	Other Clothing and Parts	101.2
4.衣着加工服务费	Clothing Manufacturing Services	102.1

项目	Item	2017
5. 鞋类	Footwear	98.2
三、居住	**Residence**	**105.7**
1. 租赁房房租	Rent of Rental Housing	108.3
2. 住房保养维修及管理	Housing Maintenance and Management	104.7
3. 水电燃料	Water, Electricity and Fuels	100.8
4. 自有住房	Private Housing	106.9
四、生活用品及服务	**Articles for Daily Use and Services**	**100.2**
1. 家具及室内装饰品	Furniture and Interior Decorations	100.4
2. 家用器具	Home Appliances	98.4
3. 家用纺织品	Home Textiles	100.1
4. 家庭日用杂品	Daily Use Household Articles	100.7
5. 个人护理用品	Personal－care Supplies	99.4
6. 家庭服务	Household Services	105.1
五、交通和通信	**Transport and Communications**	**101.5**
1. 交通	Transport	102.6
2. 通信	Communications	99.0
六、教育文化和娱乐	**Education, Culture and Recreation**	**104.1**
1. 教育	Education	103.9
2. 文化娱乐	Cultural and Recreation	104.4
七、医疗保健	**Health Care**	**101.7**
1. 药品及医疗器具	Medicine and Medical Instrument	104.3
2. 医疗服务	Medical Services	100.2
八、其他用品和服务	**Other Articles and Services**	**101.4**
1. 其他用品类	Other Articles	99.0
2. 其他服务类	Other Services	102.9

13－12 市区零售价格分类指数(2017 年)

Retail Price Indices by Category in Urban District(2017)

(上年＝100) (Preceding Year＝100)

项目	Item	2017
商品零售价格指数	**Retail Price Index**	**101.0**
一、食品	**Food**	**100.6**
1. 粮食	Grain	100.5
2. 薯类	Tubers	96.4
3. 豆类	Beans	103.7
4. 食用油	Edible Oil and Fats	100.7
5. 菜	Vegetables	90.2
6. 畜肉类	Meat of Livestock	97.6
7. 禽肉类	Meat of Poultry	98.6
8. 水产品	Aquatic Products	107.9
9. 蛋类	Eggs	97.9
10. 奶类	Milk	100.3
11. 干鲜瓜果类	Dried and Fresh Melons and Fruits	100.9
12. 糖果糕点类	Candy and Cake	103.9
13. 调味品	Flavoring	99.8
14. 其他食品类	Other Foods	104.1
15. 在外餐饮	Dining out	104.1
二、饮料、烟酒	**Beverages, Tobacco and Liquor**	**101.3**
1. 茶及饮料	Tea and Beverages	102.7
2. 烟草	Tobacco	100.7
3. 酒类	Liquor	101.2
三、服装、鞋帽	**Garments, Shoes and Hats**	**99.9**
1. 服装	Garments	100.3
2. 鞋帽袜	Footgear and Hat	98.4
3. 其他衣着配件	Other Clothing and Parts	101.0
四、纺织品	**Textiles**	**105.3**
1. 服装材料	Garments Material	118.2
2. 床上用品	Bedding	100.2
五、家用电器及音像器材	**Household Appliances, Music and Video Equipment**	**98.5**
1. 家庭设备	Household Equipment	99.0
2. 文娱用耐用消费品	Durable Consumer Goods for Entertainment	97.0

项　　目	Item	2017
3. 专业音像器材	Audio and Video Equipment	99.1
六、文化办公用品	**Cultural and office Appliances**	**97.8**
七、日用品	**Articles for Daily Use**	**99.2**
1. 日用百货	General Merchandise for Daily Use	99.1
2. 厨具餐具茶具	Kitchen Ware, Table Ware, Tea Set	100.1
3. 清洗用品	Cleaning Supplies	100.4
4. 其他日用品	Other Articles for Daily Use	97.4
八、体育娱乐用品	**Sports and Recreation Articles**	**100.7**
1. 体育户外用品	Sports Outdoor Products	98.6
2. 娱乐用品	Recreation Articles	101.6
九、交通、通信用品	**Transportation and Communication Appliances**	**99.7**
1. 交通运输机械	Transportation Vehicles	100.2
2. 通信器材	Equipment of Communication	97.4
十、家具	**Furniture**	**100.7**
十一、化妆品	**Cosmetics**	**99.9**
十二、金银饰品	**Gold and Silver Ornaments**	**100.8**
十三、中西药品及医疗保健用品	**Traditional Chinese and Western Medicine and Health Care Articles**	**104.4**
1. 医疗卫生器具	Medical Instruments and Articles	102.7
2. 中药	Traditional Chinese Medicines	104.9
3. 西药	Western Medicines	104.0
4. 保健器具及用品	Articles for Health Care	105.0
十四、书报杂志及电子出版物	**Books, Newspapers, Magazines and Electronic Publications**	**100.9**
1. 教材及参考书	Teaching Materials and Reference Books	99.1
2. 书报杂志	Books, Newspapers and Magazines	102.6
3. 计算机办公软件	Computer Office Software	100.7
十五、燃料	**Fuels**	**106.8**
1. 煤炭及制品	Coal and Coal Products	109.9
2. 石油及制品	Oil and Oil Products	106.4
十六、建筑材料及五金电料	**Building Materials and Hardware**	**100.4**
1. 建筑装璜材料	Building Decoration Materials	102.1
2. 五金水暖	Hardware	95.9

13－13 工业生产者出厂价格指数(2010－2017年)

Producer Price Indices for Industrial Products(2010－2017)

(上年＝100) (Preceding Year＝100)

项目 Item	2010	2011	2012	2013	2014	2015	2016	2017
工业生产者出厂价格总指数 Total Producer Price Indices for Industrial Products	**104.9**	**104.7**	**97.2**	**98.5**	**98.6**	**96.5**	**99.2**	**104.4**
一、按轻重工业分 Grouped by Industries								
轻工业 Light Industry	**105.0**	**105.5**	**98.1**	**99.9**	**99.2**	**97.4**	**99.8**	**104.0**
以农产品为原料 Made from Agricultural Products	103.9	104.6	99.4	100.8	99.9	98.5	99.8	102.6
以非农产品为原料 Made from Non－agricultural Products	106.0	106.8	96.1	98.4	98.2	95.8	99.8	106.1
重工业 Heavy Industry	**104.7**	**104.2**	**96.5**	**97.5**	**98.2**	**95.8**	**98.7**	**104.6**
采掘 Mining & Quarrying Industry	114.0	116.6	101.3	101.0	104.2	94.9	97.3	100.6
原料 Raw Materials Industry	110.7	108.7	96.9	97.5	96.7	92.5	96.4	106.7
加工 Manufacturing Industry	102.5	102.8	96.4	97.5	98.5	96.7	99.4	104.1
二、按二大部类分 Grouped by Means of Producting and Consumer Goods								
生产资料 Means of Production	**106.2**	**105.1**	**95.5**	**97.8**	**98.0**	**95.3**	**98.8**	**105.8**
采掘 Mining	114.0	116.6	101.3	101.0	104.2	94.9	97.3	100.6
原料 Raw Materials	114.5	110.6	92.6	96.5	95.7	91.0	96.1	109.9
加工 Manufacture	103.9	103.3	96.4	98.2	98.7	96.6	99.6	104.7
生活资料 Consumer Goods	**101.0**	**103.7**	**102.6**	**100.6**	**100.6**	**100.1**	**100.1**	**99.9**
食品 Foods	100.1	104.3	101.8	101.0	101.1	100.9	100.0	99.4
衣着 Clothing	102.4	104.5	104.6	102.0	100.1	100.1	101.1	99.9
一般日用品 Articles for Daily Use	100.8	103.9	102.3	99.8	100.7	99.9	100.5	100.4
耐用消费品 Durable Consumer Goods	100.9	101.5	102.0	99.6	100.0	99.2	99.1	99.7

(上年=100)　　13-13　续表　continued　　(Preceding Year=100)

项　　目 Item	2010	2011	2012	2013	2014	2015	2016	2017
三、按工业部门分 Grouped by Industrial Sector								
冶金工业 Metallurgical Industry	108.0	107.1	93.3	95.4	96.2	93.2	101.7	115.0
电力工业 Power Industry	105.2	102.0	101.7	99.1	99.6	98.2	97.8	100.2
煤炭及炼焦工业 Coal and Coking Industry		–						
石油工业 Petroleum Industry	117.0	110.4	103.0	100.5	100.5	92.4	87.7	97.9
化学工业 Chemical Industry	111.9	109.3	93.8	97.3	95.8	92.7	97.3	107.8
机械工业 Machine Building Industry	100.8	101.3	97.6	98.1	98.9	97.6	99.4	101.4
建材材料工业 Building Materials Industry	109.3	109.8	94.0	97.3	103.0	94.0	96.3	111.5
森林工业 Timber Industry	101.6	102.0	100.7	101.0	101.3	99.9	98.9	100.9
食品工业 Food Industry	100.1	105.1	102.0	101.2	100.5	100.2	100.2	99.6
纺织工业 Textile Industry	107.5	105.1	95.5	101.1	98.9	96.3	100.1	103.5
缝纫工业 Tailoring Industry	102.2	105.6	104.6	102.6	100.5	99.8	99.6	99.6
皮革工业 Leather Industry	102.9	101.9	103.4	101.1	101.0	100.4	100.5	101.3
造纸工业 Paper Industry	104.6	102.0	96.7	96.3	99.7	98.5	98.9	109.8
文教艺术用品工业 Cultural, Educational & Handicrafts Articles	97.3	100.9	100.1	100.0	98.8	98.9	99.5	99.7
其它工业 Others	104.7	109.0	103.9	101.3	104.6	102.9	105.5	102.5

13－14 工业生产者购进价格指数(2010－2017 年)

Purchasing Price Indices for Industrial Producers(2010－2017)

(上年＝100) (Preceding Year＝100)

项目 Item	2010	2011	2012	2013	2014	2015	2016	2017
工业生产者购进价格指数 Purchasing Price Index for Industrial Producers	**112.1**	**110.8**	**94.6**	**97.3**	**97.3**	**92.9**	**98.9**	**108.4**
燃料动力类 Fuel and Power	111.3	110.6	98.2	96.9	99.0	95.1	93.6	105.7
黑色金属材料类 Ferrous and Metals	108.6	107.0	88.7	95.0	92.4	85.9	100.9	115.5
1. 钢材 Rolled－steel	108.2	106.6	88.5	95.4	92.5	86.3	101.0	115.9
2. 其他 Other	113.0	113.1	91.2	90.1	90.3	80.5	98.2	106.8
有色金属材料及电线类 Non－ferrous Metals and Electric Wire	129.3	113.4	93.1	93.7	94.5	92.2	101.3	114.7
化工原料类 Chemical Raw Materials	113.3	114.3	94.2	97.0	97.7	91.7	100.8	110.9
木材及纸浆类 Wood and Paper Pulps	106.4	104.0	97.7	98.8	98.5	98.5	99.8	111.6
建筑材料及非金属类 Building Materials	108.8	116.8	99.5	99.4	105.7	96.9	99.0	117.1
农副产品类 Farm and Sideline Products	114.1	112.8	97.2	98.4	100.4	99.3	99.3	106.9
其他工业原材料及半成品类 Other Industrial Raw Materials and Semi－products	109.8	107.2	99.1	97.8	98.9	96.7	98.8	102.7
纺织原料类 Textile Raw Materials	110.4	110.5	96.3	101.9	99.9	97.1	98.8	104.8

13-15 住宅销售价格指数(2017年)
Residential Sales Price Indices(2017)

月份 Month	新建住宅 New Residential Building		新建商品住宅 New Residential Commodities Building		二手住宅 The Second - hand Residence	
	上月=100	上年同期=100 Preceding Year =100	上月=100	上年同期=100 Preceding Year =100	上月=100	上年同期=100 Preceding Year =100
一月 January	100	127.4	100	127.6	100.5	121.6
二月 February	99.8	125.4	99.8	125.6	100.6	121
三月 March	100.2	122.8	100.2	123	100.9	119.8
四月 April	100	119.3	100	119.5	100.7	118.5
五月 May	99.7	116.2	99.7	116.3	100.8	117.9
六月 June	100.2	114.5	100.2	114.6	100.7	117.4
七月 July	100	111.8	100	111.9	100.8	115.8
八月 August	99.8	108.1	99.8	108.2	100.7	113.5
九月 September	99.7	102.2	99.7	102.2	100.6	109.1
十月 October	100	99.1	100	99.1	100.4	106.9
十一月 November	99.9	99.4	99.9	99.4	100.2	107.1
十二月 December	100	99.4	100	99.4	100	107.2

13－16　分地区社会办福利院情况(2017 年末)

Basic Statistics on Welfare Homes by Region(End of 2017)

地区 Region	单　位 (个) Homes (unit)	职　工 (人) Staff and Workers (person)	床位数 (张) Beds (bed)	在院人数 (人) Persons Housed (person)	老　人(人) Seniors(person)
全　市 **Total**	**303**	**5393**	**70264**	**22688**	**22135**
市　区 Urban District	219	4676	58463	18903	18385
#萧山区 Xiaoshan	43	1066	12844	2766	2692
余杭区 Yuhang	21	207	7478	769	719
富阳区 Fuyang	31	230	5165	1441	1420
临安区 Lin'an	32	199	4825	1621	1601
桐庐县 Tonglu	24	269	3352	1064	1038
淳安县 Chun'an	33	280	4297	1008	1008
建德市 Jiande	27	168	4152	1713	1704

13－17　分地区优抚对象
Number of Persons Receiving

单位:人

指　标 Item	全　市 Total	市　区 Urban District	上城区 Shangcheng	下城区 Xiacheng	江干区 Jianggan
享受定期抚恤金人数 Number of Persons Receiving Periodical Commiseration	578	365	9	4	23
烈属 Number of Martyr Kinsfolk	282	153	4	2	7
牺牲军人家属 Number of the Sacrifice Soldiers	97	70	1	2	1
病故军人家属 Number of Kinsfolks of the Illness－died Soldiers	199	142	4	－	15
享受定期补助人数 Number of Persons Enjoying Regular Subsidies	38311	26431	48	54	638
在乡复员军人 Rural Demobilized Soldier	1615	1055	4	10	11
抗日 The War of Resistance Against Japan		－			
优待优抚对象带病回乡退伍军人 Number of Rural Veterans with Illness Receiving Subsiders	2744	1583	1	2	14

人员情况(2017 年)
Public Subsidies by Region(2017)

(person)

拱墅区 Gongshu	西湖区 Xihu	高新(滨江)区 Hi - Tech (Binjiang)	萧山区 Xiaoshan	余杭区 Yuhang	富阳区 Fuyang	临安区 Lin'an	桐庐县 Tonglu	淳安县 Chun'an	建德市 Jiande
6	37	3	63	51	111	58	77	74	62
4	10	3	22	21	39	41	43	49	37
1	8	-	8	10	35	4	14	5	8
1	19	-	33	20	37	13	20	20	17
169	1307	85	9079	5058	5386	4607	4485	3044	4351
13	33	20	248	245	237	234	186	176	198
1	18	11	387	189	807	153	675	137	349

13－18 市、县级社会

Basic Statistics on Institutions and

单位:个

指标	Item	全市 Total	市区 Urban District	萧山区 Xiaoshan
合计	**Total**	**3193**	**2405**	**290**
按活动区域分	**Grouped by Region**			
地级社团	City－level Societies	746	746	
县级社团	County－level Societies	2447	1659	290
按性质分	**Grouped by Category**			
科技与研究	Technology and Research	108	91	16
生态环境	Ecological Envirenment	27	23	4
教育	Education	50	39	3
卫生	Health	73	62	10
社会服务	Social Services	357	140	16
文化	Culture	227	156	31
体育	Sport	239	186	32
法律	Law	8	7	3
工商业服务	Industry and Business Services	374	318	90
宗教	Religion	36	26	7
农业及农村发展	Agricure and Rural Development	148	102	24
职业及从业组织	Vocational and Business Organizations	190	110	36
国际及涉外组织	International and Foreign Organizations	－	－	
其他	Other	1356	1145	18

团体机构情况(2017 年)
Organizations at County Level(2017)

(unit)

			桐庐县 Tonglu	淳安县 Chun'an	建德市 Jiande
余杭区 Yuhang	富阳区 Fuyang	临安区 Lin'an			
238	**217**	**219**	**229**	**321**	**238**
238	217	219	229	321	238
19	21	14	–	13	4
1	1	12	2	1	1
3	2	3	7	1	3
14	5	5	2	4	5
9	24	9	8	197	12
24	24	21	24	15	32
24	20	20	6	12	35
	1				1
66	69	21	2	20	34
4	4	4	3	3	4
26	25	14	10	20	16
7	10	49	1	22	57
41	11	47	164	13	34

13－19　社会保障情况(2010－2017 年)

Social Security(2010－2017)

单位:万人　　　　(10000 persons)

项　目 Item	2010	2011	2012	2013	2014	2015	2016	2017
城镇登记失业人员 Number of the Registered Unemployed Persons in Urban	4.85	4.40	3.97	4.60	4.03	3.67	3.72	3.76
城镇登记失业率(%) The Registered Rate of Unemployment in Urban (%)	2.19	1.86	1.63	1.85	1.84	1.74	1.72	1.70
失业人员再就业 The Re－employed Persons of Unemployment	15.54	13.17	13.29	13.13	13.50	14.22	11.48	11.04
职工基本养老保险参保人数 Number of Persons in the Basic Pension Program in Urban	383.97	428.12	492.62	530.70	559.48	569.09	575.98	628.32
失业保险参保人数 Number of Persons in the Unemployment Insurance Program	243.98	277.53	299.78	316.36	331.83	349.42	374.16	413.20
职工基本医疗保险参保人数 Number of Persons in the Basic Medical Insurance Program	345.24	386.33	425.82	448.35	469.40	500.21	529.32	580.50
工伤保险参保人数 Number of Persons in the Work－injure Insurance Program	314.95	355.28	382.21	394.82	406.65	418.17	428.41	462.44
生育保险参保人数 Number of Persons in the Bear Insurance Program	228.53	254.38	277.11	292.01	309.23	324.59	349.33	390.73
城乡居民养老保险(障)人数 Number of Persons in the Urban and Rural old－age Security	106.30	112.35	112.98	106.40	103.97	99.45	95.51	88.68
城乡居民参加医疗保险人数 Number of urban and rural residents participated in medical insurance	408.32	392.69	378.99	373.93	370.81	370.50	368.21	373.93

13 - 20 分地区社会保障情况(2017 年末)

Social Security by Region(End of 2017)

单位:人 (persons)

指标 Item	职工基本养老保险参保人数 Number of Employed Persons in the Basic Pension Program	职工基本医疗保险参保人数 Number of Persons in the Basic Medical Insurance Program	工伤保险参保人数 Number of Persons in the Work - injure Insurance Program	生育保险参保人数 Number of Persons in the Bear Insurance Program	失业保险参保人数 Number of Persons in the Unemployment Insurance Program
全　市 Total	**6283162**	**5804998**	**4624386**	**3907255**	**4131991**
市　区 Urban District	5800198	5408697	4321049	3684977	3929183
#萧山区 Xiaoshan	994809	797574	515630	508446	513368
余杭区 Yuhang	807400	716356	609966	497309	493956
富阳区 Fuyang	428288	335392	288551	185933	199685
临安区 Lin'an	255272	202421	165576	100525	106717
桐庐县 Tonglu	183921	156814	124061	93393	71501
淳安县 Chun'an	102960	103117	90319	50154	49853
建德市 Jiande	196083	136370	88957	78731	81454

主要统计指标解释

就业人员劳动报酬 指各单位在一定时期内直接支付给本单位全部就业人员的劳动报酬总额。

在岗职工工资总额 指各单位在一定时期内直接支付给本单位全部在岗职工的劳动报酬总额。

工资总额的计算原则应以直接支付给职工的全部劳动报酬为根据。各单位支付给本单位全部职工的劳动报酬,不论是计入成本的还是不计入成本的,不论是以货币形式支付还是以实物形式支付的,不论是单位自筹的资金还是上级(或政府财政部门)下拨的资金,不论是厂级单位筹集的资金还是下属车间(科室)及附属经营单位筹集的资金,均应列入工资总额计算的范围。

在岗职工平均工资 指各单位的在岗职工在一定时期内平均每人所得的工资额。它表明一定时期内在岗职工工资收入的高低程度,是反映在岗职工工资水平的主要指标。计算公式为:

$$在岗职工平均工资 = \frac{报告期实际支付的全部在岗职工工资总额}{报告期全部在岗职工平均人数}$$

全社会单位 包括独立核算的机关、事业单位,非私营企业和私营企业,但不含个体工商户。

离休、退休、退职人员 指正式办理了离休、退休、退职手续,并享受相应的离休、退休、退职待遇的人员。

保险福利费用 指企业、事业、机关单位在工资以外实际支付给职工和离休、退休、退职人员个人以及用于集体的劳动保险和福利费用。

社会福利事业单位 指集中收养社会孤、老、残、幼的机构。包括由民政部门管理的社会福利院、儿童福利院、精神病人福利院和城镇集体办的福利院,以及农村集体举办的敬老院。

社会福利事业单位收养人数 包括民政部门管理和城镇及农村集体举办的社会福利事业单位中收养的老人,少年儿童,缺乏生活自理能力的残疾人员和精神病人。

商品零售价格指数 是反映城乡商品零售价格变动趋势的一种经济指数。零售物价的调整变动直接影响到城乡居民的生活支出和国家的财政收入,影响居民购买力和市场供需平衡,影响消费与积累的比例。因此,计算零售价格指数,可以从一个侧面对上述经济活动进行观察和分析。

居民消费价格指数 是反映一定时期内城乡居民所购买的生活消费品价格和服务项目价格变动趋势和程度的相对数。是综合了城市居民消费价格指数和农民消费价格指数计算取得。利用居民消费价格指数,可以观察和分析消费品的零售价格和服务价格变动对城乡居民实际生活支出的影响程度。

工业生产者出厂价格指数 是反映全部工业产品出厂价格总水平的变动趋势和程度的相对数。其中除包括工业企业售给商业、外贸、物资部门的产品外,还包括售给工业和其他部门的生产资料以及直接售给居民的生活消费品。通过工业生产价格指数能观察出厂价格变动对工业总产值的影响。

Explanatory Notes on Main Statistical Indicators

Labour Remuneration refers to total payment by various units to their employees during a certain period of time, including total wage bill of permanent workers and staff and remuneration payment to other employees.

Total Wages of Fully Employed Staff and Workers refer to the total remuneration payment to fully employed staff and workers in various units during a certain period of time. The calculation of total wages is based on the total remuneration payment to the staff and workers. Therefore, all the wages and salaries and other payments to staff and workers are included in the total wages regardless of their sources, category, and forms (in kind or cash). (Total wages of staff and workers in this yearbook include only total wages of fully employed staff and workers, excluding the living allowances distributed to those who have left their working units while keeping their labour contract/employment relation unchanged).

Average Wage of Fully Employed Staff and Workers refers to the average wage per person during a certain period of time for fully employed staff and workers in enterprises, institutions, and government agencies, which reflects the general level of wage income during a certain period of time and is calculated as follows:

$$\text{Average Wage of Fully Employed Staff and Workers} = \frac{\text{Total wages of Fully employed staff and workers in Reference Period}}{\text{Average Number of Fully employed Staff and workers in Reference period}}$$

Units of Whole Society refers to independent accounting units of government organizations and institutions, non – private and private enterprises, but excluding individual business.

Retired and Resigned Person refers to the persons who have form ally gone through the formalities for their retirement or quitting work and enjoy the corresponding treatments.

Insurance and Welfare Funds refers to labour insurance and welf are funds paid by enterprises, organizations and institutions to their staff and workers as well as retired and resigned persons in addition to their wages and salaries.

Social Welfare Institutions refer to institutions taking care of old people without children, handicapped people and orphans. They include social welfare institutions run by civil affairs departments, children welfare institutions, social welfare institutions for mental patients, and collective – owned old people's home in rural areas.

Number of People Taken in by Social Welfare Institutions refers to the number of old people, children, totally dependent handicapped people and mental patients taken in by social welfare institutions run by civil affairs departments and those run by collective units in urban and rural areas.

Retail Price Index reflects the general change in retail prices of commodities. The change and adjustment in retail prices directly affect the living expenditure of urban and rural residents, government revenue, purchasing power of residents and the equilibrium of market supply and demand, and the ratio of consumption to accumulation. Therefore, the calculation of retail price index is useful to analyze the changes of the above economic activities.

Consumer Price Index reflects the trend and degree of changes in prices of consumer goods and services purchased by urban and rural residents, and is a composite index derived from the urban consumer price index and the rural consumer price index. Consumer price index can be used to analyze the impact of consumer price change on actual expenditure for living cost of urban and rural residents.

Ex – factory Price Index of Industrial Products reflects the trend and degree of changes in general ex – factory prices of all industrial products, including sales of industrial products by and industrial enterprise to all units outside the enterprise, as well as sales of consumer goods to residents. It can be used to analyze the impact of ex – factory prices on gross industrial output value.

HANGZHOU STATISTICAL YEARBOOK

杭州统计年鉴